Integrating Spaces

EDITORIAL ADVISORS

ASPEN COURSEBOOK SERIES

INTEGRATING SPACES: PROPERTY LAW AND RACE

ALFRED BROPHY
Reef C. Ivey II Professor of Law
University of North Carolina

ALBERTO LOPEZ
Professor of Law
Northern Kentucky University

KALI MURRAY
Assistant Professor of Law
Marquette University

www.AspenLaw.com

Aspen Publishers
Attn: Permissions Department
76 Ninth Avenue, 7th Floor
New York, NY 10011-5201

To contact Customer Care, e-mail customer.service@aspenpublishers.com, call 1-800-234-1660, fax 1-800-901-9075, or mail correspondence to:

Aspen Publishers
Attn: Order Department
PO Box 990
Frederick, MD 21705

Printed in the United States of America.

3 4 5 6 7 8 9 0

ISBN 978-0-7355-6997-3

Library of Congress Cataloging-in-Publication Data

Brophy, Alfred L.,
Integrating spaces : property law and race / Alfred L. Brophy, Alberto Lopez, Kali N. Murray.
p. cm.
ISBN 978-0-7355-6997-3
1. Discrimination in housing — Law and legislation — United States — Cases. 2. Real property — United States — Cases. 3. Race discrimination — Law and legislation — United States — Cases. I. Lopez, Alberto, 1969- II. Murray, Kali N., 1975- III. Title.
KF5740.B76 2010
344.73'0636351 — dc22

2010037725

About Wolters Kluwer Law & Business

Wolters Kluwer Law & Business is a leading provider of research information and workflow solutions in key specialty areas. The strengths of the individual brands of Aspen Publishers, CCH, Kluwer Law International and Loislaw are aligned within Wolters Kluwer Law & Business to provide comprehensive, in-depth solutions and expert-authored content for the legal, professional and education markets.

CCH was founded in 1913 and has served more than four generations of business professionals and their clients. The CCH products in the Wolters Kluwer Law & Business group are highly regarded electronic and print resources for legal, securities, antitrust and trade regulation, government contracting, banking, pension, payroll, employment and labor, and healthcare reimbursement and compliance professionals.

Aspen Publishers is a leading information provider for attorneys, business professionals and law students. Written by preeminent authorities, Aspen products offer analytical and practical information in a range of specialty practice areas from securities law and intellectual property to mergers and acquisitions and pension/benefits. Aspen's trusted legal education resources provide professors and students with high-quality, up-to-date and effective resources for successful instruction and study in all areas of the law.

Kluwer Law International supplies the global business community with comprehensive English-language international legal information. Legal practitioners, corporate counsel and business executives around the world rely on the Kluwer Law International journals, loose-leafs, books and electronic products for authoritative information in many areas of international legal practice.

Loislaw is a premier provider of digitized legal content to small law firm practitioners of various specializations. Loislaw provides attorneys with the ability to quickly and efficiently find the necessary legal information they need, when and where they need it, by facilitating access to primary law as well as state-specific law, records, forms and treatises.

Wolters Kluwer Law & Business, a unit of Wolters Kluwer, is headquartered in New York and Riverwoods, Illinois. Wolters Kluwer is a leading multinational publisher and information services company.

For my students, who've taught me so much about property, especially
Dana Jim, Michael Forton, Leah Wilson, Nic Carlisle, and Heather Fann
ALB

For my family
ABL

To my grandmothers Rosa Walker Murray and Edna Lewis Rice, and to
the memory of Donald Gaines Murray, Senior, and George Halbert Rice,
Senior, for inspiring this work
KNM

SUMMARY OF CONTENTS

CONTENTS

PREFACE

Race is often seen in property law but not heard in the property curriculum. You see race, for instance, in the struggle of the Latino migrant worker to receive access to medical care on land owned by an employer, in the conflict between Native Americans and European settlers over land during the initial settlement of the United States, and in contemporary claims that owners of property are discriminating in the terms and conditions of sale and rental of their property.

This book is inspired by students who have asked us two questions. First, why don't we hear more about the role of race in property law in the first year course? And, second, why aren't there more cases involving racial minorities (whether or not race is a factor in the outcome of the case) in our property casebook? Those two questions are related; they also suggest that students are increasingly interested in learning about how race is important in judicial decisions and in legislation. After hearing those questions over many years, we have assembled a set of readings intended to show that race is not a topic confined to courses in constitutional law or criminal law. Race also has played a vital role in the development of property law and continues to affect property law today. We also intend to show that issues of property are relevant to people of different economic, racial, and ethnic backgrounds. We hope that the cases included here will allow students to talk explicitly about the impact of race on property law, and also to see the property course populated by a greater range of voices and interests.

We wrote this book to serve as an adjunct to the traditional first-year class in property and thus help to "integrate" talk of the salience of race and ethnicity with traditional property law and theory. We also hope that this book will reach students in upper-level property classes, and even students who are looking for additional reading to expand their understanding of the race and ethnicity in property class. To that end, we have included many more cases than you will likely study in any course, to provide plenty from which teachers and students may select interesting and important cases across the spectrum, from history to contemporary common law doctrine, to contemporary civil rights law, to the property law of other countries.

We have several related goals with this book. First, we want to give you a sense of the importance of racial considerations in the historical development of property law in the United States. Chapter 1 seeks to raise and explore some key issues in property law. What is a property right? Where do property rights come from? How important are long-settled agreements that a person owns property (or, in the case of slavery, is property)? We also include a contemporary case adjudicating rights between a landlord and his tenants and their guests. Part of property law is about the boundaries of property rights; on the edges of those property rights are often other people's civil rights. Thus, as we are talking about the centrality of race, we are picking up other major themes of property law. We begin the development of a central theme of the relationship between property rights and civil rights.

Three subsequent chapters continue that historical introduction. The cases in these chapters serve two purposes. They illustrate how closely the development of property law was tied to institutional existence of slavery and segregation in the United States. Equally important, however, is uncovering how this history continues to be relevant to the way doctrine is shaped by judges and lawyers. Chapter 2 examines the impact of slavery on property. Two of the cases are about the rights of the "owner," and one deals with claims for compensation by a woman held in slavery wrongfully. While the latter case is old (it was decided toward the end of the nineteenth century), it involved a legal principle that continues to arise often today, a claim of "unjust enrichment." We hope that in learning about property's history you will learn principles that have continuing and direct application to practice today.

Chapters 3 and 4 turn to cases from the first half of the twentieth century. They deal with attempts to use the legal system to regulate public spaces where African Americans could live. Those attempts took the form of government zoning and other kinds of regulation and also private contracts, what are called in property parlance, covenants. The first two cases in Chapter 3 deal with claims that African American music — coming in once case from a jazz club and in another case from a church — is a nuisance. The doctrines of nuisance in those cases continue to this day, but they are applied in rather different ways. Another case deals with a spite fence, which is closely related to nuisance. The concluding case in Chapter 3 deals with a racially restrictive zoning ordinance, which the Supreme Court struck down in the early twentieth century. Many property scholars see in that line of precedent a fundamental principle: that property can confer rights even in the face of racial discrimination.

Chapter 4 continues to look at these themes of government and private regulation of property. We turn to the Alien Land Laws in several western states that prevented non-citizens from owning real property. Those laws were aimed largely at Asian Americans. Some of the people affected by the laws used trust law to get around them. We turn to the Supreme Court's decisions in *Oyama v. California* to discuss the expanding protections given to property rights of racial minorities. We conclude Chapter 4 by looking at the Supreme Court's invalidation of racially restrictive covenants in *Shelley v. Kraemer*. There are lessons here about the scope of constitutional protection, as well as common law principles of restraint on alienation, which continue to have salience today.

Our second goal in this book is to present contemporary cases in which race is a key deciding factor. To that end, Chapter 5 looks at the revolution in housing and neighborhood wrought by the Civil Rights Movement. We examine how the Fair Housing Act made sales and rental transactions more transparent. We also examine how the various movements that came out of the Civil Rights Movement—rights for migrants, environmental justice, and financing—have influenced notions of neighborhood in property law.

Our third goal is to introduce new cases to widely understood property doctrine. Chapter 6, then, turns to contemporary common law decisions. It is organized in the way that first-year property casebooks frequently are organized, and covers such key doctrines as adverse possession, estates and future interests, co-tenancies, landlord-tenant law, and easements, and concludes with a case of a charitable trust. Our goal here is to include common law property doctrine that deals with race, as well as cases where racial and ethnic minorities use common law property doctrines. The cases in Chapter 6 explore many basic common law property principles, but in new and unexpected contexts. So we study cases that teach basic property doctrine, but involve parties and fact situations that are different from the ones you usually encounter in property.

Finally, Chapter 7 examines issues of race and ethnicity in an international and comparative context. We examine, for instance, how the property rights of indigenous people are protected throughout the world, and how international law impacts property conflicts between indigenous people. And perhaps there are doctrines that might be helpful in analyzing domestic United States law, just as some domestic decisions may help illuminate problems elsewhere.

In developing this book, we have benefitted mightily from the extraordinary scholarship on race and ethnicity that has been produced in recent years, and from the generosity of many referees from Aspen, as well as the talented group of progressive property scholars who are remaking the field of property, as well as our students. There are many more cases and much scholarship we could have included. We very much want to hear from readers and users of this book regarding ideas for new cases, statutes, and scholarship to add. The field is vibrant and moving very quickly, and we look forward to learning from you!

Al Brophy
abrophy@email.unc.edu
Albert Lopez
lopeza@nku.edu
Kali Murray
kali.murray@marquette.edu

November 2010

ACKNOWLEDGMENTS

I would like to begin by thanking the students over many who've asked questions about why the property course doesn't talk about more issues of relevance to their communities. You are the people who inspired this book. Dana Jim was the first to ask that question years ago and others have made similar points over the years. Sometimes the question comes in the form of "Why isn't property more interesting in general?" We have tried to do something about that as well here. Anna Elizabeth Lineberger, UNC 2011, and Stacey Marlise Shepherd, UNC 2012, provided excellent research help. The support of the editorial team at Aspen has meant a great deal to us, from the moment we first started working on this book four years ago, to the final production.

This book rests on the terrific scholarship that has remade the study of property in the last generation. Our notes try to reflect that vibrant work, though we are only able to sample the literature. In addition to the numerous anonymous referees for this manuscript, we have benefitted from the counsel and scholarship of Michelle Wilde Anderson, Keith Aoki, Bernadette Atuahene, Ben Barros, Kathy Bergin, Mary Sarah Bilder, Mark Brandon, William S. Brewbaker, Carol N. Brown, David L. Callies, Carl Christensen, Stephen Clowney, Adrienne D. Davis, John Dzienkowski, James Ely, Wendy F. Greene, Daniel W. Hamilton, Daniel J. Hulsebosch, Calvin Massey, Deana Pollard-Sacks, Florence W. Roisman, Joseph Singer, Norman Stein, Asmara Tekle, Rose Cuison Villazor, Carlton Waterhouse, and Caryl Yzenbaard. Barbara Thompson has added terrifically to this project, as she has so much of my other work, and I particularly appreciate her help on the history of Hawaiian property law.

Three deans have generously supported this work: Avi Soifer of the University of Hawaii, Kenneth Randall of the University of Alabama, and Jack Boger of the University of North Carolina. Albert and Kali have been terrific, enriching this book with their enthusiasm, their scholarship, and their wise reading of cases, statutes, and culture.

ALB

I would like to thank Al Brophy for taking a chance on me!

I would also like to thank my able research assistants over the years, starting with the work of Margaret Delain, who has stuck with this work through thick and thin In addition, I would like to thank John Alarcon, Tiphany Baker-Dickerson Joan Cleven-King, J. Frank Hogue, Ashley Roth, Nicholas Russell, Benjamin Schwall, Michael Soule, and Nicole Tisdale. Your hard work on this project kept me always thinking about the audience that this book is intended to serve.

I would like to thank my amazing research assistant Sharon Hill, who keeps me sane. I would also like to thank Bernadette Wilson, who help me start this project at the University of Mississippi School of Law.

I would like to thank my current and former colleagues at the Marquette University Law School and the University of Mississippi School of Law. In particular, I would like to thank Dean Joseph Kearney at the the Marquette University Law School for his unwavering support of this project in all of its phases. I would also like to thank former Dean Sam Davis at the University of Mississippi School of Law for his support of this project in its early stages.

I would to thank the members of the Property Works in Progress, the AALS Property Section, and our unnamed peer reviewers for serving as a wonderful set of critics for this project. I would also like to thank Kristi Bowman for her thoughtful listening work on this project.

Finally, I would like to acknowledge the support of Saundra R. Murray Nettles, Donald Gaines Murray, Jr., Lucy Franklin Brown, Ronald William Bailey, Ernest "Dutch" Igoni, Alana Murray-Blue and Khalif Blue, and the members of my extended "clan" of family and friends.

KNM

The authors gratefully acknowledge the following people and institutions who gave us permission to reprint their work here.

Lindsay Robertson, *Conquest by Law: How the Discovery of America Dispossessed Indigenous Peoples of Their Land* xi-xii (Oxford University Press 2005), reprinted with permission of Lindsay Robertson.

Dana G. Jim, "Great Property Cases: *Johnson v. M'Intosh* and the South Dakota Fossil Case," 46 *St. Louis University Law Journal* 791 (2002). Reprinted with permission of the St. Louis University *Law Journal* 2002, St. Louis University School of Law, St. Louis, Missouri.

Thomas W. Mitchell, "From Reconstruction to Deconstruction: Undermining Black Landownership, Political Independence, and Community Through Partition Sales of Tenancies in Common," 95 *Northwestern University Law Review* 505 (2001), reprinted by special permission of

Northwestern University School of Law, *Journal of Criminal Law and Criminology*.

Guadalupe T. Luna, "Chicana/Chicano Land Tenure in the Agrarian Domain: On the Edge of a 'Naked Knife,'" 4 Michigan Journal of Race & Law 39 (1998), reprinted with permission of Guadalupe T. Luna and *Michigan Journal of Race & Law*.

Integrating Spaces

I

RACE IN THE MAKING OF PROPERTY LAW

1 ORIGINS: POSSESSION AND DISPOSSESSION IN PROPERTY LAW

1.1 BEGINNING PROPERTY

Often Property casebooks start with a statement from William Blackstone's *Commentaries on the Laws of England*, which describes the seemingly absolute rights associated with property:

> There is nothing which so generally strikes the imagination, and engages the affections of mankind, as the right of property; or that sole and despotic dominion which one man exercises over the external things of the world, in total exclusion of any other individual in the universe.[1]

Blackstone's classic statement of the "sole" and "despotic" dominion of property rights is appealing to those who believe they can do whatever they like with their property. They can use it however they would like; they can build whatever they would like on it; they can sell it to whomever they would like; they certainly can keep people off of it—the list goes on and on.

However, much of what we study in property class contradicts these common assumptions. We study the limitations of rights of property. One neighbor's right to use her property is limited by the other's right to be free from interference; one person may have a right (we call it an easement) to cross another's property; one neighbor may have a right to prevent building

1. 2 William Blackstone, Commentaries on the Laws of England *2 (1765). Blackstone's often-quoted statement reiterates the notion of long-standing precedent and the value of property in our society in casebooks that introduce property rights by dispelling absolutist myths. *See, e.g.*, A. James Casner et al., Cases and Text on Property 785-838 (5th ed., 2004); John E. Cribbet et al, Property: Cases and Materials 3-4 (7th ed. 1996) (same). Dwyer and Menell delay their discussion of absolutism of property until well into their book. *See* John Dwyer & Peter S. Menell, Property: An Institutional Approach 273 (1997).

on another person's property (we call it a restrictive covenant or a servitude).

Furthermore, numerous statutes and regulations affect how a property owner can use her property. From zoning regulations, to civil rights statutes, to environmental regulations, such as restrictions on development of wetlands, owners face many limitations on their rights. The array of restrictions on the rights of property owners leads one to conclude that property rights are not absolute. Property rights are limited by and exist in conjunction with the rights of others.

Understanding the complexities of these relationships is the key to understanding property law. The materials in this book expose you to the relationship between race and property law, and the impact of the law on all people, whether or not they own property. Eminent domain, for example, refers to the power of the sovereign (government) to "take" property from its citizens. However, the power of eminent domain is not unlimited. The property must be taken for "public use" and the sovereign must pay just compensation (usually the fair market value) to the dispossessed property owners. What "public use" means has been hotly debated in recent years, especially after the United States Supreme Court's 2005 decision in *Kelo v. City of New London,* 545 U.S. 469 (2005). Despite these restrictions on the sovereign's power, eminent domain has been the legal mechanism by which some communities have been torn asunder.

Yet, even Blackstone, with his vision of "sole" and "despotic" dominion, warned us not to look too closely at the origins of our treasured property rights. For if we did, we would likely find an inequitable origin—and the discomforting truth that our right of *possession* depended a great deal on others' *dispossesion.* Blackstone observed:

> Pleased as we are with the possession, we seem afraid to look back to the means by which it was acquired, as if fearful of some element in our title; or at best we rest satisfied with the decision of the laws in our favour, without examining the reason or authority upon which those laws have been built.

Blackstone's Commentaries, *supra* note 1, at *2. Blackstone accepted the utility of refusing to interrogate the source of title. For, presumably, such an inquiry might destabilize respect for property. As Blackstone wrote, "It is well if the most of mankind will obey the laws when made, without searching too nicely into the reasons of making them." Blackstone, Commentaries, *supra* note 1, at *2. Thomas Paine, in his pamphlet *Common Sense* (written at the start of the American Revolution), used such a technique to undermine the basis of heredity nobility, one of the key organizing principles of English society:

> England, since the conquest, hath known some few good monarchs, but groaned beneath a much larger number of bad ones; yet no man in his senses can say that

> their claim under William the Conqueror is a very honorable one. A French bastard landing with an armed banditti, and establishing himself king of England against the consent of the natives, is in plain terms a very paltry rascally original. It certainly hath no divinity in it.

Thomas Paine, POLITICAL WRITINGS 13 (Bruce Kuklick ed. 2000). Paine's revolutionary message was clear—if hereditary nobility had such dishonorable origins, then no respect need be accorded to such "armed banditti." Those seeking to destabilize a regime often question the legitimacy of its origins and those seeking to support the regime do not want to see it questioned.

Others, however, sought to provide a justification for property rights, even as they might appear at first glance to be inequitable. When William Paley wrote his treatise on moral philosophy in the early nineteenth century, he spoke about the seeming incoherence of property law. He asked readers to imagine a system in which some labored for others. This makes little sense at first inspection. Paley used a vignette of birds to suggest property law's hidden significance and logic:

> If you should see in a field of corn a flock of pigeons, all of whom, save one, were engaged, not in choosing for themselves the best food, but the worst, and reserving the best for that single pigeon, the weakest and perhaps the worst of the flock; and if, while that single pigeon was devouring or wasting at pleasure, you should see, when another hungry and hardy pigeon touched a grain of the hoard, all the other pigeons fly on the intruder, and peck it to death; you would then see nothing more than what is practiced every day among men. In civilized society, many persons toil to find superfluities for one, sometimes the least deserving of his species; getting for themselves only the worst and smallest share, and quietly look on, while they see the fruits of their labor spent or spoiled by that single one or his minions. They will even join to hang a man, whose necessities may have led him to take the smallest particle from the hoard so unequally distributed.

PALEY'S MORAL AND PRACTICAL PHILOSOPHY 69 (Richard Green ed. 1835). This chapter starts off in another way—exploring dispossession as an origin of property rights. The question of dispossession is a more challenging one. Chapter One looks at a variety of materials in order to explore that "hidden" story of dispossession. As we do, several issues arise:

1. How should a court deal with claims to property that has been unjustly taken?
2. Is it appropriate for a court to question the morality of title to property?
3. How should a court deal with a claim by a property owner or a non-property owner?

1.2 DISPOSSESSION: OWNERSHIP OF ANOTHER PERSON

Let us begin with a case, then, with humans as property. This is the most profound type of dispossession possible—the "taking" of individuals' freedom to control their lives. Thus, the idea of ownership of a human being obviously raises critical issues of morality. How did courts approach those fundamental issues of morality? How did they deal with claims that one person should not be owned by another? Mostly, courts did not even begin such inquiries.

To formulate some initial answers to how courts approached slavery, we begin with *The Antelope*, a case involving the origins of property in another human, the international slave trade, piracy, and the responsibility of the United States to uphold the law of nations. The complex chain of events that form the background to *The Antelope* began when a privateer ship left the port of Baltimore in 1819 and continued through 1825 when Chief Justice John Marshall of the U.S. Supreme Court decided the fate of the surviving human cargo aboard the captured slave ship.

The original vessel, the *Columbia*, sailing under a Venezuelan registry, clandestinely left Baltimore harbor with a crew of 30 to 40 Americans. The privateers changed the ship's name to the *Arraganta*, hoisted the flag of the obscure Latin American state Artega, and began preying on slave ships south of the equator along Africa's west coast. The first ship they attacked was an American ship, purportedly the *Exchange* from Bristol, Rhode Island. From this American ship, the *Arraganta* confiscated 25 newly captured slaves; the ship then proceeded to attack various Portuguese vessels and confiscate the slaves aboard them. Finally, the *Arraganta* captured *The Antelope*, a Spanish ship, carrying an estimated 160 slaves.

The privateers (whom the opinion also called "pirates") sailed the *Antelope* and the *Arraganta* to Brazil to sell their bounty of slaves. When the *Arraganta* wrecked off the coast of Brazil, many of those on board either drowned or were captured. The survivors were then transferred to the *Antelope*. Under the leadership of American John Smith, the name of the *Antelope* was changed to the *General Ramirez* and the ship sailed toward the southern United States. Off the coast of Florida, where the ship was apparently getting ready to land some of its human cargo, a United States revenue cutter under the leadership of Captain John Jackson captured the *Antelope* and brought the ship and the 280 slaves aboard to Savannah, Georgia for adjudication.

The ship's human cargo was claimed by the Spanish and Portuguese counsels and the United States. While the lower courts worked through the issues of the legality of the *Antelope*'s capture by Captain Jackson and the claims made by the American, Spanish, and Portuguese governments, approximately one-third of the slaves died in captivity. As no evidence was offered to show which of the slaves were taken from the American vessel versus the Spanish and Portuguese vessels, the district court ruled that the remaining slaves be divided by lot and the numbers of original captives be prorated (due to the subsequent deaths) for each country.

Eventually, the case was appealed to the U.S. Supreme Court, where the complex facts raised troubling issues involving how and when the U.S. courts should recognize property rights acquired through the international slave trade. The case posed a conflict, as former Attorney General William Wirt and Francis Scott Key, the author of "The Star Spangled Banner," argued for the freedom of the slaves in this case against the governments of Portugal and Spain, petitioning the Supreme Court to distinguish between "a claim to freedom [and] a claim to property." As you read the opinion, consider the relative importance of these competing claims—freedom and property—in the Court's analysis.

The Antelope

23 U.S. (10 Wheaton) 66 (1825)

MARSHALL, C.J.: In prosecuting this appeal, the United States assert no property in themselves. They appear in the character of guardians, or next friends, of these Africans, who are brought, without any act of their own, into the bosom of our country, insist on their right to freedom, and submit their claim to the laws of the lands, and to the tribunals of the nation.

The Consuls of Spain and Portugal, respectively, demand these Africans as slaves, who have, in the regular course of legitimate commerce, been acquired as property by the subjects of their respective sovereigns, and claim their restitution under the laws of the United States.

In examining claims of this momentous importance—claims in which the sacred rights of liberty and of property come in conflict with each other, . . . —this Court must not yield to feelings which might seduce it from the path of duty, and must obey the mandate of the law.

That the course of opinion on the slave trade should be unsettled, ought to excite no surprise. The Christian and civilized nations of the world with whom we have most intercourse, have all been engaged in it. However abhorrent this traffic may be to a mind whose original feelings are not blunted by familiarity with the practice, it has been sanctioned in modern times by the laws of all nations who possess distant colonies, each of whom has engaged in it as a common commercial business which no other could rightfully interrupt. It has claimed all the sanction which could be derived from long usage, and general acquiescence. That trade could not be considered as contrary to the law of nations which was authorized and protected by the laws of all commercial nations; the right to carry on which was claimed by each, and allowed by each.

The course of unexamined opinion, which was founded on this inveterate usage, received its first check in America; and, as soon as these States acquired the right of self-government, the traffic was forbidden by most of them. In the beginning of this century, several humane and enlightened individuals of Great Britain devoted themselves to the cause of the Africans; and, by frequent appeals to the nation, in which the enormity of this commerce was unveiled, and exposed to the public eye, the general sentiment was at length roused against it, and the feelings of justice and humanity, regaining their long lost ascendency, prevailed so far in the British parliament as to obtain an act for its abolition. The utmost efforts of the British government, as well as of that of the United States, have since been assiduously employed in its suppression. It has been denounced by both in terms of great severity, and those concerned in it are subjected to the heaviest penalties which law can inflict. In addition to these measures operating on their own people, they have used all their influence to bring other nations into the same system, and to interdict this trade by the consent of all.

Public sentiment has, in both countries, kept pace with the measures of government; and the opinion is extensively, if not universally entertained, that this unnatural traffic ought to be suppressed. While its illegality is asserted by some governments, but not admitted by all; while the detestation in which it is held is growing daily, and even those nations who tolerate it in fact, almost disavow their own conduct, and rather connive at, than legalize, the acts of their subjects; it is not wonderful that public feeling should march somewhat in advance of strict law, and that opposite opinions should be entertained on the precise cases in which our own laws may control and limit the practice of others. Indeed, we ought not to be surprised, if, on this novel series of cases, even Courts of justice should, in some instances, have carried the principle of suppression farther than a more deliberate consideration of the subject would justify.

The *Amedie*, (1 *Acton's Rep.* 240) which was an American vessel employed in the African trade, was captured by a British cruiser and condemned in the Vice Admiralty Court of Tortola . . . Sir William Grant, in delivering the opinion of the Court, said, that the trade being then declared unjust and unlawful by Great Britain, 'a claimant could have no right, upon principles of universal law, to claim restitution in a prize Court, of human beings carried as his slaves. He must show some right that has been violated by the capture, some property of which he has been dispossessed, and to which he ought to be restored. In this case, the laws of the claimant's country allow no right of property to such claims. There can, therefore, be no right of restitution. The consequence is, that the judgment must be affirmed.'

. . . The Diana (1 *Dodson's Rep.* 95) was a Swedish vessel, captured with a cargo of slaves, by a British cruiser, and condemned in the Court of the Vice Admiralty at Sierra Leone. This sentence was reversed on appeal, and Sir William Scott, in pronouncing the sentence of reversal, said, "the condemnation also took place on a principle which this court cannot in any manner recognize, inasmuch as the sentence affirms, 'that the slave trade, from motives of humanity, hath been abolished by most civilized nations, and is not, at the present time, legally authorized by any.' This appears to me to be an assertion by no means sustainable." The ship and cargo were restored, on the principle that the trade was allowed by the laws of Sweden.

The principle common to these cases is, that the legality of the capture of a vessel engaged in the slave trade, depends on the law of the country to which the vessel belongs. If that law gives its sanction to the trade, restitution will be decreed; if that law prohibits it, the vessel and cargo will be condemned as good prize.

. . . [Sir William Scott] also said [in *The Louis* (2 Dodson's Rep., 238)], that this [slave] trade could not be pronounced contrary to the law of nations. "A Court, in the administration of law, cannot attribute criminality to an act where the law imputes none. It must look to the legal standard of morality; and upon a question of this nature, that standard must be found in the law of nations . . ."

. . . In the United States, different opinions have been entertained in the different Circuits and Districts; and the subject is now, for the first time, before this Court.

The question whether the slave trade is prohibited by the law of nations has been seriously propounded, and both the affirmative and negative of the proposition have been maintained with equal earnestness.

That it is contrary to the law of nature will scarcely be denied. That every man has a natural right to the fruits of his own labour, is generally admitted, and that no other person can rightfully deprive him of those fruits, and appropriate them against his will, seems to be the necessary result of this admission. But from the earliest times war has existed, and war confers rights in which all have acquiesced. Among the most enlightened nations of antiquity, one of these was, that the victor might enslave the vanquished. This, which was the usage of all, could not be pronounced repugnant to the law of nations, which is certainly to be tried by the test of neutral usage. That which has received the assent of all, must be the law of all.

Slavery, then, has its origin in force; but as the world has agreed that it is a legitimate result of force, the state of things which is thus produced by general consent, cannot be pronounced unlawful.

Throughout Christendom, this harsh rule has been exploded, and war is no longer considered as giving a right to enslave captives. But this triumph of humanity has not been universal. The parties to the modern law of nations do not propagate their principles by force; and Africa has not yet adopted them. Throughout the whole extent of that immense continent, so far as we know its history, it is still the law of nations that prisoners are slaves. Can those who have themselves renounced this law, be permitted to participate in its effects by purchasing the beings who are its victims?

Whatever might be the answer of a moralist to this question, a jurist must search for its legal solution, in those principles of action which are sanctioned by the usages, the national acts, and the general assent, of that portion of the world of which he considers himself as a part, and to whose law the appeal is made. If we resort to this standard as the test of international law, the question, as has already been observed, is decided in favor of the legality of the trade. Both Europe and America embarked in it; and for nearly two centuries, it was carried on without opposition, and without censure. A jurist could not say, that a practice thus supported was illegal, and that those engaged in it might be punished, either personally, or by deprivation of property.

In this commerce, thus sanctioned by universal assent, every nation had an equal right to engage. How is this right to be lost? Each may renounce it for its own people; but can this renunciation affect others?

No principle of general law is more universally acknowledged, than the perfect equality of nations. Russia and Geneva have equal rights. It results from this equality, that no one can rightfully impose a rule on another. Each legislates for itself, but its legislation can operate on itself alone. A right, then, which is vested in all by the consent of all, can be devested only by consent; and this trade, in which all have participated, must remain lawful to those who cannot be induced to relinquish it. As no nation can prescribe a rule for others, none can make a law of nations; and this traffic remains lawful to those whose governments have not forbidden it.

If it is consistent with the law of nations, it cannot in itself be piracy. It can be made so only by statute; and the obligation of the statute cannot transcend the legislative power of the state which may enact it.

If it be neither repugnant to the law of nations, nor piracy, it is almost superfluous to say in this Court, that the right of bringing in for adjudication in time of peace, even where the vessel belongs to a nation which has prohibited the trade cannot exist. The Courts of no country execute the penal laws of another; and the course of the American government on the subject of visitation and search, would decide any case in which that right had been exercised by an American cruiser, on the vessel of a foreign nation, not violating our municipal laws, against the captors.

It follows, that a foreign vessel engaged in the African slave trade, captured on the high-seas in time of peace, by an American cruiser, and brought in for adjudication, would be restored.

The general question being disposed of, it remains to examine the circumstances of the particular case.

The *Antelope*, a vessel unquestionably belonging to Spanish subjects, was captured while receiving a cargo of Africans on the coast of Africa, by the *Arraganta*, a privateer which was manned in Baltimore, and is said to have been then under the flag of the Oriental republic. Some other vessels, said to be Portuguese, engaged in the same traffic, were previously plundered, and the slaves taken from them, as well as from another vessel then in the same port, were put on board the *Antelope*, of which vessel the

Arraganta took possession, landed her crew, and put on board a prize master and prize crew. Both vessels proceeded to the coast of Brazil, where the *Arraganta* was wrecked, and her captain and crew either lost or made prisoners.

The *Antelope*, whose name was changed to the *General Ramirez*, after an ineffectual attempt to sell the Africans on board at Surinam, arrived off the coast of Florida, and was hovering on that coast, near that of the United States, for several days. Supposing her to be a pirate, or a vessel wishing to smuggle slaves into the United States, Captain Jackson, of the revenue cutter *Dallas*, went in quest of her, and finding her laden with slaves, commanded by officers who were citizens of the United States, with a crew who spoke English, brought her in for adjudication.

She was libeled by the Vice Consuls of Spain and Portugal, each of whom claim that portion of the slaves which were conjectured to belong to the subjects of their respective sovereigns; which claims are opposed by the United States on behalf of the Africans.

. . . [Marshall affirmed the district court's award of the slaves from the Spanish ship to the Spanish claimants. However, he also placed the burden of proof as to the identity of the slaves who were on board the ship when it was captured on the Spanish claimants. Thus, the claimants were entitled only to the specific people they could prove were on the ship when it was captured by the pirates.

Marshall, moreover, questioned the claim to the slaves taken from the Portuguese ships. No one had come forward as the "probable owner" of the Portuguese slaves. Marshall thought that "irresistible testimony," that "the real owner belongs to some other nation, and feels the necessity of concealment." In fact, he considered it evidence of intent to violate the United States' prohibition on the international slave trade. Marshall concluded that the humans alleged to be owned by Portuguese citizens were entitled to freedom.]

. . . We think, then, that all the Africans, now in possession of the Marshal for the District of Georgia, and under the control of the Circuit Court of the United States for that District, which were brought in with the *Antelope*, otherwise called the *General Ramirez*, except those which may be designated as the property of the Spanish claimants, ought to be delivered up to the United States, to be disposed of according to law. So much of the sentence of the Circuit Court as is contrary to this opinion, is to be reversed, and the residue affirmed.

NOTES AND QUESTIONS

1. For a detailed history of *The Antelope*, see Professor (now Judge) John T. Noonan's *The Antelope: The Ordeal of the Recaptured Africans in the Administrations of James Monroe and John Quincy Adams* (1977).

In the end, all the slaves, except those who came from the Spanish-owned ship, were entitled to freedom. The slaves from the U.S. ship were free because the United States had outlawed the slave trade. No one from Portugal claimed the slaves who came from Portuguese vessels, and so Marshall concluded that they were free, too. Yet, those slaves from the Spanish ship (the original 93 from *The Antelope*) were brought to the United States without the consent of their owners, so a treaty with Spain protected the Spanish owners' rights. Marshall required that Spain produce evidence to prove its claim to each slave. Spain could successfully claim only about 39 of the slaves on *The Antelope*. Noonan at 132.

Among the many surprising pieces of that case was the attempt by Justice William Johnson, sitting as a circuit justice, to determine who would go free and who would be sent back to slavery by use of a lottery. The "losers" in the lottery would be assigned to the Spanish and kept in slavery; the "winners" would be freed. Johnson wrote "We can only do the best in our power. The lot must direct their fate; and the Almighty will direct the hand that acts in the selection." Noonan at 65. When the Supreme Court held that only those who could be identified as coming from the Spanish ship could be kept in slavery, the Court remanded the case to the circuit court to determine who would be freed and who enslaved. Perhaps the abandonment of the lottery signals a transition from a pre-modern sense of divine intervention to a modern sense bounded by evidence explainable to humans. *See also* Carol N. Brown, *Casting Lots: The Illusion of Justice and Accountability in Property Allocation*, 53 Buffalo L. Rev. 65 (2005).

2. What do you think Marshall's personal opinion about the slave trade was? About slavery in general? Where in the opinion does Marshall give a sense of his own opinion?

3. If Marshall may have had some opposition to slavery, then why would he uphold it in this opinion? What was his basis for upholding the slave trade? How important was the long-term existence of slavery? Did it matter that many nations engaged in it?

How important is the adoption of slavery by other countries as a guide to what is permitted under international law? What do you make of this statement: "Slavery, then, has its origin in force; but as the world has agreed that it is a legitimate result of force, the state of things which is thus produced by general consent, cannot be pronounced unlawful."

4. How did Marshall think that one person obtained the right of ownership over another person? According to Marshall, how could people be dispossessed of themselves?

5. Francis Scott Key argued another case to the Supreme Court in 1813, *Mima Queen and Child v. Hepburn*, 11 U.S. (7 Cranch) 290, on behalf of petitioners whose only proof of their great-grandmother's freedom, and thus their own freedom, was based on hearsay testimony.

The majority of the Court easily disposed of the matter by applying the established rule of law barring admission of hearsay evidence on specific facts. Chief Justice Marshall wrote, "However the feeling of the individual may be interested on the part of a person claiming freedom, the Court cannot perceive any legal distinction between the assertion of this and of any other [property] right . . . It was very justly observed by a great judge that 'all questions upon the rules of evidence are of vast importance to all orders and degrees of men: our lives, our liberty, and our property are all concerned in support of these rules, which have been matured by the wisdom of the ages, and are now revered from their antiquity and the good sense in which they are founded' . . . [i]f circumstance that the eye witnesses of any fact be dead should justify the introduction of testimony to establish that fact from hearsay, no man could feel safe in any property . . ."

Justice Duvall alone dissented, saying, "it appears to me that the reason for admitting hearsay evidence upon a question of freedom is much stronger than in cases of pedigree or in controversies relative to the boundaries of land. It will be universally admitted that the right to freedom is more important than the right to property.

And people of color from their helpless condition under the uncontrolled authority of a master, as entitled to all reasonable protection. A decision that hearsay evidence in such cases shall not be admitted, cuts up by the roots all claims of the kind, and puts a final end to them, unless the claim should arise from a fact of recent date, and such a case will seldom, perhaps never, occur."

How does the majority's statement that "all questions upon the rules of evidence are of vast importance to all orders and degrees of men: our lives, our liberty, and our property are all concerned in support of these rules" demonstrate the value it places on the petitioner's claim?

Compare this to the rationale offered by the dissent. At this point in your study of property law, what value do you see in the rationale offered by the majority? What similarities do you see in the reasoning of the majority between this case and *The Antelope*?

6. Two proslavery arguments were common before the Civil War: first, that slavery was the product of the ages, and second, that abolishing slavery would be a financial and social disaster. Senator John Bell of Tennessee used those common arguments during debates over the Fugitive Slave Act of 1850:

> As to the lawfulness or sinfulness of the institution of slavery—whatever . . . the disciples of a transcendental creed of any kind may hold or teach . . . I must claim the privilege of interpreting the law of nature by what I see revealed in the history of mankind from the earlier period of recorded time, uncontradicted by Divine authority. But above all I have seen here, on this continent, and in these United States, the original lords of the soil subdued . . . and the remnant still held in subordination; and all this under an interpretation of the law of nature which holds good at this day among our northern brethren . . . three millions of the African race, whose labor is subject to the will of masters, under such circumstances that their condition cannot be changed, though their masters should will it, without destruction alike to the interests

> and welfare of both master and slave. These are the lights by which I read and understand the law of nature.

Congressional Globe, 31st Cong., 1st Sess. 1105 (1850). The Fugitive Slave Act of 1850 expanded the rights of slaveholders to recover fugitive slaves. For instance, it denied alleged fugitives the right of a jury trial before they were returned to their owners and it made it a federal crime to interfere with the recapture of a fugitive slave.

Harriet Beecher Stowe's 1852 novel *Uncle Tom's Cabin* sought to undermine support for slavery and the Fugitive Slave Act. In the early twentieth century her son Charles Edward Stowe commented in looking back on the struggle to end slavery: "An attack on any form of property is an assault on the whole basis of civilized society, and seen as revolutionary and dangerous in the highest degree." *The Religion of Slavery*, 5 The Crisis 36 (1912).

Should such arguments about the possibility of reform or about long-standing precedent constrain judges or legislators? Should they constrain judges more than legislators?

7. Compare those arguments to another slavery case, *The Amistad*, argued 16 years after *The Antelope*. It was the subject of a Stephen Spielberg movie (called *Amistad*) released in 1997. Professor Brant Lee uses *The Amistad* case to introduce the concepts of possession and ownership to his students. He describes the case this way:

> In 1841, a Cuban slave ship called the *Amistad* was captured and taken into custody near Long Island. The forty-five Black people on board were alleged to be slaves, who had mutinied, murdered the captain, killed or expelled the crew and taken over the ship. Two Cubans found on the ship claimed to be their owners. There were salvage claims by the officers who captured the ship and its passengers and miscellaneous other claims by parties claiming a property interest in the ship or its cargo. The United States government intervened on behalf of the Queen of Spain in support of treaty rights regarding the restoration of the lost property of Spanish subjects, thus taking the side of the alleged slave owners. Astonishingly, the alleged slaves intervened on their own behalf, claiming not to be Cuban slaves at all, but illegally kidnapped free Africans, and the United States Supreme Court was eventually called upon to determine their fate.

Brant T. Lee, *Teaching The Amistad*, 46 St. Louis U. L.J. 775 (2002).

Whether the Africans were slave or free turned in large part on whether they were free at the time their ship was found off Long Island. The Africans' lawyer argued they were free at the time they were found:

> The Africans, when found by Lieutenant Gedney, were in a free state, where all men are presumed to be free, and were in the actual condition of freemen. The burden of proof, therefore, rests on those who assert them to be slaves. . . . When they call on the courts of the United States to reduce to slavery men who are apparently free, they must show some law, having force in the place where they were taken, which makes

> them slaves, or that the claimants are entitled in our courts to have some foreign law, obligatory on the Africans as well as on the claimants, enforced in respect to them, and that by such foreign law they are slaves. It is not pretended, that there was any law existing in the place where they were found, which made them slaves, but it is claimed, that by the laws of Cuba, they were slaves to Ruiz and Montez [the alleged owners of Africans on the *Amistad*]; and that those laws are to be here enforced. But before the laws of Cuba, if any such there be, can be applied, to affect the personal status of individuals within a foreign jurisdiction, it is very clear, that it must be shown that they were domiciled in Cuba.

40 U.S. 518, 561.

This argument posed substantial risk if the court followed it, for it meant that slaves who were found without owners might claim freedom. The U.S. Attorney General argued precisely this point. When they left Cuba, he wrote, the Africans were "in the actual possession of the persons claiming to be their owners." The Attorney General continued, "they may be regarded as slaves, as much as the Negroes who accompany a planter between any two ports of the United States. This, then, is the first evidence of property—their actual existence in a state of slavery, and in the possession of their alleged owners, in a place where slavery is recognized, and exists by law." 40 U.S. at 583.

Justice Joseph Story wrote for the majority of the U.S. Supreme Court. He concluded that the Africans were not slaves at the time they left Cuba and, therefore, were not subject to the treaty with Spain that required their rendition:

> They are natives of Africa, and were kidnapped there, and were unlawfully transported to Cuba, in violation of the laws and treaties of Spain, and the most solemn edicts and declarations of that government. By those laws and treaties, and edicts, the African slave trade is utterly abolished; the dealing in that trade is deemed a heinous crime; and the Negroes thereby introduced into the dominions of Spain, are declared to be free. Ruiz and Montez are proved to have made the pretended purchase of these Negroes, with a full knowledge of all the circumstances. And so cogent and irresistible is the evidence in this respect, that the district-attorney has admitted in open court, upon the record, that these Negroes were native Africans, and recently imported into Cuba, as alleged in their answers to the libels in the case. The supposed proprietary interest of Ruiz and Montez is completely displaced, if we are at liberty to look at the evidence, or the admissions of the district-attorney.
>
> If then, these Negroes are not slaves, but are kidnapped Africans, who, by the laws of Spain itself, are entitled to their freedom, and were kidnapped and illegally carried to Cuba, and illegally detained and restrained on board the *Amistad*; there is no pretense to say, that they are pirates or robbers. We may lament the dreadful acts by which they asserted their liberty, and took possession of the *Amistad*, and endeavored to regain their native country; but they cannot be deemed pirates or robbers, in the sense of the law of nations, or the treaty with Spain, or the laws of Spain itself; at least, so far as those laws have been brought to our knowledge. Nor do the libels of Ruiz or Montez assert them to be such.

40 U.S. at 593-94.

The Antelope and *The Amistad* are similar cases involving the international slave trade and the implications of the Spanish law regarding such trade. In 1817, Spain signed a treaty with Great Britain to abolish the slave trade north of the equator with a commitment to abolish the entire trade after May 30, 1820. Only slave traders with a special license from the King were allowed to operate south of the equator after the signing of the treaty in 1817. Noonan at 56. In addition, the United States had a separate treaty, the Treaty of San Lorenzo el real, which guaranteed protection of Spanish vessels and citizens and the return of any stolen property recovered by the United States.

How do these two treaties affect the decisions in *The Antelope* and *The Amistad*? Whom did the United States represent in each case and why? What is the burden of proof in each case?

1.3 DISPOSSESSION: CONQUEST AND NATIVE AMERICAN PROPERTY RIGHTS

Conquest was also used to justify dispossession of Native American claims to property. In the next case, *Johnson v. M'Intosh*, as in *The Antelope*, time, agreement among nations, and the protection of existing property rights supported Chief Justice John Marshall's opinion. Similar to his opinion in *Marbury v. Madison*, Marshall recognizes the opportunity to address an emerging and formative issue in property law through a relatively simple case that he could have succinctly disposed of in a brief opinion. Instead, the entire opinion is crafted to leave no room to doubt the historical validity of the reasoning and to duly influence western expansion in the early nineteenth century.

Johnson v. M'Intosh

21 U.S. (8 Wheaton) 543 (1823)

ERROR to the District Court of Illinois. This was an action of ejectment for lands in the State and District of Illinois, claimed by the plaintiffs under a purchase and conveyance from the Piankeshaw Indians, and by the defendant, under a [subsequent] grant from the United States. . . . [J]udgment below [was] for the defendant . . . .

MARSHALL, C.J.: The plaintiffs in this cause claim the land, in their declaration mentioned, under two grants, purporting to be made, the first in 1773, and the last in 1775, by the chiefs of certain Indian tribes, constituting the Illinois and the Piankeshaw nations; and the question is, whether this title can be recognized in the Courts of the United States?

The facts, as stated in the case agreed, show the authority of the chiefs who executed this conveyance, so far as it could be given by their own people; and likewise show, that the particular tribes for whom these chiefs acted were in rightful possession of the land they sold. The inquiry, therefore, is, in a great measure, confined to the power of Indians to give, and of private individuals to receive, a title which can be sustained in the Courts of this country.

As the right of society, to prescribe those rules by which property may be acquired and preserved is not, and cannot be drawn into question; as the title to lands, especially, is and must be admitted to depend entirely on the law of the nation in which they lie; it will be necessary, in pursuing this inquiry, to examine, not singly those principles of abstract justice, which the Creator of all things has impressed on the mind of his creature man, and which are admitted to regulate, in a great degree, the rights of civilized nations, whose perfect independence is acknowledged; but those principles also which our own government has adopted in the particular case, and given us as the rule for our decision.

On the discovery of this immense continent, the great nations of Europe were eager to appropriate to themselves so much of it as they could respectively acquire. Its vast extent offered an ample field to the ambition and enterprise of all; and the character and religion of its inhabitants afforded an apology for considering them as a people over whom the superior genius of Europe might claim an ascendency. The potentates of the old world found no difficulty in convincing themselves that they made ample compensation to the inhabitants of the new, by bestowing on them civilization and Christianity, in exchange for unlimited independence. But, as they were all in pursuit of nearly the same object, it was necessary, in order to avoid conflicting settlements, and consequent war with each other, to establish a principle, which all should acknowledge as the law by which the right of acquisition, which they all asserted, should be regulated as between themselves. This principle was, that discovery gave title to the government by whose subjects, or by whose authority, it was made, against all other European governments, which title might be consummated by possession.

The exclusion of all other Europeans, necessarily gave to the nation making the discovery the sole right of acquiring the soil from the natives, and establishing settlements upon it. It was a right with which no Europeans could interfere. It was a right which all asserted for themselves, and to the assertion of which, by others, all assented.

Those relations which were to exist between the discoverer and the natives, were to be regulated by themselves. . . .

In the establishment of these relations, the rights of the original inhabitants were, in no instance, entirely disregarded; but were necessarily, to a considerable extent, impaired. They were admitted to be the rightful occupants of the soil, with a legal as well as just claim to retain possession of it, and to use it according to their own discretion; but their rights to complete sovereignty, as independent nations, were necessarily diminished, and their power to dispose of the soil at their own will, to whomsoever they pleased, was denied by the original fundamental principle, that discovery gave exclusive title to those who made it.

While the different nations of Europe respected the right of the natives, as occupants, they asserted the ultimate dominion to be in themselves; and claimed and exercised, as a consequence of this ultimate dominion, a power to grant the soil, while yet in possession of the natives. These grants have been understood by all, to convey a title to the grantees, subject only to the Indian right of occupancy.

The history of America from its discovery to the present day proves, we think, the universal recognition of these principles.

Spain did not rest her title solely on the grant of the Pope. Her discussions respecting boundary, with France, with Great Britain, and with the United States all show that she placed in on the rights given by discovery. Portugal sustained her claim to the Brazils by the same title.

France also founded her title to the vast territories she claimed in America on discovery. . . .

No one of the powers of Europe gave its full assent to this principle, more unequivocally than England. The documents upon this subject are ample and complete. So early as the year 1496, her monarch granted a commission to the Cabots, to discover countries then unknown to *Christian people*, and to take possession of them in the name of the king of England. Two years afterwards, Cabot proceeded on this voyage, and discovered the continent of North America, along which he sailed as far south as Virginia. To this discovery the English trace their title.

In this first effort made by the English government to acquire territory on this continent, we perceive a complete recognition of the principle which has been mentioned. The right of discovery given by this commission, is confined to countries "then unknown to all Christian people;" and of these countries Cabot was empowered to take possession in the name of the king of England. Thus asserting a right to take possession, notwithstanding the occupancy of the natives, who were heathens, and, at the same time, admitting the prior title of any Christian people who may have made a previous discovery. . . .

Thus has our whole country been granted by the crown while in the occupation of the Indians. These grants purport to convey the soil as well as the right of dominion to the grantees. In those governments which were denominated royal, where the right to the soil was not vested in individuals, but remained in the crown, or was vested in the colonial government, the king claimed and exercised the right of granting lands, and of dismembering the government at his will. The grants made out of the two original colonies, after the resumption of their charters by the crown, are examples of this. The governments of New England, New York, New Jersey,

Pennsylvania, Maryland, and a part of Carolina, were thus created. In all of them, the soil, at the time the grants were made, was occupied by the Indians. Yet almost every title within those governments is dependent on these grants. In some instances, the soil was conveyed by the crown unaccompanied by the powers of government, as in the case of the northern neck of Virginia. It has never been objected to this, or to any other similar grant, that the title as well as possession was in the Indians when it was made, and that it passed nothing on that account.

These various patents cannot be considered as nullities; nor can they be limited to a mere grant of the powers of government. A charter intended to convey political power only, would never contain words expressly granting the land, the soil, and the waters. Some of them purport to convey the soil alone; and in those cases in which the powers of government, as well as the soil, are conveyed to individuals, the crown has always acknowledged itself to be bound by the grant. . . .

Further proofs of the extent to which this principle has been recognized, will be found in the history of the wars, negotiations, and treaties, which the different nations, claiming territory in America, have carried on, and held with each other. . . .

Thus, all the nations of Europe, who have acquired territory on this continent, have asserted in themselves, and have recognised in others, the exclusive right of the discoverer to appropriate the lands occupied by the Indians. Have the American States rejected or adopted this principle? . . .

It has never been doubted, that either the United States, or the several States, had a clear title to all the lands within the boundary lines described in the treaty [which concluded the war of our revolution], subject only to the Indian right of occupancy, and that the exclusive power to extinguish that right, was vested in the government which might constitutionally exercise it . . .

The ceded territory was occupied by numerous warlike tribes of Indians; but the exclusive right of the United States to extinguish their title, and to grant the soil, has never, we believe been doubted. . . .

The United States, then, have unequivocally acceded to that great and broad rule by which its civilized inhabitants now hold this country. They hold, and assert in themselves, the title by which it was acquired. They maintain, as all others have maintained, that discovery gave an exclusive right to extinguish the Indian title of occupancy, either by purchase or by conquest; and gave also a right to such a degree of sovereignty, as the circumstances of the people would allow them to exercise.

The power now possessed by the government of the United States to grant lands, resided, while we were colonies, in the Crown, or its grantees. The validity of the titles given by either has never been questioned in our Courts. It has been exercised uniformly over territory in possession of the Indians. The existence of this power must negative the existence of any right which may conflict with, and control it. An absolute title to lands cannot exist, at the same time, in different persons, or in different governments. An absolute, must be an exclusive title, or at least a title which excludes all others not compatible with it. All our institutions recognize the absolute title of the crown, subject only to the Indian right of occupancy, and recognize the absolute title of the crown to extinguish that right. This is incompatible with an absolute and complete title in the Indians.

We will not enter into the controversy, whether agriculturists, merchants, and manufacturers, have a right, on abstract principles, to expel hunters from the territory they possess, or to contract their limits. Conquest gives a title which the courts of the conqueror cannot deny, whatever the private and speculative opinions of individuals may be, respecting the original justice of the claim which has been successfully asserted. The British government, which was then our government, and whose rights have passed to the United States, asserted title to all the lands occupied by Indians, within the chartered limits of the British colonies. It asserted also a limited sovereignty over them, and the exclusive right of extinguishing the title which occupancy gave to them. These claims have been maintained and established as far west as the river Mississippi, by the sword. The title to a vast portion of the lands we now hold, originates in them. It is not for the Courts of this country to question the validity of this title or to sustain one which is incompatible with it.

Although we do not mean to engage in the defense of those principles which Europeans have applied to Indian title, they may, we think, find some excuse, if not justification, in the character and habits of the people whose rights have been wrested from them.

The title by conquest is acquired and maintained by force. The conqueror prescribes its limits. Humanity, however, acting on public opinion, has established, as a general rule, that the conquered shall not be wantonly oppressed, and that their condition shall remain as eligible as is compatible with the objects of the conquest. Most usually, they are incorporated with the victorious nation, and become subjects or citizens of the government with which they are connected. The new and old members of the society mingle with each other; the distinction between them is gradually lost, and they make one people. Where this incorporation is practicable, humanity demands, and a wise policy requires, that the rights of the conquered to property should remain unimpaired; that the new subjects should be governed as equitably as the old, and that confidence in their security should gradually banish the painful sense of being separated from their ancient connections, and united by force to strangers.

When the conquest is complete, and the conquered inhabitants can be blended with the conquerors, or safely governed as a distinct people, public opinion, which not even the conqueror can disregard, imposes these restraints upon him; and he cannot neglect them without injury to his fame, and hazard to his power.

But the tribes of Indians inhabiting this country were fierce savages, whose occupation was war, and whose subsistence was drawn chiefly from the forest. To leave them in possession of their country, was to leave the country a wilderness; to govern them as a distinct people, was impossible, because they were as brave and as high spirited as they were fierce, and were ready to repel by arms every attempt on their independence.

What was the inevitable consequence of this state of things? The Europeans were under the necessity either of abandoning the country, and relinquishing their pompous claims to it, or of enforcing those claims by the sword, and by the adoption of principles adapted to the condition of a people with whom it was impossible to mix, and who could not be governed as a distinct society, or of remaining in their neighborhood, and exposing themselves and their families to the perpetual hazard of being massacred.

Frequent and bloody wars, in which the whites were not always the aggressors, unavoidably ensued. European policy, numbers, and skill prevailed. As the white population advanced, that of the Indians necessarily receded. The country in the immediate neighborhood of agriculturists became unfit for them. The game fled into thicker and more unbroken forests, and the Indians followed. The soil to which the Crown originally claimed title, being no longer occupied by its ancient inhabitants, was parceled out according to the will of the sovereign power and taken possession of by persons who claimed immediately from the Crown or mediately through its grantees or deputies.

That law which regulates and ought to regulate in general the relations between the conqueror and conquered was incapable of application to a people under such circumstances. The resort to some new and different rule better adapted to the actual state of things was unavoidable. Every rule which can be suggested will be found to be attended with great difficulty.

However extravagant the pretension of converting the discovery of an inhabited country into conquest may appear; if the principle has been asserted in the first instance, and afterwards sustained; if a country has been acquired and held under it; if the property of the great mass of the community originates in it, it becomes the law of the land, and cannot be questioned. So, too, with respect to the concomitant principle, that the Indian inhabitants are to be considered merely as occupants, to be protected, indeed, while in peace, in the possession of their lands, but to be deemed incapable of transferring the absolute title to others. However this restriction may be opposed to natural right, and to the usages of civilized nations, yet, if it be indispensable to that system under which the country has been settled, and be adapted to the actual condition of the two people, it may, perhaps, be supported by reason, and certainly cannot be rejected by Courts of justice. . . .

This opinion conforms precisely to the principle which has been supposed to be recognized by all European governments, from the first settlement of America. The absolute ultimate title has been considered as acquired by discovery, subject only to the Indian title of occupancy, which title the discoverers possessed the exclusive right of acquiring . . .

It has never been contended, that the Indian title amounted to nothing. Their right of possession has never been questioned. The claim of government extends to the complete ultimate title, charged with this right of possession, and to the exclusive power of acquiring that right. . . .

After bestowing on this subject a degree of attention which was more required by the magnitude of the interest in litigation, and the able and elaborate arguments of the bar, than by its intrinsic difficulty, the Court is decidedly of opinion, that the plaintiffs do not exhibit a title which can be sustained in the Courts of the United States; and that there is no error in the judgment which was rendered against them in the District Court of Illinois.

NOTES AND QUESTIONS

1. The Native Americans in question conveyed their land to white people back in the 1770s. So, while there is a lot of talk about whether Native Americans could convey title to the property they occupied, the lawsuit was actually between two groups of white people: some claiming from the Natives and others claiming from a grant from the United States.

Professor Lindsay Robertson, in his extensive research into the background of *Johnson*, demonstrated that the parties actually contrived the lawsuit to test the validity of their title:

> The story it tells is unsettling. *Johnson* was a collusive case, an attempt by speculators in Indian lands to take advantage of since-closed loopholes in the early federal judicial system to win a judgment from the Supreme Court recognizing their claim to millions of acres. To achieve this the speculators brought onto their payroll many of the leading figures of the early republic, including former congressman Robert Goodloe Harper, Daniel Webster, first secretary of the navy Benjamin Stoddert, and General William Winder, the lawyer who represented William M'Intosh, the Companies' *Johnson* opponent, before the Supreme Court. Their efforts might well have succeeded had not Chief Justice John Marshall been guided by his own interests at the time the case finally came before him. Marshall saw *Johnson* as a vehicle for removing an obstacle standing between his former colleagues in Virginia's Revolutionary War militia and bounty lands promised them in western Kentucky. To resolve an ongoing dispute over title to these lands, Marshall incorporated the discovery doctrine into his opinion in the *Johnson* case, converting what might have been a one-paragraph decision into one comprising more than thirty-three pages. Traveling far beyond the question presented in a case was typical of Marshall, was contemporaneously criticized, and, as a method of adjudication, is excused today largely because scholars have on the whole sympathized with Marshall's perceived ends. In the case of *Johnson*, as the chief justice himself came to realize, traveling beyond the question presented was a tragic mistake.
>
> Marshall's incorporation of the discovery doctrine into the *Johnson* opinion led to political catastrophe for Native Americans. To Marshall's distress, Georgians seized on the doctrine as justification for the passage of an act imposing Georgia law on the Cherokees. This action inspired Congress to pass the Indian Removal Act of 1830, and

> the forced migration of the eastern tribes began. When the legitimacy of the doctrinal theory underlying these acts came before the Court in *Worcester v. Georgia* in 1832, Marshall repudiated the discovery doctrine, but by then it was too late. Marshall's death in 1835 and the filling of the Court with Andrew Jackson's appointees prevented the securing of this repudiation, and the United States has inherited a legal regime dependent on their subsequent politically driven resurrection of a wrongly decided, collusive case. Perhaps even more troubling, other former British colonial states have imported the doctrine, establishing it as a baseline for indigenous relations throughout the English-speaking world.

Lindsay Robertson, CONQUEST BY LAW: HOW THE DISCOVERY OF AMERICA DISPOSSESSED INDIGENOUS PEOPLES OF THEIR LANDS xi-xii (2005).

2. Why is "discovery" important? What rights does the "discoverer" have? Why is "conquest" important? What is the relationship between discovery and conquest? Why does Marshall talk about what western European countries believed about "discovered" land? Is there any legal significance to this? How does Marshall define the doctrine of discovery?

3. Substantial commentary exists on *Johnson*, much of it (unsurprisingly) quite critical. Marshall's Doctrine of Discovery has been criticized as denying "fundamental human rights and self-determination" because it vests "superior rights of sovereignty over non-Western indigenous peoples and their territories in European-descended government." Robert Williams, THE AMERICAN INDIAN IN WESTERN LEGAL THOUGHT: DISCOURSES OF CONQUEST 325-26 (1990).

Jedediah Purdy interprets *Johnson* as part of a broader policy of imperialism. He calls *Johnson* "one of the stranger opinions in American jurisprudence":

> In the course of ruling that purchasers of land from Native American tribes did not acquire title enforceable in the courts of the United States, Chief Justice Marshall is elegiac, triumphal, and recurrently ambivalent toward his own reasoning. Marshall acknowledged that the principle of his holding "may be opposed to natural right, and to the usages of civilized nations," but, in one of those moments of judicial candor that might convince a vulgar Legal Realist to declare (Pyrrhic) victory and go home, declared that "[c]onquest gives a title which the Courts of the conqueror cannot deny." He also spun a narrative tapestry of dicta, describing an agentless ethnic cleansing in which Native Americans "necessarily receded," along with the deer and the unbroken forests, before the axe and plough of the American frontier. By the end of the opinion, the Euro-American expropriation of North America has emerged as (1) lawful and (2) inevitable, even though the basis of its legality was "opposed to natural right" and Marshall stressed that the inevitability of the displacement gave "excuse" but not "justification" to expulsion.

Jedediah Purdy, *Property and Empire: The Law of Imperialism in Johnson v. M'Intosh*, 75 GEO. WASH. L. REV. 329, 330-31 (2007). Purdy then asks, "What is the relationship between the relentless march forward of the legal judgment and the ambivalent tone and sometimes paradoxical movements of the discussions of historical necessity and natural right?" *Id.* at 331.

4. Nevertheless, in a widely discussed article, *"The Dark Side of Efficiency: Johnson v. M'Intosh and the Expropriation of Amerindian Lands,"* 148 U. Pa. L. Rev. 1065 (2000), Eric Kades employs an economic analysis to explain the rule in *Johnson.* According to Kades, governments often pursued purchases rather than conquest because purchase allowed expropriation of Native American land at a lower cost than conquest. Kades explains expropriation "in terms of minimizing the costs, broadly defined (for example, value of lives, risks borne, and time spent on unproductive warfare), to the European colonizers." *Id.* at 1071. Kades argues that

> colonists established rules to minimize the costs associated with dispossessing the natives. If it had been cheaper to be more brutal, then Europeans would have been more brutal. Such brutality, however, was not cheap at all.
>
> Likewise, if it had been cheaper to show more humanity, the Europeans would have exhibited more, such as extending Indians full rights to sell (or keep) their land. Such a legal rule, however, would have been far from cheap. *Johnson v. M'Intosh* was an essential part of the regime of efficient expropriation because it ensured that Europeans did not bid against each other to acquire Indian lands, thus keeping prices low. The *M'Intosh* rule was neither the beginning nor the end of the means by which Europeans obtained American soil at minimal cost. . . . [W]ars of conquest were unappealing and rare, and how disease and the destruction of the Indians' stocks of wild game played a much larger role in efficient expropriation. . . . [L]egal rules channeled settlement to maximize the effect of these "natural allies" and shows how the Europeans' greater ability to maintain a united front yielded a set of tools for efficient expropriation, from *M'Intosh* to powerful advantages in negotiation.

Id. at 1071-72.

How much do you think *Johnson* is about acquiring land at an inexpensive price from the Natives? How much is it about the United States government maintaining control over who acquires land from Natives?

5. Stuart Banner argues in *How the Indians Lost Their Land* (2005) that Marshall incorrectly interpreted the historical background in *Johnson.* Contrary to Marshall's claim that our country had uniformly operated on the principle that individuals could not purchase title from Native Americans, in the eighteenth century individuals routinely bought property from them. This established practice was well understood in the 1790s but by the 1820s when *Johnson* was decided, the new truth that Marshall proclaimed in 1823 had become a "well known fact" according to Congressional records of 1827.

Marshall was actually writing his own history book of colonial America about the time of *Johnson.* Marshall references several of the colonial charters from the English government that "convey[ed] the soil as well as the right of dominion to the grantees" (*id.* at 184), but Banner points out that this "actual colonial land policy looked very different from the charters, which were drafted in England before colonial settlement took place, before local conditions could have any effect on practice. The rules that in fact governed colonial land acquisition were not taken from the charters, and indeed contradicted the charters . . . Marshall appears not to have known this . . . he mistook the [legal] fiction for the reality . . . having set forth a wrong account of British land policy, Marshall wrongly concluded that recent American practice was nothing new." (*Id.* at 184.) Interestingly enough, almost 200 years later, this misunderstanding that guided the rule set forth by the Court continues to serve as a foundational cornerstone to the origins of American Property law.

6. Did Justice Marshall think it was unjust to take land away from the Natives? What is the evidence for these particular injustices?

7. What rights do the Native Americans retain? What does "Indian title of occupancy" mean?

8. Less than a decade after *Johnson*, Chief Justice Marshall addressed a claim to several thousand acres of land in Florida, which presented similar issues in *United States v. Percheman*, 32 U.S. 51 (1833). Don Juan Percheman, an ensign in the Spanish corps of dragoons, claimed the land under an 1815 grant from the Spanish governor of Florida.

The territory of Florida was ceded, by treaty, from Spain to the United States in 1819. Percheman then claimed against the U.S. government that his grant continued even after the treaty. Marshall held that the treaty explicitly preserved Percheman's property. However, he also observed that international law would have preserved the rights of property held by people in conquered nations:

> It may not be unworthy of remark, that it is very unusual, even in cases of conquest, for the conqueror to do more than to displace the sovereign and assume dominion over the country. The modern usage of nations, which has become law, would be violated; that sense of justice and of right which is acknowledged and felt by the whole civilized world would be outraged, if private property should be generally confiscated, and private rights annulled. The people change their allegiance; their relation to their ancient sovereign is dissolved; but their relations to each other, and their rights of property, remain undisturbed. If this be the modern rule, even in cases of conquest, who can doubt its application to the case of an amicable cession of territory? Had Florida changed its sovereign by an act containing no stipulation respecting the property of individuals, the right of property in all those who became subjects or citizens of the new government would have been unaffected by the change; it would have remained the same as under the ancient sovereign. The language of the second article conforms to this general principle: 'His Catholic Majesty cedes to the United States in full property and sovereignty, all the territories which belong to him, situated to the eastward of the Mississippi, by the name of East and West Florida.' A cession of territory is never understood to be a cession of the property belonging to its inhabitants. The king cedes that only which belonged to him; lands he had previously granted, were not his to cede. Neither party could so understand the cession; neither party could consider itself as attempting a wrong to individuals, condemned by the practice of the whole civilized world. The cession of a territory by its name from one sovereign to another, conveying the compound idea of surrendering at the same time the lands and the people who inhabit them, would be necessarily understood to pass the sovereignty only, and not to interfere with private property. If this could be doubted, the doubt would be removed by the particular enumeration which follows: "The adjacent islands, dependent on said provinces, all public lots and squares, vacant lands, public edifices, fortifications, barracks and other building which are not private

> property, archives and documents which relate directly to the property and sovereignty of the said provinces, are included in this article."
>
> This special enumeration could not have been made, had the first clause of the article been supposed to pass not only the objects thus enumerated, but private property also. The grant of buildings could not have been limited by the words 'which are not private property,' had private property been included in the cession of the territory.

32 U.S. at 86-88.

Later, Marshall returns to this line of reasoning, with reference to the "usages of the civilized world":

> If, as we think must be admitted, the security of private property was intended by the parties; if this security would have been complete without the article, the United States could have no motive for insisting on the interposition of government in order to give validity to titles which, according to the usages of the civilized world, were already valid.

Id. at 88.

The 1819 treaty governing this case protected Percheman's claim against the United States' claim to the same property. Does Marshall's statement about the "modern usage of nations" contradict what the Supreme Court did in *Johnson* or is it merely *dicta*? What do you make of Marshall's statement that "A cession of territory is never understood to be a cession of the property belonging to its inhabitants. The king cedes that only which belonged to him; lands he had previously granted, were not his to cede"?

1.4 DISPOSSESSION: OF NON-PROPERTY AND EVICTIONS

Our first two cases, *The Antelope* and *Johnson v. M'Intosh*, addressed how judges rationalize property ownership. There are other ways we might think about beginning the study of property. One other way involves studying what it means to own something. At the center of the right of property is the right of exclusion, which is also known in common parlance as the right to keep people off your property. We began this chapter by emphasizing the "sole" and "despotic" from William Blackstone, but another key is his usage of the term "total exclusion" in reference to the rights of the individual property owner.

Notably, Blackstone's focus in talking about property rights is on the person who excludes others from his or her property. One might alternatively begin a class on property law by asking about the treatment of people without property.

Perhaps we should begin property class not with Blackstone, but with the eviction scene from Ralph Ellison's 1952 novel *Invisible Man*. Ellison illustrates how the rights of property conflict with ideas of humanity.

The Invisible Man comes upon an elderly couple who are being evicted from a tiny apartment in Harlem. The couple's meager possessions, including the husband's manumission papers, a card dedicated to grandma, a ticket to the St. Louis World's Fair, a breast pump, and pictures of Abraham Lincoln and Marcus Garvey, are strewn in the street outside their apartment. *Id.* at 271-72.

Invisible Man wonders why the couple is being evicted. "Dispossessed?" he cried. "'Dispossessed'! 'Dispossessed,' eighty-seven years and dispossessed of what? They ain't *got* nothing, they caint *get* nothing, they never *had* nothing. So who was dispossessed?" The dispossession took place by order of the "laws"—law enforcement officers. Ellison set up a conflict between the law-abiding couple and the dictates of "laws":

> Look at them, they look like my mama and my papa and my grandma and grandpa, and I look like you and you look like me. Look at them but remember that we're a wise, law-abiding group of people. And remember it when you look up there in the doorway at that law standing there with his forty-five. Look at him, standing with his blue steel pistol and his blue serge suit, or one forty-five, you see ten for every one of us, ten guns and ten warm suits and ten fat bellies and ten million laws.

Id. at 278.

Ellison illustrated the stark contrast between the landlord's property rights, as enforced by police officers, and the poverty of the nameless tenants. The eviction scene, like most of *Invisible Man*, contains much wisdom about the nature of legal thought and reminds us of the centrality of property rights in American thought. Ellison points out the contradictions between the law as dictated by "laws"—law enforcement officers—and the promises of equality in the Constitution. The old couple had, he observes, "a dream book, but the pages went blank and it failed to give them the number. It was called the Seeing Eye, the Great Constitutional Dream Book, The Secrets of Africa, The Wisdom of Egypt. . . . All we have is the Bible and this Law here rules that out."

The eviction scene is a vehicle for beginning to study the right of exclusion and its meaning for tenants, as well as the means by which the state protects property and the mechanisms by which eviction takes place. It used to be that many states permitted landlords to exercise "self help" to evict tenants. That is, they allowed landlords to oust tenants without resorting to the courts. Almost all states have now prohibited self-help. They require landlords to get a court order before evicting a tenant.

You will likely learn a lot about landlord-tenant law in your property course, probably including something about eviction. Right now, however, we to turn to another aspect of the landlord-tenant relationship: landlords' rights to prevent their tenants from having visitors. The question of visitors on a landlord's property turns to a critical question about what it means to be an owner (or renter) of property.

1.5 PROPERTY RIGHTS AND CIVIL RIGHTS

We now take up a case dealing with a landlord who prosecuted a health care provider and a lawyer for trespass when they visited tenants on the landlord's property. Those tenants also happened to be migrant farm workers, employed by the landlord. This case points up the conflict between the property rights of the landlord and the civil rights of the tenants. As you read this case, you may want to ask how much the landlord's rights are affected by having tenants on his property.

State v. Shack

277 A.2d 369 (N.J. 1971)

WEINTRAUB, J.

Defendants entered upon private property to aid migrant farmworkers employed and housed there. Having refused to depart upon the demand of the owner, defendants were charged with violating N.J.S.A. 2A:170-31 which provides that "[a]ny person who trespasses on any lands . . . after being forbidden so to trespass by the owner . . . is a disorderly person and shall be punished by a fine of not more than $50." Defendants were convicted in the Municipal Court of Deerfield Township and again on appeal in the County Court of Cumberland County on a trial de novo. . . .

Before us, no one seeks to sustain these convictions. The complaints were prosecuted in the Municipal Court and in the County Court by counsel engaged by the complaining landowner, Tedesco. However Tedesco did not respond to this appeal, and the county prosecutor, while defending abstractly the constitutionality of the trespass statute, expressly disclaimed any position as to whether the statute reached the activity of these defendants.

Complainant, Tedesco, a farmer, employs migrant workers for his seasonal needs. As part of their compensation, these workers are housed at a camp on his property. Defendant Tejeras is a field worker for the Farm Workers Division of the Southwest Citizens Organization for Poverty Elimination, known by the acronym SCOPE, a nonprofit corporation funded by the Office of Economic Opportunity pursuant to an act of Congress, 42 U.S.C.A. §§2861-2864. The role of SCOPE includes providing for the "health services of the migrant farm worker."

Defendant Shack is a staff attorney with the Farm Workers Division of Camden Regional Legal Services, Inc., known as "CRLS," also a nonprofit corporation funded by the Office of Economic Opportunity pursuant to an act of Congress, 42 U.S.C.A. §2809(a)(3). The mission of CRLS includes legal advice and representation for these workers.

Differences had developed between Tedesco and these defendants prior to the events which led to the trespass charges now before us. Hence when defendant Tejeras wanted to go upon Tedesco's farm to find a migrant worker who needed medical aid for the removal of 28 sutures, he called upon defendant Shack for his help with respect to the legalities involved. Shack, too, had a mission to perform on Tedesco's farm; he wanted to discuss a legal problem with another migrant worker there employed and housed. Defendants arranged to go to the farm together.

Defendants entered upon Tedesco's property and as they neared the camp site where the farmworkers were housed, they were confronted by Tedesco who inquired of their purpose. Tejeras and Shack stated their missions. In response, Tedesco offered to find the injured worker, and as to the worker who needed legal advice, Tedesco also offered to locate the man but insisted that the consultation would have to take place in Tedesco's office and in his presence. Defendants declined, saying they had the right to see the men in the privacy of their living quarters and without Tedesco's supervision. Tedesco thereupon summoned a State Trooper who, however, refused to remove defendants except upon Tedesco's written complaint. Tedesco then executed the formal complaints charging violations of the trespass statute.

I.

The constitutionality of the trespass statute, as applied here, is challenged on several scores. It is urged that the First Amendment rights of the defendants and of the migrant farmworkers were thereby offended. Reliance is placed on *Marsh v. Alabama,* 326 U.S. 501 (1946), where it was held that free speech was assured by the First Amendment in a company-owned town which was open to the public generally and was indistinguishable from any other town except for the fact that the title to the property was vested in a private corporation. Hence a Jehovah's Witness who distributed literature on a sidewalk within the town could not be held as a trespasser. Later, on the strength of that case, it was held that there was a First Amendment right to picket peacefully in a privately owned shopping center which was found to be the functional equivalent of the business district of the company-owned town in *Marsh. Amalgamated Food Employees Union Local 590 v. Logan Valley Plaza, Inc.,* 391 U.S. 308 (1968). . . . Those cases rest upon the fact that the property was in fact opened to the general public. There may be some migrant camps with the attributes of the company town in Marsh and of course they would come within its holding. But there is nothing of that character in the case before us, and hence there would have to be an extension of Marsh to embrace the immediate situation. . . .

These constitutional claims are not established by any definitive holding. We think it unnecessary to explore their validity. The reason is that we are satisfied that under our State law the ownership of real property does not include the right to bar access to governmental services available to migrant workers and hence there was no trespass within the meaning of the penal statute. The policy considerations which underlie that conclusion may be much the same as those which would be weighed with respect to one or more of the constitutional challenges, but a decision in nonconstitutional terms is more satisfactory, because the interests of migrant workers are more expansively served in that way than they would be if they had no more freedom than these constitutional concepts could be found to mandate if indeed they apply at all.

II.

Property rights serve human values. They are recognized to that end, and are limited by it. Title to real property cannot include dominion over the destiny of persons the owner permits to come upon the premises. Their well-being must remain the paramount concern of a system of law. Indeed the needs of the occupants may be so imperative and their strength so weak, that the law will deny the occupants the power to contract away what is deemed essential to their health, welfare, or dignity.

Here we are concerned with a highly disadvantaged segment of our society. We are told that every year farmworkers and their families numbering more than one million leave their home areas to fill the seasonal demand for farm labor in the United States. The Migratory Farm Labor Problem in the United States (1969 Report of Subcommittee on Migratory Labor of the United States Senate Committee on Labor and Public Welfare), p. 1. The migrant farmworkers come to New Jersey in substantial numbers . . .

The migrant farmworkers are a community within but apart from the local scene. They are rootless and isolated. Although the need for their labors is evident, they are unorganized and without economic or political power. It is their plight alone that summoned government to their aid. In response, Congress provided under Title III-B of the Economic Opportunity Act of 1964 (42 U.S.C.A. §2701 et seq.) for "assistance for migrant and other seasonally employed farmworkers and their families." . . .

These ends would not be gained if the intended beneficiaries could be insulated from efforts to reach them. It is in this framework that we must decide whether the camp operator's rights in his lands may stand between the migrant workers and those who would aid them. The key to that aid is communication. Since the migrant workers are outside the mainstream of the communities in which they are housed and are unaware of their rights and opportunities and of the services available to them, they can be reached only by positive efforts tailored to that end. . . .

A man's right in his real property of course is not absolute. It was a maxim of the common law that one should so use his property as not to injure the rights of others. . . . Although hardly a precise solvent of actual controversies, the maxim does express the inevitable proposition that rights are relative and there must be an accommodation when they meet. Hence it has long been true that necessity, private or public, may justify entry upon the lands of another. . . . The subject is not static. As pointed out in 5 Powell, *Real Property* (Rohan 1970) §745, pp. 493-494, while society will protect the owner in his permissible interests in land, yet ". . . [S]uch an owner must expect to find the absoluteness of his property rights curtailed by the organs of society, for the promotion of the best interests of others for whom these organs also operate as protective agencies. The necessity for such curtailments is greater in a modern industrialized and urbanized society than it was in the relatively simple American society of fifty, 100, or 200 years ago. The current balance between individualism and dominance of the social interest depends not only upon political and social ideologies, but also upon the physical and social facts of the time and place under discussion."

Professor Powell added in §746, pp. 494-496:

> As one looks back along the historic road traversed by the law of land in England and in America, one sees a change from the viewpoint that he who owns may do as he pleases with what he owns, to a position which hesitatingly embodies an ingredient of stewardship; which grudgingly, but steadily, broadens the recognized scope of social interests in the utilization of things. . . .

To one seeing history through the glasses of religion, these changes may seem to evidence increasing embodiments of the golden rule. To one thinking in terms of political and economic ideologies, they are likely to be labeled evidences of 'social enlightenment,' or of 'creeping socialism' or even of 'communistic infiltration,' according to the individual's assumed definitions and retained or acquired prejudices. With slight attention to words or labels, time marches on toward new adjustments between individualism and the social interests."

This process involves not only the accommodation between the right of the owner and the interests of the general public in his use of his property, but involves also an accommodation between the right of the owner and the right of individuals who are parties with him in consensual transactions relating to the use of the property. Accordingly substantial alterations have been made as between a landlord and his tenant. . . .

The argument in this case understandably included the question whether the migrant worker should be deemed to be a tenant and thus entitled to the tenant's right to receive visitors, *Williams v. Lubbering,*

73 N.J.L. 317, 319-320 (Sup. Ct. 1906), or whether his residence on the employer's property should be deemed to be merely incidental and in aid of his employment, and hence to involve no possessory interest in the realty. . . . These cases did not reach employment situations at all comparable with the one before us. Nor did they involve the question whether an employee who is not a tenant may have visitors notwithstanding the employer's prohibition.

[Therefore] [w]e see no profit in trying to decide upon a conventional category and then forcing the present subject into it. That approach would be artificial and distorting. The quest is for a fair adjustment of the competing needs of the parties, in the light of the realities of the relationship between the migrant worker and the operator of the housing facility.

Thus approaching the case, we find it unthinkable that the farmer-employer can assert a right to isolate the migrant worker in any respect significant for the worker's well-being. The farmer, of course, is entitled to pursue his farming activities without interference, and this defendants readily concede. But we see no legitimate need for a right in the farmer to deny the worker the opportunity for aid available from federal, State, or local services, or from recognized charitable groups seeking to assist him. Hence representatives of these agencies and organizations may enter upon the premises to seek out the worker at his living quarters. So, too, the migrant worker must be allowed to receive visitors there of his own choice, so long as there is no behavior hurtful to others, and members of the press may not be denied reasonable access to workers who do not object to seeing them.

It is not our purpose to open the employer's premises to the general public if in fact the employer himself has not done so. We do not say, for example, that solicitors or peddlers of all kinds may enter on their own; we may assume for the present that the employer may regulate their entry or bar them, at least if the employer's purpose is not to gain a commercial advantage for himself or if the regulation does not deprive the migrant worker of practical access to things he needs.

And we are mindful of the employer's interest in his own and in his employees' security. Hence he may reasonably require a visitor to identify himself, and also to state his general purpose if the migrant worker has not already informed him that the visitor is expected. But the employer may not deny the worker his privacy or interfere with his opportunity to live with dignity and to enjoy associations customary among our citizens. These rights are too fundamental to be denied on the basis of an interest in real property and too fragile to be left to the unequal bargaining strength of the parties. . . .

It follows that defendants here invaded no possessory right of the farmer-employer. Their conduct was therefore beyond the reach of the trespass statute. The judgments are accordingly reversed and the matters remanded to the County Court with directions to enter judgments of acquittal.

NOTES AND QUESTIONS

1. *State v. Shack* is famous for Justice Weintraub's statement that "property rights serve human values." From what you know so far, how much to you believe that statement?

2. What if a minister wants to come to Tejeras' property to preach to the migrant farm workers. Is that permitted under *Shack*?

3. One of the farm workers' theories was that they had a first amendment right to access to lawyers. That theory is hard to sustain, because a private party (the farmer) is limiting access, rather than the government. (You may recall that the First Amendment protects only against governmental interference with free speech and association rights, not the actions of private parties. Hence, there is much focus on whether a "state actor" is involved or only private parties.) There is one old case, *Marsh v. Alabama*, 326 U.S. 501 (1946), that treated a company town as essentially a "state actor." However, the New Jersey Supreme Court does not rest its decision on that theory. Why not?

4. There are other cases that protect the right to be on private property. Sometimes that happens in the context of labor union organizing. *See Hudgens v. NLRB*, 424 U.S. 507 (1976). In some states, there is a constitutional right to free speech on some private property, like a shopping mall. *See Pruneyard Shopping Center v. Robbins*, 447 U.S. 74 (1980); *New Jersey Coalition v. J.M.R. Realty Corp.*, 650 A.2d 757 (N.J. 1994). New Jersey has protected the right to leaflet on a private college campus. *See State v. Schmid*, 423 A.2d 615 (N.J. 1980). More commonly, protesters have no right to protest on private property. *See Right to Life Protestors v. Aaron Women's Clinic*, 737 S.W. 2d 564 (Tex. Ct. App. 1987) (denying right to anti-abortion protesters to protest on private property).

5. Chief Justice Weintraub claims "[a] man's right in his real property is not absolute. It was a maxim of the common law that no one should so use his property as not to injure the rights of others." Aside from prohibiting access to medical care or legal assistance, what are other practical examples of how this principle could be violated?

6. Another part of the opinion, states "[t]he necessity for such curtailments is greater in a modern industrialized and urbanized society than it was in the relatively simple American society of fifty, 100 or 200 years ago . . . [and] depends not only upon political and social ideologies, but also upon the physical and social facts of the time and place under discussion." As we progress through this course, you will see that this case may have been decided differently in places like Texas. Aside from the fact that this case deals with migrant workers, why might this affect the outcome?

7. If Chief Justice Marshall grounded his opinion in the law in *The Antelope* and *Johnson v. M'Intosh*, how does Justice Weintraub rationalize his opinion? Why didn't he ground it in the Constitution, as the defendants hoped he would? In an article written shortly after this opinion,

Boyd Mangrum opines that "the complete lack of a constitutional holding makes uncertain what value the decision will have as general precedent in future cases involving migrant farm worker access rights . . . had the decision been based on some constitutional ground . . . its value as solid precedent for other jurisdictions would have been enhanced." Why does this matter? See Boyn Mangrum, *Granting Poverty Workers Access to Farmworkers Housed on Private Property*, 25 SOUTHWESTERN L. J. 780 (1971).

2 PROPERTY RULES AND SLAVERY

2.1 PROPERTY RIGHTS IN HUMANS

The experience of slavery in the United States (and elsewhere throughout the African Diaspora, such as in Brazil and the Caribbean) influenced the development of property law in these areas. We have already read one case, *The Antelope,* about how courts justified ownership of human beings. We suggested that Chief Justice Marshall's opinion drew on and contributed to major themes in property law, like the importance of international recognition of property rules.

Yet, most of the work of courts was much more mundane than the larger issues discussed in *The Antelope.* Courts frequently heard cases between owners regarding the sale or rental of enslaved people. Those cases often addressed issues of property law, running from adverse possession to breach of warranties. For example, litigation often arose from the sale of a person who turned out to have some "defect" in the opinion of the buyer. This chapter includes a number of cases that show the difficulties regulating people caused for courts. We put the cases here with two big goals in mind. First, we hope to illustrate the ways that property law is called upon to deal with issues of morality. Second, one case at the end of the chapter deals with a freed slave who sought compensation for her time as a slave. It illustrates the principle of unjust enrichment, which courts continue to employ in widely varying situations.

As you read these cases, consider the following questions:

1. How did courts reconcile the ownership interests of the master with the autonomy and dignity interests of the enslaved person?
2. How did courts regulate competing ownership interests between two potential slave owners? Who typically had priority in these conflicts? Why?

3. What are the ways in which current property law may be affected by the legal system's experience with slavery? What are some current conflicts that may reflect some of the same tensions? Do you think that the legal methods used to resolve these conflicts can be used now?

2.2 THE OWNER'S EXERCISE OF DOMINION OVER ENSLAVED PEOPLE

Justice Thomas Ruffin's 1830 opinion in *State v. Mann* released a man from criminal liability for abusing a slave he rented. *State v. Mann* is a criminal law case; however, it illuminates the rights of an owner (or in this case a renter) over property. Ruffin provides a classic statement of the rights of the owner and the non-rights of the owned, and was widely discussed by abolitionists before the Civil War as evidence of the control that owners had over enslaved people.

State v. Mann

13 N.C. 263 (1830)

Ruffin, J.

A Judge cannot but lament, when such cases as the present are brought into judgment. It is impossible that the reasons on which they go can be appreciated, but where institutions similar to our own, exist and are thoroughly understood. The struggle, too, in the Judge's own breast between the feelings of the man, and the duty of the magistrate is a severe one, presenting strong temptation to put aside such questions, if it be possible. It is useless however, to complain of things inherent in our political state. And it is criminal in a Court to avoid any responsibility which the laws impose. With whatever reluctance therefore it is done, the Court is compelled to express an opinion upon the extent of the dominion of the master over the slave in North-Carolina.

The indictment charges a battery on Lydia, a slave of Elizabeth Jones . . .

Here the slave had been hired by the Defendant, and was in his possession; and the battery was committed during the period of hiring. With the liabilities of the hirer to the general owner, for an injury permanently impairing the value of the slave, no rule now laid down is intended to interfere. That is left upon the general doctrine of bailment. The enquiry here is, whether a cruel and unreasonable battery on a slave, by the hirer, is indictable. The Judge below instructed the Jury, that it is. He seems to have put it on the ground, that the Defendant had but a special property. Our laws uniformly treat the master or other person having the possession and command of the slave, as entitled to the same extent of authority. The object is the same—the services of the slave; and the same powers must be confided. In a criminal proceeding, and indeed in reference to all other persons but the general owner, the hirer and possessor of a slave, in relation to both rights and duties, is, for the time being, the owner. This opinion would, perhaps dispose of this particular case; because the indictment, which charges a battery upon the slave of Elizabeth Jones, is not supported by proof of a battery upon Defendant's own slave; since different justifications may be applicable to the two cases. But upon the general question, whether the owner is answerable criminaliter, for a battery upon his own slave, or other exercise of authority or force, not forbidden by statute, the Court entertains but little doubt.—That he is so liable, has never yet been decided; nor, as far as is known, been hitherto contended. There have been no prosecutions of the sort. The established habits and uniform practice of the country in this respect, is the best evidence of the portion of power, deemed by the whole community, requisite to the preservation of the master's dominion. If we thought differently, we could not set our notions in array against the judgment of every body else, and say that this, or that authority, may be safely lopped off. This has indeed been assimilated at the bar to the other domestic relations; and arguments drawn from the well established principles, which confer and restrain the authority of the parent over the child, the tutor over the pupil, the master over the apprentice, have been pressed on us. The Court does not recognize their application. There is no likeness between the cases. They are in opposition to each other, and there is an impassable gulf between them.—The difference is that which exists between freedom and slavery—and a greater cannot be imagined. In the one, the end in view is the happiness of the youth, born to equal rights with that governor, on whom the duty devolves of training the young to usefulness, in a station which he is afterwards to assume among freemen. To such an end, and with such a subject, moral and intellectual instruction seem the natural means; and for the most part, they are found to suffice. Moderate force is superadded, only to make the others effectual. If that fail, it is better to leave the party to his own headstrong passions, and the ultimate correction of the law, than to allow it to be immoderately inflicted by a private person. With slavery it is far otherwise. The end is the profit of the master, his security and the public safety; the subject, one doomed in his own person, and his posterity, to live without knowledge, and without the capacity to make any thing his own, and to toil that another may reap the fruits. What moral considerations shall be addressed to such a being, to convince him what, it is impossible but that the most stupid must feel and know can never be true—that he is thus to labor upon a principle of natural duty, or for the sake of his own personal happiness, such services can only be expected from one who has no will of his own;

who surrenders his will in implicit obedience to that of another. Such obedience is the consequence only of uncontrolled authority over the body. There is nothing else which can operate to produce the effect. The power of the master must be absolute, to render the submission of the slave perfect. I most freely confess my sense of the harshness of this proposition, I feel it as deeply as any man can. And as a principle of moral right, every person in his retirement must repudiate it. But in the actual condition of things, it must be so. There is no remedy. This discipline belongs to the state of slavery. They cannot be disunited, without abrogating at once the rights of the master, and absolving the slave from his subjection. It constitutes the curse of slavery to both the bond and free portions of our population. But it is inherent in the relation of master and slave.

. . .

We cannot allow the right of the master to be brought into discussion in the Courts of Justice. The slave, to remain a slave, must be made sensible, that there is no appeal from his master; that his power is in no instance, usurped; but is conferred by the laws of man at least, if not by the law of God. The danger would be great indeed, if the tribunals of justice should be called on to graduate the punishment appropriate to every temper, and every dereliction of menial duty. No man can anticipate the many and aggravated provocations of the master, which the slave would be constantly stimulated by his own passions, or the instigation of others to give; or the consequent wrath of the master, prompting him to bloody vengeance, upon the turbulent traitor—a vengeance generally practiced with impunity, by reason of its privacy. The Court therefore disclaims the power of changing the relation in which these parts of our people stand to each other.

We are happy to see, that there is daily less and less occasion for the interposition of the Courts. The protection already afforded by several statutes, that all powerful motive, the private interest of the owner, the benevolences towards each other, seated in the hearts of those who have been born and bred together, the frowns and deep execrations of the community upon the barbarian, who is guilty of excessive and brutal cruelty to his unprotected slave, all combined, have produced a mildness of treatment, and attention to the comforts of the unfortunate class of slaves, greatly mitigating the rigors of servitude, and ameliorating the condition of the slaves. The same causes are operating, and will continue to operate with increased action, until the disparity in numbers between the whites and blacks, shall have rendered the latter in no degree dangerous to the former, when the police now existing may be further relaxed. This result, greatly to be desired, may be much more rationally expected from the events above alluded to, and now in progress, than from any rash expositions of abstract truths, by a Judiciary tainted with a false and fanatical philanthropy, seeking to redress an acknowledged evil, by means still more wicked and appalling than even that evil.

. . . Let the judgment below be reversed, and judgment entered for the Defendant.

NOTES AND QUESTIONS

1. *Mann* deals with a person who rented a slave, Lydia, and then abused her. What do you make of Justice Ruffin's opening statement in the case? Why is he lamenting this decision? What is the struggle "in the Judge's own breast between the feelings of the man and the duty of the magistrate?" We saw in *Johnson v. M'Intosh* a similar statement by Chief Justice Marshall, which suggested he understood the conflict between the morality of what he was doing and the law. How does Ruffin resolve that conflict?

2. What is Ruffin's justification for releasing masters from criminal liability?

3. What constraints, beyond the law, does Ruffin believe exist? Does public sentiment really constrain masters?

4. Justice Ruffin does not speak to whether Lydia's owner might recover in a tort action against Mann for the abuse Lydia suffered. What is the theory of recovery that Ruffin suggests that the owner of Lydia could use to recover against the person who rented her?

In some cases, owners of slaves recovered from people who had abused slaves they had rented. Ruffin provided a standard for an owner's recovery for abuse of a slave by a person who had rented him in *Jones v. Glass*, 35 N.C. 308, 311 (1852). In a concurrence to an opinion finding the renter liable for severely injuring a slave he had rented, Ruffin wrote that a hirer of a slave was liable to the owner when he used an "unreasonable and dangerous blow . . . instead of resorting only to such moderate and usual correction as would have reduced the slave to subordination and been of good example to the other slaves."

Owners could recover against the renter when slaves were not abused, but were used outside of the terms of their lease and injured. *See, e.g., Jones v. Fort*, 36 Ala. 449 (1860) (permitting recovery for a slave killed in the process of building a gin-house, which was beyond the scope of the duties for which he was leased).

5. The North Carolina Supreme Court retreated from the *Mann* standard for criminal liability a few years later. In *State v. Hoover*, 20 N.C. 500, 500-01 (1839), Justice Ruffin decided the appeal of a slave owner who had killed his slave. The reporter summarized the gruesome facts:

> The prisoner was put upon his trial . . . for the murder of his own female slave, a woman, named Mira. The witnesses, called on the part of the State, testified to a series of the most brutal and barbarous whippings, scourgings and privations, inflicted by the prisoner upon the deceased, from about the first of December, to the time of her

> death in the ensuing March, while she was in the latter stages of pregnancy, and afterwards, during the period of her confinement and recovery from a recent delivery. A physician, who was one of the coroner's inquest, called to view the body of the deceased, stated that there were five wounds on the head of the deceased, four of which appeared to have been inflicted a week or more before her death: that the fifth was a fresh wound, about one and a half inches long, and to the bone, and was, in his opinion, sufficient to have produced her death: that there were many other wounds on different parts of her body, which were sufficient, independent of those on the head, to have caused death. The reasons assigned by the prisoner to those who witnessed his inhuman treatment of the deceased, were, at one time, that she stole his turnips and sold them to the worthless people in the neighborhood, and that she had attempted to burn his barn, and was disobedient and impudent to her mistress; at another, that she had attempted to burn his still house, and had put something in a pot to poison his family. There was no evidence except her own confessions, extorted by severe whippings, that the deceased was guilty of any of the crimes imputed to her; nor did it appear that she was disobedient or impertinent to her master or mistress; on the contrary, she seemed, as some of the witnesses testified, to do her best to obey the commands of her master, and that when she failed to do so, it was from absolute inability to comply with orders to which her condition and strength were unequal. The prisoner offered no testimony.

Justice Ruffin limited *State v. Mann* in *Hoover* with this statement: "A master may lawfully punish his slave; and the degree must, in general, be left to his own judgment and humanity, and cannot be judicially questioned. . . . . But the master's authority is not altogether unlimited. He must not kill. There is, at the last, this restriction upon his power: he must stop short of taking life."

6. Ruffin's opinion drew attention from abolitionists. Harriet Beecher Stowe, author of *Uncle Tom's Cabin*, published *A Key to Uncle Tom's Cabin* (1853) shortly afterward to provide the factual background of *Uncle Tom's Cabin*. Stowe wrote extensively about Ruffin's opinion in *State v. Mann*. She wrote of Ruffin that "No one can read this decision, so fine and clear in expression, so dignified and solemn in its results, without feeling at once deep respect for the man and horror for the system." *Id.*, at 78. What was it about Ruffin that Stowe—a committed abolitionist—would respect?

Stowe thought people like Ruffin were aware of the inhumanity of slave law, but "if they are going to preserve the THING, they have no recourse but to make the laws, and to execute them faithfully after they are made." *Id.*, at 71. Such people, in Stowe's mind, recognized that if slavery were to survive, the laws must be severely enforced:

> Like Judge Ruffin, men of honor, men of humanity, men of kindest and gentlest feelings, are obliged to interpret these severe laws with inflexible severity. In the perpetual reaction of that awful force of human passion and human will, which necessarily meets the compressive power of slavery,—in that seething, boiling tide, never wholly repressed, which rolls its volcanic stream underneath the whole frame—work of society so constituted, ready to find vent at the least rent or fissure or

> unguarded aperture, — there is a constant necessity which urges to severity of law and inflexibility of execution.

Id., at 71.

Stowe came to admire Ruffin's legal reasoning; she thought that "one cannot but admire the unflinching calmness with which a man, evidently possessed of honorable feelings, walks through the most extreme and terrible results and conclusions, in obedience to the laws of legal truth." *Id.*, at 77.

Stowe held out some hope that Ruffin, once he recognized the humanity of the slaves, might modify the law. "So abhorrent is the slave-code to every feeling of humanity that just as soon as there is any hesitancy in the community about perpetuating the institution of slavery, judges begin to listen to the voice of their honorable nature, and by favorable interpretations to soften its necessary severities." *Id.*, at 71. But Ruffin did not listen to the voice in drafting his opinion; instead, he applied cold logic to the issue. It was the cold logic that led to so many perverse conclusions:

> Every act of humanity of every individual owner is an illogical result from the legal definition; and the reason why the slave-code of America is more atrocious than any ever before exhibited under the sun, is that the Anglo-Saxon race are a more coldly and strictly logical race, and have an unflinching courage to meet the consequences of every premise which they lay down, and to work out an accursed principle, with mathematical accuracy, to its most accursed result. The decisions of American law-books show nothing so much as this severe, unflinching accuracy of logic.

Id., at 82.

Stowe concluded her discussion of the law of slavery with a statement that illuminates her fascination with Ruffin's ability to separate his legal mind from his feelings: "There is but one sole regret; and that is that such a man, with such a mind, should have been merely an expositor and not a reformer of the law." *Id.*, at 79.

7. One of the many ways abolitionists attacked slavery was by attacking property rights. Abolitionist criticism of *State v. Mann* focused on its embrace of a "logical" conclusion to crimes committed under a slave regime. For instance, William Goodell's *American Slave Code in Theory and Practice* 170-74 (1853) reprinted the opinion and concluded the following:

> Here is a document that will repay profound study. The moral wrong of slavery is distinctly and repeatedly admitted, along with the most resolute determination to support it, by not allowing the rights of the master to come under judicial investigation, betraying a consciousness that they would not abide the test of the first principles of legal science. The struggle between the man and the magistrate, implying that slavery requires of its magistrates to trample upon their own manhood; the cool

> and deliberate decision to do this, and to elevate the law of slavery above the law of nature and of nature's God, are painful but instructive features of the exhibition.

Id. at 174.

2.3 THE EMANCIPATION OF ENSLAVED PERSONS

Despite the general recognition of property rights that lay at the base of the institution of slavery, sometimes legislatures restricted owners' rights to dispose of their "property." One example of this is the restriction on emancipation. Legislatures frequently restricted the rights of owners to emancipate their slaves. These restrictions gave rise to *Hinds v. Brazealle,* a case about a slave owner who fathered a child with one of his slaves. He then took both the child and the child's mother to Ohio and freed them and together they all returned to Mississippi. When the man died, he left his estate to his child. Then the owner's relatives sued to get the property. *Hinds v. Brazealle* limits the rights of an owner to free his slaves (who also happen to be his family) and leave them his property. In this conflict between property rights and the community's right to control slave property, the property rights lose.

Hinds v. Brazealle

3 Miss. (2 How.) 837 (1838)

Mr. Chief Justice Sharkey delivered the opinion of the court.

The complainants, who are the appellees, claim the property mentioned in the bill as heirs at law of Elisha Brazealle. The allegations in the bill disclose these facts. Elisha Brazealle left this state, where he permanently resided, some time in the year 1826, and took with him to the state of Ohio, a negro woman and her son, John Munroe Brazealle, for the purpose of emancipating them, and with the intention of then bringing them back to this state. That he accordingly executed the deed of emancipation whilst in Ohio, and returned with the negroes to his residence in Jefferson county, where he continued to reside until his death. By his will executed after the deed, he recited the fact that such a deed had been executed, and declared his intention to ratify it, and devised his property to the said John Munroe, acknowledging him to be his son. His executors proved the will and took charge of the estate, and have continued to hold it and receive the profits. The complainants claim the estate on the ground, that the deed of emancipation was void as being contrary to the laws and policy of this state, and that being so the said John Monroe is still a slave and incapable of taking by devise, or holding property. The respondents demurred to the bill, which was overruled by the chancellor and this appeal taken.

The deed of emancipation is not made an exhibit, but the bill alleges it to have been made in the manner and for the purpose described, and it is referred to and ratified by the will. The validity of this deed is the main question in the controversy.

Upon principles of national comity, contracts are to be construed according to the laws of the country or state where they are made, and the respective rights and duties of parties are to be defined and enforced accordingly. As these laws derive their force entirely from comity, they are not to be adopted to the exclusion of state laws by which the great and fundamental policy of the state is fixed and regulated. And hence it follows that this rule is subject to exceptions. No state is bound to recognize or enforce a contract made elsewhere, which would injure the state or its citizens; or which would exhibit to the citizens an example pernicious and detestable. . . .

Let us apply these principles to the deed of emancipation. To give it validity would be, in the first place, a violation of the declared policy, and contrary to a positive law of the state. The policy of a state is indicated by the general course of legislation on a given subject, and we find that free negroes are deemed offensive, because they are not permitted to emigrate to, or remain in the state. They are allowed few privileges, and subject to heavy penalties for offences. They are required to leave the state within thirty days after notice, and in the meantime give security for good behavior, and those of them who can lawfully remain, must register and carry with them their certificates, or they may be committed to jail. It would also violate a positive law, passed by the legislature, expressly to maintain this settled policy, and to prevent emancipation. No owner can emancipate his slave, but by a deed or will properly attested, or acknowledged in court, and proof to the legislature, that such slave has performed some meritorious act for the benefit of the master, or some distinguished service for the state; and the deed or will can have no validity until ratified by special act of the legislature. It is believed that this law and policy are too essentially important to the interests of our citizens, to permit them to be evaded.

The state of the case shows conclusively, that the contract had its origin in an offence against morality, pernicious and detestable as an example. But above all, it seems to have been planned and executed with a fixed design to evade the rigor of the laws of this state. The acts of the party in going to Ohio with the slaves, and there executing the deed, and his immediate return with them to this state, point with unerring certainty to his purpose and object. The laws of this state cannot be thus defrauded of their operation by one of our own citizens. If we could have any doubts about the principle, the case reported in 1 Randolph, 15, would remove them.

As we think the validity of the deed must depend upon the laws of this state, it becomes unnecessary to inquire whether it could have any force by the laws of Ohio. If it were even valid there, it can have no force here. The consequence is, that the negroes John Munroe and his mother, are still slaves, and a part of the estate of Elisha Brazealle. They have not acquired a right to their freedom under the will; for, even if the clause in the will were sufficient for that purpose, their emancipation has not been consummated by an act of the legislature.

John Munroe being a slave, cannot take the property as devisee; and I apprehend, it is equally clear, that it cannot be held in trust for him. 4 Desaus. Rep. 266. Independent of the principles laid down in adjudicated cases, our statute law prohibits slaves from owning certain kinds of property, and it may be inferred, that the legislature supposed they were extending the act as far as it could be necessary to exclude them from owning any property, as the prohibition includes, that kind of property, which they would most likely be permitted to own without interruption, to wit, hogs, horses, cattle, ... They cannot be prohibited from holding such property in consequence of its being of a dangerous or offensive character, but because it was deemed impolitic for them to hold property of any description.

It follows, therefore, that the heirs are entitled to the property.

As the deed was void, and the devisee could not take under the will, the heirs might, perhaps, have had a remedy at law; but as an account must be taken for the rents and profits, and for the final settlement of the estate, I see no good reason why they should be sent back to law. The remedy is, doubtless, more full and complete than it could be at law.

The decree of the chancellor overruling the demurrer must be affirmed, and the cause remanded for further proceedings.

NOTES AND QUESTIONS

1. We usually think that people who own property can do what they would like with it. Why, in this case, are there so many restrictions on the "owner's" rights? Why did Justice Sharkey not uphold Ohio's emancipation?

2. The question of emancipation via a testator's will was litigated frequently. Some famous cases include *Fisher's Negroes v. Dabbs,* 14 Tenn. 119 (1834) (upholding emancipation) and *Cleland v. Waters,* 16 Ga. 496 (1854) (concluding that will may provide for emancipation of slaves outside of Georigia). For more on such cases, see Bernie D. Jones, *Fathers of Conscience: Mixed-Race Inheritance in the Antebellum South* (2009).

2.4 TRUSTS FOR EMANCIPATION

Southern courts frequently cited *Hinds* in the years before the Civil War, for the principle that states could restrict the emancipation of slaves. Even in some slave states, however, creative lawyers found ways to get around state statutes prohibiting emancipation. One popular method involved the use of a "trust." A trust is a legal arrangement in which a "trustee" is given the legal title to property, to manage that property for the "beneficiary" (or beneficiaries) of the trust. The trustee has legal title to the property, but we say the beneficiary has equitable title to the property. Trusts are extremely common; many people use these devices to control property and you will likely take a course dealing with them in the upper level curriculum. You may study a little bit about them in a basic property course, as alternatives to leaving property in a legal life estate.

The trust for emancipation placed enslaved people into trust and the trustee was instructed to take the enslaved people to a Northern state (or sometimes to Liberia) and free them. In some cases, the owners placed their enslaved humans into trust with the American Colonization Society, an organization popular from the 1820s to the 1840s, which promoted emancipation and then colonization of enslaved people in Africa. One famous case was *American Colonization Society v. Wade*, 15 Miss. (7 Smedes and Marshall) 663 (1846). It upheld a trust that provided for transporting enslaved people to Liberia and freeing them. The case percolated through the Mississippi courts for years. Why, you might ask, would the Mississippi court uphold a gift to the American Colonization Society in *Wade*, even though it had prohibited the emancipation in *Hinds*? The fact that the enslaved people would leave the state was critical in upholding the trust.

Another example of a trust to free slaves comes from the will of Revolutionary War hero—and Polish patriot—Tadeuz Kosciuszko (also known as Thaddeus Koscuiszko). Kosciuszko returned to the United States in 1797, where he was greeted as a hero and where Congress passed a statute giving him some $15,000 in back wages and interest owed him for the Revolution. Koscuiszko gave Thomas Jefferson power of attorney over his back wages and also wrote a will that made Jefferson the trustee of Koscuiszko's property in the United States (the wages voted him by Congress), along with the power to use the money to free as many slaves as possible. The will of May 5, 1798 is as follows:

> I, Thaddeus Kosciuszko, being just on my departure from America, do hereby declare and direct that, should I make no other testamentary disposition of my property in the United States, I hereby authorize my friend Thomas Jefferson to employ the whole thereof in purchasing negroes from among his own or any others, and giving them liberty in my name; in giving them an education in trades, or otherwise, and in having them instructed for their new condition in the duties of morality, which may make

> them good neighbors, good fathers or mothers, husbands or wives, and in their duties as citizens, teaching them to be defenders of their liberty and country, and of the good order of society, and in whatsoever may take them happy and useful. And I make the said Thomas Jefferson my executor of this.
>
> T. KOSCIUSZKO. 5th day of May 1798.

A codicil of 1806 modified the 1798 will, to provide $3,704 to Kosciuszko Armstrong, the son of the United States minister in Paris. It reads as follows:

> Know all men by these presents, that I, Thade Kosciuszko, formerly an officer of the United States of America in their revolutionary war against Great Britain, and a native of Lilourui, in Poland, at present residing at Paris, do hereby will and direct, that, at my decease, the sum of three thousand seven hundred and four dollars, currency of the aforesaid United States, shall of right be possessed by, and delivered over to the full enjoyment and use of Kosciuszko Armstrong, the son of general John Armstrong, minister plenipotentiary of the said States at Paris. For the security and performance whereof, I do hereby instruct and authorize my only lawful executor in the said United States, Thomas Jefferson, president thereof, to reserve in trust for that special purpose, of the funds he already holds belonging to me, the aforesaid sum of three thousand seven hundred and four dollars, in principal; to be paid by him, the said Thomas Jefferson, immediately after my decease, to him, the aforesaid Kosciuszko Armstrong; and in case of his death, to the use and benefit of his surviving brothers.

Armstrong v. Lear, 33 U.S. 52, 55-56 (1834).

After Kosciuszko's death in 1817, Jefferson relinquished his position as executor of the estate, apparently because of his own reluctance to carry out the provisions of the will. Litigation over the will, codicil, and an alleged other will, which would have revoked both the 1798 will and 1806 codicil and left most of Kosciuszko's property to Francis Xavier Zeltner, with whom Kosciuszko lived at the time of his death, lasted until the 1830s. *See Armstrong v. Lear*, 33 U.S. 52 (1834); *Armstrong v. Lear*, 25 U.S. 169 (1827). The case involved frustrating complexities of jurisdiction and of evidence, which caused Justice Joseph Story to ask for the parties to clarify the record in 1834: "Under the complicated circumstances of the present case, and the important bearings of foreign law upon it, it is very desirable, that if it should come again before us, all the facts, and all the lights necessary for a final decision may be furnished, without submitting it to farther embarrassments," *Armstrong*, 33 U.S. at 74. For further discussion of this fascinating and complex story, see Gary Nash and Graham Hodges, *Friends of Liberty: Thomas Jefferson, Thaddeus Kosciuszko, and Agrippa Hull* (2008).

Other courts were not always so willing to enforce gifts or trusts to free slaves. For example, *American Colonization Society v. Gartrell*, 23 Ga. 448 (1857), decided by the Georgia Supreme Court shortly before the Civil War, refused to uphold a bequest of slaves to the American Colonization Society. The will bequeathed all the testator's slaves to the Society "for the purpose of sending them to Liberia, in Africa, all his slaves." Where the

Wade court had construed the American Colonization Society's powers broadly, the *Gartrell* court did not. What accounts for the difference?

Chief Justice Joseph Henry Lumpkin of the Georgia Supreme Court believed that the gift was beyond the powers of the American Colonization Society to accept. The Society had only limited powers—to colonize free people. Lumpkin construed those powers narrowly. "By their constitution, the association is empowered to receive property by bequest or otherwise: and to use it or dispose of it at their discretion, 'for the purpose of colonizing, with their own consent, in Africa, the free people of color residing in the United States, and for no other purpose whatsoever.'" Because the slaves were not yet free, Lumpkin thought that the Society could not free them, for that would be beyond the Society's charter:

> That these negroes were slaves in this State, cannot be questioned, talk as we may about their inchoate right to freedom. They were slaves before the will of Gideon was executed. They cannot be any thing else, here, afterwards. Any attempt made to change their condition here, by deed or will, would be nugatory. Being then, bondsmen here, do they become freemen when they cross the Savannah river? Do they become so in any State, slave or free, in their transit to Africa? Surely not. The Society itself, has no power, either by their charter, or by the will, to bestow freedom upon these slaves, in this or any other county, except Africa. It is doubtful whether by removing them to a free State, this trustee could, by operation of law, enable these slaves to acquire their freedom. No such power has been delegated to the Society to do this; and they would be acting in violation of their trust.

20 Ga. at 453. Lumpkin's real fear was likely that as soon as the enslaved people were free, they could not be forced to go back to Africa. He asked, "[w]hat certainty is there that the slaves would give their consent to go to Africa? And being free, it is indisputable that they could not be transported and colonized against their will. At any rate, force could not be employed for this purpose by the American Colonization Society. The basis and apex of this institution, being one of persuasion, not of force." *Id.*

Lumpkin, thus, took a narrow view of the Society's powers and affirmed the trial court's dismissal of the Society's petition to have the slaves to be turned over to them. He grimly concluded with a stark statement about his opposition to emancipation:

> I was once, in common with the great body of my fellow citizens of the South, the friend and patron of this enterprise. I now regard it as a failure, if not something worse; as I do every effort that has been made, for the abolition of negro slavery, at home or abroad, Liberia was formed of emancipated slaves, many of them partially trained and prepared for the change, and sent thousands of miles from all contact with the superior race; and given a home in a country where their ancestors were natives, and supposed to be suited to their physical condition. Arrived there, they have been for a number of years in a state of pupilage to the Colonization Society, in order that they might learn "to walk alone and by themselves." And at the end of a half a century what do we see? A few thousand thriftless, lazy semi-savages, dying of famine, because they will not work! To inculcate care and industry upon the descendants

> of Ham, is to preach to the idle winds. To be the "servant of servants" is the judicial curse pronounced upon their race. And this Divine decree is un-reversible. It will run on parallel with time itself.

Id. at 464.

2.5 RECOVERY FOR BEING WRONGFULLY HELD IN SLAVERY: UNJUST ENRICHMENT

In recent years there has been talk in some circles about the idea of "reparations" for slavery and for loss of Native American land. Often we think of this only in terms of making "payments" in an attempt to correct past wrongs, but reparations can take many forms. South Africa formed a Truth and Reconciliation Commission after apartheid ended. Civil rights legislation was passed in the United States in the 1960s and affirmative action programs were created. Community development programs continue to target those who arguably are still affected by the negative effects of slavery. Sometimes these issues appear in property class; for example, *United States v. Platt*, 730 F.Supp. 318 (D.Az. 1990), which appears in Chapter Six, establishes the "right" of a Native American tribe in Arizona to cross land now owned by others to get to a religious site that has been important to the tribe for centuries.

There are also some cases of direct relevance to reparations for slavery, and those cases tell us something about the contemporary law of unjust enrichment. That series of now-forgotten cases allowed people who had been enslaved to sue to recover money. Even before the Civil War, a few southern courts confronted claims by people who had been wrongfully held in slavery. In some instances, they gave compensation to those people. In *Aleck v. Tevis*, 34 Ky. (4 Dana) 242 (1836), for instance, the Kentucky Supreme Court awarded damages to Aleck, a young man who was wrongfully put into slavery. The award of damages, however, was only for the value of Aleck's labor to the person who enslaved him. In that case, the damages were measured by the theory of "unjust enrichment." You will likely study this many times in law school—in contracts, in property, and in an upper-level course in remedies. One key aspect of "unjust enrichment" is the idea that it provides a recovery based on the value of services provided rather than the harm to the plaintiff.

Even after the Civil War, courts confronted the question whether there was a right to restitution for services performed as a slave. Thus, we have *Hickam v. Hickam*, decided by the Missouri Appellate Court at the end of the nineteenth century, several decades after slavery ended. (You may recall that President Lincoln's Emancipation Proclamation was in 1863 and that slavery as a legal institution ended everywhere in the United States by the close of the Civil War in April 1865.)

Hickam v. Hickam

46 Mo. App. 496 (1891)

GILL, J.

At the December term, 1889, the plaintiff presented to the probate court of Cooper county, for allowance against the estate of Joseph Hickam, deceased, the following account:

> "The Estate of Joseph Hickam, deceased, To Eda Hickam (colored), Dr.: To services rendered by said Eda Hickam for the said Joseph Hickam as house and general servant from the eighteenth day of February, 1865, to the twenty-third day of February, 1889, being twenty-four years and five days, at the rate of $5 per month, amounting in the aggregate to the sum of $1,440.85."

The case was tried before a jury in the probate court, and judgment rendered for the plaintiff for $785.29, from which the defendant appealed to the circuit court of Cooper county, where a trial was had before a jury, resulting in a verdict for the defendant, whereupon the plaintiff sued out her writ of error, and brought the case to this court. We make the following brief statement of the facts as set out in counsel's brief upon which plaintiff's demand is based:

Prior to the Civil War and up to the date of the emancipation of slaves in Missouri, the plaintiff was the property of Joseph Hickam, now deceased, who lived in Moniteau county, Missouri, from whence he removed to Cooper county, where he died in the year 1889. At the time of the abolition of slavery in Missouri the plaintiff was about twenty-three years old. From childhood she had been the slave of said Joseph Hickam; had no education, and had had very little intercourse with anyone outside of the family of her owner. She claims (and there is some evidence to sustain her) that during the war and until the death of her "old master," Joseph Hickam, she was not allowed to, and never did, leave his premises except in the company of a member of the Hickam family; that she was not allowed to visit any of her own race, and no colored person, not even her stepfather, was allowed to talk to her alone; that she was never permitted to go to church or public gatherings of any kind, and lived in absolute ignorance of the fact that the negroes had been set free, or that she was a free woman, until after the death of her master, Joseph Hickam. During the whole of the time, from the abolition of slavery in Missouri until the death of Joseph Hickam (twenty-four years and five days), she lived and served as his slave in total ignorance of her rights, and without any remuneration or reward for her services, except what she had received while she was in fact a slave, to-wit, her food and clothing. The theory upon which plaintiff's claim is based is, that if by fraud, deceit or duress she was kept in ignorance of her rights by the said Joseph Hickam, whereby she was induced to and did render him services, then she is entitled to pay for the same, although he may not have intended to pay her, and she may not have expected to charge for such services. . . .

Of the instructions given by the court at the request of the defendant, we call attention to the following: "3. The jury are instructed that there is no evidence in this case that there was an express contract between the plaintiff and Joseph Hickam for the payment of wages to her, and the sole and only issue submitted to the jury is whether or not there was any implied contract between the plaintiff and said Joseph Hickam. And although the jury may believe that the plaintiff continued to live with the said Joseph Hickam after she became free, and she rendered valuable and meritorious services, still, unless they further believe from the evidence that at the time she rendered the services she expected to charge wages therefor, and the said Joseph Hickam knew that she intended to make said charge, there can be no recovery in this case.

4. The jury are instructed that even though they may believe that the plaintiff continued to live with and work in the family of the said Joseph Hickam after the legal emancipation of the slaves, and after she became free, and that she did this in ignorance of the enactment of the law making her a free woman, still this will not authorize a recovery against the said Joseph Hickam's estate in this case if the services were rendered without expectation upon her part of receiving wages therefor, and without the intention on his part of paying therefor.

5. The jury are instructed that, although they may believe that the plaintiff continued to live with Joseph Hickam, deceased, for twenty-four years after she became free, and that during that time she worked for, and rendered to him valuable services, still she cannot recover in this case, no matter how meritorious her services may have been, unless the jury shall believe from the evidence that at the time she was rendering said services she intended to charge Joseph Hickam therefor, and that said Joseph Hickam understood at the time said services were being rendered that she expected to make said charges, and the burden of showing that the services were rendered under the expectation on the part of the plaintiff of charging, and on the part of Joseph Hickam of paying therefor, is upon the plaintiff, and unless this proof has been made the finding must be for the defendant.

6. The jury are instructed that the plaintiff cannot recover for any services rendered more than five years prior to the death of the said Joseph Hickam, as the right to recover for any services rendered more than five years prior to his death is barred by the statute of limitations."

I. It will be seen by a comparison of plaintiff's refused instruction with the instruction given for defendant, that the trial court declined to adopt the theory that if the negro girl, Eda, was induced by the fraudulent concealment of her rights by the said Joseph Hickam to labor for his benefit without pay, that then she ought to recover the value of such services; but held that the plaintiff could not recover, however valuable the services may have been, unless "the jury should believe from the evidence that at the time she was rendering said services she intended to charge Joseph Hickam therefor, and that the said Joseph Hickam understood at the time said services were being rendered that she expected to make said charge," etc. In other words, the jury was advised that, even admitting the charge that Joseph Hickam did by his fraudulent practices hold the said Eda in practical bondage years after the emancipation, and that, in utter ignorance that she was free, the plaintiff performed valuable labor for said Joseph Hickam, yet that there was no implied obligation on him to pay therefor, because she, the plaintiff, at the time expected no reward, nor did Hickam expect to pay anything therefor.

We do not understand this to be the law in this character of case. An implied promise does not always depend upon the existence of intention in fact of the one to pay and the other to receive. The law frequently affixes a promise to pay even contrary to actual intention. As well expressed by an eminent author: "The law implies from men's conduct and actions contracts and promises as forcible and binding as those made by express words, and such contracts are implied sometimes in furtherance of the intention, or presumed intention, of the parties, and sometimes in furtherance of justice without regard to the intention of the parties. Thus a promise to pay for services rendered, or for goods received, or money obtained, will be implied against the wrongdoer who never intended to pay or intended deceptively to avoid payment." 3 Add. on Cont., sec. 1399; 1 Hilliard on Contracts, sec. 20, p. 65.

II. But it is suggested by defendant's counsel that the ignorance, on account of which plaintiff seeks relief, is that of law and not of fact, and hence, under the well-known maxim, Ignorantia legis neminem excusat, she cannot complain of the deception alleged to have been practiced by Joseph Hickam. Generally, it is true, a misrepresentation of the law affords no ground of redress; the misrepresentation should relate to a question of fact. However, this harsh and arbitrary rule is not without its exception. All men are not always presumed to know the law. Misrepresentation of the law is sometimes binding on the party who makes it. This is true in transactions between parties occupying fiduciary and confidential relations. "Indeed," it is said, "where one who has had superior means of information professes a knowledge of the law, and thereby obtains an unconscionable advantage of another who is ignorant, and has not been in a situation to become informed, the injured party is entitled to relief as well as if the misrepresentation had been concerning matter of fact."

Justice Story thus concludes a recital of exceptions to the above rule that there is no relief from an ignorance of the law. He says: "It is relaxed * * * in cases of imposition, misrepresentation, undue influence, misplaced confidence and surprise." 1 Story's Eq., sec. 137; also sec. 120, et seq. Conceding, now, for the purpose only of illustrating our contention, that the facts of this case are as put by plaintiff's counsel, that this negro girl was born and raised a slave, ignorant, unable to read, kept under strict surveillance by her master during and since the momentous year of 1865, and, up to his death in 1889, guarded by watchful eyes, kept within the precincts of the Hickam home and unadvised of the history of the times and the country, and taught to believe that she was still a slave and was the property of Hickam; that her old master kept her in darkness and absolute ignorance all these twenty-four years of the fact that she was free, what an outrage on justice would it be to answer her claim for compensation for valuable services to say to her: "You all the time knew the law of the land, and there is no relief for you." No; the plaintiff's case, as claimed by her, forms an exception to the rule, and, if Joseph Hickam was guilty of this fraudulent suppression of the truth and this misrepresentation to one under his care and control, he cannot be now heard to invoke the maxim of law above quoted.

III. We conclude, then, that the case in hand should have been submitted to the jury on the theory outlined in plaintiff's first instruction, and that the defendant's instructions (which were given and numbered 3, 4 and 5) incorrectly declared the law of this case, and should not have been given. We do not mean, however, to sanction the particular wording of plaintiff's first instruction. At another trial counsel should avoid calling attention to particular portions of the evidence, and thereby giving undue prominence to certain isolated testimony. Further, we must say that, in our opinion, plaintiff's second and third instructions have no place in this case. As already held, in reference to defendant's instructions, the question of intention on plaintiff's part to charge for services rendered is not to be considered; for, in this kind of case, there can in fact be no intention one way or the other. If plaintiff recover at all, it must be regardless of actual intention on the part of one or the other; it must be for the reason, and that alone, that she was fraudulently induced, by the conduct of Joseph Hickam, to render services for him under the belief that she, the plaintiff, owed him such labor as his slave. The case is thus narrowed to the one question, and it will only confuse the triers of the fact to inject other issues not pertinent.

IV. The trial court erred also in declaring to the jury that plaintiff could only recover, if at all, for the last five years' service. If she has any cause of action, it is for the whole term. Her claim is an entirety, good as to the whole, or bad as to the whole. . . .

The judgment will be reversed, and the cause remanded for a new trial.

NOTES AND QUESTIONS

1. What is the statute of limitations for unjust enrichment (here called quasi-contract)? Why do you suppose the court allowed the plaintiff to recover for the entire period of her enslavement, even if that slavery took place before the period of the statute of limitations? In some other cases, courts have allowed for plaintiffs to sue only for benefits conferred within the statute of limitations. *See, e.g., Olwell v. Nye & Nissen*, 173 P. 2d 652 (Oregon 1946) (permitting unjust enrichment claim for use of egg-washing machine for only period of statute of limitations—in that case, three years).

2. The plaintiff requests $5 per month for 24 years she was held in slavery. Where does that figure come from? Why is the plaintiff asking for a contract-based measure of recovery, rather than a tort-based measure? What are the differences between those measures?

For more on the unjust enrichment cases brought by former slaves, see Andrew Kull, *Restitution in Favor of Former Slaves*, 84 Boston U. L. Rev. 1277 (2004).

3. Why does the defendant say that the plaintiff needed to intend to charge the defendant for her services? When a plaintiff seeks to recover in quasi-contract (which is a fancy name for instances where the court imposes contract-like terms on parties' dealings, even though they did not actually have a contract), courts typically require that plaintiffs intended to receive compensation for the benefits they conferred. *See, e.g., Vortt Exploration v. Chevron, USA*, 787 S.W.2d 942 (Tex. 1990) (concluding that there Vortt furnished information to Chevron with the understanding that "a joint operating agreement would be reached"). It is hard to see how one could think that the services were provided voluntarily in *Hickam*, but that seems to be the argument that the defendant was making.

To disentangle these confusing situations, there are instances where unjust enrichment is used as a *measure of recovery*—as in *Olwell*, where the money saved is a measure of relief for the conversion of the plaintiff's egg-washing machine. Then in other instances, unjust enrichment serves as a *substantive basis for recovery*—as in *Vortt*, where Vortt claimed it provided information to Chevron as part of what it hoped would be a joint venture. In cases where unjust enrichment is the asserted basis for recovery, plaintiffs must show that there is some expectation on the part of the plaintiffs that they will receive compensation. *See* Douglas Laycock, *The Scope and Significance of Restitution*, 67 Texas L. Rev. 1277 (1989). In *Hickam* the claim for unjust enrichment seems to be a measure of recovery for being wrongfully held in slavery. However, the defendants seem to have been thinking (or at least arguing) that the requirement of intent to confer a benefit applied in their case as well.

4. Let us change now from the setting of *Hickam* to that of families. Even when family members expected to receive compensation for helping each other, they may not be entitled to compensation because courts often find there is a pre-existing duty to assist family members. This has arisen in some cases involving promises by one family member to care for another during illness, in exchange for the ill family member leaving property to the caretaker. For example, in *Borelli v. Brusseau,* 16 Cal. Rptr.2d 16 (Cal. App. 1993), the court rejected a widow's claim for her husband's promise to convey non-marital property to her in return for caring for him at home, instead of a nursing home. The majority concluded that "a wife is obligated by marriage contract to provide nursing type care to an ill husband. Therefore, contracts whereby the wife is to receive compensation for providing such services are void as against public policy and there is no compensation for the husband's promise." *Id.* at 19. In another turn on such facts, *Dusenka v. Dusenka,* 21 N.W. 528 (Minn. 1946), found no basis for recovery by a wife who voluntarily contributed to her husband's business, a tavern, and cared for him. Upon his death, it was revealed that the husband had secretly given his son (his wife's step-son) his interest in the tavern.

Sometimes unjust enrichment is used as a measure of damages, which may provide a larger measure of relief than trespass damages. Such was the case, for instance, in *Edwards v. Lee's Administrator,* 96 S.W.2d 1028 (Ky, 1936). *Edwards* involves a cave; the entrance was on Edward's property and he began to advertise and charge admission to the cave. Unbeknownst to Lee, the interesting parts of the cave were actually under Lee's property. Then, the federal government condemned the property where the cave was located, for use as part of a national park. Lee subsequently sued for the profits that Edwards made.

You may see discussion of *Edwards,* or another famous cave case, *Marengo Cave Co. v. Ross,* 10 N.E.2d 917 (Ind. 1937), when you study adverse possession. *Marengo* dealt with the question whether the owner of a cave had adversely possessed the part of the cave that was on his neighbor's property. The court concluded the occupation was not "open and notorious" because the owner of the property did not know that people were crossing his part of the cave — or that there even was a cave on his property. *Edwards,* however, dealt with apportioning profits between the operators of the cave and the owner of the property.

2.6 ANTI-FEUDALISM

Among the many critiques of slavery was that it was anti-republican. That is, that slavery — like feudalism — interfered with republican values. Those values included economic independence, widely distributed property holdings, and some semblance of equality. Slavery, however, made some people lords of others and that led them to have economic dominance over whites as well as African Americans. Moreover, slavery interfered with equality among white people, in part because slave labor crowded out free labor.

It was not just slavery, however, that interfered with republican values. Landlords can exercise extraordinary power over their tenants. In New York in the 1830s there emerged an important protest movement, known as the Anti-Rent Movement. Along the Hudson River Valley in upstate New York there lived thousands of people who were on long-term (and low-rent) "leases." The "leases" (some might also call them covenants) required "tenants" to perform minimal services or pay yearly rents to their landlords. Some "leases" also contained provisions that if the land was transferred, the renters had to pay a transfer fee (known as a quarter-rent) to the landlord. The movement got underway in 1839, after the primary patroon (Stephen Van Rensselaer III) died and his two sons began to systematically enforce the terms, which their father had neglected to do for many years. The movement went through various stages for the next several decades, winning at some times great sympathy with the legislature and at other times losing such sympathy, for instance after a law enforcement officer trying to execute an order to oust a tenant from his land was killed.

The next opinion, *Overbaugh v. Patrie*, delivered after the movement had been going for more than a decade and as the legislature and New Yorkers tired of the dispute, addressed the validity (or in this case the non-validity) of the quarter-rent provisions. This is a heavily edited version of the opinion. We have omitted the sections that deal with some doctrinal reasons for the unenforceability of the quarter-rent (like the ancient restrictions against fines for alienation, which were in essence payments on alienation). What we reprint below is the section of the opinion that deals with the New York policy regarding the quarter-rent (in this case referred to as one-sixth rent) provisions.

Overbaugh v. Patrie

8 Barb. 28 (NY Sup. Ct. 1852)

By the Court, PARKER, J.

By the indenture in question, Isaac D. Verplanck reserved the right to receive, and the lessees promised to pay one-sixth part of the purchase money, whenever the premises should be sold by the lessees, their heirs or assigns. He also reserved a pre-emption right to the property, at a deduction of one-sixth of its price or value. The plaintiff claimed at the trial, to recover, on the ground that the property had been twice sold without paying over the "sixth sale" reserved; and that in both instances the sales had been made without having first offered to sell the farm to the lessor on the terms prescribed in the lease. If these were valid conditions, the forfeiture was incurred and the plaintiffs had a right to re-enter.

I think the only question here presented is, whether the sixth sale reservation was valid. The forfeiture of one-sixth of the purchase money was to be incurred whether the sale was made to the lessor or to a third person. The lessees could not therefore comply with the conditions of the lease, by first offering to sell for a reasonable price to the lessor; they were required to go further, and to submit to a sale to him for five-sixths of the value. If, therefore, the reservation of the sixth sale was invalid, it follows that the right of pre-emption on such a condition was also void.

The question is an important one. Reservations of this description, generally known as "quarter sales," "sixth sales," and "tenth sales," have been frequently made in perpetual leases in fee. The legal title to hundreds of farms now depends upon their validity; and though it may be true that forfeitures for a breach of such conditions have been rarely enforced, the question involved is none the less important in principle. It is perhaps because the claim to the quarter sale has been generally compromised for a small sum, much less than the cost of testing its validity, that this question has been so rarely, if ever, brought before the courts of this state for examination. It is claimed, on the part of the plaintiffs, that this question has been decided in the late supreme court of this state. If so, we are bound by such authority, and shall not have occasion to discuss the principle. It is important, therefore, that we first ascertain whether it is an open question.

. . . It remains to consider whether the condition is void on the ground that it is against public policy.

I do not deem it necessary to a decision of this cause to go into an examination of the feudal system, its origin, its history and its consequences upon the present tenure of land. It is enough to say, it was a system originating in a military age, and well adapted to its necessities; but utterly unsuited, every vestige of it, to the institutions under which we live, and to the personal independence and equality of political rights enjoyed by our citizens. The tenant no longer looks to his lord for protection against lawless aggressions, nor does the lord depend upon the military services of his tenants. There are no longer courts baron, nor homage, nor fealty, nor knight service. The reasons why neither the lord nor the tenant could change their relations with each other without mutual consent, ceased, centuries ago, with the necessities which imposed them. The progress of man in intelligence, in knowledge, in the arts of peace and in political advancement, now calls for tenures in accordance with perfect political equality, and entire personal freedom; and if there be vestiges of feudal tenure still remaining here, they should be eradicated as speedily as is consistent with a strict regard to the rights of property of those concerned.

Quarter sales, sixth sales, and tenth sales, and all fines for alienation, or sums required to be paid in the nature of fines upon alienation, have long been regarded as prejudicial to the public interests. Some of their evils are well stated in a report made to the legislature by Messrs. Spencer and Van Ness in 1812. (See Assembly Journal of 1812, page 110.) It is the policy of the law that lands shall not be withdrawn from commerce; but these conditions tie up estates by a species of perpetual entail, from which a temporary relief can only be obtained by the payment of a very large price for the indulgence. By the common law, the right of alienation could not be suspended for a longer time than twenty-one years and nine months, after a life or lives in being; and the revised statutes do not allow the absolute power of alienation to be suspended by any limitation or condition whatever, for a longer period than during the continuance of two lives in being at the creation of the estate. But here is a restraint upon alienation to continue for all future time. As often as the owner shall find it necessary to sell, age after age and century after century, at every alienation, one-sixth of the purchase money must be paid to the remote representatives or assigns of the lessor. After twelve alienations, they will have received twice the improved value of the farm, in addition to the price paid on the original purchase. Yet their claim will be in no respect lessened—the demand will be insatiable—its existence interminable.

Such conditions have the effect of preventing a change of occupation. They require the son to live upon and cultivate the same farm his father has tilled, though he may be unfitted for the employment, and may have been designed by nature for some other calling better adapted to his taste and capabilities. He is denied the opportunity to go abroad into the world to reap the rewards of his enterprise and industry, except at the sacrifice of a large share of the estate made valuable by the toil and industry of his fathers. In a land where the professions and trades are open to all, he is subjected to all the discouragements of caste. A freeman and a freeholder, he is not at liberty to dispose of his own property.

Such conditions depreciate the value of property, and discourage industry. It can hardly be supposed a purchaser from the tenant will pay the full value for a farm, when he knows he will be under the necessity of giving to a landlord one-sixth of what he shall receive, whenever he shall be disposed to sell it again. Nor will an owner consent to make permanent improvements or valuable erections, subject to such a loss on them by alienation. The improvement of the country is largely concerned in defeating a condition thus charged upon land for all time to come.

I think no person can be found the advocate, and few persons the apologists, of such a condition, at the present day; a condition so unconscionable, that the cases are exceedingly rare, in which the landlord has ever sought to enforce it, and so odious, that a distinguished writer in the *American Review* (2 Am. Rev. 593) says, "after a new owner had come into possession, having paid the full value of the property, if he should have occasion to sell again for the like value, we should envy no man his conscience or his character, who, under this provision would take from him the full quarter part of his purchase."

It is said that this condition formed a substantial part of the consideration for which the grant was made. If this were so, it would not affect the legal question. Where a physician covenants, in consideration of $1000 paid to him, never to practice medicine again in the state, the covenant is void, notwithstanding the consideration, as being in restraint of trade and against the policy of the law. (Nobles v. Bates, 7 Cowen, 307. 7 Mod. 230. 10 Id. 27, 85, 130. 2 Saund. 156 a, n. 1.) But though in law this condition is regarded as a part of the consideration for the grant, it was esteemed of but little value when the lease was executed. Upon this subject Messrs. Spencer and Van Ness say in their report above referred to, "covenants and conditions, which coerce the tenant to pay a penalty for leave to change his residence are generally without consideration; for it can not be pretended that in settling the terms of the lease, landlord took a lower rent on the contingency that his tenant would change his mind and become disposed to part with his lease. It may also be remarked that the tenant, in entering into stipulations to pay a fine or a quarter sale on alienation, does so under circumstances which may induce him to believe he will never be disposed to alienate; but his circumstances change, and a variety of unforseen causes impel him to a change of residence. It can never be right to suffer a landlord who is not prejudiced by the alienation of his tenant to grasp a part of his earnings for his yielding to imperious circumstances or for his changing his mind."

It is within the legitimate scope of judicial inquiry to ascertain whether such reservations are against public policy; and I have therefore thought it proper to look somewhat into their nature and character. Upon this question it seems to me there is no good reason for a difference of opinion.

I need not here repeat the authorities bearing upon this question which I have referred to under the first point. Upon both principle and authority, such a condition is condemned, as against the policy of the law. I think there should be a new trial, costs to abide the event.

New trial granted.

NOTES AND QUESTIONS

1. What was wrong with the quarter-rent system according to *Overbaugh*? Why did that provide a basis for relief?

2. Does the anti-feudalism principle have any other applications in property law? Might this apply to more standard landlord-tenant leases? *See* Joan Williams, "The Rhetoric of Property," 83 Iowa L. Rev. 277 (1999).

3. The quarter-sale restriction is what we now call an "indirect restraint on alienation." That is, it limits (although indirectly) the

alienation (sale) of land. There are also direct restraints—like the prohibition on sale during the life of a person. Property law looks with great suspicion on restraints on alienation, and with particularly great suspicion on direct restraints on alienation.

The Restatement (Third) of Property §3.1 (3) provides that a servitude is invalid if it "imposes an unreasonable restraint on alienation under §3.4 [absolute restraint on alienation] or §3.5 [indirect restraint on alienation]." Section 3.5, "Indirect restraints on Alienation and Irrational Servitudes" provides:

> (1) An otherwise valid servitude is valid even if it indirectly restrains alienation by limiting the use that can be made of property, by reducing the amount realizable by the owner on sale or other transfer of the property, or by otherwise reducing the value of the property of the property.
>
> (2) A servitude that lacks a rational justification is invalid.

Might such a quarter-sale provision be invalid today? *See, e.g., United States v. 397.51 Acres of Land*, 692 F.2d 688 (10th Cir. 1982); *Girard v. Myers*, 694 P.2d 678 (Wash. App. 1985); *White v. White*, 251 A.2d 470 (N.J. Super. 1969). They were certainly suspect at the time of the anti-rent movement. *See DePeyster v. Michael*, 6 N.Y. 467 (1852).

4. *Overbaugh* was affirmed by the New York Court of Appeals in *De Peyster v. Michael*, 6 N.Y. 467 (1852). For more on the anti-rent movement, see Charles McCurdy, *The Anti-Rent Era in New York Law and Politics, 1839-1865* (2001) and the essay review of McCurdy by Eric Kades, "The End of the Hudson Valley's Peculiar Institution: The Anti-Rent Movement's Politics, Social Relations, and Economics," 27 LAW & SOCIAL INQUIRY 941–65 (2002).

II RACE AND THE REMAKING OF PROPERTY

3 RACIAL REGULATION OF PUBLIC SPACES IN THE UNITED STATES

3.1 INTRODUCING THE REGULATION OF RACE THROUGH PROPERTY: NUISANCE AND ZONING

Our first chapter discussed the origins of property, what we protect as property and why. Then we looked more deeply at the rules regarding property in human beings—the institution of slavery—as well as one case that gave some modicum of relief to a person who had been enslaved.

Now we turn to the regulation of property as it relates to race. This chapter deals with regulation of property by public entities—either the courts or the local zoning board. We look at the regulation of public spaces through the doctrine of nuisance (what some property writers term judicial zoning) and the attempts to use zoning ordinances to isolate groups based on race. The next chapter turns to the attempts by states in the early twentieth century to restrict ownership of property by non-citizens and some of the devices that creative lawyers used to get around those restrictions. It then turns to the restrictive covenants that developers and homeowners used to restrict the sale or occupancy of property by racial minorities. Although they were effective for several decades, the Supreme Court eventually struck down the racially restrictive covenants.

We start with two cases on nuisances. Although these cases are from the early twentieth century, they deal with a doctrine that is still important as a way of regulating use of land. As you read these cases, consider the following questions:

1. How much, if at all, did the judges bend the law of nuisance? Would you decide the cases any differently today?

2. How do the nuisance cases raise different issues from racial zoning cases? How are they similar?
3. Why was property protected against racial zoning, even as the Supreme Court was upholding racial distinctions in other cases?

The first case is about a jazz club that was enjoined from operation in San Antonio, Texas. It is not clear whether the defendants — the operators of a jazz club — were African American, white, or of some other race. However, jazz was closely associated at the time with African Americans. When the court wrote of the "screeching pianos, high-keyed violins and blaring saxophones, emitting the strains of barbaric jazz, more discordant than tom-tom or Chinese gong," it tapped into a common fear of jazz. *See* Amy Leigh Wilson, *A Unifying Anthem or Path To Degradation? The Jazz Influence in American Property Law,* 55 Alabama L. Rev. 425 (2004). The second case is about an injunction against an African-American church in South Carolina.

After those two cases, we turn to a dispute over a fence that a family put up in their yard. The family claimed it was to prevent passersby, including African Americans, from looking into their yard. The neighbors, however, claimed the fence was put there to spite them. This allows us to look at the odd, but still important, doctrine of spite fences, and to try to assess the meaning of that doctrine. We finally turn to *Buchanan v. Warley,* in which the U.S. Supreme Court struck down a racial zoning ordinance.

3.2 RACE NUISANCE CASES: THE REGULATION OF JAZZ AND AFRICAN-AMERICAN CHURCHES

Trueheart v. Parker

257 S.W. 640 (Tex.Civ.App. 1923)

Fly, C.J.

This is an appeal from a judgment of the trial court denying a permanent injunction to restrain appellee from using a building on the north side of Josephine street, in the city of San Antonio, as a dance hall, and setting aside and dissolving a temporary injunction theretofore granted. Appellant sought to restrain the use of the building for purposes of a dance hall, on the ground that as conducted it was a nuisance and greatly disturbed the peace and quiet of him and his family, and depreciated the value of his property, which is situated directly across Josephine street from the property controlled by appellee.

It was alleged that Josephine street, running west from river avenue, is about 55 feet in width, and that appellee has constructed a lumber shed or barn about 40 feet wide and 90 feet long on a lot directly across Josephine street from appellant's residence property, on which appellant resides with his family, and other adjoining portions of the property owned by him, occupied by a tenement house and an apartment house; that the dance hall is in full view of the occupants of his property, and the music therein and the unchaperoned females and others who meet there and dance at night until 11 or 12 o'clock, and are boisterous and sometimes profane, greatly disturb appellant and his family.

The court presented the following issue to the jury:

> "Does the operation of defendant's dance hall do injury to plaintiff's property or person, or cause annoyance and discomfort to plaintiff and his family in the use and enjoyment of their home?"

The jury answered the question in the negative, and upon that answer the judgment was rendered in favor of appellee. No other issues were requested and none given.

A hall used for dancing is not a nuisance per se; yet, if accompanied with drunkenness, swearing, loud and boisterous language, or disorderly conduct, it may become a nuisance. Unless a dance hall is condemned by law, whether it is or is not a nuisance is a question of fact to be tried as any other fact by a jury. The dance hall of appellee was a licensed dance hall and was being conducted under authority from the city of San Antonio at the time of being closed by a temporary injunction issued in this case. It was therefore not a nuisance per se, but was or was not a nuisance under proof of the manner in which it was conducted.

A nuisance, broadly stated, is anything that works an injury, harm, or prejudice to an individual or the public. According to definitions formulated from numerous decisions, a nuisance will embrace everything that endangers life or health, offends the human senses, transgresses laws of decency, or obstructs, impairs, or destroys the reasonable, peaceful, and comfortable use of property. Personal and property rights are guaranteed by the organic and statutory law of the land, but liberty, not license, in the use of these rights is the heritage of the American citizen, and coupled with the protection and conservation of rights of person and property is the mandate, to so use them as to not trample upon, disregard, or destroy the rights of others. If the individual persists in attempts to disregard the old maxim, "Sic utere tuo ut alienum non laedas,"[1] equity stands as a sentinel over the public or individual whose rights are invaded and issues its stern commands to the offender to desist from the invasion of the rights of others. In the investigation into the question of whether certain acts constitute a nuisance, it is the general though not the invariable rule

1. [This is an ancient Latin phrase, meaning "Use your property so as to not injure others." It is unclear, however, how that phrase helps to resolve this or any case, for it does not help us define what use injures property so much that it should be prohibited. — Eds.]

that neither negligence nor the intent of the party creating the nuisance are of any great importance. Acts which are denounced as illegal by law, when the perpetration of them invade the rights of others will be nuisances per se, but other acts in their nature may not be nuisances but may become by their location, situation, surroundings, or the method in which the acts are given utterance, or the manner in which a business or performance is conducted. A thing which is at all times and under any set of circumstances a violation of the rights of others is a nuisance per se. In other cases certain facts might create a nuisance, but about which honest differences might exist. 20 R.C.L. §§1 to 6, inclusive.[2]

The charter of the city of San Antonio does not recognize the absolute right of a citizen to open and conduct what is known as a "dance hall," but permits them to be operated only when licensed by the proper authority. Common experience has taught that public places where men and women, whose characters under no system can be properly investigated, have the right upon payment of certain fees, to assemble and engage in dancing, and perhaps drinking, may become foci of moral disease and infection, from which may emanate crime, drunkenness, immorality, and disorder, and such community centers are tolerated only under strict police surveillance and control. With this experience to guide the municipality it has reserved the right to grant or refuse licenses for dance halls, and it is evident that, if such places should ever be licensed, a due regard for the rights of the home-builder would dictate the refusal to permit the operation of them in close proximity to residences. No self-respecting citizen with a home in which lives his wife and children could fail to be disturbed by the proximity of a place of assemblage at night of men and women, who to the accompaniment of screeching pianos, high-keyed violins and blaring saxophones, emitting the strains of barbaric jazz, more discordant than tom-tom or Chinese gong, transform rest and slumber into a nightmare, and render hideous the hours set apart by nature for their enjoyment.

The evidence in this case shows that the dance hall of appellee is directly across Josephine street from the residence and other property of appellant, as well as other residences; that from 75 to 150 people would assemble there at night, and a dance would be run there daily from 8 o'clock p.m. to 11:30 p.m. The entrance fee was 55 cents for men, and women were admitted without charge. Many of the women were not chaperoned. The dance was known as the Silver Leaf Club. No one swore that the music and voices in the hall could not be heard in the home of appellant. Several witnesses swore that they could be heard, and there was ample testimony to show that the street in front of appellant's house was nightly almost blocked by automobiles and that their honking and other noises were very disagreeable and disturbing.

2. [*Ruling Case Law*, a legal encyclopedia published 1914 to 1921; it is similar to *Corpus Juris Secundum* and *American Jurisprudence*. —Eds.]

All of the witnesses for appellee were either patrons of the dance hall, or women there to control the female dancers and others interested in the affairs of the dance hall. They were not disturbed of course. They went there to dance, to hear the roar of drums, and the music of the fiddle and the saxophone. It was either their business or their pleasure to be there, and they were not disturbed. The people who lived in their homes in the immediate vicinity, however, swore, and no one contradicted them, that until the din and noise had died out because the dancers had dispersed, sleep was driven away and the night robbed of its rest and comfort. To those that business or pleasure had lured to the dance, it was a terpsichorean dream of pleasure, while to the unfortunate denizens of the homes near by it was a terrible nightmare, and while the dancers chased the fleeting hours with flying feet to the sensuous strains of dance hall music, the residents tossed upon sleepless beds.

The question to be solved was not whether the dance hall disturbed the habitués of the hall, the passers-by who stopped out of curiosity, or the residents of other blocks not in the immediate vicinity, but did it disturb the peace and comfort of appellant and his family, and was it calculated to interfere with him in the full enjoyment of his property? The testimony, without contradiction, answered the question in the affirmative. Common sense and reason and universal experience combine to declare that a dance hall cannot be conducted under modern conditions in close proximity to private residences in such a way as to not disturb the occupants and not amount to an invasion of their rights of person and property. A permit from a mayor or a tax commissioner cannot sanctify a dance hall or rob it of its injurious effects on persons and property.

The attorney for appellee, in his closing speech to the jury, told them that if they answered the issue in the affirmative it would put appellee out of business and he would lose all he had invested in the dance hall, amounting to more than $3,000, for which he had worked so hard. This was objected to by appellant, and the court instructed the jury not to consider it. The argument was so improper, however, and so strongly calculated to arouse the sympathy of the jury for appellee, and create a bias in his favor and a prejudice against appellant that its effects could not be removed by an instruction of the court, and it doubtless influenced the verdict of the jury.

The judgment is reversed and judgment here rendered that a permanent injunction be issued against appellee, as prayed for in the petition, and that appellee pay all costs in this behalf expended.

NOTES AND QUESTIONS

1. What is the standard that *Trueheart* sets up for nuisance? What is it about the dance hall that is a nuisance?

2. It appears that the city of San Antonio provided a permit for the jazz hall. Why does that not immunize the hall from liability for nuisance?

3. The modern standard, given by the Restatement (Second) of Torts, is that there is liability for a private nuisance if one's

> conduct is a legal cause of an invasion of another's interest in the private use and enjoyment of land, and the invasion is either
>
> (a) intentional and unreasonable, or
> (b) unintentional and otherwise actionable under the rules controlling liability for negligent or reckless conduct, or for abnormally dangerous conditions or activities.

RESTATEMENT (SECOND) TORTS, §822.

We are interested here with the "intentional and unreasonable" part. In section 826, the *Restatement* provides two tests for "unreasonable." Conduct is unreasonable if

> (a) the gravity of the harm outweighs the utility of the actor's conduct, or
> (b) the harm caused by the conduct is serious and the financial burden of compensating for this and similar harm to others would not make the continuation of the conduct not feasible.

How would those factors fit with the dance hall in *Trueheart*?

4. Why was the dance hall not permitted to tell the jury that it had spent $3,000 and that the owners of the hall would lose their investment if it were shut down?

Now we turn to a case that deals with public nuisance. This time it is a church, rather than a dance hall, that the neighbors are complaining about. The neighbors first obtained relief from the city of Columbia, South Carolina, which determined through a legislative process (where the church had no opportunity to participate) that the church was a public nuisance. The church then challenged that legislative conclusion and the South Carolina Supreme Court overturned the legislative finding, although it upheld the injunction because it found the church was a public nuisance.

Morison v. Rawlinson

193 S.C. 25, 7 S.E.2d 635 (S.C. 1940)

FISHBURNE, Justice.

This suit was instituted and a temporary injunction obtained by the appellants for the purpose of restraining the enforcement by the respondents, the Chief of Police and the Police Department of the City of Columbia, of a resolution passed by the City Council, alleged to be invalid. By the terms of this resolution the religious worship conducted by the appellants and the other members of The House of Prayer, was declared to be a public nuisance, and the Police Department of the City of Columbia was ordered to forthwith abate the nuisance, and to close and keep closed The House of Prayer. This order was immediately carried into effect by the Police Department.

The purpose of the proceeding is to enjoin the City of Columbia and its officers from interfering with and molesting the plaintiffs in what they allege is their worship of God. This is a representative action, and a permanent injunction is sought.

The complaint alleges, in substance, that the plaintiffs are the officers and representatives of a religious denomination known as The House of Prayer, which owns valuable property in the form of a church building in the City of Columbia wherein they conduct their church services; that without notice, a petition was submitted to the City Council, asking that their church building be closed, and that the services conducted by them therein be abated as a public nuisance. It is further alleged that pursuant to this petition the City Council passed a resolution, without giving the plaintiffs an opportunity to be heard, declaring the place of worship a nuisance, and directing the Police Department to forthwith close the church.

In taking these steps the plaintiffs allege that the City Council, under the circumstances set forth, was without power or authority to declare The House of Prayer a nuisance, and that in so doing it abridged the right of plaintiffs to freedom of religious worship, and denied them due process of law as guaranteed by the State and Federal Constitutions.

By their answer and return, the respondents admit that the resolution referred to was adopted, and that under its authority the church was closed as a public nuisance. They further allege that the service or worship conducted in the church was carried on in such a disorderly and riotous manner that it constituted a public nuisance, necessary to be abated by the municipal authorities. The defendants deny that the action taken by the City Council was without power or authority of law, and they specifically allege that the City Council is clothed with power, upon petition, to declare the church a public nuisance, without notice, and that it is vested with authority to abate it.

Upon the return to a rule to show cause, the Circuit Court referred the case to the master for Richland County to take the testimony offered, and, until the case could be heard upon its merits, restrained the defendants from attempting to put into effect the resolution referred to. By this order the terms of the temporary injunction first issued were modified so as to provide that the plaintiffs should be allowed, pending the determination of the case, "to worship only up to the hour of ten o'clock P. M. on any night, and any holding of the meeting beyond said time is not protected by the terms and conditions of this or the order heretofore issued". The order further granted "the right to the defendant and those under him, peace officers of the City of Columbia, to at all times prohibit and prevent the plaintiffs from engaging in disorderly or boisterous conduct; from congregating in and about the streets outside of said house of worship, and also any violation of law which is defined either in the state law or by city ordinance."

Much testimony offered by both sides was taken before the referee. This testimony was reported to the Court, and thereafter, upon a full hearing, the Court by its decree denied the injunction prayed for by the plaintiffs, dissolved the temporary restraining order, as modified, and dismissed the complaint.

We proceed to consider the first question presented by the appeal: Do the plaintiffs and those they represent, members of the religious sect known as The House of Prayer, so conduct their service and worship as to constitute a public nuisance?

In 1933, a group of negroes, the plaintiffs and those whom they represent, purchased a lot of land in the City of Columbia, known as 2549 Cherry Street, and applied for and obtained from the City Council permission to erect thereon a building within which they proposed to conduct their services. The cost of the lot and building represent an investment of approximately $3,100. Before the building permit was issued by the Council, citizens living in the neighborhood where the church was to be built protested, upon the ground that the establishment of this church, with its accustomed form of worship, would create a nuisance in the community. Council, however, granted the building permit upon the assurance from those representing The House of Prayer that the services would not be conducted in such a manner as to give public annoyance.

Thereafter, in March, 1938, numerous white residents living in the vicinity of the church building presented a petition to the City Council setting forth, in substance, that the services or worship as conducted at The House of Prayer constituted a public nuisance, and prayed that the City Council take steps to abate it. It was upon consideration of this petition that the City Council, on March 29, 1938, adopted the resolution to which we have referred. The plaintiffs had no notice of the filing of the petition, and as already stated had no opportunity to be heard before this resolution was passed.

Many witnesses living in the neighborhood of the church were sworn, both by the plaintiffs and the defendants, who gave in repetitious detail the procedure and practice of worship followed by the church members. They do not disagree thereabout in any essential particular. Among these witnesses were five police officers, one of whom resided in the community where the church is located.

The evidence shows that the plaintiffs dance in the church, and, in the course of the meeting, give forth weird and unearthly outcries. There is loud shouting, clapping of hands in unison, and stamping of feet. The incessant use of drums, timbrels, trombones, horns, scrubbing boards and wash tubs add to the general clamor. Some of the votaries are moved to testify; others enter an hypnotic trance. The central pillars of the church are padded to protect them from injury during their transports. The tumult can be heard for many city blocks. Meetings are carried on daily from early hours in the evening until the early hours of the morning. Boisterous and disorderly throngs, unable to enter the crowded building, congregate in the adjoining streets. Fights often occur. White residents who live in the vicinity testified that life is made unbearable by the continual din, which deprives them of all peace and tranquility, and makes sleep impossible.

On more than one occasion police officers have been summoned not only by officers of The House of Prayer, but by local residents, to quell disorders among those present in the church as well as those congregated outside. On one occasion a police officer arrested fifteen persons, taken from within and from without the church, for disturbing the peace. Upon another occasion the police attempted to arrest the head usher of the church who was engaged in a fight. He resisted arrest with a blackjack and a knife. Police officers and others testified that there is attached to and adjoining the church building a stand operated by The House of Prayer, in which beer, soft drinks and food are sold. Witnesses for the plaintiffs denied the sale of beer. Plaintiffs' witnesses assert that the members of the church do not participate in the prevalent disorder, but that it is carried on by visitors attending the services. The section of the City where The House of Prayer is located is a thickly populated residential area.

The evidence leaves no room for doubt that this constant noise, with its unending repetition, accompanied by frequent breaches of the peace, tends to shatter the nervous system and impair the health of those subjected to it, or coming within its influence, except perhaps those actively participating therein.

From a very careful consideration of the testimony and the law, and despite a deep and sympathetic understanding of this type of worship carried on by the members of this negro church, it is impossible for us to escape the conclusion that the services as conducted on this location constitute a public nuisance which is detrimental to the peace, health, and good order of the community in which it is practiced. Nor can there be any doubt of the fact that if the municipal authorities were authorized and empowered to abate nuisances, it was their duty to act in the premises.

A nuisance to be a public nuisance must be in a public place or where the public frequently congregate, or where members of the public are likely to come within the range of its influence, for if the act of use of property be in a remote and infrequented locality, it will not be, unless *malum in se*, a public nuisance. *Black's Law Dictionary*, 2d Ed., page 835.

We think, however, that the lower Court erred in holding that the City Council of Columbia, as disclosed by the record, was vested with power to declare The House of Prayer a nuisance. Or, if it had the authority, that under the circumstances here, it was empowered to abate the nuisance without giving the plaintiffs an opportunity to be heard in the first instance.

The City of Columbia has no ordinance which authorizes the exercise of the power to abate nuisances. Its ordinances provide only for the criminal prosecution of those conducting or maintaining a nuisance. Revised Ordinances, City of Columbia, 1933, Section 609. It is said, however, that such power is derived from Section 7233, Code 1932, which reads: "The city councils and town councils of the cities and towns of the State shall, in addition to the powers conferred by their respective charters, have power and authority to make, ordain and establish all such rules *** and ordinances respecting the roads, streets, markets, police, health and order of said cities and towns, or respecting any subject as shall appear to them necessary and proper for the security, welfare and convenience of such cities and towns, or for preserving health, peace, order and good government within the same. ***"

In addition to this, such power is referred to an Act of the General Assembly amending the charter of the City of Columbia, approved February 26, 1870, . . . which, among other things, provides, "The said mayor and aldermen of the City of Columbia shall have power to abate and remove all nuisances in the said City".

But these sources of authority do not meet the situation here. In our opinion the proper construction of the statutory language referred to is that the city is clothed with authority to declare by general ordinance what shall constitute a nuisance, that is to say, the city may by such ordinance define, classify and enact what things or classes of things are injurious to the health or inimical to peace and good order, and under what conditions and circumstances such specified things are to constitute and be deemed nuisances. But not that the City Council may by mere resolution or motion declare any particular thing a nuisance which has not theretofore been pronounced to be such by law, or so adjudged by judicial determination. *Denver v. Mullen,* [3 P. 693 (Colo. 1884)]. . . .

We have found no authority dissenting from the general proposition that the power to declare a nuisance must be exercised by an ordinance general in its character operating uniformly upon all persons and upon all property of the same character within the city. And it is generally held that a municipal corporation cannot make a thing a nuisance by merely declaring it to be such. Such a declaration is not a final determination of the question. . .

We are also of the opinion that the person or persons who are responsible, allegedly, for the nuisance should be given reasonable notice and a fair hearing before the particular thing or the act sought to be abated is declared to be a nuisance by the City Council, in the absence of a public emergency.

We are not asserting that where the particular thing or the act sought to be abated is made a nuisance by statute or is characterized as such by the common law any inquiry or notice is necessary, because the question as to whether it is in fact a nuisance is already determined. But it is fundamental law that when the act or thing is not made so by the common or statute law, as in this case, the question as to whether it is or is not a nuisance is a judicial one, to be passed upon by the City Council having power to abate it, after notice to the party interested. 43 C.J. §§522, 527, pp. 405, 407.

In the charter provision referred to above, the general authority is given to the City of Columbia to abate and remove all nuisances, but the statute declares no particular thing to be a nuisance. It is left to the City Council to prescribe by general ordinance what shall constitute a nuisance. And the record discloses that there is not any such ordinance.

The nuisance with which we are here concerned belongs to that class of nuisances which in their nature are not nuisances per se, but which may become so by reason of their locality, surroundings, or the method in which they may be conducted or managed, and we perceive no sound reason why a general ordinance may not be passed covering this and similar situations.

However, the foregoing holding does not mean that the judgment below should be reversed. All of the parties are in a Court of equity, and where the Court of equity rightfully assumes jurisdiction for one purpose, it may grant all the relief, either legal or equitable, to which any of the parties show themselves entitled, in the subject matter of the controversy. *Heyward v. Long*, [183 S.E. 145, 147 (S.C., 1935)]. The defendants in their answer and return, upon sufficient allegations, raised the issue that the conduct of the plaintiffs constituted a public nuisance, and prayed that the complaint be dismissed, the temporary restraining order dissolved, and for such other and further relief as may be just and proper. The plaintiffs specifically consented to the order referring the whole matter to the master to take the testimony, and all of the testimony on both sides is directed to the question, whether the acts of the plaintiffs establish a nuisance. The appellants have been fully heard, and, in our opinion, have now had their day in Court.

The appellants urge with great earnestness that so much of the injunction be retained as allows them to continue their services on any night up until ten o'clock P. M. In this case we fully realize that to dissolve the injunction is severe in its consequences to the plaintiffs, and we are in full accord with the rule that the abatement of a public nuisance should not be allowed except when the necessity therefore is clearly and conclusively made out. It is not enough to show a probable, eventual or contingent injury, but it must be shown to be inevitable and undoubted. Of course a thing which merely threatens to become a nuisance will be enjoined only where the Court is satisfied that the threat will become a certainty; and, since the remedy is so severe, resulting often in wholly depriving an owner of the use of his property, the Court will proceed with the utmost caution in restraining such threatened and possible injury.

It is, however, evident from the testimony of the plaintiffs themselves that their form of worship is inseparably connected with and accompanied by unrestrained noise and consequent public disturbance. The things they do are habitual. It is an integral part of what they congregate for. That the nuisance will continue is very plainly and clearly indicated in the testimony of W. M. Morison, the pastor in charge of The House of Prayer, who in his testimony gave Biblical citations for the clapping of hands, shouting, the making of a joyful noise, and the worship of the Lord both morning and evening. Nor is there anything in the evidence which would indicate that this form of worship can be or would be changed so that noise, to the injury of the public, would constitute no part of it.

It is not a question here of prohibiting the free exercise of religious worship in any constitutional sense. It is a question of peace and public order in a thickly populated community. The plaintiffs are entitled to maintain and practice any religious belief or religious principle, or teach any religious doctrine, which does not violate the laws of morality and property, and which does not infringe upon personal rights. . . .

Judgment affirmed.

NOTES AND QUESTIONS

1. *Rawlinson* raises several important issues in the definition of nuisances. The city of Columbia at first legislatively declared The House of Prayer to be a nuisance without giving The House of Prayer a chance for a hearing. This is a problem. (Notice that it is the House of Prayer that sues here to enjoin the city from enforcement of the City Council's resolution finding that the House of Prayer was a nuisance.) The City Council can set general rules regarding what will be a nuisance or it can hold hearings to determine whether there is a nuisance in an individual case. However, as the court points out, the Council should not make determinations about the House of Prayer by itself without a hearing. Thus, *Rawlinson* illustrates a fundamental distinction between legislation (setting general rules about nuisance) and adjudication (holding a particular hearing about the application of general rules to individuals). This distinction arises again elsewhere in basic property, such as with zoning boards.

This also raises the issue of the difference between a public nuisance and a private nuisance. Public nuisances are usually defined as nuisances that cause injury to the public in general; generally only the government could seek an injunction against a public nuisance; and it is often a criminal act to create a public nuisance. In this case, the city of Columbia's legislation attempted to make the House of Prayer a public nuisance.

Once the Court strikes down the Council's legislative finding that the House of Prayer is a nuisance it then turns to the question whether there is still an enjoinable public nuisance. It concludes that there is, but why?

2. Rachel Godsil discusses *Rawlinson* in some depth in "Race Nuisance," 105 *Mich. L. Rev.* 505, 523 (2006), and relates it to two other

reported cases that sought to enjoin the construction of African American churches:

> In three instances, white communities sought to enjoin the construction or operation of black churches. The supreme courts of both Kentucky, in 1903 [*Boyd v. Bd. of Councilmen of Frankfort*, 77 S.W. 669], and Oklahoma, in 1924 [*Spencer Chapel Methodist Episcopal Church v. Brogan*, 231 P. 1074], declined to grant the white communities the relief they sought, but in South Carolina in 1940 [in *Rawlinson*], the court found the way in which the prayer services were conducted to be a nuisance in fact. In all three cases, white communities inveighed against the perceived exuberant style of black worship, which they claimed affected their use and enjoyment of their property and decreased their property's value. However, both *Boyd v. Board of Councilman of Frankfort* and *Spencer Chapel Methodist Episcopal Church v. Brogan* involved attempts to prohibit the construction of a new church facility, while *Morison v. Rawlinson* involved a city council attempt to declare the existing church a nuisance in fact.

What is the difference between seeking to enjoin a church on a nuisance theory before it is constructed and after it is operational? It is harder to make out a successful claim for nuisance during construction, because the harm is not quite so clear. In *Jack v. Torrant*, 71 A.2d 705 (Conn. 1950), the Connecticut Supreme Court upheld an injunction against construction of a funeral home on the theory that the home would depress neighbors. Presumably, that result was certain to occur, while the churches that had not yet been built might or might not cause an unreasonable disturbance to the neighbors. *But see Nicholson v. Connecticut Half-Way House*, 218 A.2d 383 (Conn. 1966) (refusal to enjoin the opening of a halfway house).

However, if plaintiffs wait to sue for an injunction until after the church (or funeral home or half-way house or whatever is being complained about) is operational, then the plaintiffs may face a claim of laches (an equitable defense saying that the plaintiffs sat on their rights). Moreover, plaintiffs seeking to enjoin a nuisance will have to show that the harm to the continued operation outweighs the harm from the injunction. Once the church is operational, then the equities will likely shift. The church in *Rawlinson* argued that they had expended $3,100 in construction; thus, they had a significant equitable argument against the injunction. Still, those equities were not enough in *Rawlinson* to prevent the injunction.

3. Sometimes plaintiffs argued that the mere presence of African Americans was a nuisance. Courts uniformly rejected those claims from the late nineteenth century when plaintiffs first tried them through the dark years of the Jim Crow era. *See, e.g., Lancaster v. Harwood*, 245 S.W. 755 (Tex. Civ. App. 1922) (rejecting claim that "the effect of building this negro servant's house within 10 feet of the sleeping quarters of white people would put the negro sleeping quarters in such close proximity to the Harwood residence as would be objectionable").

4. For more on The United House of Prayer (referred to in the case as "The House of Prayer"), an important movement in African American

religion in the early part of the twentieth century, see Marie W. Dallam, *Daddy Grace and the Foundational Years of the United House of Prayer* (2007). Consider, along those lines, the statement of Hillary Clinton back in 1997 on musicians from the United House of Prayer in Harlem:

> Last week, the Heritage Awards honored 11 uniquely American folk artists. Before I arrived in the East Room for the ceremony, I knew something out of the ordinary was going on. The doors in the White House were shaking. The chandeliers were quaking. And all because of the full-throttle, Gospel trombone music of one of the honorees—Ed Babb and his band, the McCullough Sons of Thunder from the United House of Prayer in Harlem.

http://clinton2.nara.gov/WH/EOP/First_Lady/html/columns/HRC0930.html

The Smithsonian Institution, which produces CDs to help preserve our country's musical traditions, has a recording of United House of Prayer musicians, *Saints' Paradise: Trombone Shout Bands from the United House of Prayer Smithsonian Folkways*, 1999.

3.3 A SPITE FENCE? RACE AND THE PURPOSE OF FENCES

Now we turn to a different use of nuisance doctrine—to attack what the plaintiff here terms a "spite fence"—that is, a fence that is put up to "spite" the neighbor. As you read this case, you may want to ask what the theory is behind prohibition of spite fences, and what evidence will show that a fence was put up to spite the neighbor. In addition, consider how reference to race is used to defeat the claim that the fence was put up for spite.

Bixby v. Cravens

156 P. 1184 (Okla. 1916)

GALBRAITH, C.

Tams Bixby, as complainant, commenced this action in the trial court against the defendants in error for an injunction to prevent them from maintaining, and requiring them to remove a fence erected along the north boundary of their property next to his. Cravens filed a disclaimer, and the Lesters joined issue. There was a trial to the court, and the injunction was denied. From an order overruling a motion for new trial an appeal has been duly prosecuted to this court. The parties were neighbors, and owned and lived on adjoining property near the end of Fourteenth Street, between Emporia and Fon Du Lac, in the city of Muskogee.

The plaintiff's cause of action as set out in his amended petition, upon which the trial was had, was as follows:

> "That he is, and has been for a number of years, the owner of lot numbered 17 in subdivision of lot 1 in block 226, according to the plat filed for record in June, 1906, in the city of Muskogee, Muskogee county, state of Oklahoma, which has a frontage of 265 feet, and that he has a residence on said lot facing in a south direction, the south side of said residence being 26 feet north of the south line of said lot, and that he now occupies with his family, and has for a number of years last past, the above-described property as a home.
>
> That the defendants Richard A. Lester and Nell Lester, his wife, own lots numbered 15 and 16 in the said subdivision of lot numbered 1 in block 226, according to the plat filed for record in June, 1906, in said city of Muskogee, that there is a residence thereon, and that the defendants Richard A. Lester and Nell Lester reside with their family thereon, and have for a number of years last past, which said lots lie south of the west 110 1/2 feet owned and occupied by the plaintiff, there being about an 8-foot alley between the said lots of plaintiff and defendants.
>
> That on or about the 15th day of May, 1913, the said defendants Richard A. Lester and May Lester maliciously, spitefully, and for the purpose of annoying the plaintiff and his family, erected a plank fence along the entire northerly line of their said lot and the southerly line of the alley between the said lots of plaintiff and defendants, 6 feet high; that said fence was not erected for any useful or necessary purpose on the part of defendant, but purely for the purpose of annoying plaintiff and his family; that said plaintiff has a beautiful home, and said fence presents an unsightly appearance on the side facing said home; that said fence cuts off plaintiff's view, and also cuts off the air and light from the plaintiff's premises, and greatly damages the plaintiff in the value of his said property; that said fence is a great annoyance to the plaintiff and his family, and not only cuts off the air and light, but shuts out the view from said premises of plaintiff south and southwest, and greatly detracts from the appearance of plaintiff's said premises; that plaintiff has no complete and adequate remedy at law; and that, unless this court interferes by injunction, he will suffer great and irreparable injury.
>
> Wherefore he prays that on a final hearing of this cause he may have a decree enjoining the defendants, their agents and servants, from maintaining said fence and requiring them to tear down and remove the same and every foot thereof, and he prays for all further equitable and general relief."

The Lesters answered, admitting the ownership of the property and its occupancy as a home as alleged in the petition, and, further answering, denied each and every allegation in the petition made and prayed for judgment.

. . .

Lester testified that he had no personal acquaintance with their neighbor, Bixby, and that he had never spoken to him, and had no desire to harass or annoy him, and did not think about Bixby when he built the fence, but built it for his own convenience, entirely upon his own ground, and to protect his own property and its privacy; that the fence was 5 feet and 9 inches above the sidewalk, and was built from new No. 2 pine lumber; that the alleyway along which this fence was erected was only 15 feet distant from his dining room window, and that the alleyway was a public thoroughfare much traveled by ice wagons, grocers' deliveries, and by negroes afoot going to the negro settlement out beyond Fon Du Lac, and that the privacy of his home was exposed to the gaze and view of persons passing through the alley, and by persons cutting across his yard before the fence was erected; that the traffic through the alley cut up the ground, and during dry and windy weather the dust blew into his house; that he kept in his yard chickens and pigeons, and a bulldog, and also cultivated therein flowers; and that the fence was erected in the manner it was for his own convenience and protection entirely, and to guard against the dust from the alley and to cut off their view of complainant's garden and cow and the droppings from his cow shed. This testimony was supported by that of other witnesses called on behalf of the defendants in error.

It is urged in the plaintiff in error's brief in support of this cause of action in part as follows:

> "He was beautifying his yard and making a park out of it, and while this was going on his neighbor erected this unsightly fence (unsightly on plaintiff's side, but not so on defendant's side), which is the first thing to greet him in the morning, and the recollection of which stays with him after he retires at night. It was the contrast between the appearance of plaintiff's side of this fence and the surroundings that caused it to be placed there, and it was this idea that caused such glee on the part of Mrs. Lester and prompted her to say from an overflowing heart: 'How are the mighty fallen.' What explanation do they give to this act on her part? None. There is but one answer to it, and that is the interpretation we place on it. It is the most potent fact in the case, aside from the photographs. People who have aesthetic tastes, and attempt to have a home in keeping with such tastes, are entitled to protection."

To which the defendant in error replied in defense of the usefulness of the fence as follows:

> "It shielded Mr. Lester's home, to a substantial degree, from the dust of an unpaved alley carrying considerable traffic; it made it convenient and satisfactory, if indeed it did not make it possible, for Mrs. Lester to beautify the north line of the lot with a row of roses and to attend to her flowers; it protected the privacy of their yard and dining room from the close gaze of the many people, white and black, who constantly passed through the alley; it enhanced the safety of the home and chickens and pigeons in the back yard, and to a greater degree in view of Mr. Lester's absence from home two-thirds of the time; it prevented trespassing upon the lot; it concealed a muddy or a dusty washed and rutted alley, and cut off a close view of the Bixby cow and manure pile, and the high garden weeds towards the end of summer."

And in reply to the claim of malice shown by the remarks of Mrs. Lester in regard to Mr. Bixby, it is said:

> "The third incident arose one Sunday morning as Mr. and Mrs. Lester were walking through their yard, and Mr. Bixby was hoeing weeds in the alley. Mr. Bixby alleges that she remarked: 'How are the mighty fallen.' And that she laughed. Mr. Lester remembered the occasion, but did not recall his wife's words. The record does not

> disclose whether Col. Bixby wore the hat and pants that usually attend the hoe, nor whether he sacrificed a peaceful hour in church that morning to accomplish the long deferred extermination of the tall and stately weeds which fringed the unpaved alley and in later summer claimed the Bixby garden for their own, but we submit that Mrs. Lester was in good taste when she gave vent to the words of the prophet: 'How are the mighty fallen.' 2 Samuel, xix, 25, 27. What connection is there between her remark and the fence? One must have a vivid imagination to torture this harmless and humorous incident into evidence of 'malice' in the then long-built fence."

The law of this case is well stated by the Supreme Court of Indiana in the case of *Giller v. West*, . . . 69 N. E. 548, at page 549, as follows:

> "The fact that the division fence erected by the appellant was close and high, and made of rough and unsightly materials, and that it cut off the view from appellant's lot toward Pierce street, and shaded and thereby injured her garden, did not render the fence a private nuisance, nor entitle the appellee to have it abated. The appellant had the right to build a partition fence, a house or any other structure on his premises, and along the entire length of the line dividing them from the real estate owned by the appellee. The latter had no easement of light, air, or view in or over the appellant's lots, and she had no legal cause for complaint if these were interfered with or entirely shut off by the erection of a fence, house, or other building. The appellant had the right to use his premises, and every part of them, for any lawful purpose which did not deprive the adjacent owner of any right of enjoyment of her property recognized and protected by law. The erection and maintenance of a division fence thereon was a lawful use of the appellant's land, and no legal right of the appellee was violated or invaded thereby. Had the appellant erected a house 30 feet high and 114 feet long on the part of his lot adjacent to the appellee's premises, thereby in a much more serious manner cutting off the sunlight, air, and view from appellee's lot and residence, she could not have been heard to complain of such use of his land. If appellant could lawfully construct such a building on his lot, he could, without doubt, lawfully erect and maintain a close fence, 8 feet in height, on the division line. That it was rough and unsightly made no difference. The law does not require that such fences shall be constructed of fine materials, or that they shall be attractive in appearance."

. . .

We are constrained to approve the conclusion of the trial court that the evidence in this case did not justify an injunction, inasmuch as the fence complained of did not constitute a nuisance and was not erected and maintained purely out of spite and ill will toward complainant, as in *Smith v. Speed*, 11 Okl. 95, 66 Pac. 511, . . . but was erected in the exercise of a lawful right of the owner to improve and benefit his own property. The complainant is doubtless a man of education and refinement, and evidently takes great pride in his home and in beautifying the grounds surrounding the same, for all of which he is to be commended. He was doubtless annoyed and harassed at the unsightly view that this alley fence presented. Still the defendants in error had a perfect right to erect the fence and maintain the same to protect their home and their property and add to its privacy, comfort, and convenience, and they were not compelled to consult the "aesthetic taste" of their neighbors as to the kind of a fence they should build or whether the smooth or the rough side thereof faced in or out, or the color of the paint they should use thereon. They were clearly within their rights, in consulting and satisfying their own taste in these matters.

The judgment appealed from is affirmed. . . .

NOTES AND QUESTIONS

1. Tams Bixby, the plaintiff in this action, was one of Oklahoma's most important politicians in the early years of the twentieth century. In 1897, President William McKinley appointed him Commissioner of the Five Civilized Tribes and also Commissioner of the Dawes Commission. The Bixby family then moved from Minnesota, where Bixby had been an influential Republican and sometimes newspaper publisher, to Muskogee, then one of the leading towns in the Oklahoma territory. Bixby became the acting chair of the Dawes Commission and oversaw the process of allotment, which granted tribal members individual parcels of land from tribal land. It, thus, broke up the tribes' common ownership of property.

In 1906, Bixby took over publication of the newspaper the Muskogee Phoenix. *See* Kent Carter, *Tams Bixby: Doing Government Business in the Gilded Age*, 78 Chronicles of Oklahoma 412-43 (2001).

2. What, then, is the theory used to oppose a spite fence? The theory is that conduct — even legal conduct — on one's land is a nuisance. You might think about the *Restatement of Torts'* standard for nuisance, which we discussed in note 3 to *Trueheart.* Recall that the *Restatement* provides that a nuisance is the use of property in a way that interferes *unreasonably* with a neighbor. Reasonableness turns on whether the utility of the conduct (the spite fence) outweighs the harm. Restatement (Second) Torts §826. In this case, although the builder of the fence may get great joy from the harm inflicted on the neighbor, we do not consider that a social good. Obviously, in this case "utility" means social utility. It is an intriguing doctrine that protects social values and hints at what owners can do with their property.

Cases enjoining spite fences are relatively rare. *See, e.g., Dowdell v. Bloomquist*, 847 A.2d 827 (R.I. 2004) (holding that a hedge planted to obstruct a neighbor's view of the Atlantic Ocean was a spite fence). In such cases, courts seem rather reluctant to inquire into motive. *See Roper v. Durham*, 353 S.E.2d 476 (Ga. 1987). Moreover, when courts inquire into motive, as with *Bixby*, it seems that it is difficult to make out cases of malicious intent. In some recent cases, courts have inferred an economic motive to injure a competitor in enjoining a spite fence. *See, e.g., Sundowner, Inc. v. King*, 509 P.2d 785 (Idaho 1973) (enjoining fence that obscured a neighbor's competing motel).

3. At the time *Bixby* was argued, the case law against spite fences was even weaker than it is today. So given the difficultly of obtaining an injunction for a spite fence, why did Tams Bixby even try it?

How did the Lesters respond to Bixby's allegations? If this case was controlled by precedent like *Giller v. West*, 69 N.E. 548 (Ind. 1904) and *Gusdu Blass Dry Goods v. Reinman & Wolfort*, 143 S.W. 1087 (Ark. 1912), then why did the Lesters talk about the alleyway they fenced off as "a public thoroughfare much traveled by ice wagons, grocers' deliveries, and by negroes afoot going to the negro settlement out beyond Fon Du Lac"? What role did the invocation of race play in this case? What role did the Lesters' self-description of their interest in gardens play here? How did it help defeat a claim that they established the fence for spite?

4. Sometimes courts enjoin as nuisance use of property that lowers neighbors' property values dramatically. *See, e.g., Puritan Holding Co. v. Holloschitz*, 372 N.Y.S.2d 500 (Sup. Ct. 1975) (finding abandoned apartment building that lowered neighbors' property values a nuisance).

3.4 ZONING: PRESCRIBING USES BY RACE AND ETHNICITY

Now we turn from nuisances to zoning. In *Buchanan v. Warley* we take up a U.S. Supreme Court case that struck down a racial zoning ordinance. Many have commented in recent years on how unusual the case was: decided two decades after the Supreme Court's 1896 decision upholding segregation on railway cars in *Plessy v. Ferguson*, it struck down a housing segregation ordinance. As you read *Buchanan*, see if you can figure out why the court would think segregation on railroads (and in schools) was acceptable if it is not acceptable when imposed on regulations of property.

Buchanan v. Warley

245 U.S. 60 (1917)

Mr. Justice Day delivered the opinion of the Court.

Buchanan, plaintiff in error, brought an action in the chancery branch of Jefferson circuit court of Kentucky for the specific performance of a contract for the sale of certain real estate situated in the city of Louisville at the corner of Thirty-seventh street and Pflanz avenue. The offer in writing to purchase the property contained a proviso:

> 'It is understood that I am purchasing the above property for the purpose of having erected thereon a house which I propose to make my residence, and it is a distinct part of this agreement that I shall not be required to accept a deed to the above property or to pay for said property unless I have the right under the laws of the state of Kentucky and the city of Louisville to occupy said property as a residence.'

This offer was accepted by the plaintiff.

To the action for specific performance the defendant by way of answer set up the condition above set forth, that he is a colored person, and that on the block of which the lot in controversy is a part, there are ten residences, eight of which at the time of the making of the contract were occupied by white people, and only two (those nearest the lot in question) were occupied by colored people, and that under and by virtue of the ordinance of the city of Louisville, approved May 11, 1914, he would not be allowed to occupy the lot as a place of residence.

In reply to this answer the plaintiff set up, among other things, that the ordinance was in conflict with the Fourteenth Amendment to the Constitution of the United States, and hence no defense to the action for specific performance of the contract. . . .

The title of the ordinance is:

> 'An ordinance to prevent conflict and ill-feeling between the white and colored races in the city of Louisville, and to preserve the public peace and promote the general welfare, by making reasonable provisions requiring, as far as practicable, the use of separate blocks, for residences, places of abode, and places of assembly by white and colored people respectively.'

. . .

This ordinance prevents the occupancy of a lot in the city of Louisville by a person of color in a block where the greater number of residences are occupied by white persons; where such a majority exists colored persons are excluded. This interdiction is based wholly upon color; simply that and nothing more. In effect, premises situated as are those in question in the so-called white block are effectively debarred from sale to persons of color, because if sold they cannot be occupied by the purchaser nor by him sold to another of the same color.

This drastic measure is sought to be justified under the authority of the state in the exercise of the police power. It is said such legislation tends to promote the public peace by preventing racial conflicts; that it tends to maintain racial purity; that it prevents the deterioration of property owned and occupied by white people, which deterioration, it is contended, is sure to follow the occupancy of adjacent premises by persons of color.

The authority of the state to pass laws in the exercise of the police power, having for their object the promotion of the public health, safety and welfare is very broad as has been affirmed in numerous and recent decisions of this court. Furthermore the exercise of this power, embracing nearly all legislation of a local character is not to be interfered with by the courts where it is within the scope of legislative authority and the means adopted reasonably tend to accomplish a lawful purpose. But it is equally well established that the police power, broad as it is, cannot justify the passage of a law or ordinance which runs counter to the limitations of the Constitution; that principle has been so frequently affirmed in this court that we need not stop to cite the cases. . . .

The concrete question here is: May the occupancy, and, necessarily, the purchase and sale of property of which occupancy is an incident, be inhibited by the states, or by one of its municipalities, solely because of the color of the proposed occupant of the premises? That one may dispose of his property, subject only to the control of lawful enactments curtailing that right in the public interest, must be conceded. The question now presented makes it pertinent to inquire into the constitutional right of the white man to sell his property to a colored man, having in view the legal status of the purchaser and occupant.

Following the Civil War certain amendments to the federal Constitution were adopted, which have become an integral part of that instrument, equally binding upon all the states and fixing certain fundamental rights which all are bound to respect. The Thirteenth Amendment abolished slavery in the United States and in all places subject to their jurisdiction, and gave Congress power to enforce the amendment by appropriate legislation. The Fourteenth Amendment made all persons born or naturalized in the United States, citizens of the United States and of the states in which they reside, and provided that no state shall make or enforce any law which shall abridge the privileges or immunities of citizens of the United States, and that no state shall deprive any person of life, liberty, or property without due process of law, nor deny to any person the equal protection of the laws.

The effect of these amendments was first dealt with by this court in *Slaughter House Cases,* 16 Wall. 36. . . . The reasons for the adoption of the amendments were elaborately considered by a court familiar with the times in which the necessity for the amendments arose and with the circumstances which impelled their adoption. In that case Mr. Justice Miller, who spoke for the majority, pointed out that the colored race, having been freed from slavery by the Thirteenth Amendment, was raised to the dignity of citizenship and equality of civil rights by the Fourteenth Amendment, and the states were prohibited from abridging the privileges and immunities of such citizens, or depriving any person of life, liberty, or property without due process of law. While a principal purpose of the latter amendment was to protect persons of color, the broad language used was deemed sufficient to protect all persons, white or black, against discriminatory legislation by the states. This is now the settled law. In many of the cases since arising the question of color has not been involved and the cases have been decided upon alleged violations of civil or property rights irrespective of the race or color of the complainant. In *Slaughter House Cases* it was recognized that the chief inducement to the passage of the amendment was the desire to extend federal protection to the recently emancipated race from unfriendly and discriminating legislation by the states. . . .

In giving legislative aid to these constitutional provisions Congress enacted in 1866, chapter 31, §1, 14 Stat. 27 (Comp. St. 1916, §3931), that:

> 'All citizens of the United States shall have the same right, in every state and territory, as is enjoyed by white citizens thereof to inherit, purchase, lease, sell, hold and convey real and personal property.'

And in 1870, by chapter 114, §16, 16 Stat. 144 (Comp. St. 1916, §3925), that:

> 'All persons within the jurisdiction of the United States shall have the same right in every state and territory to make and enforce contracts to sue, be parties, give evidence, and to the full and equal benefit of all laws and proceedings for the security of person and property as is enjoyed by white citizens, and shall be subject to like punishment, pains, penalties, taxes, licenses and exactions of every kind, and none other.'

In the face of these constitutional and statutory provisions, can a white man be denied, consistently with due process of law, the right to dispose of his property to a purchaser by prohibiting the occupation of it for the sole reason that the purchaser is a person of color intending to occupy the premises as a place of residence?

The statute of 1866, originally passed under sanction of the Thirteenth Amendment, 14 Stat. 27, and practically re-enacted after the adoption of the Fourteenth Amendment, 16 Stat. 144, expressly provided that all citizens of the United States in any state shall have the same right to purchase property as is enjoyed by white citizens. Colored persons are citizens of the United States and have the right to purchase property and enjoy and use the same without laws discriminating against them solely on account of color. *Hall v. De Cuir*, 95 U. S. 485, 508. . . . The Fourteenth Amendment and these statutes enacted in furtherance of its purpose operate to qualify and entitle a colored man to acquire property without state legislation discriminating against him solely because of color.

The defendant in error insists that *Plessy v. Ferguson*, 163 U. S. 537 . . ., is controlling in principle in favor of the judgment of the court below. In that case this court held that a provision of a statute of Louisiana requiring railway companies carrying passengers to provide in their coaches equal but separate accommodations for the white and colored races did not run counter to the provisions of the Fourteenth Amendment. It is to be observed that in that case there was no attempt to deprive persons of color of transportation in the coaches of the public carrier, and the express requirements were for equal though separate accommodations for the white and colored races. In *Plessy v. Ferguson*, classification of accommodations was permitted upon the basis of equality for both races.

In the *Berea College Case*, 211 U. S. 45 . . ., a state statute was sustained in the courts of Kentucky, which, while permitting the education of white persons and negroes in different localities by the same incorporated institution, prohibited their attendance at the same place, and in this court the judgment of the Court of Appeals of Kentucky was affirmed solely upon the reserved authority of the Legislature of Kentucky to alter, amend, or repeal charters of its own corporations, and the question here involved was neither discussed nor decided.

In *Carey v. City of Atlanta,* [84 S. E. 456 (Ga. 1916)] the Supreme Court of Georgia, holding an ordinance, similar in principle to the one herein involved, to be invalid, dealt with *Plessy v. Ferguson,* and *Berea College Case,* in language so apposite that we quote a portion of it:

> 'In each instance the complaining person was afforded the opportunity to ride or to attend institutions of learning, or afforded the thing of whatever nature to which in the particular case he was entitled. The most that was done was to require him as a member of a class to conform to reasonable rules in regard to the separation of the races. In none of them was he denied the right to use, control, or dispose of his property, as in this case. . . . 'The effect of the ordinance under consideration was not merely to regulate a business or the like, but was to destroy the right of the individual to acquire, enjoy, and dispose of his property. Being of this character it was void as being opposed to the due process clause of the Constitution.'

That there exists a serious and difficult problem arising from a feeling of race hostility which the law is powerless to control, and to which it must give a measure of consideration, may be freely admitted. But its solution cannot be promoted by depriving citizens of their constitutional rights and privileges.

As we have seen, this court has held laws valid which separated the races on the basis of equal accommodations in public conveyances, and courts of high authority have held enactments lawful which provide for separation in the public schools of white and colored pupils where equal privileges are given. But in view of the rights secured by the Fourteenth Amendment to the federal Constitution such legislation must have its limitations, and cannot be sustained where the exercise of authority exceeds the restraints of the Constitution. We think these limitations are exceeded in laws and ordinances of the character now before us.

It is the purpose of such enactments, and, it is frankly avowed it will be their ultimate effect, to require by law, at least in residential districts, the compulsory separation of the races on account of color. Such action is said to be essential to the maintenance of the purity of the races, although it is to be noted in the ordinance under consideration that the employment of colored servants in white families is permitted, and nearby residences of colored persons not coming within the blocks, as defined in the ordinance, are not prohibited.

The case presented does not deal with an attempt to prohibit the amalgamation of the races. The right which the ordinance annulled was the civil right of a white man to dispose of his property if he saw fit to do so to a person of color and of a colored person to make such disposition to a white person.

It is urged that this proposed segregation will promote the public peace by preventing race conflicts. Desirable as this is, and important as is the preservation of the public peace, this aim cannot be accomplished by laws or ordinances which deny rights created or protected by the federal Constitution. . . .

We think this attempt to prevent the alienation of the property in question to a person of color was not a legitimate exercise of the police power of the state, and is in direct violation of the fundamental law enacted in the Fourteenth Amendment of the Constitution preventing state interference with property rights except by due process of law. That being the case, the ordinance cannot stand. . . .

Reversed.

NOTES AND QUESTIONS

1. The Supreme Court emphasizes that the right of the plaintiff (a white man) was limited by the zoning ordinance, "because it was held in effect that he could not sell the lot to a person of color who was willing and ready to acquire the property, and had obligated himself to take it." Why is that the case? The zoning ordinance only prohibits the *occupancy* of the property in question by an African American.
2. What is the claim by the plaintiff? How does the zoning ordinance affect his property rights?
3. Did you notice the name of the zoning ordinance? How does the city try to justify the ordinance under its police power?
4. This is how the Supreme Court framed this case:

> May the occupancy, and, necessarily, the purchase and sale of property of which occupancy is an incident, be inhibited by the states, or by one of its municipalities, solely because of the color of the proposed occupant of the premises?

This turns the case into one of property rights. How does the court distinguish cases like *Plessy v. Ferguson*, which permitted segregation on railroad cars, and *Berea College*, which upheld segregation in higher education? Does it turn on whether the Court thinks segregation on a railroad car is still providing similar treatment, but the flat prohibition on occupancy (which seems to be essentially a prohibition on sale) is denying the right to buy or sell property altogether? Perhaps so. *Buchanan* relies on *Carey v. City of Atlanta*, 84 S.E. 456 (Ga. 1916), which struck down a similar zoning ordinance, employing such reasoning.

Is there something special about property that accounts for the different outcomes in *Buchanan* and *Plessy*? If so, do you believe that property rights led the way for subsequent expansion of other civil rights?

5. Is this decision really based on the Civil Rights Act of 1866 or the Civil Rights Act of 1870?

6. When you study *Shelley v. Kraemer* in the next chapter, try to pick out the similarities (and differences) with *Buchanan. Shelley* struck down private covenants (rather than a public zoning ordinance) that prohibited the occupancy of the property by African Americans (and some other races as well). *Shelley* emphasizes that there was a willing buyer and a willing seller and the only thing standing in the way was a covenant prohibiting African Americans from occupying the property. When you get to *Shelley*, you might ask, how much does *Buchanan*'s emphasis on the zoning ordinance as prohibiting the occupancy influence the Supreme Court's opinion in the case?

7. There is extensive literature on *Buchanan*; much of it celebrates the role of property rights in leading the way for subsequent expansion of other civil rights. *See* David Bernstein, *Philip Sober Controlling Philip Drunk: Buchanan v. Warley in Historical Perspective*, 51 VAND. L. REV. 797-879 (1998); Alexander M. Bickel and Benno C. Schmidt, THE JUDICIARY AND RESPONSIBLE GOVERNMENT 789-817 (1984).

8. Even after *Buchanan*, there were continued efforts at racial zoning. The Supreme Court struck down a Richmond, Virginia ordinance in 1930. *See City of Richmond v. Deans*, 281 U.S. 704 (1930). State and lower federal courts also struck down attempts at racial zoning. *See, e.g., Allen v. Oklahoma City*, 52 P.2d 1054 (Okla. 1935); *City of Birmingham v. Monk*, 185 F.2d 859 (5th Cir. 1950).

DISCRIMINATION AND THE SALE OR OCCUPANCY OF REAL PROPERTY

In this chapter, we turn our attention to public laws and private agreements that promoted racial discrimination involving the purchase or lease of real property. During the early twentieth century, a number of western states enacted statutory barriers to the sale or lease of land to individuals belonging to certain races. In addition to these public law barriers, private individuals entered into covenants that barred the sale of private property to persons of specific races identified in the written agreement. Courts fielded a large number of legal challenges to public and private prohibitions on the sale or lease of real property based on the race of the parties involved in the transaction. As the materials demonstrate, courts struggled to overcome doctrinal obstacles that blocked relief for individuals affected by these laws and agreement; however, courts eventually found a way to overcome these doctrinal hurdles by the mid-twentieth century.

Consider the following questions as you read through this chapter:

1. What were the ways in which private actors would discriminate in the purchase or lease of real property?
2. Why was resort to constitutional protections limited in this era?

4.1 STATUTORY PROHIBITIONS ON THE PURCHASE OR LEASE OF REAL PROPERTY: ALIEN LAND LAWS

The first section of this chapter focuses on public laws that not only barred the sale of real property, but also limited the duration of leases that could be extended to certain individuals. Collectively, these statutes are known as the Alien Land Laws. California became the first state to enact an Alien Land Law in 1913 in response to growing concerns about immigration and the state's agricultural economy. After California passed its law in 1913, other states enacted similar restrictions on the ability of some individuals to own or lease real property. Arkansas, Arizona, Idaho, Kansas, Montana, Oregon, Utah, Washington, and Wyoming all enacted restrictions on who could own or lease property in the state. A number of the Alien Land Laws enacted in other states were almost identical to California's 1913 statute. However, some states, such as Arizona, employed slightly different language to block land ownership for certain persons. Regardless of the text of the statute, Alien Land Laws had a singular purpose.

> *Alien Land Law Act, Cal. ch. 113 (1913)*
> Section 1. All aliens eligible to citizenship under the laws of the United States may acquire, possess, enjoy, transmit and inherit real property, or any interest therein, in this state, in the same manner and to the same extent as citizens of the United States, except as otherwise provided by the laws of this state.
> Section 2. All aliens other than those mentioned in section one of this act may acquire, possess, enjoy and transfer real property, or any interest therein, in this state, in the manner and to the extent and for the purposes proscribed by any treaty now existing between the government of the United States and the nation or country of which such alien is a citizen or subject, and not otherwise, and may in addition thereto lease lands in this state for agricultural purposes for a term not exceeding three years.

> *Alien Land Law Act, Ariz. ch. 43 (1917)*
> Section 2. An alien shall not own land or take or hold title thereto. No person shall take or hold land or title to land for an alien. Land now held by or for aliens in violation of the constitution of the state is forfeited to and declared to be the property of the state. Land hereafter conveyed to or for the use of aliens in violation of the constitution or of this Act shall thereby be forfeited to and be come the property of the state. Nothing herein contained shall be construed to destroy or limit existing or vested rights of any person at the time of passage of this Act.

NOTES AND QUESTIONS

1. What is the specific distinction comprehended by the California and Arizona statutes regarding those eligible to purchase or lease property? How does one decide who is and who is not covered by the restrictions imposed by such laws? As you can see from the language of these statutes, the text of the alien land laws generally did not identify specific racial groups for differential treatment. However, the 1943 Arkansas legislature enacted a statute declaring that "no Japanese or a descendent of a Japanese shall ever purchase or hold title to any lands in the State of Arkansas." 1943 ARK. ACTS 75. Interestingly, the statute in Arkansas seems to have run afoul of the Fourteenth Amendment of the U.S. Constitution as it applied to Japanese citizens of the United States. Furthermore, the Arkansas law may have violated the Constitution of the State of Arkansas because it

stated that "[n]o distinction shall ever be made by law between resident aliens and citizens in regard to possession, enjoyment, and descent of property." ARK. CONST. OF 1874, art. II, §20. For more on these laws generally and more information on the legal irony of the Arkansas law, see Dudley O. McGovney, *The Anti-Japanese Land Laws of California and Ten Other States*, 35 CAL. L. REV. 7 (1947).

2. What was the ultimate goal of the legislation in states like California and Arizona? One answer to that difficult question comes from California's attorney general at the time of California's passage of its statute. According to California's Attorney General Ulysses S. Webb,

> The fundamental basis of all legislation upon this subject, State and Federal, has been, and is, race undesirability. It is unimportant and foreign to the question under discussion whether a particular race is inferior. The simple and single question is, is the race desirable. . . . [The Alien Land Law] seeks to limit their presence by curtailing their privileges which they may enjoy here; for they will not come in large numbers and long abide with us if they may not acquire land. And it seeks to limit the numbers who will come by limiting the opportunities for their activity here when they arrive.

Yamato Ichihashi, JAPANESE IN THE UNITED STATES 275 (1969).

3. Do you think that such legislation was effective? Can you think of any way that people may have circumvented the strictures imposed by such laws? According to Brant T. Lee,

> From 1913 to 1920 the amount of agricultural land owned by Japanese in California increased by 150 percent, and the total amount of land farmed by Japanese, either by ownership, lease, or contract, grew from under 300,000 acres to over 450,000 acres. Japanese farmers during this period managed to exploit the loose wording of the statute. The most popular method was for the Issei, or immigrant Japanese, to purchase property in the name of their American-born minor children, or Nisei. Then they would be appointed the trustee or guardian for their children's property and thereby retain control. Or they could get an adult American citizen who was willing to lend his or her name to be put on a deed. Or they could form a landholding corporation in which two nissei children and a white American attorney would be the majority shareholders and the issei parents minority shareholders.

A Racial Trust: The Japanese YWCA and the Alien Land Law, 7 UCLA ASIAN PAC. AM. L.J. 1, 19 (2001).

In response to the shortcomings of the 1913 statute, California voters passed a new alien land law by initiative in 1920. Keith Aoki describes the modifications in the 1920 law:

> The 1920 Initiative barred guardianships and trusteeships in the name of "aliens ineligible to citizenship" who would be prohibited from owning such properties, barred all leases of agricultural land, barred corporations with a majority of shareholders who were "aliens ineligible to citizenship" from owning agricultural land and classified sharecropping contracts as "interests in land," making them off-limits to first-generation Japanese.

> . . . In 1923 and 1927, the California legislature added additional amendments to the 1920 Initiative, making escheat effective immediately upon the conclusion of a transaction involving agricultural land with an "alien ineligible to citizenship," rather than at the successful conclusion of an escheat action by the State Attorney General (a citizen buyer could lose one's property thus acquired). The Amendments also required "aliens ineligible to citizenship" to sell inherited property or it would escheat to the state, made escheat actions commencible by the County District Attorney, barred "aliens ineligible to citizenship" from owning stock in a corporation that owned agricultural land and created a rebuttable presumption that any real estate transaction involving an "alien ineligible to citizenship" was to be treated as a criminal conspiracy to evade the Alien Land Law.

No Right to Own: The Early Twentieth-Century "Alien Land Laws" as a Prelude to Internment, 40 B.C. L. Rev. 37, 56-59 (1998-99) (footnotes omitted).

4. Passage of statutes like those in California and Washington spurred legal challenges on a variety of legal grounds. In *Terrace v. Thompson*, 263 U.S. 197 (1923), Washington's Alien Land Law barred two citizens of the United States and the State of Washington from leasing their farmland to a "subject of the emperor of Japan." As a result, they challenged Washington's Alien Land Law on due process and equal protection grounds. The Court observed that

> The Fourteenth Amendment, as against the arbitrary and capricious or unjustly discriminatory action of the State, protects the owners in their right to lease and dispose of their land for lawful purposes and the alien resident in his right to earn a living by following ordinary occupations of the community, but it does not take away from the State those powers of police that were reserved at the time of the adoption of the Constitution. And in the exercise of such powers the State has wide discretion in determining its own public policy and what measures are necessary for its own protection and properly to promote the safety, peace and good order of its people.
>
> And, while Congress has exclusive jurisdiction over immigration, naturalization and the disposal of the public domain, each State, in the absence of any treaty provision to the contrary, has power to deny to aliens the right to own land within its borders. . . .
>
> State legislation applying alike and equally to all aliens, withholding from them the right to own land, cannot be said to be capricious or to amount to an arbitrary deprivation of liberty or property, or to transgress the due process clause.
>
> This brings us to a consideration of appellants' contention that the act contravenes the equal protection clause. That clause secures equal protection to all in the enjoyment of their rights under like circumstances. But this does not forbid every distinction in the law of a State between citizens and aliens resident therein. . . .
>
> By the statute in question all aliens who have not in good faith declared intention to become citizens of the United States, as specified in §1 (a), are called "aliens," and it is provided that they shall not "own" "land," as defined in clauses (d) and (b) of §1 respectively. The class so created includes all, but is not limited to, aliens not eligible to become citizens. Eligible aliens who have not declared their intention to become citizens are included, and the act provides that unless declarants be admitted to citizenship within seven years after the declaration is made, bad faith will be presumed. This leaves the class permitted so to own land made up of citizens and aliens who may, and who intend to, become citizens, and who in good faith have made the declaration required by the naturalization laws. The inclusion of good faith declarants in the same class with citizens does not unjustly discriminate against aliens who are

> ineligible or against eligible aliens who have failed to declare their intention. The classification is based on eligibility and purpose to naturalize. Eligible aliens are free white persons and persons of African nativity or descent. . . . Generally speaking, the natives of European countries are eligible. Japanese, Chinese and Malays are not. Appellants' contention that the state act discriminates arbitrarily against Nakatsuka and other ineligible aliens because of their race and color is without foundation. All persons of whatever color or race who have not declared their intention in good faith to become citizens are prohibited from so owning agricultural lands. . . .
>
> And we think it is clearly within the power of the State to include nondeclarant eligible aliens and ineligible aliens in the same prohibited class. Reasons supporting discrimination against aliens who may but who will not naturalize are obvious. . . .
>
> The Terraces, who are citizens, have no right safeguarded by the Fourteenth Amendment to lease their land to aliens lawfully forbidden to take or have such lease. The state act is not repugnant to the equal protection clause and does not contravene the Fourteenth Amendment.

Id. at 216-22.

5. During the same week that the Supreme Court decided *Terrace,* the Court upheld California's Alien Land Law of 1920 against an equal protection challenge in *Porterfield v. Webb,* 263 U.S. 225 (1923). Two other cases upheld other aspects of the Alien Land Law. In *Webb v. O'Brien,* 263 U.S. 313 (1923), the Court construed the law broadly to apply to cropping contracts, and in *Frick v. Webb,* 263 U.S. 326 (1923), the Court upheld the bar on land ownership by corporations with a majority of shareholders who were aliens ineligible for citizenship.

Forty-five years after upholding California's Alien Land Law in *Porterfield,* California's limitations on who could own or lease real property in the state again arrived at the Supreme Court. By the time California's Alien Land Law made it back to Court, however, the legal and social landscape of the country had changed. The Court cited to California Attorney General Webb's comments in a footnote, but the outcome proved to be rather different from the first time they were offered to the Court.

Oyama v. California

332 U.S. 633 (1948)

Mr. Chief Justice Vinson delivered the opinion of the Court.

Petitioners challenge the constitutionality of California's Alien Land Law as it has been applied in this case to effect an escheat of two small parcels of agricultural land. One of the petitioners is Fred Oyama, a minor American citizen in whose name title was taken. The other is his father and guardian, Kajiro Oyama, a Japanese citizen not eligible for naturalization, who paid the purchase price.

Petitioners press three attacks on the Alien Land Law as it has been applied in this case: first, that it deprives Fred Oyama of the equal protection of the laws and of his privileges as an American citizen; secondly, that it denies Kajiro Oyama equal protection of the laws; and, thirdly, that it contravenes the due process clause by sanctioning a taking of property after expiration of the applicable limitations period. Proper foundation for these claims has been laid in the proceedings below. . . .

In broad outline, the Alien Land Law forbids aliens ineligible for American citizenship to acquire, own, occupy, lease, or transfer agricultural land. It also provides that any property acquired in violation of the statute shall escheat as of the date of acquisition and that the same result shall follow any transfer made with "intent to prevent, evade or avoid" escheat. In addition, that intent is presumed, prima facie, whenever an ineligible alien pays the consideration for a transfer to a citizen or eligible alien.

The first of the two parcels in question, consisting of six acres of agricultural land in southern California, was purchased in 1934, when Fred Oyama was six years old. Kajiro Oyama paid the $4,000 consideration, and the seller executed a deed to Fred. The deed was duly recorded.

Some six months later, the father petitioned the Superior Court for San Diego County to be appointed Fred's guardian, stating that Fred owned the six acres. After a hearing, the court found the allegations of the petition true and Kajiro Oyama 'a competent and proper person' to be appointed Fred's guardian. The appointment was then ordered, and the father posted the necessary bond. . . .

The second parcel, an adjoining two acres, was acquired in 1937, when Fred was nine years old. It was sold by the guardian of another minor, and the court supervising that guardianship confirmed the sale 'to Fred Oyama' as highest bidder at a publicly advertised sale. A copy of the court's order was recorded. Fred's father again paid the purchase price, $1,500.

From the time of the two transfers until the date of trial, however, Kajiro Oyama did not file the annual reports which the Alien Land Law requires of all guardians of agricultural land belonging to minor children of ineligible aliens. . . .

In 1942, Fred and his family were evacuated from the Pacific Coast along with all other persons of Japanese descent. And in 1944, when Fred was sixteen and still forbidden to return home, the State filed a petition to declare an escheat of the two parcels on the ground that the conveyances in 1934 and 1937 had been with intent to violate and evade the Alien Land Law. At the trial the only witness, other than a court official testifying to records showing the facts set forth above, was one John Kurfurst, who had been left in charge of the land at the time of the evacuation. He testified that the Oyama family once lived on the land but had not occupied it for several years before the evacuation. After the evacuation, Kurfurst and those to whom he rented the property drew checks to Fred Oyama for the rentals (less expenses), and Kurfurst transmitted them to Fred Oyama through the War Relocation Authority. The canceled checks were returned endorsed 'Fred Oyama,' and no evidence was offered to prove that the signatures were not by the son. Moreover, the receipts issued by the War Relocation Authority for the funds transmitted by Kurfurst were for the account of Fred Oyama, and Kurfurst identified a letter signed 'Fred Oyama' directing him to turn the property over to a local bank for management. . . .

From this evidence the trial court found as facts that the father had had the beneficial use of the land and that the transfers were subterfuges effected with intent to prevent, evade or avoid escheat. Accordingly, the court entered its conclusion of law that the parcels had vested in the State as of the date of the attempted transfers in 1934 and 1937. . . .

We agree with petitioners' first contention, that the Alien Land Law, as applied in this case, deprives Fred Oyama of the equal protection of California's laws and of his privileges as an American citizen. In our view of the case, the State has discriminated against Fred Oyama; the discrimination is based solely on his parents' country of origin; and there is absent the compelling justification which would be needed to sustain discrimination of that nature.

By federal statute, enacted before the Fourteenth Amendment but vindicated by it, the states must accord to all citizens the right to take and hold real property. California, of course, recognizes both this right and the fact that infancy does not incapacitate a minor from holding realty. It is also established under California law that ineligible aliens may arrange gifts of agricultural land to their citizen children. Likewise, when a minor citizen does become the owner of agricultural land, by gift or otherwise, his father may be appointed guardian of the estate, whether the father be a citizen, an eligible alien, or an ineligible alien. And, once appointed, a guardian is entitled to have custody of the estate and to manage and husband it for the ward's benefit. To that extent Fred Oyama is ostensibly on a par with minors of different lineage.

At this point, however, the road forks. The California law points in one direction for minor citizens like Fred Oyama, whose parents cannot be naturalized, and in another for all other children—for minor citizens whose parents are either citizens or eligible aliens, and even for minors who are themselves aliens though eligible for naturalization.

In the first place, for most minors California has the customary rule that where a parent pays for a conveyance to his child there is a presumption that a gift is intended; there is no presumption of a resulting trust, no presumption that the minor takes the land for the benefit of his parent. When a gift is thus presumed and the deed is recorded in the child's name, the recording suffices for delivery, and, absent evidence that the gift is disadvantageous, acceptance is also presumed. Thus the burden of proving that there was in fact no completed bona fide gift falls to him who would attack its validity.

In the second place, when it came to rebutting this statutory presumption, Fred Oyama ran into other obstacles which, so far as we can ascertain, do not beset the path of most minor donees in California. Fred Oyama, on the other hand, faced at the outset the necessity of overcoming a statutory presumption that conveyances financed by his father and recorded in Fred's name were not gifts at all. Something very akin to a resulting trust was presumed and, at least prima facie, Fred was presumed to hold title for the benefit of his parent.

Thus the California courts said that the very fact that the transfer put the land beyond the father's power to deal with it directly—to deed it away, to borrow money on it, and to make free disposition of it in any other way—showed that the transfer was not complete, that it was merely colorable. The fact that the father attached no strings to the transfer was taken to indicate that he meant, in effect, to acquire the beneficial ownership himself. The California law purports to permit citizen sons to take gifts of agricultural land from their fathers, regardless of the fathers' nationality. Yet, as indicated by this case, if the father is ineligible for citizenship, facts which would usually be considered indicia of the son's ownership are used to make that ownership suspect; if the father is not an ineligible alien, however, the same facts would be evidence that a completed gift was intended. . . .

The only basis for this discrimination against an American citizen, moreover, was the fact that his father was Japanese and not American, Russian, Chinese, or English. But for that fact alone, Fred Oyama, now a little over a year from majority, would be the undisputed owner of the eight acres in question.

The State argues that racial descent is not the basis for whatever discrimination has taken place. The argument is that the same statutory presumption of fraud would apply alike to any person taking agricultural land paid for by Kajiro Oyama, whether the recipient was Fred Oyama or a stranger of entirely different ancestry. We do not know how realistic it is to suppose that Kajiro Oyama would attempt gifts of land to others than his close relatives. But in any event, the State's argument ignores the fact that the generally applicable California law treats conveyances to the transferor's children differently from conveyances to strangers. Whenever a Chinese or English parent, to take an example, pays a third party to deed land to a stranger, a resulting trust is presumed to arise, and the stranger is presumed to hold the land for the benefit of the person paying the consideration; when the Alien Land Law applies a similar presumption to a like transfer by Kajiro Oyama to a stranger, it appears merely to reiterate the generally applicable law of resulting trusts. When, on the other hand, the same Chinese or English father uses his own funds to buy land in his citizen son's name, an indefeasible title is presumed to vest in the boy; but when Kajiro Oyama arranges a similar transfer to Fred Oyama, the Alien Land Law interposes a presumption just to the contrary. Thus, as between the citizen children of a Chinese or English father and the citizen children of a Japanese father, there is discrimination; as between strangers taking from the same transferors, there appears to be none. . . .

There remains the question of whether discrimination between citizens on the basis of their racial descent, as revealed in this case, is justifiable. Here we start with the proposition that only the most exceptional circumstances can excuse discrimination on that basis in the face of the equal protection clause and a federal statute giving all citizens the right to own land. In Hirabayashi v. United States this Court sustained a war measure which involved restrictions against citizens of Japanese descent. But the Court recognized that, as a general rule, 'Distinctions between citizens solely because of their ancestry are by their very nature odious to a free people whose institutions are founded upon the doctrine of equality.' 1943, 320 U.S. 81, 100, 1385.

The only justification urged upon us by the State is that the discrimination is necessary to prevent evasion of the Alien Land Law's prohibition against the ownership of agricultural land by ineligible aliens. This reasoning presupposes the validity of that prohibition, a premise which we deem it unnecessary and therefore inappropriate to reexamine in this case. But assuming, for purposes of argument only, that the basic prohibition is constitutional, it does not follow that there is no constitutional limit to the means which may be used to enforce it. In the light most favorable to the State, this case presents a conflict between the State's right to formulate a policy of landholding within its bounds and the right of American citizens to own land anywhere in the United States. When these two rights clash, the rights of a citizen may not be subordinated merely because of his father's country of origin.

Since the view we take of petitioners' first contention requires reversal of the decision below, we do not reach their other contentions: that the Alien Land Law denies ineligible aliens the equal protection of the laws, and that failure to apply any limitations period to escheat actions under that law takes property without due process of law.

Reversed.

NOTES AND QUESTIONS

1. How does the Court's decision in *Oyama* compare with its decision in *Terrace*? What social changes, if any, might explain the difference in the outcomes of the two cases? In another case decided in 1948, the Supreme Court also scrutinized and struck down a California statute that denied non-citizens the right to engage in commercial fishing. *See Takahashi* v. *Fish and Game Commission,* 334 U.S. 410 (1948).

2. The effects of the Alien Land Laws and the mechanisms by which individuals circumvented their strictures have not been forgotten. In an

article entitled *Rebellious Lawyering, Settlement, and Reconciliation: Soko Bukai v. YWCA*, 5 Nev. L.J. 172 (2004-05), Bill Ong Hing discusses a case filed against the YWCA when it attempted to evict the tenants of a YWCA building in San Francisco and then sell it for $1.65 million. Arguing against eviction, the tenants maintained that the building, which had been paid for in part by contributions from the Japanese community in San Francisco in the early 1920s, was held in trust by the YWCA for the community. *Id.* at 177-78. As Hing describes it:

> On May 28, 1920, the SF YWCA board minutes noted a proposal that:
>
> > *[T]he Japanese people rai[se] funds to purchase a house to be used for the Japanese Y.W.C.A. This property to be bought by the local Association and held in trust for the Japanese Y.W.C.A. . . .*
>
> Records from the 1930s reveal the intent to treat the property as being held in trust for the benefit of the Japanese American community. In 1932, the Japanese YWCA published a twenty year retrospective that stated: "'[I]n January of 1931, we completed the payments for the full amount of the purchase' of the property, which the SF YWCA had financed through a . . . bank . . . 'this building of ours belongs not only to us but also to the Japanese community in general.'"

Id. In addition to records that suggested the existence of a charitable trust, the actions of the YWCA suggested that it acted as a charitable trustee of a charitable trust to benefit Japanese-Americans. For example, YWCA not only housed young Japanese women following World War II, but also held community-related programs designed to benefit Japanese-Americans. *Id.* at 179.

In 1996, the YWCA faced significant financial problems; therefore, the YWCA attempted to close the building and sell it. *Id.* at 180. Soko Bukai filed a suit to enforce what it characterized as a charitable trust in 1997. *Id.* at 180-81. Shortly before trial in 2002, the parties settled the case. *Id.* at 192. As part of the settlement, the YWCA deeded title to a community group in exchange for a payment of $733,000 from the community and another similar payment from an undisclosed third party. *Id.* Hing speculates that the undisclosed party might have been the YWCA's insurance company. *Id.*

4.2 RACIALLY RESTRICTIVE COVENANTS PRE-*SHELLEY*

In this section, we will explore the nexus between property law and private acts of discrimination associated with land sale transactions. The primary tool of discrimination addressed in the materials that follow is the covenant. Simply put, a covenant is a promise to do or not do something with one's real property. Because it grants the holder an interest in land, a covenant must comply with the Statute of Frauds and satisfy certain legal requirements before benefiting or burdening subsequent purchasers of real property. As students of property law recognize, the elements that must be satisfied for the burden of a real covenant to run with the land include a written instrument, intent for the burden to run with the land, horizontal and vertical privity, the burden must touch and concern the land, and the successor in interest must have notice of the burden. Alternatively, covenants are more easily enforced as equitable servitudes and the associated injunctive relief because the requirements to enforce equitable servitudes against subsequent owners do not include horizontal or vertical privity.

In many cases, owners of real property entered into covenants to protect the value of their properties by restricting physical characteristics of those properties. For example, a subdivider of real property might insert a clause in the deeds conveyed to buyers that restricts the height of buildings that can be built on lots in the subdivision or specifies setback requirements for structures on the subdivision lots. However, a more pernicious use of running covenants developed during the early part of the twentieth century—racially restrictive covenants.

Racially restrictive covenants did not represent a restriction on the use to which property was put in the sense that restrictions barred owners from constructing certain structures on their lands. Instead, racially restrictive covenants equated to restrictions on *who* used the land subject to the sale. To that end, individuals in a variety of racial groups found themselves subject to the constraints of racially restrictive covenants when they sought to own or occupy parcels of real property. A covenant in California, for example, specified that

> neither said premises, nor any part thereof, shall be used in any manner whatever or occupied by any Negro, Chinese, Japanese, Hindu, Armenian, Asiatic, or native of the Turkish Empire, or descendent of above named persons, provided however, that such a person may be employed by a resident upon said property as a servant for such resident.

Dudley O. McGovney, *Racial Residential Segregation by State Court Enforcement of Restrictive Agreements, Covenants, or Conditions in Deeds is Unconstitutional,* 33 Cal. L. Rev. 5, 15 (1945).

From a theoretical perspective, restricting the uses that a landowner could make of the land by use of a covenant cut against two deeply held notions about private property ownership. First, restrictive covenants infringed on the liberty of the landowner to do what she pleased with her property and property ownership has long been equated to freedom. Second, restrictive covenants reduced the marketability of property and the justification for many property rules, such as the Rule Against Perpetuities, is that they promote the marketability of property. As a result, restrictive covenants of any sort were unpopular among both buyers and sellers during the late nineteenth and early twentieth century.

From a practical perspective, however, a decline in property sales increased the stock of unsold property and took a bite out of developers' profits. Sellers eventually discovered that some restrictions on land use provided buyers with a greater degree of comfort about their investments as compared to unrestricted lands; therefore, the historical apprehension about land use restrictions eroded. For example, a purchaser need not worry that her neighbor might add on to his/her house in an objectionable fashion if a covenant banned such construction.

Parmalee v. Morris

188 N.W. 330 (Mich. 1922)

MOORE, J. The chancellor who heard this case filed a written opinion therein which so clearly states the questions involved that we reproduce it here:

> At the time the Ferry Farm Addition to the city of Pontiac was platted the lots were sold subject to the following uniform restrictions:
>
> > No building shall be built within twenty feet of the front line of the lot. Said lot shall not be occupied by a colored person, nor for the purpose of doing a liquor business thereon.
>
> Defendant Morris and Anna Morris, his wife, both colored, have entered into a contract to purchase a lot in the subdivision, and the bill of complaint was filed by plaintiffs, who are owners of lots on the same subdivision and residents of the neighborhood, to restrain defendants from violating the restriction by occupying the premises in question. The record presents the sole question as to whether or not the restriction against the occupancy of the premises by a colored person is void as contravening the provisions of the 13th and 14th Amendments to the Constitution of the United States, while plaintiffs insist that the provisions of the Federal Constitution have no application and that the restriction is a matter of a purely personal action of the owner of the premises and is valid and enforceable.
>
> Every owner of land in fee is invested with full right, power and authority, when he conveys a portion away, to impose such restrictions and limitations on its use as will in his judgment prevent the grantee, or those claiming under him, from making such use of the premises conveyed as will impair the use or diminish the value of the part which he retains. The only limitation on this right is the requirements that the restrictions be reasonable; not contrary to public policy and not create an unlawful restraint on alienation. These rights have been repeatedly recognized by our Supreme Court. . . .
>
> The reasons urged on behalf of defendants, why these general rules are not decisive of the issue, are: (1) Because the restriction contravenes rights granted to defendants by the 13th and 14th Amendments to the Constitution of the United States. (2) Because the restriction is contrary to public policy. These reasons will be discussed in their order. . . .
>
> 1. It would seem settled . . . that the provisions of the 13th and 14th Amendments cannot be invoked in the present case. The issue presented arises out of individual rather than State action and is to be determined wholly as a domestic issue. . . .
> 2. Is the restriction contrary to public policy?

It has been said that certain acts are contrary to public policy so that the law will refuse to recognize them when they have a mischievous tendency so as to be injurious to the interests of the State. This brings up the question as to what interests of the State are likely to be injured if an owner of property, for reasons which are satisfactory to himself, refuses to sell himself, or permit his assignors to sell to certain persons who may be distasteful to him as neighbors. Are there any interests of the State which will be promoted or advanced compelling the creation of such a condition in the community? The law is powerless to eradicate racial instincts or to abolish distinctions which some citizens do draw on account of racial differences in relation to their matter of purely private concern. For the law to attempt to abolish these distinctions in the private dealings between individuals would only serve to accentuate the difficulties which the situation presents.

One of the purposes of the restriction in the instant case was apparently to preserve the subdivision as a district unoccupied by negroes. Whether this action on the part of the owner was taken to make the neighborhood more desirable in his estimation or to promote the better welfare of himself and his grantees is a consideration which I do not believe enters into a decision of the case. So far as I am able to discover there is no policy of the State which this action contravenes. Were defendants' claim of rights based upon any action taken by the authority of the State an entirely different question would be presented.

Defendant's motion to dismiss the bill of complaint will therefore be denied. The injunction heretofore issued is however broader than warranted by the provisions of the restriction. The restriction covers the occupancy of the property by a colored person only. In terms at least it would not be violated by leasing the same to a colored person so long as such person did not occupy it. The temporary injunction heretofore issued will therefore be modified to the extent of prohibiting defendant from occupying the premises himself, or from permitting the same to be occupied by a colored person, and as so modified, will be made permanent.

Glenn C. Gillespie, Circuit Judge.

A decree was made in accordance with the opinion. The case is brought here for review by appeal. . . .

We quote 18 C.J. p. 397, as follows:

While restrictions against the use of property held in fee are not favored, yet where the intention of the parties is clearly manifested in the creation of the restrictions, they will be enforced in equity. Any use in contravention of the terms and objects of such covenants will constitute a breach for which relief may be obtained. Covenants restraining the use of real property afford an instance of that class of cases in which equity will charge the conscience of a grantee of land with an agreement relating to the land, although the agreement neither creates an easement nor runs with the land. The jurisdiction is not confined to cases in which an action at law can be maintained, but such covenants, although not binding at law, may be enforced in equity provided the grantee has taken with notice of the covenants. . . .

Counsel say in the brief:

Under the theory of our American democracy and citizenship, negroes, or any other race or class, ought not now to be forced to stand and plead for right, justice and equity which ought to be the common heritage of all men by virtue of their citizenship and domicile within the jurisdiction of the United States. If the opinion of the learned trial judge is affirmed it will open a wedge to all kinds of discrimination, wrongs and injustice to a vast number of American citizens of African descent. Slavery was once defended by church and statesmen, but who today would want to be classified as an upholder of such a vile institution?

Such a restriction as the one referred to, if upheld, would place the negro and people of other sects and creeds in the same category as slaughter houses, livery stables, tanneries, garages, etc., and brand them as a nuisance, loathsome and undesirable in neighborhoods.

Would the learned trial judge's decision stand the test of time? Will there always exist in this country conditions whereby judicial decision will band ten millions of people, as it affects the negro, three millions as it affects the Jew, and about thirty millions, as it affects the foreigner, and equally as many as it affects the Catholic, thus placing all of these classes in the list of undesirables?

We think the learned trial judge's decision in this case, if affirmed, would in a short period of time take the course of the *Dred Scott* decision written by Mr. Justice Taney.

We think the counsel has entirely misapprehended the issue involved. Suppose the situation was reversed, and some negro who had a tract of land platted it and stated in the recorded plat that no lot should be occupied by a Caucasian, and that the deeds that were afterwards executed contained a like restriction, would any one think that dire results to the white race would follow an enforcement of the restrictions? In the instant case the plat of land containing the restriction was of record. It was also a part of defendant's deed. He knew or should have known all about it. He did not have to buy the land and he should not have bought it unless willing to observe the restrictions it contained.

The issue involved in the instant case is a simple one, *i.e.*, shall the law applicable to restrictions as to occupancy contained in deeds to real estate be enforced or shall one be absolved from the provisions of the law simply because he is a negro? The question involved is purely a legal one and we think it was rightly solved by the chancellor under the decisions found in his opinion.

The decree is affirmed, with costs to the appellees.

Porter v. Johnson

115 S.W.2d 529 (Mo. Ct. App. 1938)

SPERRY, J. This is an action brought by plaintiffs below, who will be known here as plaintiffs, against Carl R. Johnson and Carrie Johnson, as defendants. The latter will be referred to in this opinion as defendants. Plaintiffs are the owners of certain tracts of land, particularly described in the petition, same being a part of the land described in a restrictive agreement hereinafter set out in full.

> The owner of one parcel of the land mentioned in the restrictive agreement, and a signer of same, on October 7, 1935, sold and delivered possession of said property, same being located at 2602 Tracy, . . . to defendants, Carl R. and Carrie Johnson, persons of the Negro race.

This sale to negroes was in violation of the restrictions. They entered into immediate possession and now occupy and claim title to said property. This they did with full knowledge of the restrictive agreement. Plaintiffs prayed for relief by mandatory injunction, requiring defendants to vacate said property, and that their deed thereto be cancelled. Before conclusion of the trial two of the plaintiffs withdrew from the case as parties . . . leaving these appealing plaintiffs. The case was tried in equity and the trial court refused plaintiffs the relief prayed for, or any relief, and entered judgment for defendants. From this judgment the remaining plaintiffs prosecute this appeal. The restrictive agreement above mentioned was pleaded and was in evidence. It is, in words and figures, as follows:

> AGREEMENT.
> The undersigned owners of land improved and unimproved described as follows:
>
> 1. No part of said property at said time shall be owned, occupied or used by or permitted or suffered to be owned, occupied or used by any person or persons of the Negro race or descent.
> 2. No part of said property shall be by any or either of the parties hereto their respective heirs and assigns or by anyone in their name or behalf conveyed, deeded, leased, willed, sold, rented or in anywise transferred to any person or persons of the Negro race or descent.
>
> The restrictions herein set forth shall run with the land and bind the present owners their respective heirs, successors and assigns and all parties claiming by, through or under them and whether said restrictions be expressed in deeds thereof or not shall be taken to hold, agree and covenant with the owners of said lots their heirs, successors and assigns and with each of them to comply with and observe said restrictions. . . .

It is suggested that the restrictive agreement should be strictly construed in favor of freeing the property. The rules governing construction of restrictive agreements are the same general rules to be followed in construing any contract or covenant. The prime rule of construction is that when there is no ambiguity in the language used, then there is no room for construction. The plain every day meaning of the language of the contract governs. That is this case. Defendants do not claim any ambiguity, but they urge that enforcement of the covenant will work a hardship on 50,000 negroes in Kansas City because they are said to be having difficulty in finding homes. We cannot agree that the property of any person may be confiscated for private purposes simply because some one, regardless of race or color, fancies a particular house, and covets it and no other. The social and economic rights of every citizen are guaranteed by the constitution of the United States; but such rights are not infringed by restrictive covenants such as the one at bar. The property rights of every citizen, black or white, are equally under the protection of the constitution. Defendants' position, if sustained on the ground urged, would result in overriding the very constitutional and statutory provisions upon which the Negro race places chief reliance for safety and security. To establish a precedent on the excuse offered would be to start a boomerang on its vicious circuit. Such a weapon, it is said, invariably returns to its starting point.

We come, finally, to the only contention of defendants that has any real merit. It is urged that the conditions which induced the execution of the agreement have so materially changed as to render it inequitable to enforce it. "The general rule is that equity will enjoin the violation of restrictive covenants irrespective of the amount of damage which would result from a breach and even though there be no substantial monetary damage. The covenantee may stand upon his contract and the law will enforce it. . . .

"When, however, the restrictive agreement is induced by the then existing condition and surroundings of the realty in the covenanted area, and assumes its continued availability for particular uses, if a radical change takes place in the whole neighborhood such as defeats the purpose of the restrictions and renders their enforcement inequitable and oppressive, equity will not enforce them, but will leave the complainant to his remedy at law. This is not on the theory that the contract, as such fails to cover the situation . . . ; but it is because the changed condition forbid equitable intervention."

The evidence here is that at the time the covenant was entered into, negroes had completely taken over the residence property on Tracy Avenue up to a point two blocks North of the North side of the area restricted; but only white people then lived along this street from that point South, to, including, and beyond this district. The evidence also discloses that negroes have since taken over all of the property along Tracy, Northward from the North line of this district; that one house on the North side of the block out of which the district is carved, was bought by a negro just prior to the adoption of the covenant; that this negro still resides there; that his advent in the block occasioned the execution of the covenant; that the South lot in this district is vacant and is not within the restricted district; that the property across the street from the district is vacant, unrestricted and is advertised for sale to negroes for residential property; that at the time the agreement was signed this last mentioned property was restricted, as was also the block North of this area; that negroes occupy the properties back of this area, as well as that back of the vacant lot across the street; that the trend of Negro migration in Kansas City is Southward in this neighborhood, along Tracy Avenue; that only eighteen new residences for Negro occupancy have been built in Kansas City during the past fifteen years, and that the Negro population is increasing and negroes have, for many years, been moving Southward in this general neighborhood, gradually abandoning residences formerly occupied by them to the North, for the reason that owners could not afford to keep property occupied by them in repair on the rental received. The above facts are admitted by both sides in oral argument. There seems to be no doubt but that conditions in the surrounding neighborhood, on three sides, outside of the restricted district, have changed materially with reference to Negro occupancy since the restrictive agreement was made and entered into.

However, it would seem that the property owners, in 1921, anticipated these very changes in the surrounding neighborhood, and believed that unless they protected themselves against it the block would be invaded by colored residents. They acted to enforce the covenant promptly after the first negro moved into the block. They adopted these restrictions, so far as this record shows, independently of the action of residents of other similar areas that adopted restriction at about that same time. In other words, the residents of this area did not join with owners of other property in this general neighborhood in adopting restrictions. We cannot say that they would not have so restricted their district had they fully anticipated that every house in the neighborhood, outside of this particular district, would eventually be occupied by negroes. It would seem that a majority would have so acted in the face of that certain knowledge, because, even in 1936, before the first fifteen year period had expired, according to the record, the owners of a majority of the frontage in the district failed to sign the formal release, although such a release was being circulated. . . .

We think plaintiffs are entitled to stand on their contract and have it enforced at equity. Their remedy at law, under the circumstances of this case, would be wholly inadequate. To deny them equitable relief would be to permit the violation of the restrictive agreement and permit property adjoining theirs to be occupied by persons of the Negro race, and, in the case of the former owner of the property now owned by defendants, compel plaintiffs to go outside of this jurisdiction to recover damages from her. . . .

Defendants cannot complain of the harshness of the rule, if it seems harsh, because they bought with full knowledge, actual as well as constructive, of the restrictions. They admit in evidence that they took a chance on being able to break the covenant. They will be required to abide by their decision. . . .

The judgment of the circuit court is, accordingly, reversed, and the cause remanded, with directions that the circuit court set aside its former judgment and decree in this case, and enter judgment in favor of plaintiffs as against defendants, enjoining their continued occupancy of the property described in this opinion until May 1, 1951; enjoining them from leasing, selling, or delivering possession of it to persons of the Negro race until on and after May 1, 1951; and ordering, and directing defendants to vacate said property forthwith; and adjudging that defendants pay all costs of this action.

NOTES AND QUESTIONS

1. As each of the previous cases suggests, one of the arguments commonly asserted to challenge racially restrictive covenants was that such covenants violate public policy. What public policy is violated by the covenants? How would a court identify and apply such a public policy if one, in fact, exists? What evidence might you offer of the public policy at stake in these cases?

2. One of the underlying themes of the law of property is to promote the free alienability of real property. Do racially restrictive covenants inhibit or promote the free alienability of real property? Why or why not?

3. California's history regarding the enforcement of racially restrictive covenants is particularly noteworthy. In *Gandolfo v. Hartman*, 49 F. 181 (C.C.S.D. Cal. 1892), distinguished by the court in *Parmalee*, the Circuit Court for the Southern District of California refused to enforce a restrictive covenant that barred Chinese individuals from leasing property by relying, in part, on the guarantees of the Fourteenth Amendment. *Id.* Discussing the application of the Fourteenth Amendment to racially restrictive covenants, the court explained that

> [i]t would be a very narrow construction of the constitutional amendment in question and of the decisions based upon it, and a very restricted application of the broad principles upon which both the amendment and the decisions proceed, to hold that, while state and municipal legislatures are forbidden to discriminate against the Chinese in their legislation, a citizen of the state may lawfully do so by contract, which the courts may enforce. Such a view is, I think, entirely inadmissible. Any result inhibited by the constitution can no more be accomplished by contract of individual citizens than by legislation, and the courts should no more enforce the one than the other. This would seem to be very clear.

Id. at 182. Twenty-five years later, in *Title Guarantee & Trust Co. v. Garrott*, a California state court asserted that

> [t]he fourteenth amendment, in so far as it prohibits any abridgment of the privileges or immunities of citizens of the United States and guarantees the equal protection of the laws to all persons, addresses itself to the state government and its instrumentalities, to its legislative, executive, and judicial authorities, and not to contracts between individuals. It is state action of a particular character that is prohibited. Individual invasion of individual rights is not the subject matter of the amendment.

183 P. 470, 471 (Cal. Ct. App. 1910). However, the court held that the racially restrictive covenant in the case violated the principle of free alienability of property. The court explained that

> [i]f the continuation of the estate in the grantee may be made to depend upon his not selling or leasing to persons of African, Chinese, or Japanese descent, it may be made to depend upon his not selling or leasing to persons of Caucasian descent, or to any but

> albinos from the heart of Africa or blond Eskimos. It is impossible, on any known principle, to say that a condition not to sell to any of a very large class of persons, such as those embraced within the category of descendants from African, Chinese, or Japanese ancestors, shall not be deemed an unreasonable restraint upon alienation, but that the proscribed class may be so enlarged that finally the restriction becomes unreasonable and void. Where shall the dividing line be placed? . . . No matter how large or how partial and infinitesimal the restraint may be, the principles of natural right, the reasons of public policy, and that principle of the common law which forbids restraints upon the disposition of one's own property, are as effectually overthrown by the one as by the other. The difference is of degree, not principle.

Id. at 473. Shortly thereafter, the Supreme Court of California weighed in on the issue in *Los Angeles Inv. Co. v. Gary*, 186 P. 596 (Cal. 1919). The court agreed with Garrott's holding that such covenants unduly restricted the alienability of property, but the court upheld usage and occupancy restraints. *Id.* at 597. In other words, the court struck down covenants insofar as they restricted sellers from conveying ownership of land by race of the buyers, but upheld such covenants insofar as they prevented those buyers from using or occupying the purchased property. Who received the primary benefit of decisions like *Gary*?

4. What happened to buyers following an unsuccessful challenge to racially restrictive covenants? If the buyer had taken possession of the property, one result, as *Porter* suggests, was that the buyer/owner had to vacate the property. *See also, e.g., Porter v. Pryor*, 164 S.W.2d 353, 355 (Mo. 1942) (noting that ouster suits had been filed against those occupying property in violation of a racially restrictive covenant). Alternatively, courts had the power to enjoin a buyer from taking possession of restricted property even after signing a contract for the purchase of property, *see, e.g., Dury v. Neely*, 69 N.Y.S.2d 677 (Sup. Ct. 1942).

5. In addition to arguments against the enforcement of racially restrictive covenants on public policy grounds, challengers often asserted that courts should refuse to enforce the restrictions because of a change in circumstances. Although the change of circumstances argument failed in *Porter*, a number of challenges based on a change of circumstances were successful. *See, e.g., Letteau v. Ellis*, 10 P.2d 496 (Cal. Ct. App. 1932); *Clark v. Vaughan*, 292 P. 783 (Kan. 1930). Furthermore, individuals also attacked racially restrictive covenants on the ground that they had not been legally executed. For example, courts refused to enforce racially restrictive covenants if they construed the covenant as requiring the signatures of all beneficiaries as a condition precedent to enforcement or against sellers who failed to sign the covenant. *See, e.g., Oberwise v. Poulos*, 12 P.2d 156 (Cal. Ct. App. 1932); *Mueninghaus v. James*, 24 S.W.2d 1017 (Mo. 1930). One intriguing case involving a permutation of the lack of execution attack is *Christie v. Lyons*, 47 P.2d 128 (Okla. 1935). In *Christie*, a white seller and an African-American buyer entered into a contract for the purchase of the seller's real property. *Id.* However, the African-American buyer refused

to perform, which prompted a suit for specific performance by the seller. *Id.* Defending against the lawsuit, the African-American buyer pointed to a racially restrictive covenant in the seller's deed that prohibited the sale. *Id.* The white seller countered that the covenant had never become operative because it had failed to acquire the support of nine-tenths of the owners of the affected properties as specified by the explicit terms of the covenant. *Id.* at 128-29. The court ruled in favor of the white seller and required the African-American buyer to perform. *Id.* at 128.

4.3 *SHELLEY V. KRAEMER* AND THE REFUSAL TO ENJOIN VIOLATIONS OF RACIALLY RESTRICTIVE COVENANTS

Despite the legal setbacks, individuals continued to challenge the constitutionality of racially restrictive covenants. Eventually, the Supreme Court addressed the issue in a case from Missouri in which that state's highest court upheld a racial covenant against an attack based on the Fourteenth Amendment. In *Kraemer v. Shelley,* 198 S.W.2d 679 (Mo. 1946), the Supreme Court of Missouri observed that:

> [a]greements restricting property from being transferred to or occupied by negroes have been consistently upheld by the courts of this state as one which the parties have the right to make and which is not contrary to public policy. . . .
>
> The restriction does not contravene the guaranties of civil rights of the Constitution of the United States. . . .
>
> Such living conditions bring deep concern to everyone, and present a grave and acute problem to the entire community. . . . But their correction is beyond the authority of the courts generally, and in particular in a case involving the determination of contractual rights between parties to a law suit. If their correction is sought in the field of government, the appeal must be addressed to its branches other than the judicial.

198 S.W.2d 679, 682-83 (Mo. 1946). After it wound its way through the state courts, the Supreme Court granted certiorari and penned one of its most famous property law decisions.

Shelley v. Kraemer

334 U.S. 1 (1948)

Mr. Chief Justice Vinson delivered the opinion of the Court.

These cases present for our consideration questions relating to the validity of court enforcement of private agreements, generally described as restrictive covenants, which have as their purpose the exclusion of persons of designated race or color from the ownership or occupancy of real property. Basic constitutional issues of obvious importance have been raised.

The first of these cases comes to this Court on certiorari to the Supreme Court of Missouri. On February 16, 1911, thirty out of a total of thirty-nine owners of property fronting both sides of Labadie Avenue between Taylor Avenue and Cora Avenue in the city of St. Louis, signed an agreement, which was subsequently recorded, providing in part:

> the said property is hereby restricted to the use and occupancy for the term of Fifty (50) years from this date . . . that hereafter no part of said property or any portion thereof shall be, for said term of Fifty-years, occupied by any person not of the Caucasian race, it being intended hereby to restrict the use of said property for said period of time against the occupancy as owners or tenants of any portion of said property for resident or other purpose by people of the Negro or Mongolian Race. . . .

On August 11, 1945, pursuant to a contract of sale, petitioners Shelley, who are Negroes, for valuable consideration received from one Fitzgerald a warranty deed to the parcel in question. The trial court found that petitioners had no actual knowledge of the restrictive agreement at the time of the purchase.

On October 9, 1945, respondents, as owners of other property subject to the terms of the restrictive covenant, brought suit in the Circuit Court of the city of St. Louis praying that petitioners Shelley be restrained from taking possession of the property and that judgment be entered divesting title out of petitioners Shelley and revesting title in the immediate grantor or in such other person as the court should direct. . . .

Petitioners have placed primary reliance on their contentions, first raised in the state courts, that judicial enforcement of the restrictive agreements in these cases has violated rights guaranteed to petitioners by the Fourteenth Amendment of the Federal Constitution and Acts of Congress passed pursuant to that Amendment. Specifically, petitioners urge that they have been denied the equal protection of the laws, deprived of property without due process of law, and have been denied privileges and immunities of citizens of the United States. We pass to a consideration of those issues. . . .

It cannot be doubted that among the civil rights intended to be protected from discriminatory state action by the Fourteenth Amendment are the rights to acquire, enjoy, own and dispose of property. Equality in the enjoyment of property rights was regarded by the framers of that Amendment as an essential pre-condition to the realization of other basic civil rights and liberties which the Amendment was intended to guarantee. Thus, §1978 of the Revised Statutes, derived from §1 of the Civil Rights

Act of 1866 which was enacted by Congress while the Fourteenth Amendment was also under consideration, provides:

> All citizens of the United States shall have the same right, in every State and Territory, as is enjoyed by white citizens thereof to inherit, purchase, lease, sell, hold, and convey real and personal property.

This Court has given specific recognition to the same principle *Buchanan v. Warley*, 245 U.S. 60 (1917).

It is likewise clear that restrictions on the right of occupancy of the sort sought to be created by the private agreements in these cases could not be squared with the requirements of the Fourteenth Amendment if imposed by state statute or local ordinance. We do not understand respondents to urge the contrary.

But the present cases . . . do not involve action by state legislatures or city councils. Here the particular patterns of discrimination and the areas in which the restrictions are to operate, are determined, in the first instance, by the terms of agreements among private individuals. Participation of the State consists in the enforcement of the restrictions so defined. The crucial issue with which we are here confronted is whether this distinction removes these cases from the operation of the prohibitory provisions of the Fourteenth Amendment.

Since the decision of this Court in the *Civil Rights Cases*, 109 U.S. 3 (1883), the principle has become firmly embedded in our constitutional law that the action inhibited by the first section of the Fourteenth Amendment is only such action as may fairly be said to be that of the States. That Amendment erects no shield against merely private conduct, however discriminatory or wrongful.

We conclude, therefore, that the restrictive agreements standing alone cannot be regarded as violative of any rights guaranteed to petitioners by the Fourteenth Amendment. So long as the purposes of those agreements are effectuated by voluntary adherence to their terms, it would appear clear that there has been no action by the State and the provisions of the Amendment have not been violated.

But here there was more. These are cases in which the purposes of the agreements were secured only by judicial enforcement by state courts of the restrictive terms of the agreements. The respondents urge that judicial enforcement of private agreements does not amount to state action; or, in any event, the participation of the State is so attenuated in character as not to amount to state action within the meaning of the Fourteenth Amendment. Finally, it is suggested, even if the States in these cases may be deemed to have acted in the constitutional sense, their action did not deprive petitioners of rights guaranteed by the Fourteenth Amendment. We move to a consideration of these matters. . . .

Against this background of judicial construction, extending over a period of some three-quarters of a century, we are called upon to consider whether enforcement by state courts of the restrictive agreements in these cases may be deemed to be the acts of those States; and, if so, whether that action has denied these petitioners the equal protection of the laws which the Amendment was intended to insure.

We have no doubt that there has been state action in these cases in the full and complete sense of the phrase. The undisputed facts disclose that petitioners were willing purchasers of properties upon which they desired to establish homes. The owners of the properties were willing sellers; and contracts of sale were accordingly consummated. It is clear that but for the active intervention of the state courts, supported by the full panoply of state power, petitioners would have been free to occupy the properties in question without restraint.

These are not cases, as has been suggested, in which the States have merely abstained from action, leaving private individuals free to impose such discriminations as they see fit. Rather, these are cases in which the States have made available to such individuals the full coercive power of government to deny to petitioners, on the grounds of race or color, the enjoyment of property rights in premises which petitioners are willing and financially able to acquire and which the grantors are willing to sell. The difference between judicial enforcement and non-enforcement of the restrictive covenants is the difference to petitioners between being denied rights of property available to other members of the community and being accorded full enjoyment of those rights on an equal footing. . . .

We hold that in granting judicial enforcement of the restrictive agreements in these cases, the States have denied petitioners the equal protection of the laws and that, therefore, the action of the state courts cannot stand. We have noted that freedom from discrimination by the States in the enjoyment of property rights was among the basic objectives sought to be effectuated by the framers of the Fourteenth Amendment. That such discrimination has occurred in these cases is clear. Because of the race or color of these petitioners they have been denied rights of ownership or occupancy enjoyed as a matter of course by other citizens of different race or color. . . .

For the reasons stated, the judgment of the Supreme Court of Missouri and the judgment of the Supreme Court of Michigan must be reversed.

NOTES AND QUESTIONS

1. What limits, if any, exist on the state action doctrine as described by the Court in *Shelley*? Does judicial enforcement of any private agreement equate to state action sufficient to trigger constitutional inquiry? For evidence that courts have not construed *Shelley's* language so broadly

and an argument that the Court should have decided *Shelley* on the basis of the Thirteenth Amendment, see Mark D. Rosen, *Was Shelley v. Kraemer Incorrectly Decided? Some New Answers*, 95 CAL. L. REV. 451 (2007). *Shelley* and its state action analysis has been a popular source of academic investigation and criticism; *see, e.g.*, Shelley Ross Saxer, *Shelley v. Kraemer's Fiftieth Anniversary: "A Time for Keeping or a Time for Throwing Away"?*, 47 KAN. L. REV. 61 (1998-99); *Symposium on the State Action Doctrine of Shelley v. Kraemer*, 67 WASH. U. L. Q. 671 (1989); Mark Tushnet, *Shelley v. Kraemer and Theories of Equality*, 33 N.Y.L. SCH. L. REV. 383 (1988).

2. Can you imagine any circumstances under which the discriminating party *should* prevail against the party suffering the discrimination? For an argument that such circumstances exist, see Louis Henkin, *Shelley v. Kraemer: Notes for a Revised Opinion*, 110 U. PA. L. REV. 473 (1961-62) (arguing in favor of a balancing test to determine when the state is sufficiently involved to transform private discrimination into state action such that the protection of the Due Process Clause outweighs Equal Protection concerns).

3. If courts were prohibited from enforcing racially restrictive covenants by injunction, were monetary damages available as an alternative remedy for violations of the covenants? In *Barrows v. Jackson*, 346 U.S. 249 (1953), the Supreme Court ruled that a state court's award of damages for the violation of a racially restrictive covenant amounted to state action for purposes of the Fourteenth Amendment. Citing to *Shelley*, the Court reasoned that:

> [i]f a state court awards damages for breach of a restrictive covenant, a prospective seller of restricted land will either refuse to sell to non-Caucasians or else will require non-Caucasians to pay a higher price to meet the damages which the seller may incur. Solely because of their race, non-Caucasians will be unable to purchase, own, and enjoy property on the same terms as Caucasians. Denial of this right by state action deprives such non-Caucasians, unidentified but identifiable, of equal protection of the laws in violation of the Fourteenth Amendment.

Id. at 254. Despite its reliance on *Shelley*, Chief Justice Vinson, who authored the Court's decision in *Shelley*, dissented from the Court's decision in *Barrows*.

According to Chief Justice Vinson,

> in the *Shelley* case, it was not the covenants which were struck down but judicial enforcement of them against Negro vendees. The question which we decided was simply whether a state court could decree the ouster of Negroes from property which they had purchased and which they were enjoying. We held that it could not. We held that such judicial action, which operated directly against the Negro petitioners and deprived them of their right to enjoy their property solely because of their race, was state action and constituted a denial of "equal protection."
>
> This case is different.
>
> The majority identifies no non-Caucasian who has been injured or could be injured if damages are assessed against respondent for breaching the promise which

> she willingly and voluntarily made to petitioners, a promise which neither the federal law nor the Constitution proscribes. Indeed, the non-Caucasian occupants of the property involved in this case will continue their occupancy undisturbed, regardless of the outcome of the suit. The state court was asked to do nothing which would impair their rights or their enjoyment of the property.

Id. at 261-62.

4. One week after it issued its decision in *Shelley,* the Court implemented the decision to reverse a case from Ohio and send two California cases back to that state for opinions consistent with *Shelley. Trustees of the Monroe Ave. Church of Christ v. Perkins,* 334 U.S. 813 (1948); *Amer v. Superior Ct.,* 334 U.S. 813 (1948); *Kim v. Superior Ct.,* 334 U.S. 813 (1948). Furthermore, *Shelley* served as the controlling precedent to strike down covenants that barred the sale of real property to Mexican-Americans. In *Clifton v. Puente,* a covenant prohibited landowners from selling or leasing property "to persons of Mexican descent." 218 S.W.2d 272, 273 (Tex. Civ. App. 1948). In an action to enforce the covenant against a buyer who was a naturalized American citizen born in Mexico, the court relied on *Shelley* to rule against those seeking to bar the sale. The court simply stated that "[u]nder the decision of the Supreme Court, above referred to, judicial recognition or enforcement of the racial covenant involved here by a state court is precluded by the 'equal protection of the laws' clause of the Fourteenth Amendment." *Id.* at 274. For another case similar to *Puente* involving a racially restrictive covenant aimed at Mexican-Americans with a similar result, see *Matthews v. Andrade,* 198 P.2d 66 (Cal. Dist. Ct. App. 1948).

4.4 THE APPLICATION OF *SHELLEY* IN A DIFFERENT CONTEXT

In addition to limiting available housing before *Shelley,* racial covenants also restricted the availability of burial plots. In fact, the language of the covenants that restricted access to cemetery plots by race looked strikingly similar to those deemed unconstitutional in *Shelley.* For example, a public cemetery in Alabama conveyed deeds to its burial plots with the restriction that

> [c]emetery lots shall be owned only by human beings of the white and/or Caucasian race and the said lots shall be used only for burial of human bodies of the white and/or Caucasian race, and such ownership and use shall at all times be subject to the Rules and Regulations and By-Laws . . . now or hereafter in force. Any attempted transfer of a lot or interest in a lot to one not authorized to own same shall be invalid and of no force and effect and the corporation shall not be obligated to honor such transfer.

Terry v. Elmwood Cemetery, 307 F. Supp. 369, 370 (N.D. Ala. 1969).

The last two cases in this chapter examine the application of *Shelley* to these racially restrictive covenants.

Rice v. Sioux City Memorial Park Cemetery

60 N.W.2d 110 (Iowa 1953)

Larson, J. Plaintiff in her petition alleges that on or about August 17, 1951, she entered into a written contract, Exhibit A, for the purchase of three cemetery lots belonging to defendant corporation, one lot to be used for the burial of her deceased husband, Sergeant Rice, whose body was being shipped home from Korea. This contract contains a racial restrictive clause and provides . . . as follows:

> This agreement is assignable only with the consent of seller, and burial privileges accrue only to members of the Caucasian race, and before any burial can be made the grave space or spaces so used shall be paid in full.

Plaintiff alleged that her deceased husband, Sergeant John Rice, killed in combat on active duty in Korea, had 11/16 Winnebago Indian blood and 5/16 white blood, and that defendant cemetery refused to permit the body of her deceased husband to be lowered into the ground, after graveside services were held, caused the body to be removed from the grave site and advised her that the refusal was because "he was not a Caucasian." . . .

Plaintiff relies upon and argues six alleged errors, but her main contention is that the court erred in holding, as a matter of law, that the racial restrictive clause in the admitted contract was not void, and that the action of the court in permitting the defendants to stand upon its terms and defend thereunder this action for damages in court would not amount to nor constitute state or federal action contrary to the Fifth Amendment or the Fourteenth Amendment to the United States Constitution or the Constitution of Iowa (section 1, Article I, or section 6, Article I).

We shall discuss this contention first and address ourselves to the contract rather than tort features of plaintiff's complaint.

I. It is strongly contended by plaintiff that the whole field of law on the subject of restrictive covenants was completely changed by pronouncements of the United States Supreme Court in the cases of *Shelley v. Kraemer*, 334 U.S. 1, and *Hurd v. Hodge*, 334 U.S. 24, which hold in effect that affirmative action of state courts by granting injunctions, specific performance and other active aids to the enforcement of restrictive covenants based on color or race was state action and violated the Fifth and Fourteenth Amendments to the United States Constitution. In this group of cases it is to be noted that the state has lent its power in support of the actions of private individuals or corporations and, of course, in so doing has clothed the private acts with the character of state action. While we must recognize an evolution of our society as disclosed by these recent decisions, all of the previous decisions may be distinguished from our present case in that they disclose the exertion of governmental power *directly* to aid in discrimination, or other deprivation of right. Certainly that factor is not presented here, where the state has maintained neutrality.

But plaintiff would have us go one step further than the United States Supreme Court and declare any private contract, which contains any restrictive covenants, void as to the covenants. She is asking more. She asks us to reform the contract voluntarily agreed to with another private party. She asks that we remove the restrictive covenant in her contract which she repudiates and permit her to recover damages from the other party; in other words, extend the theory announced in the Shelley v. Kraemer and Hurd v. Hodge cases, supra, to indirect as well as direct support of private agreements containing restrictive covenants; to bar the recognition of such clauses in contracts between private parties even though no active aid is given their enforcement. This theory the district court would not adopt and we think properly declined to do so. Our sympathy must not be allowed to carry us to the aid of either party in circumstances of this nature unless the restriction is clearly one against public policy. It may be desirable to hold that state action can be discerned in any case where the state has tolerated discrimination by inaction, or otherwise, in matters of public importance, and we are in sympathy with the ideals of race equality. But there is danger in attempting a remedy by such constitutional expansion. Invocation of the constitution then might depend upon a balance of two asserted values—the privilege of the private corporation versus the right of the plaintiff to equality of treatment which is another well-known constitutional safeguard. It must be clear that a clash would result between such expansion of the Fourteenth Amendment and the decisions of long standing in the Civil Rights Cases. 109 U.S. 3. Both demand that the states protect the rights defined in the amendment against the wrongful actions of private individuals. This most states do by appropriate legislation, and it is just and proper that state authorities furnish appropriate means of extending these moral rights into areas when they have not heretofore been asserted rather than to try an extension of the coverage of the Fourteenth Amendment to fields that will abridge other individual rights and violate other constitutional guarantees. . . .

II. But plaintiff further urges that the restrictive covenants violate "public policy" . . .

Plaintiff lays great stress on her claim that a racial restriction in a private agreement such as we have here must be declared void as violating public policy. This is a typical argument in cases of this kind and admittedly has caused courts some difficulty. The greatest of these difficulties is that of determining the meaning of "public policy." . . .

In general throughout the United States, covenants or agreements restricting real property from ownership or occupancy by persons of a certain race, or by anyone not of the Caucasian race, have been held not contrary to public policy.

We are in doubt that the restrictive clause here contravenes sound public policy, and must therefore hold that there has been no such violation of public policy such as would justify the holding of the restrictive agreement void in the contract.

It is fundamental in our law that a private individual may, unless expressly forbidden by police power enactments, deal freely with whom he pleases, and his reasons or policy are not the concern of the state. The state may not aid him in certain of his restrictive or arbitrary agreements, and so here if plaintiff had herself lowered her deceased husband's body into the ground, in violation of her agreement with defendants, the State would have had to deny defendants aid in restraining her, nor could it have helped in punishing her for violating that agreement.

[After considering and rejecting the appellant's contract and tort claims, the court affirmed the decision of the lower court.]

Spencer v. Flint Memorial Park Association

144 N.W.2d 622 (Mich. Ct. App. 1966)

Lesinski, C.J. The sole question to be determined here is: Whether it is a denial of equal protection under the 14th Amendment to the United States Constitution for a State to enforce a restrictive agreement of a cemetery association which would deny the owner of a cemetery plot, who is a Negro, the right to bury a non-Caucasian therein.

The excellent opinion filed in this cause by the learned trial judge, Stewart A. Newblatt, leaves nothing further to be said. We enthusiastically adopt the reasoning and conclusions therein. The opinion is as follows:

> This court is now being asked to pass on the question of whether a cemetery association may refuse to permit an owner of a lot the right to bury a Negro in that lot. In a sense, it seems highly grotesque to spend such time and legal effort in considering the rights of dead soulless bodies when we have not as a society yet secured full rights for the living.
>
> This cause has been submitted upon a joint statement of facts which need not be repeated herein except to note that the plaintiff is the owner of a cemetery plot — right of sepulture in the language of the trade — in defendant cemetery which cemetery was organized as a nonprofit corporation under P.A. 1869, No. 12, as a rural cemetery. The plaintiff's ownership of this plot was previously determined in an earlier case between these parties in this circuit, which determination was not appealed and which therefore is final. When a burial right is purchased, one of the conditions thereof provides that:
>
>> In no instance shall the cemetery be utilized for the burial of dead bodies of other than the human race and of the Caucasian race only, or of the ashes thereof.
>
> . . . The statute under which the defendant was organized provides that lands set aside for cemetery purposes and the rights of burial therein are wholly tax exempt,

C.L. 1948, §456.108 (Stat. Ann. 1963 Rev. §21.878), and that such rights are transferable and as fully alienable as any other personal property in this State subject only to such conditions as shall be prescribed by the board of directors (C.L.S. 1961, §456.112 [Stat. Ann. 1963 Rev. §21.882]).

The owner of the lot, the plaintiff, is a Negro and the body tendered and which was refused was that of a Negro. It is in this general context that this cause must be decided. . . .

The law having been established as to restrictive covenants and the ban upon their enforceability by the State courts, is there any reason why such ban should not be applied to a cemetery lot, be it ownership thereof in fee simple, a mere right of burial or sepulture, a license, franchise or easement? The defendant asserts that burial rights are different and that such racially discriminatory clauses as are here involved are permissible. In support of this contention, defendant cites 14 C.J.S., Cemeteries, §31, pp 90, 91, and 10 Am. Jur., Cemeteries, §30, pp 507, 508, both of which state that a cemetery corporation may validly pass a regulation stating that the remains of persons of the white race only may be admitted to burial. . . . In response to such assertion, it need only be pointed out that both quotations are out of date, the quotation from *American Jurisprudence* having been written in 1937, and that from *Corpus Juris Secundum* in 1939, 11 and 9 years respectively before *Shelley*. The supplements to these works do not refer to *Shelley* nor is any editorial comment changed or added. In short, such out of date encyclopedic authority cannot be relied upon.

Both plaintiff and defendant cite *Rice v. Sioux City Memorial Park Cemetery* (1953), 245 Iowa 147 (60 N.W.2d 110). . . .

This case cannot be considered as authority for the defendant's view in the instant case for three reasons: . . .

Third: The *Rice Case* is not authority in the instant case because the State of Michigan is committed to the doctrine that indirect enforcement of such covenants is equally prohibited under *Shelley v. Kraemer, supra,* as direct enforcement.

Should the fact that the property involved is a cemetery lot require a conclusion different from *Shelley?* We have seen that on the basis of a difference in the nature of the property interest, there was no distinction drawn even in *Rice* and the 'restrictive covenant — State action' analysis was applied by the Court in reaching its decision. But going further, this question should be asked: Is the private covenant any less restrictive because it deals with a cemetery lot or with personal property? The answer appears obvious — No. Is the enforcement by State courts of such private covenants as to a cemetery lot any less State action than if the covenant dealt with real property? Again the answer should be obvious — No.

As pointed out by the defendant, the interest of the plaintiff herein is a burial right or right of sepulture. There is no question but that such burial right is a peculiar interest incapable of being pushed into the convenient pigeonhole lawyers and judges are so wont to place difficult concepts. It is not a fee interest, but rather a right of burial which is transferable and the rights of holders thereof are legally enforceable. Regardless of what label we hang on this interest, it is a property right. . . .

It appears therefore clear that the 'restrictive covenant — State action — 14th Amendment' approach applies to cemetery lots to the same extent that such analysis applies to more conventional property interest. . . .

And finally, defendant asserts that 'there is nothing to prevent the plaintiff from choosing a place of burial among his own kind.' In this connection please note the language of the Supreme Court previously quoted on page 164 of this opinion indicating that the rights under the 14th Amendment are personal rights that are not attached to white persons or to Negroes or to Indians, et cetera, but to individuals. I repeat:

> Equal protection of the law is not achieved through the indiscriminate imposition of inequality.

. . . It is a bizarre interpretation of the equal protection of the laws clause of the 14th Amendment to conclude that this protection is to afford a white person what all white people would want—burial among whites; and to the Negro a burial 'among his own kind.' The law of this land looks to enforcement of the rights of individuals without presuming to force upon the individual what we imagine such individuals want and without assuming that there is recognized in the law a social, economic, racial, religious or political caste system with a different set of rights and desires for all members of each group. When the law recognizes the philosophy represented by 'his own kind,' we are only a step away from adopting the racist philosophy which World War II was fought to eliminate.

This opinion must close and this writer can think of no better way than to quote the language of Mr. Justice Dooling in *Long v. Mountain View Cemetery Association* (1955), 130 Cal. App. 2d 328, also quoted at page 535 of *Erickson*:

> I cannot believe that a man's mortal remains will disintegrate any less peaceably because of the close proximity of the body of a member of another race, and in that inevitable disintegration I am sure that the pigmentation of the skin cannot long endure. It strikes me that the carrying of racial discrimination into the burial grounds is a particularly stupid form of human arrogance and intolerance. If life does not do so, the universal fellowship of death should teach humility. The good people who insist on the racial segregation of what is mortal in man may be shocked to learn when their own lives end that God has reserved no racially exclusive position for them in the hereafter.

Judgment for the Plaintiff and an appropriate judgment order shall be tendered by plaintiff's counsel forthwith for signature.

NOTES AND QUESTIONS

1. Which of the opinions, *Rice* or *Spencer*, is more convincing as it pertains to the applicability of *Shelley*?

2. What does the court in *Rice* mean by its statement that *Shelley* was a case involving an "exertion of governmental power *directly* to aid in discrimination" while *Rice* involved "indirect" exertion by comparison? Do you agree with the distinction drawn by the court in *Rice*?

3. African Americans and Native Americans were not the only racial groups who encountered discrimination by cemeteries. A cemetery in Texas refused to accept the body of a Mexican-American serviceman for burial in 1948. Eventually, the serviceman was buried in Arlington National Cemetery after efforts by Texas civil rights activist Dr. Hector Garcia and then–U.S. Representative Lyndon B. Johnson. Lupe S. Salinas, Gus Garcia & Thurgood Marshall, *Two Legal Giants Fighting for Justice*, 28 T. Marshall L. Rev. 145, 160-61 (2002-03). Similarly, some cemeteries in Denver, Colorado barred Japanese-Americans from interment. Tom I. Romero, II, *Uncertain Waters and Contested Lands: Excavating the Layers of Colorado's Legal Past*, 73 U. Colo. L. Rev. 521, 575 n.310 (2002).

RACE AND CONTEMPORARY PROPERTY

5 REDEFINING HOME AND NEIGHBORHOOD: CIVIL RIGHTS AND ITS IMPACT ON PROPERTY LAW

In this chapter, we explore how property law changed in response to the Civil Rights Movement, which lasted roughly from 1948 until 1980. The Civil Rights Movement, in some sense, "federalized" a number of key property concepts by subjecting the housing market to significant regulation that sought to ameliorate racial and ethnic discrimination.

The Civil Rights Movement fundamentally shifted property norms in two key ways. First, the Fair Housing Act (FHA) expanded the ability of parties to transfer property by sale, lease, or other means within the housing market. These protective measures require property owners to ensure property transfers occur without category-based discrimination. Thus, the Civil Rights Movement significantly expanded access to housing by ensuring a transparent marketplace. Second, the Civil Rights Movement prompted an ongoing debate: What are the rights of property owners with respect to a clean, healthy, and economically viable neighborhood? Debates over the *colonias* communities of Texas, the environmental justice movement, and mortgage financing have raised issues over how the law can effectively address racial and ethnic disparities in access to clean, healthy, and economically viable neighborhoods.

This chapter, then, explores two key questions:

1. What are the responsibilities of a society to alleviate social inequities, such as discrimination in the purchase or transfer of a home? Are there more effective measures that do not impinge on a property owner's rights?
2. What are the responsibilities of a society to ensure safe, secure, and economically viable neighborhoods?

5.1 SECTION 1982 OF THE CIVIL RIGHTS ACT OF 1866

The advent of urban industrialization in the late nineteenth century, coupled with a significant increase in domestic migrant and immigrant populations, prompted a number of discriminatory trends in the transfer of property. Private parties refused to sell or rent to minority tenants and buyers. Real estate agents engaged in "block-busting," whereby the entry of minority groups, such as African-Americans or Hispanics, into the housing market was accompanied by scare tactics that induced whites in the same area to sell their property.

Discriminatory governmental policies often worsened these practices. Beginning with the introduction of federal housing programs in the 1930s, the federal government implemented a number of practices that discriminated against minority homeowners. These practices included the use of discriminatory appraisals of homes constructed in minority neighborhoods, the use of mortgage practices that favored construction in largely white suburban neighborhoods at the expense of heterogeneous urban cores, and, until the Supreme Court's decision in *Shelley v. Kraemer,* the requirement that federally approved mortgages contain racially restrictive covenants. *See* Kenneth T. Jackson, Crabgrass Frontier: The Suburbanization of the United States 190-218 (1985); *see also* James A. Kushner, *Apartheid in America: A Historical and Legal Analysis of Contemporary Racial Residential Segregation in the United States,* 22 How. L.J. 547 (1979).

However, in 1968, two events changed the structure of housing policy in the United States. First, the Supreme Court held in *Jones v. Mayer* that Section 1982 of the Civil Rights Act of 1866 outlawed private discrimination in the housing market. Section 1982 states that

> All citizens of the United States shall have the same right, in every State and Territory, as is enjoyed by white citizens thereof to inherit, purchase, lease, sell, hold, and convey real and personal property.

42 U.S.C. §1982. Second, Congress passed the FHA, 42 U.S.C. §§3601-3619 (2006), which sought to prevent discrimination in real estate transactions.

Jones v. Mayer

392 U.S. 409 (1968)

Mr. Justice Stewart delivered the opinion of the Court.

In this case we are called upon to determine the scope and constitutionality of an Act of Congress, 42 U.S.C. §1982, which provides that:

> "All citizens of the United States shall have the same right, in every State and Territory, as is enjoyed by white citizens thereof to inherit, purchase, lease, sell, hold, and convey real and personal property."

On September 2, 1965, the petitioners filed a complaint in the District Court for the Eastern District of Missouri, alleging that the respondents had refused to sell them a home in the Paddock Woods community of St. Louis County for the sole reason that petitioner Joseph Lee Jones is a Negro. Relying in part upon §1982, the petitioners sought injunctive and other relief. The District Court sustained the respondents' motion to dismiss the complaint, and the Court of Appeals for the Eighth Circuit affirmed, concluding that §1982 applies only to state action and does not reach private refusals to sell. We granted certiorari to consider the questions thus presented. For the reasons that follow, we reverse the judgment of the Court of Appeals. We hold that §1982 bars all racial discrimination, private as well as public, in the sale or rental of property, and that the statute, thus construed, is a valid exercise of the power of Congress to enforce the Thirteenth Amendment.

I.

At the outset, it is important to make clear precisely what this case does not involve. Whatever else it may be, 42 U.S.C. §1982 is not a comprehensive open housing law. In sharp contrast to the Fair Housing Title (Title VIII) of the Civil Rights Act of 1968, Pub.L. 90-284, 82 Stat. 81, the statute in this case deals only with racial discrimination and does not address itself to discrimination on grounds of religion or national origin. It does not deal specifically with discrimination in the provision of services or facilities in connection with the sale or rental of a dwelling. It does not prohibit advertising or other representations that indicate discriminatory preferences. It does not refer explicitly to discrimination in financing arrangements or in the provision of brokerage services. It does not empower a federal administrative agency to assist aggrieved parties. It makes no provision for intervention by the Attorney General. And, although it can be enforced by injunction it contains no provision expressly authorizing a federal court to order the payment of damages.

Thus, although §1982 contains none of the exemptions that Congress included in the Civil Rights Act of 1968, it would be a serious mistake to suppose that §1982 in any way diminishes the significance of the law recently enacted by Congress. . . .

III.

We begin with the language of the statute itself. In plain and unambiguous terms, §1982 grants to all citizens, without regard to race or color, "the same right" to purchase and lease property "as is enjoyed by white citizens." As the Court of Appeals in this case evidently recognized, that right can be impaired as effectively by "those who place property on the market" as by the State itself. For, even if the State and its agents lend no support to those who wish to exclude persons from their communities on racial grounds, the fact remains that, whenever property "is placed on the market for whites only, whites have a right denied to Negroes." So long as a Negro citizen who wants to buy or rent a home can be turned away simply because he is not white, he cannot be said to enjoy "the same right . . . as is enjoyed by white citizens . . . to . . . purchase (and) lease . . . real and personal property." 42 U.S.C. §1982.

On its face, therefore, §1982 appears to prohibit all discrimination against Negroes in the sale or rental of property-discrimination by private owners as well as discrimination by public authorities. Our examination of the relevant history . . . persuades us that Congress meant exactly what it said.

IV.

In its original form, 42 U.S.C. §1982 was part of §1 of the Civil Rights Act of 1866. That section was cast in sweeping terms:

> "Be it enacted by the Senate and House of Representatives of the United States of America in Congress assembled, That all persons born in the United States and not subject to any foreign power, . . . are hereby declared to be citizens of the United States; and such citizens, of every race and color, without regard to any previous condition of slavery or involuntary servitude, . . . shall have the same right, in every State and Territory in the United States, to make and enforce contracts, to sue, be parties, and give evidence, to inherit, purchase, lease, sell, hold, and convey real and personal property, and to full and equal benefit of all laws and proceedings for the security of person and property, as is enjoyed by white citizens, and shall be subject to like punishment, pains, and penalties, and to none other, any law, statute, ordinance, regulation, or custom, to the contrary notwithstanding."

The crucial language for our purposes was that which guaranteed all citizens "the same right, in every State and Territory in the United States, . . . to inherit, purchase, lease, sell, hold, and convey real and personal property . . . as is enjoyed by white citizens. . . ." To the Congress that passed the Civil Rights Act of 1866, it was clear that the right to do these things might be infringed not only by "State or local law" but also by "custom, or prejudice." Thus, when Congress provided in §1 of the Civil Rights Act that the right to purchase and lease property was to be enjoyed equally throughout the United States by Negro and white citizens alike, it plainly meant to secure that right against interference from any source whatever, whether governmental or private. . . .

V.

The remaining question is whether Congress has power under the Constitution to do what §1982 purports to do: to prohibit all racial discrimination, private and public, in the sale and rental of property. Our starting point is the Thirteenth Amendment, for it was pursuant to that constitutional provision that Congress originally enacted what is now §1982. The Amendment consists of two parts. Section 1 states:

> "Neither slavery nor involuntary servitude, except as a punishment for crime whereby the party shall have been duly convicted, shall exist within the United States, or any place subject to their jurisdiction."

Section 2 provides: "Congress shall have power to enforce this article by appropriate legislation."

As its text reveals, the Thirteenth Amendment "is not a mere prohibition of state laws establishing or upholding slavery, but an absolute declaration that slavery or involuntary servitude shall not exist in any part of the United States." Civil Rights Cases, 109 U.S. 3, 20, 3 S.Ct. 18, 28, 27 L.Ed. 835. It has never been doubted, therefore, "that the power vested in Congress to enforce the article by appropriate legislation," ibid., includes the power to enact laws "direct and primary, operating upon the acts of individuals, whether sanctioned by state legislation or not." Id., at 23, 3 S.Ct., at 30.

Thus, the fact that §1982 operates upon the unofficial acts of private individuals, whether or not sanctioned by state law, presents no constitutional problem. If Congress has power under the Thirteenth Amendment to eradicate conditions that prevent Negroes from buying and renting property because of their race or color, then no federal statute calculated to achieve that objective can be thought to exceed the constitutional power of Congress simply because it reaches beyond state action to regulate the conduct of private individuals. The constitutional question in this case, therefore, comes to this: Does the authority of Congress to enforce the Thirteenth Amendment "by appropriate legislation" include the power to eliminate all racial barriers to the acquisition of real and personal property? We think the answer to that question is plainly yes. . . .

The judgment is reversed.

Mr. Justice Douglas, concurring.

Enabling a Negro to buy and sell real and personal property is a removal of one of many badges of slavery.

"Slaves were not considered men. . . . They could own nothing; they could make no contracts; they could hold no property, nor traffic in property; they could not hire out; they could not legally marry nor constitute families; they could not control their children; they could not appeal from their master; they could be punished at will." W. Dubois, Black Reconstruction in America 10 (1964). . . .

Some badges of slavery remain today. While the institution has been outlawed, it has remained in the minds and hearts of many white men. Cases which have come to this Court depict a spectacle of slavery unwilling to die. We have seen contrivances by States designed to thwart Negro voting, e.g.,

Lane v. Wilson, 307 U.S. 268, 59 S.Ct. 872, 83 L.Ed. 1281. Negroes have been excluded over and again from juries solely on account of their race, e.g., Strauder v. West Virginia, 100 U.S. 303, 25 L.Ed. 664, or have been forced to sit in segregated seats in courtrooms, Johnson v. State of Virginia, 373 U.S. 61, 83 S.Ct. 1053, 10 L.Ed.2d 195. They have been made to attend segregated and inferior schools, e.g., Brown v. Board of Education, 347 U.S. 483, 74 S.Ct. 686, 98 L.Ed. 873, or been denied entrance to colleges or graduate schools because of their color, e.g., Commonwealth of Pennsylvania v. Board of Directors of City of Trusts, 353 U.S. 230, 77 S.Ct. 806, 1 L.Ed.2d 792; Sweatt v. Painter, 339 U.S. 629, 70 S.Ct. 848, 94 L.Ed. 1114. Negroes have been prosecuted for marrying whites, e.g., Loving v. Commonwealth of Virginia, 388 U.S. 1, 87 S.Ct. 1817, 18 L.Ed.2d 1010. They have been forced to live in segregated residential districts, Buchanan v. Warley, 245 U.S. 60, 38 S.Ct. 16, 62 L.Ed. 149 and residents of white neighborhoods have denied them entrance, e.g., Shelley v. Kraemer, 334 U.S. 1, 68 S.Ct. 836, 92 L.Ed. 1161. Negroes have been forced to use segregated facilities in going about their daily lives, having been excluded from railway coaches, Plessy v. Ferguson, 163 U.S. 537, 16 S.Ct. 1138, 41 L.Ed. 256; public parks, New Orleans City Park Improvement Assn. v. Detiege, 358 U.S. 54, 79 S.Ct. 99, 3 L.Ed.2d 46; restaurants, Lombard v. State of Louisiana, 373 U.S. 267, 83 S.Ct. 1122, 10 L.Ed.2d 338; public beaches, Mayor and City Council of Baltimore v. Dawson, 350 U.S. 877, 76 S.Ct. 133, 100 L.Ed. 774; municipal golf courses, Holmes v. City of Atlanta, 350 U.S. 879, 76 S.Ct. 141, 100 L.Ed. 776; amusement parks, Griffin v. State of Maryland, 378 U.S. 130, 84 S.Ct. 1770, 12 L.Ed.2d 754; buses, Gayle v. Browder, 352 U.S. 903, 77 S.Ct. 145, 1 L.Ed.2d 114; public libraries, Brown v. State of Louisiana, 383 U.S. 131, 86 S.Ct. 719, 15 L.Ed.2d 637. A state court judge in Alabama convicted a Negro woman of contempt of court because she refused to answer him when he addressed her as "Mary," although she had made the simple request to be called "Miss Hamilton." Hamilton v. State of Alabama, 376 U.S. 650, 84 S.Ct. 982, 11 L.Ed.2d 979. . . .

This recital is enough to show how prejudices, once part and parcel of slavery, still persist. The men who sat in Congress in 1866 were trying to remove some of the badges or "customs" of slavery when they enacted §1982. . . .

Mr. Justice Harlan, whom Mr. Justice White joins, dissenting.

The decision in this case appears to me to be most ill-considered and ill-advised.

For reasons which follow, I believe that the Court's construction of §1982 as applying to purely private action is almost surely wrong, and at the least is open to serious doubt. The issues of the constitutionality of §1982, as construed by the Court, and of liability under the Fourteenth Amendment alone, also present formidable difficulties. Moreover, the political processes of our own era have, since the date of oral argument in this case, given birth to a civil rights statute embodying "fair housing" provisions which would at the end of this year make available to others, though apparently not to the petitioners themselves, the type of relief which the petitioners now seek. . . .

A.

The Court's opinion focuses upon the statute's legislative history, but it is worthy of note that the precedents in this Court are distinctly opposed to the Court's view of the statute.

In the Civil Rights Cases, 109 U.S. 3, 3 S.Ct. 18, 27 L.Ed. 835, decided less than two decades after the enactment of the Civil Rights Act of 1866, from which §1982 is derived, the Court said in dictum of the 1866 Act:

> "This law is clearly corrective in its character, intended to counteract and furnish redress against state laws and proceedings, and customs having the force of law, which sanction the wrongful acts specified. . . . The civil rights bill here referred to is analogous in its character to what a law would have been under the original constitution, declaring that the validity of contracts should not be impaired, and that if any person bound by a contract should refuse to comply with it, under color or pretence that it had been rendered void or invalid by a state law, he should be liable to an action upon it in the courts of the United States, with the addition of a penalty for setting up such an unjust and unconstitutional defence." Id., at 16-17, 3 S.Ct., at 25.

In Corrigan v. Buckley, 271 U.S. 323, 46 S.Ct. 521, 70 L.Ed. 969, the question was whether the courts of the District of Columbia might enjoin prospective breaches of racially restrictive covenants. . . . The Court reasoned, inter alia, that the statutes, including the immediate predecessor of §1982, were inapplicable because "they, like the Constitutional Amendment under whose sanction they were enacted, do not in any manner prohibit or invalidate contracts entered into by private individuals in respect to the control and disposition of their own property." 271 U.S., at 331, 46 S.Ct. at 524.

In Hurd v. Hodge, 334 U.S. 24, 68 S.Ct. 847, 92 L.Ed. 1187, the issue was again whether the courts of the District might enforce racially restrictive covenants. At the outset of the process of reasoning by which it held that judicial enforcement of such a covenant would violate the predecessor of §1982, the Court said:

> "We may start with the proposition that the statute does not invalidate private restrictive agreements so long as the purposes of those agreements are achieved by the parties through voluntary adherence to the terms. The action toward which the provisions of the statute under consideration is (sic) directed is governmental action. Such was the holding of Corrigan v. Buckley . . ." 334 U.S., at 31, 68 S.Ct., at 851.

B.

Like the Court, I began analysis of §1982 by examining its language.

The Court finds it "plain and unambiguous . . . that this language forbids purely private as well as state-authorized discrimination." With all respect, I do not find it so. For me, there is an inherent ambiguity in the term "right," as used in §1982. The "right" referred to may either be a right to equal status under the law, in which case the statute operates only against state-sanctioned discrimination, or it may be an "absolute" right enforceable against private individuals. To me, the words of the statute, taken alone, suggest the former interpretation, not the latter. . . .

C.

The Court rests its opinion chiefly upon the legislative history of the Civil Rights Act of 1866. I shall endeavor to show that those debates do not, as the Court would have it, overwhelmingly support the result reached by the Court, and in fact that a contrary conclusion may equally well be drawn.

D.

Many of the legislators who took part in the congressional debates inevitably must have shared the individualistic ethic of their time, which emphasized personal freedom and embodied a distaste for governmental interference which was soon to culminate in the era of laissez-faire. It seems to me that most of these men would have regarded it as a great intrusion on individual liberty for the Government to take from a man the power to refuse for personal reasons to enter into a purely private transaction involving the disposition of property, albeit those personal reasons might reflect racial bias. It should be remembered that racial prejudice was not uncommon in 1866, even outside the South. Although Massachusetts had recently enacted the Nation's first law prohibiting racial discrimination in public accommodations, Negroes could not ride within Philadelphia streetcars or attend public schools with white children in New York City. Only five States accorded equal voting rights to Negroes, and it appears that Negroes were allowed to serve on juries only in Massachusetts. Residential segregation was the prevailing pattern almost everywhere in the North. There were no state "fair housing" laws in 1866, and it appears that none had ever been proposed. In this historical context, I cannot conceive that a bill thought to prohibit purely private discrimination not only in the sale or rental of housing but in all property transactions would not have received a great deal of criticism explicitly directed to this feature. The fact that the 1866 Act received no criticism of this kind is for me strong additional evidence that it was not regarded as extending so far.

II.

[T]his is one of those rare instances in which an event which occurs after the hearing of argument so diminishes a case's public significance, when viewed in light of the difficulty of the questions presented, as to justify this Court in dismissing the writ as improvidently granted.

The occurrence to which I refer is the recent enactment of the Civil Rights Act of 1968, Pub.L. 90-284, 82 Stat. 73. Title VIII of that Act contains comprehensive "fair housing" provisions, which by the terms of §803 will become applicable on January 1, 1969, to persons who, like the petitioners, attempt to buy houses from developers. Under those provisions, such persons will be entitled to injunctive relief and damages from developers who refuse to sell to them on account of race or color, unless the parties are able to resolve their dispute by other means. Thus, the type of relief which the petitioners seek will be available within seven months' time under the terms of a presumptively constitutional Act of Congress. In these circumstances, it seems obvious that the case has lost most of its public importance, and I believe that it would be much the wiser course for this Court to refrain from deciding it.

For these reasons, I would dismiss the writ of certiorari as improvidently granted.

NOTES AND QUESTIONS

1. How does the majority opinion address the question of whether state action is necessary to invoke Section 1982? How does the dissenting opinion address the same issue?

In *Jones*, the majority opinion rejected the state action requirement as to Section 1982. The Supreme Court held that the Section 1982 could apply to the behavior of private parties in the housing market because Congress passed Section 1982 pursuant to the Thirteenth Amendment of the Constitution, which sought to eliminate slavery and involuntary servitude in the United States. Is the use of the Thirteenth Amendment to address these issues a more comfortable framework than the one outlined by the Court in *Shelley v. Kraemer*?

2. The Supreme Court considered *Jones* during the passage of the FHA. What are the differences between the two statutes identified in *Jones*? Typically, Section 1982 is understood to be both narrower and broader in scope than the FHA. *See* James A. Kushner, FAIR HOUSING: DISCRIMINATION IN REAL ESTATE, COMMUNITY DEVELOPMENT AND REVITALIZATION 6-8 (2nd ed. 1995). Section 1982 protects individuals from only racial discrimination within the housing market, whereas the FHA protects individuals against discrimination based on race as well as color, sex, religion, national origin, familial status (which has been interpreted to extend to age), and disability (and third parties who assist a protected disabled person). *See* 42 U.S.C. §3604(a) (outlining protected classes under FHA); §3604(f) (designating the disabled as a protected class under the FHA); §3604(f)(2)(C) (designating persons who aid the disabled as a protected class). Moreover, unlike Section 1982, which requires individuals to prove a personal injury to

recover under its provisions, the FHA contemplates that the government will engage in independent affirmative enforcement efforts. *See* 42 U.S.C. §3608 (delegating authority to review housing discrimination to administrative law judges appointed by the Department of Housing and Urban Development (HUD)); §3610 (reviewing administrative procedures associated with the affirmative enforcement of the act). Section 1982, however, can be applied to a wide range of behavior that does not involve the sale or lease of a property. *See, e.g., Terry v. Elmwood Cemetery,* 307 F. Supp. 369 (N.D. Ala. 1969) (transactions involving cemetery graves could be considered property under Section 1982). In practice, this difference has been significantly lessened by broad application of Section 3604(a).

3. Federal statutes and provisions other than Section 1982 and the FHA also address fair housing issues. *See, e.g.,* U.S. Const. amend. XIV, §1 (prevents governmental action or private entities acting with the government from discriminating based on race or other suspect classifications); Civil Rights Act of 1964, 42 U.S.C. §2000d (2006) (which prohibits discrimination based on race, color, and national origin in programs that receive any federal funding); Civil Rights Act of 1866, 42 U.S.C. §1981 (2006) (prohibits discrimination based on race in the making and enforcement of contracts).

4. As we will discuss throughout this text, the relationship of individual housing to a given neighborhood is a complex one. Intentional discrimination in housing does not simply affect one individual; it can have an impact on how an entire community is perceived. According to Charles R. Lawrence III, "[o]ur culture attaches racial meaning to residential segregation. When we see an all-white neighborhood in close proximity to an all-black one, we do not imagine that it is white because its inhabitants' forbears settled there generations ago or that blacks have chosen not to live there." *The Id, the Ego, and Equal Protection: Reckoning with Unconscious Racism,* 39 Stan. L. Rev. 317, 369 (1986). Rather, he argues our first impression is that the neighborhood is white "because nonwhites have been excluded." *Id.* The Supreme Court took up the issue of racially segregated neighborhoods in *Village of Arlington Heights v. Metropolitan Housing Development Corp.,* 429 U.S. 252 (1977), although the conflict is couched in terms of rezoning based on socioeconomic status. A nonprofit real estate developer filed suit when "a predominantly white, upper middle class Chicago suburb prevented the construction of a proposed housing development for low and moderate income families by refusing to rezone the projected site to allow multifamily units." Lawrence, *supra,* at 347. The Supreme Court analyzed this case under the Equal Protection Clause of the Fourteenth Amendment. While the Court recognized the decision not to rezone had racially discriminatory effects, *Arlington Heights,* 429 U.S. at 269, it rejected the equal protection claim on the ground that the black plaintiffs "simply failed to carry their burden of proving that discriminatory purpose was a motivating factor in the Village's decision." *Id.* at 270. For further discussion of *Arlington Heights,* see Kenneth L. Karst, *Foreword: Equal Citizenship under*

the Fourteenth Amendment, 91 HARV. L. REV. 1 (1977); Michael J. Perry, *Disproportionate Impact Theory of Racial Discrimination*, 125 U. PA. L. REV. 540 (1976).

5. Darrell A.H. Miller has examined the background of *Jones v. Mayer*. Darrell A.H. Miller, *White Cartels, The Civil Rights Act of 1866, and the History of Jones v. Alfred H. Mayer Co.*, 77 FORDHAM L. REV. 999 (2008). Miller proposes that *Jones* may be used as precedent to address the disparate impact of facially neutral practices that have discriminatory effects by utilizing the Thirteenth Amendment, *id.* at 1044-50. Miller does this by first providing a thorough history of the case, *id.* at 1004-14, and next linking the historical record of the Civil Rights Act of 1866 with economic theories, asserting that the Act was meant to be a market-corrective action, *id.* at 1023-38.

5.1.1 The Fair Housing Act

The FHA, 42 U.S.C. §§3601-3619 (2006), seeks to provide, within constitutional limitations, "fair housing" throughout the United States. The FHA makes it unlawful to discriminate in the sale or rental of housing based on race, color, religion, sex, familial status, national origin, or handicap. *See* 42 U.S.C. §3604.

The vagueness of the term *fair housing* exposes the tensions in the scope of the FHA. Does *fair housing* mean the absence of discrimination in the decision to rent, sell, market, or lend? Or does it mean the absence of neighborhoods segregated by race or national origin? *See* James A. Kushner, *An Unfinished Agenda: The Federal Fair Housing Enforcement Effort*, THE FAIR HOUSING ACT AFTER TWENTY YEARS 49 (Robert G. Shwemm ed., 1989).

The primary sections of the FHA are Section 3604, which regulates the transfer of real property, and Section 3606, which regulates the financing of real property.

Fair Housing Act

42 U.S.C. §3604 (2006)

As made applicable by section 3603 of this title and except as exempted by sections 3603 (b) and 3607 of this title, it shall be unlawful—

(a) To refuse to sell or rent after the making of a bona fide offer, or to refuse to negotiate for the sale or rental of, or otherwise make unavailable or deny, a dwelling to any person because of race, color, religion, sex, familial status, or national origin.

(b) To discriminate against any person in the terms, conditions, or privileges of sale or rental of a dwelling, or in the provision of services or facilities in connection therewith, because of race, color, religion, sex, familial status, or national origin.

(c) To make, print, or publish, or cause to be made, printed, or published any notice, statement, or advertisement, with respect to the sale or rental of a dwelling that indicates any preference, limitation, or discrimination based on race, color, religion, sex, handicap, familial status, or national origin, or an intention to make any such preference, limitation, or discrimination.

(d) To represent to any person because of race, color, religion, sex, handicap, familial status, or national origin that any dwelling is not available for inspection, sale, or rental when such dwelling is in fact so available.

(e) For profit, to induce or attempt to induce any person to sell or rent any dwelling by representations regarding the entry or prospective entry into the neighborhood of a person or persons of a particular race, color, religion, sex, handicap, familial status, or national origin.

(f)(1) To discriminate in the sale or rental, or to otherwise make unavailable or deny, a dwelling to any buyer or renter because of a handicap of—

(A) that buyer or renter,

(B) a person residing in or intending to reside in that dwelling after it is so sold, rented, or made available; or

(C) any person associated with that buyer or renter.

NOTES AND QUESTIONS

1. The FHA exempts (1) any single-family home sold or rented by an owner without the use of an intermediary, such as real estate broker, and without any advertisement or notice; (2) any multi-family home, in which the owner of the home occupies one unit; (3) any rental or occupancy dwelling maintained by religious organizations, non-profit institutions, or organizations related to religious organizations; and (4) any non-commercial lodging maintained by a private club for its members. *See* 42 U.S.C. §3603(b)(1-2); 42 U.S.C. §3607(a).

2. The FHA contemplates two types of enforcement—governmental enforcement and private-party enforcement—under Sections 3504 and 3605, respectively. The government can bring actions under the FHA in two ways. First, the Department of Justice can bring an action under Section 3613 alleging a defendant has engaged in a both pattern and practice of discrimination or, in the alternative, in a pattern of discrimination alone. *See* 42 U.S.C. §3613. Second, HUD can bring an administrative complaint under Section 3610 alleging the defendant has engaged in discriminatory practices under the FHA. *See* 42 U.S.C. §3610(a).

A private plaintiff challenging a discriminatory practice under the FHA can (1) bring an administrative complaint to HUD under Section 3610; (2) bring a district court action under Section 3613; or (3) bring a private suit under the Administrative Procedure Act, alleging that HUD has failed to undertake its affirmative duty to collect data on the use of race and ethnicity in housing decision-making. *See* 42 U.S.C. §§3610(a), 3612, 3608(a).

3. As of July 1, 2003, many states and localities have been recognized by HUD as having laws equal to Title VIII. *See, e.g.*, Arizona (Ariz. Rev. Stat. Ann. §41-1491.14 (2008)), Arkansas (Ark. Code Ann. §16-123-201(2009)), California (Cal. Civ. Code §51 (West 2009)), Colorado (Colo. Rev. Stat. §24-34-502 (2008)), Connecticut (Conn. Gen. Stat. §46a-64 (2008)), Delaware (Del. Code Ann. Tit. 6, §4601 (2009)), Florida (Fla. Stat. §760.23 (2009)), Georgia (Ga. Code Ann. §8-3-202 (2009)), Hawaii (Haw. Rev. Stat. §515-3 (2009)), and Illinois (65 Ill. Comp. Stat. 5/11-11.1-1 (2009)).

Section 3604 has a broad scope and has been applied in a variety of contexts. The following case, *Whisby-Myers v. Kiekenapp*, 293 F. Supp. 2d 845 (2003), explores the scope and limits of Section 3604(a).

Whisby-Myers v. Kiekenapp

293 F.Supp.2d 845 (N.D. Ill. 2003)

Plaintiff Lisa Whisby-Myers and her husband Christopher Myers brought this action on their own behalf and on behalf of their children Kenny Whisby, Kenshell Whisby, and Christian Myers against defendant Robert Kiekenapp, alleging violations of 42 U.S.C. §1982 and the Fair Housing Act, 42 U.S.C. §§3604 & 3617, as well as state law claims for assault, civil hate crime, and intentional infliction of emotional distress. Kiekenapp has moved to dismiss plaintiffs' federal claims for failure to state a claim, to strike their requests for injunctive relief and prejudgment interest, to dismiss the complaint for failing to contain a separate and proper prayer for relief and the state claims for lack of a viable federal claim, and to strike certain unnumbered narrative paragraphs in the complaint. On October 8, 2003, the Court advised the parties that the motion to dismiss was denied. The purpose of this Opinion is to explain the Court's ruling.

FACTS

We take the following from plaintiffs' complaint, the allegations of which we take as true for purposes of Kiekenapp's motion.

At the times relevant to this lawsuit, the plaintiffs, who are African-American, lived in the same Calumet City neighborhood as Kiekenapp, who is Caucasian. Plaintiffs were the only African-American family on the block.

Around 10:15 p.m. on May 1, 2001, Whisby-Myers was driving through her neighborhood on her way to work. As she passed Kiekenapp's home, she heard a loud explosion that rocked her vehicle. She exited her car and was confronted by Kiekenapp, who came running toward her from his home. Kiekenapp allegedly swung his arms and screamed racial epithets at Whisby-Myers, calling her "black bitch" and "n bitch."

Officers of the Calumet City police department, having heard the explosion, showed up at Kiekenapp's home shortly thereafter. Kiekenapp allegedly told the police that he "tried to blow [Whisby-Myers'] ass up" and would "do it again," and that the police should "take this n bitch to jail," and also claimed that Whisby-Myers was "not registered." The police searched Kiekenapp's garage and found numerous weapons and bomb-making materials. The police department's bomb squad later identified the device that Kiekenapp detonated as a U.S. Military M21 Flash Simulator.

After the confrontation, Whisby-Myers returned to her home, located directly across the street from Kiekenapp's home, and called her workplace to advise that she would not be coming in that evening. Because the plaintiffs feared future attacks, the Whisby-Myers children were told not to play in front of the house, and the family and its visitors stopped parking their cars in front of the home. Plaintiffs allege that they were humiliated, embarrassed and emotionally and economically harmed by Kiekenapp's actions, and that their injuries included "deprivation of their right to equal housing opportunities." Cmpl. ¶25. . . .

A. *Section 1982 claim*

Count One is a claim under 42 U.S.C. §1982, which provides:

> All citizens of the United States shall have the same right, in every State and Territory, as is enjoyed by white citizens thereof to inherit, purchase, lease, sell, hold, and convey real and personal property.

Kiekenapp argues that §1982 bars racial discrimination only in property transactions such as the sale or rental of property. Though the Seventh Circuit has not addressed this issue, this Court agrees with those courts that have rejected this proposed limitation on the statute's coverage.

Section 1982's reference to the right to "hold" property indicates that it is not confined to property transactions. *See Stirgus v. Benoit,* 720 F.Supp. 119, 123 (N.D.Ill.1989). When interpreting a statute, a court must attempt to provide meaning to every word in the statute. *Reiter v. Sonotone Corp.,* 442 U.S. 330, 339, 99 S.Ct. 2326, 60 L.Ed.2d 931 (1979). To give effect to each term in the statute, the term "hold" must have a meaning different from the terms "purchase," "lease," "sell," and "convey." *Bryant v. Polston,* No. IP 00-1064-C, 2000 WL 1670938, at 6 (S.D.Ind. Nov. 2, 2000). We agree with those courts that have concluded that section 1982's protection of the right "to hold" property includes the right to use one's property. . . .

As the Supreme Court has stated, section 1982 is concerned with "the right of black persons to hold and acquire property on an equal basis with white persons and [to provide for] the right of blacks not to have property interests impaired because of their race." *City of Memphis v. Greene*, 451 U.S. 100, 122, 101 S.Ct. 1584, 67 L.Ed.2d 769 (1981). Kiekenapp's narrow reading of section 1982 is at odds with the broad scope of the protection intended by Congress when it adopted the statute. *See Jones v. Mayer Co.*, 392 U.S. 409, 437, 443, 88 S.Ct. 2186, 20 L.Ed.2d 1189 (1968) (finding that the language of §1982 reflects Congress' desire to secure for black citizens the "right to live wherever a white man can live").

To state a claim under §1982, plaintiffs must allege that the defendant had a racial animus, intended to discriminate against the plaintiff, and deprived the plaintiff of protected rights because of the plaintiff's race. *Kundacina v. Concession Services, Inc.*, No. 96 C 4422, 1997 WL 222943, at 6 (N.D.Ill. Apr. 30, 1997). Plaintiffs have alleged all the elements of a section 1982 claim. Whisby-Myers alleges that Kiekenapp had racial animus by asserting that he called her a "black bitch" and a "n bitch" after she exited her car. *Id.* ¶ 15. Kiekenapp's intent to discriminate against plaintiffs is adequately alleged in the assertions that he detonated the bomb as Whisby-Myers passed his home, *id.* ¶ 15, and he told police "I tried to blow her ass up and I'll do it again." *Id.* ¶ 17. Finally, plaintiffs adequately allege that Kiekenapp deprived plaintiffs of rights protected by §1982: they allege they feared future attacks, their children could no longer play in the front yard of their home, and plaintiffs and their visitors could not park on the street in front of their home. Cmpl. ¶ 24. Count One states a claim.

B. Fair Housing Act claims

In Count Two, plaintiffs seek damages in violation of the Fair Housing Act, 42 U.S.C. §§3604 & 3617. Kiekenapp argues that this claim is deficient because plaintiffs can sue under these provisions only for prohibited discrimination in real estate transactions, and that the Act's prohibitions do not apply to single family homes. The Court disagrees.

The purpose of the Fair Housing Act is to ensure fair and equal housing opportunities and to eliminate segregated housing throughout the United States. 42 U.S.C. §3601; *see South Suburban Housing Center v. Board of Realtors*, 935 F.2d 868, 882 (7th Cir.1991). Section 3613, the provision of the Act that authorizes the filing of suit by a private person, states that an aggrieved person can sue "after the occurrence or the termination of an alleged discriminatory housing practice, or the breach of a conciliation agreement entered into under this subchapter . . . to obtain appropriate relief. . . ." 42 U.S.C. §3613(a)(1)(A). Kiekenapp argues that the use of the phrase "discriminatory housing practice" reflects that sections 3604 and 3617 apply only to real estate *transactions*. This is a *non sequitur*. A "discriminatory housing practice" is defined in the Act to include conduct that is prohibited under sections 3604 and 3617. 42 U.S.C. §3602(f). Thus we must look to those provisions to determine the scope of their coverage.

Section 3604(a) makes it unlawful to refuse to sell or rent after the making of a bona fide offer, or to refuse to negotiate for the sale or rental of or *otherwise make unavailable or deny*, a dwelling to any person because of race, color, religion, sex, familial status, or national origin. 42 U.S.C. §3604 (emphasis added). Kiekenapp first argues that the Act does not apply to single family homes like the one in which the plaintiffs live. He relies on section 3603(b), which states that "[n]othing in section 3604 of this title (other than subsection (c)) shall apply to . . . any single-family house sold or rented by an owner," provided that certain other conditions are met. 42 U.S.C. §3603(b). First of all, this exemption is limited to section 3604, and would not preclude plaintiffs' claim under section 3617 even were the Court to read the exemption in the manner urged by Kiekenapp. *See United States v. Pospisil*, 127 F.Supp.2d 1059, 1064 (W.D.Mo.2000). But the Court does not agree with Kiekenapp's reading of section 3603(b). The exemption's text indicates that it was meant by Congress to be limited to actions by a homeowner in selling or renting his home, not post-sale actions by a non-owner (like Kiekenapp) designed to deprive a homeowner of the use of the home. The legislative history of the provision leads to a similar conclusion. *See, e.g., Hogar Agua y Vida en el Desierto v. Suarez-Medina*, 36 F.3d 177, 184-85 (1st Cir.1994); *Singleton v. Gendason*, 545 F.2d 1224, 1226-27 (9th Cir.1976). *Accord, Pospisil*, 127 F.Supp.2d at 1064. Because the Fair Housing Act is to be given a "generous construction" in view of its purpose, *Trafficante v. Metropolitan Life Ins. Co.*, 409 U.S. 205, 209, 212, 93 S.Ct. 364, 34 L.Ed.2d 415 (1972), and because the Act's exemptions, for the same reason, are to be narrowly construed, *Hogar Agua y Vida*, 36 F.3d at 181 (citing cases), the Court concludes that §3603(b) does not exempt the activity alleged in this case.

Kiekenapp's second argument regarding plaintiffs' section 3604 claim is similar to his argument regarding the scope of section 1982; he contends that the statute bars discrimination only in connection with a real estate transaction. Again, the Court disagrees. As the Seventh Circuit and other courts have concluded, the prohibitions of section 3604 extend beyond mere sales and rentals of real estate. . . . As in those cases, the plaintiffs in this case have alleged that their dwelling was made unavailable to them, at least in certain respects, because of racially discriminatory conduct.

Kiekenapp likewise argues that claims under section 3617 are limited to those involving discriminatory practices in real estate transactions. Section 3617 makes it unlawful to "coerce, intimidate, threaten, or interfere with any person in the exercise or enjoyment of . . . any right granted or protected by section . . . 3604." 42 U.S.C. §3617. Courts have consistently applied section 3617 to "threatening, intimidating, or extremely violent discriminatory conduct designed to drive an individual out of his home. . . ."

Kiekenapp's alleged detonation of an explosive device simulator to intimidate the plaintiffs is of like kind to the conduct held in these cases to give rise to a claim under section 3617.

For these reasons, the Court rejects Kiekenapp's motion to dismiss plaintiffs' Fair Housing Act claims. . . .

NOTES AND QUESTIONS

1. Why did the Court uphold the Whisby-Myers' claim under Section 1982? What is the burden of proof for a plaintiff under Section 1982 as discussed in *Whisby*? Was there a substantive difference between the Whisby-Myers' claims under Section 1982 as opposed to the FHA?

2. Why does the Court determine that Section 3604 is not limited to real estate transactions under the law? How did Kiekenapp allegedly deprive the Whisby-Myers family of its rights under Section 3604? How does the Court outline the way the relationship of Section 3617 aids in the enforcement of Section 3604?

3. The FHA has adopted a liability framework from other areas of civil rights law. Two paths to showing liability exist under the FHA. See *Doe v. City of Butler, PA*, 892 F.2d 315 (3rd Cir. 1989). A plaintiff can allege, through direct or circumstantial evidence, that the defendant acted in an intentionally discriminatory manner. See *Kormoczy v. Secretary, U.S. Department of Urban Development on Behalf of Briggs*, 53 F.3d 821, 824 (7th Cir. 1995) (outlining the contours of the discriminatory treatment claim within the context of the FHA). Alternatively, if such evidence of intentional discrimination is absent, a plaintiff can attempt to prove discrimination under the inferential, burden-shifting method of *McDonnell-Douglas Corp. v. Green*, 411 U.S. 792 (1973). Under the *McDonnell-Douglas* framework, a plaintiff must come forward with a prima facie case of discrimination. Then, the burden shifts to the defendant to prove the alleged discriminatory practice was motivated by legitimate non-racial considerations. Finally, once the defendant brings forth evidence that articulates non-discriminatory reasons, the burden shifts back to the plaintiff to show that the proffered reasons were a mere pretext. The elements of the prima facie case differ depending on the alleged violations of the FHA. See, e.g., *Asbury v. Brougham*, 866 F.2d 1276, 1280 (10th Cir. 1989) (outlining prima facie case for refusal to rent claim under Section 3604, which involves showing that plaintiff is a member of a protected class and was qualified to rent, that she was denied the

opportunity to rent, and that the apartment was remained available for rent).

In addition to the broad scope of Section 3604(a), the FHA requires property owners to take a number of affirmative steps to ensure integrated neighborhoods. In particular, Section 3604(c) requires that marketing efforts be conducted without preference, limitation, or discrimination. This has raised a number of interesting issues as to the full scope of the FHA, as well as to its interaction with other constitutional provisions, such as the First Amendment.

Ragin v. Harry Macklowe Real Estate Co.

6 F.3d 898 (2nd Cir. 1993)

Plaintiffs-appellants-cross-appellees Luther M. Ragin, Jr., Deborah Fish Ragin, Renaye Cuyler, Jerome F. Cuyler and the Open Housing Center ("OHC") appeal from a judgment entered in the United States District Court for the Southern District of New York (Sweet, *J.*) after a bench trial with an advisory jury. The plaintiffs commenced this action for damages and injunctive relief in August of 1988, alleging that defendant-appellee-cross-appellant Harry Macklowe Real Estate Company ("HMRE") and HMRE's sole owner and president, defendant-appellee-cross-appellant Harry Macklowe, violated section 804(c) of the Fair Housing Act, 42 U.S.C. §3604(c) (1988) (the "FHA" or the "Act"). The gravamen of the plaintiffs' complaint was that the defendants' placement of display advertising for residential apartments in *The New York Times* violated the Act's prohibition against racial discrimination in residential housing advertising because all the models portrayed in the advertisements were white.

After a fourteen-day trial, the advisory jury recommended: that only HMRE be found liable for violating the Act; that each individual plaintiff receive $25,000 in compensatory damages for emotional distress; that the OHC receive $100,000 in compensatory damages for the resources it was required to allocate to counteract the effects of the defendants' advertisements; and that HMRE be required to pay $62,500 in punitive damages to the plaintiffs. On August 25, 1992, the district court issued an opinion: finding that both HMRE and Macklowe violated the Act; awarding each individual plaintiff $2500 in compensatory damages for emotional distress; and awarding the OHC $20,000 in compensatory damages for the resources it was required to allocate to counteract the effects of the defendants' advertisements. *See Ragin v. Harry Macklowe Real Estate Co.*, 801 F.Supp. 1213, 1230-34 (S.D.N.Y. 1992). The district court declined to award punitive damages but entered an injunction prohibiting the defendants from violating the Act by using display advertising that indicated a racial preference. . . .

Background

We assume familiarity with the facts set forth in the district court's published opinion, *see Ragin v. Harry Macklowe Real Estate Co.*, 801 F.Supp. 1213 (S.D.N.Y. 1992), and therefore provide only a brief summary of the facts and circumstances giving rise to this action. The individual plaintiffs are two married couples who reside in New York City. All four are African Americans who hold graduate degrees in the fields of law, public policy, medicine or speech pathology. The OHC is a nonprofit corporation located in New York City. Its "mission" is to reduce the amount of segregation in, and to eliminate all discrimination from, the metropolitan residential housing market.

HMRE was the leasing agent and managing agent for two luxury residential apartment complexes in Manhattan. The first building, Riverterrace, is located at 515 East 72nd Street. Between May of 1986 and April of 1987, HMRE placed six half-page or full-page display ads for Riverterrace in *The New York Times*. One of these ads ("HOME") featured a photograph of three single white models engaging in sports or recreational activities and a photograph of a white couple embracing. A second ad ("New Year at 5:15") portrayed four white models gathering around a piano on New Year's Eve. A third ad ("Live It Up at 5:15") included three photographs: the scene depicted in the New Year at 5:15 ad, two white models at a swimming pool and a white couple on a terrace. The last three ads ("5:15 is the Time") also each included three photographs: the scene featured in the New Year at 5:15 ad, a white couple in a swimming pool and a white model at a gym.

The second building, Riverbank West, is located at 555 West 42nd Street. Between April of 1987 and December of 1988, HMRE placed twenty-eight half-page or full-page display advertisements for Riverbank West in *The New York Times*. Three of the ads ("3-D") featured a recreation of a famous *Life* magazine photograph depicting a movie audience of seventy-five white men and women wearing 3-D eyeglasses. All the individuals pictured in the 3-D ad were employees of either HMRE or the advertising agency that created the ad. Three advertisements ("Lying on Beach") depicted a young white woman lying in the sun next to an image of Riverbank West. Four ads ("Beach Bag") showed a young white woman walking on a beach and swinging a bag with an image of Riverbank West rising out of the surf. Nine of the ads ("Lipstick") depicted a white woman's lips and fingers applying a lipstick in the shape of Riverbank West. Two ads ("Skier") featured a white man skiing against a background of mountains among which was nestled Riverbank West. Two of the ads

("Get It") depicted a white woman wearing a bathing suit and lying in the ocean in front of an image of Riverbank West. The remaining five advertisements ("Beauty & the Best") showed a glamorous white woman "leaning toward a miniature image of Riverbank West." 801 F.Supp. at 1221. The Beauty & the Best ads ran from September to December of 1988 and were the only HMRE advertisements that included an Equal Housing Opportunity logo.

The target group for Riverterrace consisted of individuals in the thirty-five to fifty-five-year-old age group with household incomes in excess of $75,000. The target group for Riverbank West consisted of individuals in the twenty-five to forty-five-year-old age group with household incomes in excess of $50,000. All the human models for these advertisements were chosen from stock photograph books, which included both black and white models. The defendants never requested that black models be used in, or excluded from, the display ads for the two buildings.

In addition to placing ads in the print media, HMRE also advertised the two buildings by using direct mail, press releases, classified advertising, on-site brochures and signs, and radio advertisements and by placing ads on the sides of buses, which ran throughout Manhattan, including Harlem. None of the ads contained any language that either explicitly or implicitly conveyed a discriminatory message. Finally, there was no evidence presented that the defendants discriminated against minorities in the leasing of apartments in the two buildings.

The plaintiffs saw the defendants' ads in *The New York Times* between August of 1985 and late 1988. In June of 1987, the plaintiffs filed a complaint with the New York State Division of Human Rights ("SDHR") against The Harry Macklowe Organization (the "Organization"). In their SDHR complaint, the plaintiffs alleged that the Organization had engaged in unlawful, discriminatory housing practices. In response to the plaintiffs' administrative complaint, the SDHR initiated an administrative proceeding against the Organization. The administrative complaints were dated June 15, 1987, and contained allegations that the display advertisements for Riverbank West and Riverterrace appearing in 1987 violated the New York State Human Rights Law because they did not include any black models. After receiving notice of the administrative complaints, Macklowe directed HMRE's in-house counsel to conduct an investigation of their obligations under the relevant housing statutes.

On May 10, 1988, the SDHR issued a finding of probable cause against the Organization and recommended that a public hearing be held to determine if further action was warranted. A public hearing never was held, and no further administrative action was taken by the SDHR. After HMRE received notice of the probable cause finding in May of 1988, all new layouts of display ads published in *The New York Times* included the Equal Housing Opportunity logo, which apparently was smaller than the size prescribed by United States Department of Housing and Urban Development ("HUD") regulations. *See* 24 C.F.R. §109.30(a) & app. I (1992). The logo also was placed on the existing bus posters, and a radio advertisement for Riverbank West included the Equal Housing Opportunity slogan. A video advertisement for Riverbank West also displayed the logo and showed a black man using the health club with three other tenants.

The evidence introduced at trial indicated that the other real estate advertisements published on the same pages of *The New York Times* as the HMRE display ads also did not use black models and that most of the ads did not have the Equal Housing Opportunity logo. In addition to the testimony of the individual plaintiffs that they were offended when they saw these ads over a period of time, both sides presented expert testimony concerning whether the "ordinary" reader would view the defendants' ads as expressing a racial preference. The defendants also offered the testimony of a black tenant from each of the two buildings. Both tenants testified that they saw some of the defendants' ads but did not believe that they conveyed a racially exclusionary message.

At the conclusion of the trial, the district court entered judgment for the plaintiffs; awarded less compensatory damages than those recommended by the advisory jury; declined to award punitive damages; entered an injunction prohibiting the defendants from continuing to use display ads that expressed a racial preference; and declined to award attorneys' fees. Both sides timely appealed.

Discussion

B. Liability

Two years ago, in *Ragin v. New York Times Co.*, 923 F.2d 995, 999 (2d Cir.), *cert. denied,* 502 U.S. 821, 112 S.Ct. 81, 116 L.Ed.2d 54 (1991), we held that a plaintiff could bring an action against a defendant for violating section 804(c) of the Act if the defendant's housing ads "suggest[ed] to an ordinary reader that a particular race [was] preferred or dispreferred for the housing in question," regardless of the defendant's intent, *id.*, at 1000. We defined the ordinary reader as "neither the most suspicious nor the most insensitive of our citizenry. Such a reader does not apply a mechanical test to every use of a model of a particular race." *Id.* at 1002. Although we indicated that the intent of the defendant "may be relevant to a factual determination of the message conveyed," the message conveyed to the ordinary reader was the "touchstone" of our inquiry. *Id.* at 1000.

In concluding that the defendants' display ads violated the FHA, the district court found that HMRE, through its agents, arranged for the ads[,] . . . that Macklowe was actively involved in conceptualizing and approving the ads as president of HMRE . . . [and] that, viewing the ads as many times and over the same period as they did, an ordinary reader would naturally interpret the ads to 'indicate' a racial preference. 801 F.Supp. at 1231. The district court based these findings both on the fact that there were no black models in any of the ads, including the ad portraying seventy-five movie viewers, and on the number of occasions (between fourteen and twenty-five) when the individual plaintiffs viewed the ads between 1986 and 1988. *See id.* at 1232. Moreover, the district court noted that the advisory jury's finding of liability also was probative of the ads' effect on the ordinary reader. *See id.*

In reaching its conclusion, the district court did not rely on the expert testimony presented by the parties, finding such testimony to be inconclusive. *See id.* at 1231. The district court also gave limited weight to the individual plaintiffs' testimony because of their "commitment to their cause and heightened sensitivity attributable to an awareness of historical patterns of housing discrimination and personal experiences with segregation." *Id.* The district court declined to credit the testimony of the two black residents living in the defendants' buildings because "they did not view the same variety or number of ads over the same duration as the Plaintiffs" and because their testimony was affected by their experiences after having lived in the buildings. *Id.* at 1232. Finally, the district court declined to consider evidence of the racial composition of Riverterrace and Riverbank West because that evidence was "not probative of the ordinary reader's interpretation of the ads." *Id.*

In their cross appeal, the defendants argue that the district court erred in finding them liable for violating section 804(c) because the plaintiffs failed to present any expert testimony or survey evidence regarding whether the ordinary reader (rather than the ordinary *black* reader) would find that their ads indicated a racial preference; there was no evidence of discriminatory intent on their behalf; and there was no evidence that the ads had a discriminatory effect on the racial composition of their buildings. We find these arguments to be unpersuasive.

We never have held that a plaintiff is required to submit survey evidence or expert testimony to prove whether the ordinary reader would find an advertisement to express a racial preference, and we decline to do so here. Defendants' reliance on our requirement that plaintiffs submit such evidence to prove confusion in trademark infringement cases, *see, e.g., Johnson & Johnson * Merck Consumer Pharmaceuticals Co. v. Smithkline Beecham Corp.*, 960 F.2d 294, 298 (2d Cir. 1992), is misplaced. In trademark infringement cases, the inquiry focuses on whether there is a likelihood that a defendant's mark will confuse a group of customers. *Id.* at 297-98. In contrast, the inquiry directed by *Ragin* is whether a *hypothetical ordinary reader* would find that a defendant's ads expressed an impermissible racial preference. Like the inquiry in negligence cases concerning whether a defendant's conduct conformed with that of the reasonable person, this question is one that the factfinder can answer by viewing the ads and the defendants' conduct and then applying common sense. *Cf. Washington Hosp. Ctr. v. Butler*, 384 F.2d 331, 336 (D.C. Cir. 1967) (no need for expert testimony to resolve issue that would not "extend the jury beyond the range of ordinary lay knowledge and experience"). No expert testimony or survey evidence is necessary, although such evidence no doubt is admissible.

In *Ragin* we explicitly rejected the argument that a showing of discriminatory intent or discriminatory effect is required to prove a prima facie violation of section 804(c). *See* 923 F.2d at 1000 (intent is relevant but not dispositive). Our holding in *Soules v. United States Department of Housing & Urban Development,* 967 F.2d 817 (2d Cir. 1992), does not, as defendants argue, require a showing of intent. Relying on *Ragin,* the *Soules* court observed that "factfinders may examine intent, *not because a lack of design constitutes an affirmative defense* to an FHA violation, but because it helps determine the manner in which a statement was made and the way an ordinary listener would have interpreted it." *Id.* at 825 (emphasis added). Here, Judge Sweet considered the defendants' lack of discriminatory intent and the absence of any discriminatory effect in determining liability and still concluded that an ordinary reader would find that their ads expressed a racial preference. We agree with that conclusion. *See Saunders,* 659 F.Supp. at 1058 ("plaintiffs need not establish that defendants intended to express a racial preference" to prove that the Act was violated).

C. *Compensatory damages*

1. *Damages Awarded to Individual Plaintiffs*

It is axiomatic that civil rights plaintiffs may recover compensatory damages for emotional distress. *See, e.g., Baskin v. Parker,* 602 F.2d 1205, 1209 (5th Cir.1979) (per curiam); *Fort v. White,* 530 F.2d 1113, 1116 (2d Cir.1976); *Steele v. Title Realty Co.,* 478 F.2d 380, 384 (10th Cir.1973). The district court awarded $2500 to each of the four individual plaintiffs to compensate them for the emotional distress they suffered as a result of viewing the defendants' ads. In determining the damages suffered by the individual plaintiffs, the district court found that "[t]heir testimony credibly established that they took offense at the ads and that the indignation, humiliation and distress they suffered was directly attributable, at least in part, to the Defendants' conduct." 801 F.Supp. at 1233. However, the district court declined to credit their testimony that their distress was caused only by the defendants' ads. Instead, the district court found that the individual plaintiffs' emotional distress partly was caused by viewing display ads that were not published by the defendants and that their distress was aggravated by their past experiences with, and heightened sensitivities to, racial discrimination. *See id.* at 1234. Finally, the district court found that the emotional distress sustained by the individual plaintiffs was not so severe as to justify a damage award larger than $2500 per person. *See id.*

Plaintiffs principally argue that the district court's damages award should be set aside for two reasons, neither of which we find persuasive.

First, plaintiffs argue that, in discounting their past experiences with racial discrimination, the district court ignored the well-established principle of tort law that a tortfeasor "takes the plaintiff as he finds him." *Maurer v. United States,* 668 F.2d 98, 100 (2d Cir. 1981) (per curiam); *see also Restatement (Second) of Torts* §435, at 454 (1965); W. Page Keeton et al., *Prosser and Keeton on the Law of Torts* §43, at 292 (5th ed. 1984). This argument ignores the fact that the "eggshell skull" doctrine has been applied only in cases where the plaintiff suffered physical injuries. *See, e.g., Munn v. Algee,* 924 F.2d 568, 576 (5th Cir.), *cert. denied,* 502 U.S. 900, 112 S.Ct. 277, 116 L.Ed.2d 229 (1991); Keeton et al., *supra,* §43, at 291 ("[t]he defendant is held liable when the defendant's negligence operates upon a concealed *physical* condition") (emphasis added).

Plaintiffs also argue that the district court's finding that they failed to establish a strong causal link between the distress they suffered as a result of viewing the defendants' ads and the distress they suffered as a result of viewing other ads was based on a misinterpretation of their testimony. In *Ragin,* we emphasized that "liability may not be based on an aggregation of advertisements by different advertisers." 923 F.2d at 1001-02. The district court's findings with respect to the issue of causation were based on its assessment of the plaintiffs' credibility. After reviewing the trial transcript, we see no basis for disturbing the district court's assessment of the plaintiffs' credibility. . . .

In affirming the damages awarded by the district court for emotional distress, we echo the view expressed by the *Ragin* court that there exists a "potential for large numbers of truly baseless claims for emotional injury," that "there appears to be no ready device, other than wholly speculative judgments as to credibility, to separate the genuine from the baseless," and that it is the responsibility of district courts to "keep such awards within reason." 923 F.2d at 1005. Although the *Ragin* court expressed this view in the context of the potential for unreasonably high damage awards against newspapers, we find it pertinent to all section 804(c) cases in which plaintiffs recover damages only for emotional distress. *Cf. Housing Opportunities Made Equal, Inc. v. Cincinnati Enquirer, Inc.,* 943 F.2d 644, 666 n. 12 (6th Cir.1991) (Keith, J., dissenting) (where an FHA violation is "based only upon the use of white models, individual emotional distress damages would, in the ordinary case, be too speculative as a matter of law").

Finally, we agree with the district court that the damages awarded were appropriate in light of the plaintiffs' failure to prove severe emotional distress. . . .

2. *Damages Awarded to OHC*

The OHC argues that the district court committed clear error in declining to award it damages to compensate it for the cost of the time and effort it must devote in the future to counteract the adverse effects of the defendants' ads. [T]here was no evidence that the OHC was forced to increase its educational, counselling or referral services due to the Defendants' ads in particular. . . . we cannot say that Judge Sweet clearly erred in his analysis of the evidentiary record that was before him.

D. Punitive damages

In declining to award punitive damages, the district court held that the absence of any intent to discriminate on the part of the defendants in placing the ads precluded, as a matter of law, "a finding of wanton, willful or malicious behavior." 801 F.Supp. at 1235. The district court also found that the defendants' continued use of display advertisements that failed to include any black models after the SDHR determination of probable cause did not constitute a reckless or callous disregard for plaintiffs' rights or an intentional violation of federal law. *See id.* The district court did not abuse its discretion in declining to award punitive damages.

E. Injunctive relief

The district court's injunction prohibited the defendants from continuing to use advertisements that "violate[ ] [the FHA], and indicate [ ] to the ordinary reader any preference, limitation or discrimination based upon race or color, or an intention to make such preference, limitation or discrimination or that the housing or dwelling being advertised is not open to all without regard to race or color." We review the scope of a district court's injunction for abuse of discretion. *Nikon Inc. v. Ikon Corp.*, 987 F.2d 91, 94 (2d Cir. 1993).

The plaintiffs argue that the injunction was inadequate because it did not require that "the models should be clearly definable as *reasonably representing* majority and minority groups in the metropolitan area," Appellants' Brief at 35 (quoting 24 C.F.R. §109.30(b)) (emphasis added in Appellants' Brief), and because it did not require that defendants' ads include the Equal Housing Opportunity logo, as required by 24 C.F.R. §109.30(a). Notwithstanding plaintiffs' contention that these provisions often are included in consent decrees resolving section 804(c) litigation, we do not believe the district court abused its discretion in declining to include the requested HUD regulation language or logo in the injunction. As the district court wisely observed, entering an injunction requiring the use of proportional representation for blacks in real estate display advertising would put district courts in the position of becoming "an abettor to discrimination against other groups." 801 F.Supp. at 1236. . . .

Conclusion

The district court's findings with respect to standing, liability, damages and injunctive relief are affirmed.

NOTES AND QUESTIONS

1. How did the court define the "ordinary reader" under Section 3604(c)? Why did the court not require evidence of expert testimony as to the state of mind of the ordinary reader?

2. The FHA contemplates various remedies, as seen in *Ragin (II)*, many of which were strengthened by the Fair Housing Amendments of 1988. If a suit involves a private litigant under Section 3613, the remedies include (1) actual and punitive damages; (2) permanent and temporary injunctive relief; and (3) reasonable attorney's fees. *See* 42 U.S.C. §3613 (c)(1-2). If a suit involves an administrative complaint brought before an administrative law judge under Section 3610, the remedies include: (1) actual damages suffered by the plaintiff; and (2) a range of civil penalties, dependant on the length of time that the alleged discriminatory practice was undertaken by the defendant. *See* 42 U.S.C. §3612.

3. *Ragin (II)* raises an interesting question: Do the requirements of Section 3604(c) impinge on the free speech rights of the property owner? Does the property owner have a First Amendment right to advertise in a manner that may have the consequence of excluding a racial or ethnic group? For further discussion of these issues see Michael E. Rosman, *Ambiguity and the First Amendment: Some Thoughts on All-White Amendments,* 61 Tenn. L. Rev. 289 (1993-94) (contending that commercial speech such as housing advertisements enjoys limited protection under the First Amendment, and therefore, damages awards should only be awarded in limited circumstances under the FHA); Robert G. Schwemm, *Discriminatory Housing Statements and §3604(c): A New Look at the Fair Housing Act's Most Intriguing Provision,* 29 Fordham Urb. L. J. 187 (2001-02) (contending that strong implementation of Section 3604(c) does not violate the First Amendment); Helen L. Norton, *You Can't Ask (Or Say) That: The First Amendment and Civil Rights Restrictions on Decisionmaker Speech,* 11 Wm. & Mary Bill Rts. J. 727 (2002-03) (analyzing free speech concerns raised by §3604(c)).

5.2 REDEFINING NEIGHBORHOOD: PLACE, PROPERTY, AND THE LAW IN A POST–CIVIL RIGHTS CONTEXT

The societal responsibility for ensuring the ability to purchase property, and the subsequent habitability of the property (in particular, through landlord-tenant law), has been commonly accepted. Recently, the issues surrounding the ability to purchase property have been extended to the context of neighborhoods and communities, and the following question has arisen: Do individuals have a right to a healthy neighborhood?

We first consider what responsibility the government has to provide basic resources for a community by examining the experience of *colonias* at the Texas–Mexico border. We next consider the environmental justice movement, which claims that individuals deserve neighborhoods that are free from unfairly distributed environmental risks, such as sitting toxic waste. Finally, we consider the impact of governmental regulation in shaping and shifting urban space. This section addresses two ways in which the government has attempted to reinvigorate potentially blighted urban areas—redevelopment and credit financing. These redevelopment efforts, for a variety of reasons, may be difficult to enact and may create significant costs for the impacted community.

Each of these concerns raise issues regarding what Judith E. Koons has called *locational justice,* that is, *justice* "grounded in land, home, and community, with regional connections and local participation in government." *See* Judith E. Koons, *Locational Justice: Race, Class, and The Grassroots Protest of Property Takings,* 46 Santa Clara L. Rev. 811 (2005).

5.2.1 A Basic Right to Community: The Colonias *Experience in Texas*

Along the international border between the United States and Mexico, one can find communities consisting of ramshackle homes, dirt roads, and makeshift water systems. These communities, known as *colonias,* are most prevalent along the Texas–Mexico border and are home to an estimated 400,000 Texans. Federal Reserve Bank of Dallas, Texas Colonias: A Thumbnail Sketch of the Conditions, Issues, Challenges and Opportunities 1, *available at* http://www.dallasfed.org/ca/pubs/colonias.pdf (last visited September 10, 2010). *Colonias* are characterized by a lack of necessities like potable water, sewer systems, electricity, paved roads, and safe and sanitary housing. *Id.* at 3. These conditions are comparable to conditions found in underdeveloped countries. *Id.* at 7. Ninety-seven percent of *colonia* residents are Hispanic and eighty-five percent are United States citizens. U.S. Department of Housing and Urban Development, Facts About Farmworkers and Colonias, *available at* http://www.hud.gov/groups/farmwkercolonia.cfm (last visited June 29, 2009).

Traditionally, most *colonia* residents have acquired their property through a contract for deed. *Id.* at 7. This financing method is common among residents because they often do not have the credit history or proper resources to qualify for traditional financing from a bank or credit institution. *Id.* Contracts for deed are reminiscent of rent-to-own programs. The purchaser pays the seller in installments, which often have very high interest rates, and the seller retains the title to the land until the purchaser pays the entire purchase price. *Id.*

The Texas legislature has passed various measures designed to improve the infrastructure and quality of life in *colonias*. The following case addresses problems that may arise when a purchaser obtains property through a contract for deed.

Arturo de la Cruz v. Columbus P. Brown a/k/a C.P. Brown

109 S.W.3d 73 (Tex. App. 2003)

Opinion

In this case of first impression, we consider whether statutory protections afforded to the residents of *colonias* may give rise to a private cause of action for monetary damages. Because we conclude that the Legislature intended to create a private cause of action, we reverse and remand.

Fact Summary

On December 3, 1984, Arturo de la Cruz purchased from Columbus P. Brown by executory contract a parcel of land described as Lot 3, Block 5, Roseville Subdivision, El Paso County, Texas, also known as 320 Bauman Road, El Paso County, Texas. De La Cruz made the final payment on June 9, 1997. In January 2001, he filed suit for damages arising from Brown's failure to transfer recorded legal title to the property in question. He argued that Section 5.102 of the Texas Property Code provided for the imposition of fines on the seller of real property if the seller failed to transfer recorded legal title within thirty days of receipt of the purchaser's final payment. Tex. Prop. Code Ann. §5.079 (Vernon's Supp. 2003).[1] Brown recorded the deed to the property on March 30, 2001, nearly four years after final payment was tendered.

De La Cruz filed a motion for summary judgment claiming that he had established as a matter of law his entitlement to the sum of $648,500 in penalties for a violation of Section 5.102. By amended motion, he adjusted the penalty to $664,500. In his first amended answer, Brown claimed that Section 5.102 did not provide a private cause of action and that the penalties sought to be imposed would amount to an excessive fine. He alternatively alleged the affirmative defenses of waiver, estoppel and laches, and contended that De La Cruz had failed to mitigate his damages, if any. [Both Brown and De La Cruz filed motions for summary judgment.] The trial court granted Brown's motion, denied De La Cruz's motion, and rendered a take-nothing judgment in favor of Brown.

1. [Eds. Act of June 17, 1995, 74th Leg., R.S., ch. 994, §3, *amended by* Act of June 13, 2001, 77th Leg., R.S., ch. 693, §1, eff. Sept. 1, 2001.]

This appeal follows. De La Cruz brings seven issues challenging the granting of Brown's motion for summary judgment and the denial of his own. The main issue before us—the interpretation and construction of Section 5.102 of the Texas Property Code—is one of first impression. . . .

The Statute at Issue

Section 5.102 provided:

> (a) The seller shall transfer recorded, legal title of the property covered by the executory contract to the purchaser not later than the 30th day after the date the seller receives the purchaser's final payment due under the contract.
>
> (b) A seller who violates Subsection (a) is subject to a penalty of:
>
> (1) $250 a day for each day the seller fails to transfer the title to the purchaser during the period that begins the 31st day and ends the 90th day after the date the seller receives the purchaser's final payment due under the contract; and
>
> (2) $500 a day for each day the seller fails to transfer title to the purchaser after the 90th day after the date the seller receives the purchaser's final payment due under the contract.
>
> (c) In this section, 'seller' includes a successor, assignee, personal representative, executor; [sic] or administrator of the seller.

Act of June 17, 1995, 74th Leg., R.S., ch. 994, §3 (amended 2001) (current version at Tex.Prop.Code Ann. §5.079 (Vernon Supp. 2003)).

Legislative History of the Statute

Section 5.102 of the Texas Property Code was introduced during the 74th Legislative Session as part of S.B. 336. Senate Committees on International Relations, Trade & Technology, Bill Analyses, Tex. S.B. 336, 74th Leg., R.S. (1995). S.B. 336 sought to establish notice and cure provisions required for a defaulting purchaser under a contract for deed and to establish requirements for and loans associated with a contract for deed transaction in certain counties. *Id.* S.B. 336 was signed in the Senate and House on May 27, 1995, and by the Governor on June 17, 1995. It became effective on September 1, 1995.

The bill was targeted to address subdivisions known as *colonias*, described as "substandard, generally impoverished, rural subdivisions that typically lack one or more of the basic amenities of water, wastewater service, paved streets, drainage or electric service." Senate Committees on International Relations, Trade & Technology, Bill Analyses, Tex. S.B. 336, 74th Leg., R.S. (1995). While *colonias* exist in the greatest concentration along the Texas-Mexico border, particularly in the lower Rio Grande Valley and El Paso County, there are similarly substandard subdivisions in virtually every area of Texas. *Id.*

Residents of *colonias* almost always acquire lots by means of an executory contract, generally known as a "contract for deed" or "contract for sale." *Id.* This type of conveyance is unlike a typical deed of trust transaction in several notable respects. First, the property being conveyed generally is land only, with no house, structure or improvements included. Second, under a contract for deed, legal title does not transfer until all payments are made, and the purchaser may not accrue any equity in a tract even though substantial payments have been tendered. Third, contracts for deed are not required to be recorded; and fourth, virtually none of the state and federal protections afforded conventional home buyers apply to a purchaser under a contract for deed. *Id.*

This paucity of remedies led to abusive practices by sellers in *colonias*. *Id.* For example, sellers have sold individual tracts to two or more buyers, sold lots without a written contract, and placed liens on lots subsequent to the sale without informing the purchaser. *Id.* Sellers have also misrepresented the availability of water, sewer service and other utilities, and purchasers are often not informed that the property lies in a flood plain or is otherwise unsuitable for habitation. *Id.*

The magnitude of problems stemming from the development of *colonias* and the role that contracts for deed play in allowing these problems to develop led some parties to call for an outright prohibition on these conveyances. *Id.* However, low income families needing housing currently have no other alternatives, as few, if any, banks or other conventional financial institutions are willing to lend, and few insurers will provide coverage for *colonias*. *Id.* . . .

While numerous changes were made to this chapter of the Texas Property Code, the amendments to Section 5.102, renumbered as Section 5.079, are the focus of the issue at bar. Section 5.079(b) provides that the seller who fails to transfer title upon receipt of the final payment is liable for reasonable attorney's fees and liquidated damages. Senate Comm. on Intergovernmental Relations, Bill Analyses, Tex. S.B. 198, 77th Leg., R.S. (2001). Thus, the "penalty" language of Section 5.102 was replaced with "liquidated damages" and provision was made for recovery of reasonable attorney's fees. This statutory change applies only to a violation occurring on or after September 1, 2001. *Id.* A violation pre-dating the effective date of the amendment is governed by the law in effect when the violation occurred, and the former law is continued in effect for that purpose. *Id.* Thus, for purposes of this appeal, we must look to Section 5.102(b).

Is There a Private Cause of Action?

. . . Brown was required to transfer to De La Cruz recorded legal title no later than July 9, 1997, the thirtieth day after Brown received the final payment.

The change in law made by Section 5.079(b) applies only to a violation that occurred on or after September 1, 2001; the language of Section 5.102(b) remains in effect for the case at bar. *Id.* Brown is subject to a penalty of $250 a day for each day he failed to transfer title during the period beginning July 10, 1997 and ending September 9, 1997; and $500 per day for each day after September 10, 1997 until March 30, 2001, when title was finally transferred. Brown contends that this statutory penalty applies to enforcement by the State of Texas through the Office of the Attorney General and does not give rise to a private cause of action. He relies on amended Section 5.079, which explicitly provides that the seller "is liable to the purchaser . . . for liquidated damages" in arguing that the Legislature obviously did not intend a private cause action to be available until after the 2001 amendments. Tex.Prop.Code Ann. §5.079. . . .

Section 5.102 does not contain any language from which it can be concluded that the Legislature intended the State to collect the penalty in a suit filed by the Attorney General. Significantly, there is no language specifically obligating or authorizing the Attorney General to enforce the penalty by a civil suit. By contrast, there are numerous statutes which not only provide for a civil penalty but further specify that the Attorney General is authorized to file suit to collect the penalty on behalf of the State. . . . In the absence of specific legislation, the Attorney General is not authorized to file suit to collect the penalty provided for by Section 5.102(a).

In reviewing the circumstances under which the original statute was enacted and legislative history, it is clear that the Legislature was addressing the problems an individual purchaser faced when entering into an executory contract to purchase land in a *colonia.* Senate Committees on International Relations, Trade & Technology, Bill Analyses, Tex. S.B. 336, 74th Leg., R.S. (1995). The bill's history noted that a purchaser had very few rights or remedies under a contract for deed, and that abusive practices by sellers of *colonia* lots were common. *Id.* With the 2001 amendments, the Legislature made the contract for deed protections applicable statewide. Senate Comm. on Intergovernmental Relations, Bill Analyses, Tex. S.B. 198, 77th Leg., R.S. (2001). These amendments buttress our conclusion that the purpose of this legislation was to provide a measure of protection and legal recourse to the purchasers who have been victimized in the past.

We have already determined that Section 5.102 did not authorize the Attorney General to file suit on behalf of the State to collect the penalty. If we accept Brown's argument that Section 5.102 did not provide a private cause of action to a purchaser, then the statute is rendered meaningless and unenforceable as no one would be authorized to file suit to collect the penalty. Such a construction is impermissible as the Legislature is never presumed to have done a useless thing. *Hunter v. Fort Worth Capital Corp.*, 620 S.W.2d 547, 551, 24 Tex. Sup. Ct. J. 500 (Tex. 1981); *Collins v. County of*

El Paso, 954 S.W.2d 137, 147 (Tex.App.–El Paso 1997, pet. denied). Further, in construing a statute, it is presumed that the entire statute is intended to be effective and a result feasible of execution is intended. Tex. Gov't Code Ann. §311.021. We therefore conclude that the Legislature intended that purchasers such as De La Cruz would have the ability to maintain a private cause of action to recover the civil penalty established by Section 5.102. Issues One through Seven are sustained.

Posture of Affirmative Defenses

... Because the trial court rendered a take-nothing judgment, it is apparent that the trial court addressed only the argument pertaining to the construction of Section 5.102 and did not address Brown's affirmative defenses raised in his response to the motion for summary judgment. Therefore, remand rather than rendition is the appropriate remedy. Having sustained Issues One through Seven, we reverse the judgment of the trial court and remand this cause for further proceedings consistent with this opinion.

NOTES AND QUESTIONS

1. On appeal, the Supreme Court of Texas reversed the Court of Appeals decision, concluding that Section 5.102 did not provide a private cause of action. The court determined that the statute expressly provided for a penalty but was silent about who may collect it. The court concluded that there was no private cause of action based on prior precedent that interpreted similar statutes, the subsequent 2001 amendments that created a private cause of action, and the ambiguity of legislative silence. In its decision, the court recognized that the statute in its present form, as amended in 2001 and renumbered Property Codes section 5.079, clearly provides a private cause of action for purchasers. *See Brown v. De La Cruz*, 156 S.W.3d 560 (Tex. 2004).

2. Compare Section 5.102, which was the applicable version in this case, to the current version of the Title Transfer statute, which reflects the 2001 amendments.

Tex. Prop. Code Ann. §5.079 (Vernon 2009)

§5.079. Title Transfer

(a) The seller shall transfer recorded, legal title of the property covered by the executor contract to the purchaser no later than the 30th day after the date the seller receives the purchaser's final payment due under the contract.

(b) A seller who violates Subsection (a) is liable to the purchaser for:
(1) liquidated damages in the amount of:
(A) $250 a day for each day the seller fails to transfer the title to the purchaser during the period that begins the 31st day and ends the 90th day after the date the seller receives the purchaser's final payment due under the contract; and
(B) $500 a day for each day the seller fails to transfer title to the purchaser after the 90th day after the date the seller receives the purchaser's final payment due under the contract; and
(2) reasonable attorney's fees.

3. Despite the poor condition of many *colonias*, these communities offer residents certain advantages. The system provides residents with a pathway to homeownership, which may otherwise be unavailable to low-income residents. M. Isable Medina, *At the Border: What Tres Mujeres Tells Us About Walls and Fences*, 10 J. Gender Race & Just. 245, 252 (2007). Additionally, the lack of zoning regulations in some *colonias* allows residents to build their homes as they are able without having to worry about building restrictions, building with nonstandard materials, or conventional use restrictions. Medina, *supra* note 35.

4. For additional information on *colonias* see, for example, Federal Reserve Bank of Dallas, Texas Colonias: A Thumbnail Sketch of the Conditions, Issues, Challenges and Opportunities 1, *available at* http://www.dallasfed.org/ca/pubs/colonias.pdf; Texas Secretary of State Hope Andrade, About the Colonias Program, *available at* http://www.sos.state.tx.us/border/colonias/index.shtml (last visited June 29, 2009); Jane E. Larson, *Informality, Illegality, and Inequality*, 20 Yale L. & Pol'y Rev. 137 (2002).

5. The *colonias* experience raises issues in relationship to the question of the impact of the failure to deliver basic municipal services to communities. Michelle Wilde Anderson has argued that *colonias* share similar experiences with rural, low-income communities that border municipalities. Michelle Wilde Anderson, *Cities Inside Out: Race, Poverty and Exclusion at the Urban Fringe*, 55 UCLA L. Rev. 1095 (2008). She notes that:

> Linking colonias and black rural poverty through the broader concept of unincorporated urban areas reveals widespread common ground among all three patterns from the vantage point of local government and land-use law. Such communities tend to originate as highly unregulated subdivisions on unincorporated land, and they lack adequate public investment in the physical state of the neighborhood. They have experienced segregation and racial discrimination, tenacious poverty, a scarcity of housing alternatives, and in many cases, vulnerable or damaged land. The predominance of self-built housing, with improvised materials and construction methods, has resulted in poor and uneven building standards. As a consequence of these characteristics, such communities' unusually high rates of homeownership do not create the same prospects for financial stability and upward mobility as homeownership in other contexts.

Id. at 1195.

5.2.2 Environmental Justice: A Right to a Healthy Community?

> You know, when I was a little boy we used to catch tadpoles in the ditches and save them and trade them. Yeah, we did all that. But young people, do not go in the ditches out there. Ditches here are highly polluted. Contaminants can get into your feet. Understand you got to take care of you. We need y'all healthy.

Arthur Smith, *Speech in* Melissa Checker, Polluted Promises: Environmental Racism and the Search for Justice in a Southern Town 2 (2005).

South Camden Citizens in Action v. New Jersey Department of Environmental Protection

254 F.Supp.2d 486 (D.C.N.J. 2003)

Approximately two years ago, South Camden Citizens in Action, and the individual Plaintiffs who reside in a South Camden, New Jersey neighborhood, known as "Waterfront South," asked this Court to issue a preliminary injunction enjoining the construction and operation of a proposed cement grinding facility, which they claimed would have a disparate impact on the residents of their community in violation of Title VI of the Civil Rights Act of 1964, 42 U.S.C. §2000d-1. Since then, the boundaries of Title VI jurisprudence have been narrowed well beyond what was initially thought to be appropriate by this Court. As observed by Edmund, the protagonist in Shakespeare's *King Lear* who met an untimely demise, "The wheel is come full circle." With this lawsuit now before this Court for the second time, I must consider the Defendants' motions to dismiss Plaintiffs' remaining claims pursuant to Fed.R.Civ.P. 12(b)(6). Plaintiffs' remaining claims are: (1) intentional discrimination in violation of both §601 of Title VI of the Civil Rights Act of 1964, 42 U.S.C. §2000d, and 42 U.S.C. §1983 and the Fourteenth Amendment (First and Third Counts, Second Amended Complaint); (2) discriminatory impact on the basis of race, color, and national origin in violation of the Fair Housing Act, Title VIII of the Civil Rights Act of 1968, 42 U.S.C. §§3601 *et seq.* (Fourth Count, Second Amended Complaint); (3) Private Nuisance and Public Nuisance against the Defendant-Intervenor, St. Lawrence Cement Co., LLC only (Fifth and Sixth Counts, respectively, Second Amended Complaint)....

II. Legal Standard Governing Motions to Dismiss Pursuant to Fed. R. Civ. P. 12(b)(6)

Under Federal Rule of Civil Procedure 12(b)(6), a defendant may move to dismiss a complaint for "failure to state a claim upon which relief can be granted." Fed.R.Civ.P. 12(b)(6). A complaint should not be dismissed for failure to state a claim "unless it appears beyond doubt that the plaintiff can prove no set of facts in support of his claim which would entitle him to relief." . . .

IV. Discussion

A. *Intentional discrimination under §601 of title VI and the equal protection clause*

The SCCIA Plaintiffs first allege that the NJDEP Defendants, "who are the recipients of federal financial assistance and subject to the requirements of Title VI, intentionally discriminated against the plaintiffs and other African-American and Hispanic residents of Waterfront [South] and the adjoining communities on the basis of race, color, and national origin" in violation of §601 of Title VI. Second Amended Compl. ¶ 101. FN4 Section 601 of Title VI provides:

> No person in the United States shall, on the ground of race, color, or national origin, be excluded from participation in, be denied the benefits of, or be subjected to discrimination under any program or activity receiving Federal financial assistance.

42 U.S.C. §2000d. In addition, the SCCIA Plaintiffs allege that by intentionally discriminating against them on the basis of race, color, and national origin, the NJDEP Defendants violated the Equal Protection Clause of the Fourteenth Amendment and §1983. Compl. ¶¶ 109-13.

Section 1983 provides, in relevant part:

> Every person who, under color of any statute, ordinance, regulation, custom, or usage, of any State . . . subjects, or causes to be subjected, any citizen of the United States or other person within the jurisdiction thereof to the deprivation of any rights, privileges, or immunities secured by the Constitution and laws, shall be liable to the party injured in an action at law, suit in equity, or other proper proceeding for redress. . . .

42 U.S.C. §1983.

The Supreme Court has made it clear that "the reach of Title VI's protection extends no further than the Fourteenth Amendment." *United States v. Fordice,* 505 U.S. 717, 732 n. 7, 112 S.Ct. 2727, 120 L.Ed.2d 575 (1992) (citing *Regents of Univ. of Cal. v. Bakke,* 438 U.S. 265, 287, 98 S.Ct. 2733, 57 L.Ed.2d 750 (1978)). In order to state a claim upon which relief can be granted under either §601 of Title VI or the Equal Protection Clause of the Fourteenth Amendment and §1983, a party must allege that he or she was the target of purposeful, invidious discrimination. . . . In order to conclude that the SCCIA Plaintiffs have failed to state a claim of intentional discrimination, I must find "beyond a doubt" that no set of facts alleged in the Second Amended Complaint would entitle them to relief. *Pryor,* 288 F.3d at 564.

A plaintiff who seeks recovery under a theory of purposeful discrimination must demonstrate that governmental authority implemented the facially neutral policy at issue "'because of,' not merely 'in spite of,' its adverse effects upon an identifiable group." *Id.* at 562 (quoting *Feeney,* 442 U.S. at 279, 99 S.Ct. 2282). *See also Stehney v. Perry,* 101 F.3d 925, 937-38 (3d Cir.1996) (upholding lower court's dismissal pursuant to Rule 12(b)(6) because plaintiff had merely alleged that a facially neutral policy had a discriminatory effect).

Determining whether invidious discrimination was a motivating factor demands a sensitive inquiry into such circumstantial and direct evidence of intent as may be available. The impact of the official action whether "it bears more heavily on one race than another," *Washington v. Davis, supra,* 426 U.S. at 242, 96 S.Ct. at 2049 may provide an important starting point. Sometimes a clear pattern, unexplainable on other grounds than race, emerges from the effect of the state action even when the governing legislation appears neutral on its face. *Arlington Heights,* 429 U.S. at 266, 97 S.Ct. 555. The Supreme Court, however, has recognized that "disproportionate impact is not the sole touchstone of invidious racial discrimination," *id.* at 265, 97 S.Ct. 555, but rather, "is often probative of why the action was taken in the first place since people usually intend the natural consequences of their actions." *Pryor,* 288 F.3d at 563 (quoting *Reno v. Bossier Parish Sch. Bd.,* 520 U.S. 471, 117 S.Ct. 1491, 137 L.Ed.2d 730 (1997)).

In addition to disproportionate impact, the other factors indicative of a discriminatory animus include: (1) the "historical background of the decision," *Arlington Heights,* 429 U.S. at 267, 97 S.Ct. 555 (observing that the historical background of a state action is an "evidentiary source, particularly if it reveals a series of official action taken for invidious purposes"); (2) any "departures from the normal procedural sequence also might afford evidence that improper purposes are playing a role," *id.*; (3) any "[s]ubstantive departures . . . particularly if the factors usually considered important by the decisionmaker strongly favor a decision contrary to the one reached," *id.*; and (4) the foreseeability of the consequences of the state action, *see Columbus Bd. of Educ. v. Penick,* 443 U.S. 449, 465, 99 S.Ct. 2941, 61 L.Ed.2d 666 (1979) ("[A]ctions having foreseeable and anticipated disparate impact are relevant evidence to prove the ultimate fact, forbidden purpose."). *See also Baker v. City of Kissimmee,* 645 F.Supp. 571, 585 (M.D.Fl.1986) ("These factors, probative of discriminatory intent include: (1) the nature and magnitude of the disparity itself . . . ; (2) foreseeability of the consequences of the [state] actions; (3) legislative and administrative history of the decision-making process; and (4) knowledge, in that a defendant's actions would be known to have caused [a] discriminatory impact. . . .") (citing *Ammons v. Dade City,* 783 F.2d 982, 987-88 (11th Cir.1986), and *Dowdell v. City of Apopka,* 698 F.2d 1181, 1186 (11th Cir.1983)).

Once a plaintiff has established that the state actor harbored a discriminatory intent, the burden shifts to the state actor to show that the same decision would have resulted in the absence of a discriminatory animus. *See id.* at 271 n. 21, 97 S.Ct. 555. Proof that the decision by the Village was motivated in part by a racially discriminatory purpose would not necessarily have required invalidation of the challenged decision. Such proof would, however, have shifted to the Village the burden of establishing the same decision would have resulted even had the impermissible purpose not been considered. If this were established, the complaining party in a case of this kind could no longer attribute the injury complained of to improper consideration of a discriminatory purpose. In such circumstances, there would be no justification for judicial interference with the challenged decision. *Id.*

In their motion to dismiss, the NJDEP Defendants contend that the SCCIA Plaintiffs have failed to state a claim of intentional discrimination upon which relief can be granted under the applicable statutory and constitutional provisions. Specifically, the NJDEP Defendants argue that the SCCIA Plaintiffs' allegations are legally deficient because they have merely alleged that Defendants knew or were deliberately indifferent to the disparate impact the siting of the cement grinding facility would have on the residents of Waterfront South. *See* Defs. NJDEP and Bradley M. Campbell's Br. in Support of Motion to Dismiss under Fed.R.Civ.P. 12(b)(6) at 11 ("NJDEP Br."). According to the NJDEP Defendants, "these allegations [do not] meet the legal test for a private cause of action under Title VI because they do not contend that the New Jersey Defendants issued the permits for St. Lawrence *because* the area's residents are Black or Hispanic." *Id.* at 12 (emphasis in original). The NJDEP Defendants further argue that "an intentionally discriminatory motive [cannot] be reasonably inferred from the complaint because it is incontrovertible that the air pollution criteria that were applied in South Camden to St. Lawrence are uniformly applicable throughout New Jersey and even nationally." *Id.* at 12-13.

In response, the SCCIA Plaintiffs contend that not only are allegations of disparate impact "highly relevant and probative of discriminatory motive," but also that they have alleged "numerous other circumstances which support a finding of intent, including DEP's historical practices and the specific sequence of events leading to the issuance of the permit," as well as NJDEP's "knowledge of the discriminatory impact of its actions. . . ." Pls.' Br. in Opposition to Defs.' Motion to Dismiss at 4-5 ("SCCIA Br."). Moreover, the SCCIA Plaintiffs contend that the NJDEP's justification for issuing the permits, namely that it acted within the parameters of federal environmental laws and did not violate the National Ambient Air Quality Standards ("NAAQS"), goes to the merits of the case, and has no bearing upon whether the SCCIA Plaintiffs have stated a claim upon which relief can be granted pursuant to Fed.R.Civ.P. 12(b)(6).

I agree with the SCCIA Plaintiffs that the Second Amended Complaint contains allegations sufficient to state a cause of action of intentional discrimination under both §601 of Title VI and the Fourteenth Amendment.

In support of their claim that the NJDEP Defendants purposefully and invidiously discriminated against them on the basis of their race, color, and national origin, the SCCIA Plaintiffs allege facts which, if proven true, would show not only that the operation of the cement grinding facility would have a disparate impact upon the predominantly minority community of Waterfront South, but also that the NJDEP was well-aware of the potential disproportionate and discriminatory burden placed upon that community and failed to take measures to assuage that burden. . . .

B. Unlawful discrimination under the fair housing act

The SCCIA Plaintiffs' allegation that the NJDEP Defendants violated the Fair Housing Act presents a more difficult issue. Specifically, the SCCIA Plaintiffs contend that: "By granting the permits to SLC, DEP has caused a diminution in both the quantity and quality of the available housing stock in the Waterfront South neighborhood, which has a discriminatory impact on the Waterfront South residents on the basis of race, color, and national origin in violation of Title VIII [of the Civil Rights Act of 1968, 42 U.S.C. §3604(a)]." Second Amended Compl. ¶ 117. Whether the SCCIA Plaintiffs have stated a claim upon which relief can be granted under the Fair Housing Act is contingent upon one issue: Does the NJDEP provide a service to the residents of Waterfront South in a manner contemplated by the Fair Housing Act? While the question is not free from doubt, I ultimately conclude that the NJDEP does not provide such a service.

The Fair Housing Act, Title VIII of the Civil Rights Act of 1968, 42 U.S.C. §§3601 *et seq.*, prohibits "both direct discrimination and practices with significant discriminatory effects" on the availability of housing. *See Southend Neighborhood Improvement Ass'n v. County of St. Clair,* 743 F.2d 1207, 1209 (7th Cir.1984). The relevant provisions of Title VIII make it unlawful:

> (a) To refuse to sell or rent after the making of a bona fide offer, or to refuse to negotiate for the sale or rental of, or otherwise make unavailable or deny, a dwelling to any person because of race, color, religion, sex, familial status, or national origin.
>
> (b) To discriminate against any person in the terms, conditions, or privileges of sale or rental of a dwelling, or in the provision of services or facilities in connection therewith, because of race, color, religion, sex, familial status, or national origin.

42 U.S.C. §3604(a)-(b). . . .

1. Have the SCCIA Plaintiffs Stated a Claim under §3604(a) of the Fair Housing Act?

That being said, however, it is not true that the tentacles of Title VIII extend beyond the availability of housing or related services. The NJDEP Defendants contend that they have taken no action to deny the residents of Waterfront South the sale or rental of residential property or to evict them from their homes. In response, the SCCIA Plaintiffs maintain in their moving papers that their situation is analogous to a "constructive eviction." SCCIA Br. at 22. According to the SCCIA Plaintiffs, the permitting of the cement grinding facility by the NJDEP is an act which rendered the Waterfront South neighborhood uninhabitable.

The SCCIA Plaintiffs' arguments, although creative, are unavailing. First, the SCCIA Plaintiffs have not alleged facts in their Second Amended Complaint that, if true, would state a claim of "constructive eviction." The SCCIA Plaintiffs have failed to allege the most obvious element of "constructive eviction" — that residents vacated the Waterfront South community. *See Reste Realty Corp. v. Cooper,* 53 N.J. 444, 461, 251 A.2d 268, 277 (1969) ("The general rule is, of course, that a tenant's right to claim a constructive eviction will be lost if he does not vacate the premises within a reasonable time after the right comes into existence.").

I conclude that in granting SLC permits to operate a cement grinding facility, the NJDEP's actions at most had an indirect effect on the availability of housing in the Waterfront South community. A survey of the case law in this area reveals that, in order to have a cognizable claim under §3604(a), plaintiffs must establish a far closer nexus between housing availability and the challenged action. . . .

2. *Have the SCCIA Plaintiffs Stated a Claim Under §3604(b) of the Fair Housing Act?*

More interestingly, the SCCIA Plaintiffs claim that the NJDEP was providing a service to the residents of Waterfront South, which in turn would bring the NJDEP under the umbrella of §3604(b) of Title VIII. Specifically, they maintain that because the NJDEP "is responsible for the promotion of environmental protection and the prevention of pollution of the environment of the State . . . [and] oversees sanitary engineering and sewerage systems in New Jersey," it "qualifies as a 'governmental unit' which provides services [directly related to housing] much like garbage collection." SCCIA Br. at 19-20. The SCCIA Plaintiffs analogize the circumstances in this case to those presented in *Campbell v. City of Berwyn,* 815 F.Supp. 1138, 1144 (N.D.Ill.1993), where the district court held that citizens who alleged that the city's termination of police protection interfered with their right to fair housing sufficiently stated a claim under §3604(b). The *Campbell* court further observed that §3604(b) "applies to services generally provided by governmental units such as police and fire protection or garbage collection." *Id.* at 1143-44 (quoting *Southend Neighborhood Improvement Ass'n,* 743 F.2d at 1210).

The NJDEP Defendants contend, on the other hand, that the NJDEP does not provide the type of services contemplated by §3604(b), and, therefore, the SCCIA Plaintiffs have failed to state a cognizable claim under that provision of Title VIII. The NJDEP Defendants maintain that significant parallels exist between the SCCIA Plaintiffs' claim and the claims presented in both *Jersey Heights,* 174 F.3d at 193, and *Laramore,* 722 F.Supp. at 452-53. The NJDEP Defendants point out that both courts, in considering whether Title VIII was applicable to either the siting of a state highway or a sports stadium, held that Title VIII does not extend to every service which may have an effect on residents of a neighborhood. *Jersey Heights,* 174 F.3d at 192-93; *Laramore,* 722 F.Supp. at 452. Similar to their argument that the SCCIA Plaintiffs failed to state a claim under §3604(a), the NJDEP Defendants contend that the granting of industrial air pollution permits is simply too far removed to fall within the scope of the remedial objectives of §3604(b).

I conclude that the NJDEP Defendants have the better argument. If I were to accept the SCCIA Plaintiffs' argument that §3604(b) extends to the decision of every governmental agency that may have an indirect impact on housing, Title VIII would be a civil rights statute of general applicability rather than one dealing with the specific problems of fair housing." *Jersey Heights,* 174 F.3d at 193. Although the NJDEP clearly provides a number of valuable services to the citizens of the State of New Jersey by enacting regulations and overseeing their implementation, it does not follow that it provides specific residential services. The NJDEP is not responsible for door-to-door ministrations such as those provided by police departments, fire departments, or other municipal units. The SCCIA Plaintiffs, therefore, have failed to state a cognizable claim under §3604(b) . . .

C. Nuisance

Finally, the SCCIA Plaintiffs allege that SLC, "through the operation of its [cement grinding] facility, and through the associated use of diesel trucks," has created both a public and private nuisance in the Waterfront South neighborhood. Second Amended Compl. ¶¶ 120-34. SLC moves to dismiss the nuisance claims on the basis that, because the SCCIA Plaintiffs have failed to allege that the construction of the cement grinding facility was in violation of regulations promulgated under the Clean Air Act, 42 U.S.C. §7409(1) ("CAA"), and permits issued by the NJDEP, they have failed to state a valid claim of either private or public nuisance.

1. Have the SCCIA Plaintiffs Stated a Claim of Private Nuisance?

In the Second Amended Complaint, the SCCIA Plaintiffs allege sufficient facts that, if true, could lead a factfinder to conclude that the operation of the cement grinding facility causes substantial harm to the residents of the Waterfront South community. More specifically, the SCCIA Plaintiffs maintain that emissions from the cement grinding facility have increased the level of pollution in the air to the point that their health and safety, as well as that of their children and families, is significantly endangered. In addition, the SCCIA Plaintiffs allege that the annual ingress and egress of nearly 80,000 delivery trucks, in addition to threatening the health of those residing in the Waterfront South neighborhood, will also create noise, vibrations, and dust which will "affect the quality of life, interfere with sleep, cause property damage, and lower the self-esteem of plaintiffs. . . ." *Id.* ¶¶ 51-57. New Jersey courts have recognized the existence of a private nuisance when similar factors have been present. For these reasons, I conclude that the SCCIA Plaintiffs have stated a claim of private nuisance upon which relief can be granted. Accordingly, I shall deny SLC's motion to dismiss the Fifth Count of the Second Amended Complaint which alleges a claim of private nuisance.

2. *Have the SCCIA Plaintiffs Stated a Claim of Public Nuisance?*

Not only can the argument be made that the emission of pollutants is fully regulated under both federal and state laws and the implementing regulations promulgated thereunder, *see* 42 U.S.C. §§7401 *et seq.* (Clean Air Act); N.J.S.A. §§26:2C-1 *et seq.*, but also, in this case, the activities in which SLC engaged were affirmatively sanctioned by the NJDEP by way of air permits. Because the SCCIA Plaintiffs have not alleged that SLC's activities were not fully regulated, I conclude that the SCCIA Plaintiffs cannot state a claim of public nuisance. Accordingly, I shall grant SLC's motion to dismiss the Sixth Count of the Second Amended Complaint which alleges a claim of public nuisance. . . .

NOTES AND QUESTIONS

1. Three key terms have been used when analyzing environmental risks faced by low-income and minority communities: (1) **environmental racism**, which broadly refers to any policy, practice, or directive that disproportionately affects the environment of individuals, groups, or communities based on race; (2) **environmental equity**, which argues that environmental risks should be not disproportionately allocated among specific segments of the population (which can include a focus on racial groups, but does not refer to them exclusively); and (3) **environmental justice**, which encompasses both of these concerns. James P. Lester, David W. Allen & Kevin Hill, Environmental Justice in the United States: Myth and Realities 21-22 (2001).

2. No freestanding law of "environmental justice" exists. Litigants have used a range of different strategies within the environmental justice context. Typically, the litigant can raise either a civil rights claim or an environmental rights claim. Litigants have raised environmental justice claims within a civil rights context on four bases: (1) an equal protection claim under the Fourteenth Amendment in which the claimant alleges that the government actor has acted in a purposefully discriminatory manner in assessing a particular environmental risk; (2) a claim under Section 601 and Section 602 of Title VI of the Civil Rights Act of

1964 that a state or local government actor, which has received federal financial assistance, has acted in a discriminatory fashion; (3) a claim under the FHA under Section 3604 that the disputed practice prevents the claimant from obtaining housing; and (4) a claim under Section 1982 of the Civil Rights Act of 1866 that suggests a member of a racial or ethnic minority has been intentionally discriminated against in his or her ability to assert a property right. Stringent requirements of intentionality have made it difficult for litigants to raise civil rights claims within the environmental justice context. For further review of these types of claims, see THE LAW OF ENVIRONMENTAL JUSTICE: THEORIES AND PROCEDURES TO ADDRESS DISPROPORTIONATE RISKS (Micheal B. Gerrad & Sheila R. Foster eds., 1999).

3. Litigants have increasingly brought claims based on common-law and statutory violations. Two categories of environmental statutes have supported environmental justice claims. First, litigants may claim that the government actor failed to properly conduct the decision-making process under the National Environmental Policy Act, its state equivalent, or other provisions of environmental statutes. *See, e.g., El Pueblo Para El Aire y Agua Limpio v. County of Kings,* 22 ELR 20357 (Cal. 1991) (final environmental impact report that resulted in a conditional use permit was inadequate under the California Environmental Quality Act because of failure to provide materials in Spanish to the impacted community). Second, litigants, like those in *South Camden,* may raise a common-law claim under private or public nuisance. For further review of these types of claims, see Rachel D. Godsil, *Viewing The Cathedral From Behind the Color Line: Property Rules, Liability Rules, and Environmental Racism,* 53 EMORY L. J. 1807 (2004) (analyzing common law nuisance remedies within the environmental justice context); Carlos A. Ball, *The Curious Intersection of Nuisance and Takings Law,* 86 B.U. L. REV. 819 (2006) (reviewing the use of nuisance and takings law within an environmental justice context); Sheila R. Foster, *Justice From the Ground Up: Distributive Inequities, Grassroots Resistance, and The Transformative Politics of the Environmental Justice Movement,* 86 CAL. L. REV. 775 (1998) (reviewing the shift from a civil rights paradigm to a process-oriented environmental rights paradigm).

4. Why did the Court reject a broad interpretation of Section 3604(a), as seen in *Whisby,* in the environmental justice context? Do you think that the goals of FHA would support a different interpretation?

5. Why did the court reject the plaintiffs' claim of public nuisance? Why did the court uphold the claim of private nuisance?

6. Yale Rabin has described the process of locating undesirable uses in low-income and minority neighborhoods as "expulsive zoning." Expulsive zoning, argues Rabin, is the process of permitting and promoting the intrusion into low income and minority neighborhoods of "disruptive incompatible uses that have diminished the quality and undermined the

stability of those neighbourhoods." Yale Rabin, *Expulsive Zoning: The Inequitable Legacy of Euclid, in* ZONING AND THE AMERICAN DREAM 101 (Charles M. Haar & Jerold S. Kayden eds., 1989). Expulsive zoning practices can include: (1) approval of uses, such as manufacturing and retail, that result in significant household displacement for particular minority groups; (2) zoning ordinances that locate predominantly industrial or high-density uses in low-income and minority neighborhoods, while maintaining residential uses in majority neighborhoods; (3) use of historic designation districts that fail to take into account long-term use by African-Americans; and (4) failure to provide equal access to municipal services such as water, sewer, or paved streets. Rabin, *supra,* at 107-18. To what extent do you think the claims of environmental justice are a response to practices that constitute expulsive zoning? Are these claims better addressed by relevant property theories?

5.2.3 Drawing Lines: Real Estate Transactions and Neighborhoods

The recent housing crisis has demonstrated the complex relationship between real estate financing for individual purchase of a home and its broader impact on neighborhoods, in particular within communities of color in the United States. A study published in 2008 by the California Reinvestment Corporation, Community Reinvestment Association of North Carolina, Empire Justice Center, Massachusetts Affordable Housing Alliance, Ohio Fair Lending Coalition, Neighborhood Economic Development Advocacy, and the Woodstock Institute, concluded that

> Defaults and foreclosures also directly and indirectly impact neighborhoods and cities that see mounting vacant and abandoned properties, decreased property values, and losses to their tax bases and local economies. One foreclosed home can lower the property values of all neighboring homes, decreasing local property values by thousands of dollars. Decreased property values mean that neighboring homeowners may be less able to refinance their own loans or sell their homes, putting them at greater risk of foreclosure and potentially creating a vicious and repeating cycle of neighborhood decline.

PAYING MORE FOR THE AMERICAN DREAM: THE SUBPRIME SHAKE-OUT AND ITS IMPACT ON LOWER-INCOME AND MINORITY COMMUNITIES 6 (2008).

A number of discriminatory practices have impacted neighborhoods of communities of color, including the following:

- **Redlining** is the practice by which a bank draws a red line around a neighborhood on a map and refuses to lend there because of perceived credit risks associated with the neighborhood. Richard

D. Marico, DEMOCRATIZING CAPITAL: THE HISTORY, LAW, AND REFORM OF THE COMMUNITY REINVESTMENT ACT 12 (Carolina Academic Press 2005). As Carol N. Brown has stated, the practice of redlining has "reduced the supply of financing in targeted neighborhoods and therefore demand for these homes, resulting in a slower rate of home appreciation compared to non-targeted neighborhoods." Carole N. Brown, *Intent and Empirics: Race to the Sub-Prime,* 93 MAR. L. REV. 93, 12 (2010).

- **Reverse redlining** is "the practice of denying the extension of credit to specific geographic areas due to the income, race or ethnicity of its resident." *United Cos. Corp. v. Sergeant,* 20 F. Supp. 2d 192 (D. Mass. 1998).
- **Predatory lending,** which does not have a commonly defined definition, but, as Deborah Goldstein notes, what a number of these definitions, share is a focus on "a set of a loan terms and practices that fall between appropriate risk-based pricing by subprime lending and blatant fraud." Deborah Goldstein, UNDERSTANDING PREDATORY LENDING: MOVING TOWARDS A COMMON DEFINITION AND WORKABLE SOLUTIONS (2008).

These discriminatory practices are long-standing. For instance, in 1939, the Federal Housing Administration initiated the practice of redlining to retain property values in certain districts. Kenneth T. Jackson, CRABGRASS FRONTIER: THE SUBURBANIZATION OF THE UNITED STATES 207 (Oxford University Press 1985). "It feared that an entire area could lose its investment value if rigid white-black separation was not maintained." *Id.* at 208. Even when the Federal Housing Administration shifted its policies to help make mortgage insurance available to inner-city neighborhoods, it simply enabled white families to finance their escape from the area. *Id.* at 215.

A number of "fair lending" statutes have sought to address these practices. These statutes fall into roughly two types of categories. The first set of statutes seeks to prohibit intentional discrimination within real estate transactions and provide transparent mechanisms to monitor the transactional market.

Initially, the FHA itself contains Section 3605, which forbids intentional discrimination in real-estate transactions.

Fair Housing Act

42 U.S.C. §3605 (2006)

In general

It shall be unlawful for any person or other entity whose business includes engaging in residential real estate-related transactions to discriminate against any person in making available such a transaction, or in the terms or conditions of such a transaction, because of race, color, religion, sex, handicap, familial status, or national origin.

(b) "Residential real estate-related transaction" defined

As used in this section, the term "residential real estate-related transaction" means any of the following:

(1) The making or purchasing of loans or providing other financial assistance—

(A) for purchasing, constructing, improving, repairing, or maintaining a dwelling; or

(B) secured by residential real estate.

(2) The selling, brokering, or appraising of residential real property.

Section 3605 has been used to address any intentional discrimination that impacts housing availability for those protected categories under the FHA. For instance, in *Honorable v. Easy Life Real Estate Sys.*, 100 F. Supp. 2d 885 (N.D. Ill. 2000), Judge Elaine Bucko denied the defendants' motion for summary judgment, where the plaintiffs had made a claim that the defendants, by utilizing deceptive sales and lending practices, had intentionally discriminated under the FHA. She concluded that the defendants' motion for summary judgment must be denied because:

> It does not address the plaintiffs' intentional discrimination claims about "reverse redlining." Redlining is the practice of denying the extension of credit to specific geographic areas due to the income, race, or ethnicity of its residents. Reverse redlining is the practice of extending credit on unfair terms to those same communities. See Strep. No. 103-169, at 21 (1993), *reprinted in* 1994 U.S.C.C.A.N. 1881, 1905; *see also Reverse Redlining: Problems in Home Equity Lending,* before the Senate Committee on Banking, Housing, and Urban Affairs, 103rd Cong. 243-471 (1993).
>
> The term was derived from the actual practice of drawing a red line around certain areas in which credit would be denied. *United Companies Lending Corp. v. Sergeant, 20 F. Supp. 2d 192, 203 n.5 (D. Mass. 1998).*
>
> These sort of practices come within the ambit of the Fair Housing Act; *see NAACP v. American Family Mutt. Ins. Co., 978 F.2d 287, 301 (7th Cir. 1992)* (discriminatory denials of insurance and discriminatory pricing), which is to be read broadly. Courts have construed the statute to cover "mortgage 'redlining,' insurance redlining, racial steering, exclusionary zoning decisions, and other actions by individuals or governmental units which directly affect the availability of housing to minorities." *Southend Assoc., 743 F.2d at 1209-10* & n.3 (citing cases). The law is "violated by discriminatory actions, or certain actions with discriminatory effects, that affect the availability of housing." *Id. at 1210.* If so, the law would also prohibit reverse redlining. Although *sections 1981*

> and *1982* are narrower, *id.*, they may be construed to prohibit some or all of the practices of which the plaintiffs produce evidence here; the defendants have at least waived the right to argue the contrary here by failing to do it.

Id. at 892.

Recent court cases have used the intentional discrimination standard of Section 3605 in an innovative manner to address the potential excesses of the subprime mortgage crisis.

McGlawn v. Pennsylvania Human Relations Committee

891 A.2d 757 (2006)

This case involves an issue of first impression: whether the Pennsylvania Human Relations Act (Act) extends to a mortgage broker's predatory lending activities known as "reverse redlining." We affirm the Commission's holding that the Act prohibits reverse redlining. However, we vacate part of the Commission's award of actual damages and remand for further proceedings. . . .

I. Background

Broker, a corporation which brokers mortgage loans, refinancing and insurance for its customers, was founded in 1985 by its chief officers, Reginald McGlawn, and his brother, Anthony McGlawn. Reginald McGlawn is Broker's mortgage loan specialist, and Anthony McGlawn is Broker's insurance specialist. Broker also employs other McGlawn family members.

Broker specializes in arranging sub-prime mortgage loans for its customers. The prime lending market provides credit to those considered good credit risks. The sub-prime lending market provides credit to people the financial industry considers enhanced credit risks. These people generally have a flawed credit history or a debt-to-income ratio outside the range the financial industry considers acceptable for prime credit. As discussed hereafter, sub-prime interest rates are usually two to three percentage points higher than prime rates.

In 1998-2000, Broker arranged sub-prime mortgage loans for Complainants, who own real property in Philadelphia County. Broker is an African American-owned company. Complainants are African Americans who reside in predominantly African American neighborhoods.

In April 2001, Complainant Lucrecia Taylor (Taylor) filed a verified complaint with the Commission alleging Broker unlawfully discriminated against her in the terms and conditions of a real estate-related transaction and loan of money because of her race and the racial composition of her neighborhood, African American. Specifically, Taylor alleged Broker targeted her, as an African American, for a mortgage loan transaction containing predatory and unfair terms in violation of the Act's loan and real estate transaction provisions. . . .

[**Editor's Note**: Other complainants were added to Ms. Taylor's initial complaint. We have not excerpted that material here.]

B.

In its decision, the Commission found Broker engaged in predatory brokering activities regarding all Complainants. Those actions resulted in unfair and predatory mortgage loans. It also found Broker engaged in an aggressive marketing plan targeting African Americans and African American neighborhoods in the Philadelphia area. Nearly all of Complainants contacted Broker in response to radio, television and newspaper advertisements.

Broker's predatory practices, the Commission noted, included arranging loans containing onerous terms such as high interest rates, pre-payment penalties, balloon payments and mandatory arbitration clauses. In addition, Broker charged Complainants high broker fees, undisclosed fees, yield spread premiums and various other additional closing costs. Broker's predatory practices also included falsification of information on loan documents, failure to disclose information regarding terms of the loan, and high pressure sales tactics.

Because there are no state appellate court decisions addressing the issue of whether reverse redlining and/or predatory lending constitutes prohibited housing discrimination under the Act, the Commission relied on several federal court decisions. Those decisions hold reverse redlining and related discriminatory practices violate the Fair Housing Act (FHA), *42 U.S.C. §§3601-3631.*

The seminal case prohibiting reverse redlining is *Hargraves v. Capital City Mortgage Corp., 140 F. Supp. 2d 7 (D. D.C. 2000)*. . . . the Commission concluded Complainants established a prima facie reverse redlining claim against Broker under the *Hargraves* test. The Commission rejected Broker's arguments that (1) it did not discriminate because it did not arrange loans for non-African Americans on more preferable terms, (2) it had a legitimate business necessity for its actions, (3) it is not responsible for the terms and conditions of the loans or the disclosure of information relating to the loans, and (4) all mortgage brokers are predators.

As a result, the Commission held Respondents violated the loan provisions and the real estate transaction provisions of the Act by unlawfully discriminating against Complainants in the terms and conditions of real estate-related transactions. The Commission therefore entered the order previously described, and Respondents' petitioned this Court for review.

Before this Court . . . Respondents challenge the Commission's authority to implement a new cause of action for discrimination for reverse redlining under the loan provisions and real estate transaction provisions of the Act. . . . Respondents challenge support for the conclusion that Broker engaged in reverse redlining. . . .

II. Cause of Action

Respondents first argue the Commission lacked the jurisdiction and authority to create a cause of action for reverse redlining under the Act. They contend the Commission's authority is limited by the Act. Any doubtful powers do not exist. Respondents maintain it is the responsibility of courts, not the Commission, to recognize a new cause of action.

In response, the Commission contends this is a housing discrimination case. Section 3 of the Act recognizes an individual's civil right to obtain any housing accommodation without discrimination because of race. *43 P.S. ß 953*. The Act is an exercise of the Commonwealth's police power "for the protection of the public welfare, prosperity, health and peace of the people of the Commonwealth . . . ." Section 2(c) of the Act, *43 P.S. ß 952(c)*. . . . Reverse redlining is a recognized, if new, form of housing discrimination. *Hargraves*. Section 5(h) of the Act, *43 P.S. ß 955(h)*, addresses housing discrimination. *Section 5(h)(4)*, the loan provision, prohibits discrimination "against any person in the terms and conditions of any loan of money, whether or not secured by mortgage or otherwise for the acquisition, construction, rehabilitation, repair or maintenance of housing accommodations . . . ." *43 P.S. ß 955(h)(4)*. Further, *Section 5(h)(8)(i)*, the real estate transaction provision, makes it unlawful for a business engaged in real estate-related transactions to discriminate in the terms and conditions of those transactions.

In view of the foregoing, we conclude under the Act, the Commission has both the jurisdiction and the authority to investigate, prosecute and remedy unlawful housing discrimination practices in the Commonwealth, including claims of reverse redlining. Respondents' contrary assertion lacks merit.

Respondents contend, however, the Commission impermissibly broadened the scope of the Act by creating a new cause of action for reverse redlining. Conceding this issue is one of first impression in the Commonwealth, the Commission based its decision on federal court decisions on reverse redlining. As discussed above, federal courts conclude reverse redlining is a form of housing discrimination that violates the FHA and other related civil rights statutes. *Hargraves*. . . .

The FHA and the Act share the objective to prohibit discrimination. In particular, like the FHA, Section 2(a) of the Act recognizes that housing discrimination is injurious to the public health and leads to racial segregation and its related evils. *43 P.S. ß 952(a)*.

Also, the FHA and the Act share language addressing discrimination in real estate transactions. Section 3605(a) of the FHA provides "it shall be unlawful for any person or other entity whose business includes engaging in residential real estate-related transactions to discriminate against any person in making available such a transaction, or in the terms or conditions of such a transaction, because of race. . . ." *42 U.S.C. ß 3605(a).* Importantly, the real estate transaction provision of the Act contains identical language.

In *Hargraves*, the District Court determined housing discrimination in the form of reverse redlining is prohibited under *Section 3605(a) of the FHA.* In light of the shared objectives of the FHA and the Act, to ban housing discrimination, and the identical language in both statutes prohibiting discrimination in real estate-related transactions, we agree with the Commission that the Act provides a cause of action for discrimination based on reverse redlining. . . .

For the foregoing reasons, we reject Respondents' challenges to the Commission's decision based on jurisdiction and authority to address a claim of reverse redlining.

III. Substantial Evidence

Respondents next challenge support for the Commission's findings. They assert the Commission's conclusion Broker engaged in reverse redlining is not supported by substantial evidence. In particular, Respondents maintain the evidence does not show Broker engaged in predatory lending practices or targeted African Americans.

To establish a discrimination claim based on reverse redlining, the plaintiff must show "the defendants' lending practices and loan terms were 'predatory' and 'unfair.'" *Hargraves, 140 F. Supp. 2d at 20.* The plaintiff must also show "the defendants either intentionally targeted on the basis of race, or that there is a disparate impact on the basis of race." *Id.*

A. *Predatory lending*

Respondents first argue Broker did not engage in predatory or unfair lending practices because it did not approve Complainants' loans or lend them the money. Therefore, they were not responsible either for the terms and conditions of Complainants' loans or for the disclosure of information related to the loans. Those responsibilities belong to the lending institutions that set the terms and approved the loans.

The Commission accepted the testimony of Complainants' expert witnesses. Michelle Lewis, President and Chief Executive Officer of Northwest Counseling Service, Inc. (Complainants' first expert), stated that a mortgage broker is significantly involved in making the loan. The broker is the middleman who creates the loan opportunity. *Id.* The broker's customer relies on the broker's expertise in lending matters and has an expectation that the broker will be able to obtain the best available deal.

The Commission also relied on Ira Goldstein, Director of Public Policy and Program Assessment for the Reinvestment Fund (Complainants' second expert), who testified that, in brokered transactions, the broker's customer—the borrower, never actually meets the lender. As a result, in the borrower's mind, the broker is the lender. Complainants' second expert also testified that in loan transactions where a yield spread premium is used, the broker plays a significant role in establishing the interest rate of the loan.

As additional support for its determination, the Commission cited Reginald McGlawn's testimony. He testified, "When people come to us, I provide loans." Reginald McGlawn also testified he chooses which lender receives the borrower's loan application. He also stated he sets the broker fee and gives the borrower the option of using a yield spread premium, which has the effect of increasing the interest rate.

1.

There is substantial evidence to support the Commission's determination that Respondents engaged in brokering [*769] activities that resulted in predatory and unfair loans.

First, it is noted that a mortgage broker owes a fiduciary duty to its customers. *See In re Barker, 251 B.R. 250 (Bankr. E.D. Pa. 2000)* (mortgage broker is borrower's agent; borrower has a reasonable expectation broker will attempt to secure the most advantageous loan for borrower).

Second, application of the loan and real estate transaction provisions of the Act are not restricted to a lending institution. Rather, the provisions apply to any "person," which is defined to specifically include a "broker, salesman, agent . . . ." Section 4(a) of the Act, *43 P.S. ß 954(a).*

Third, Broker's activities were a substantial part of the loan transactions at issue. In particular, Broker selected which lender received Complainants' loan applications. Broker was the sole negotiator for Complainants with the ultimate lender. Also, Broker influenced the ultimate interest rates in loans involving yield spread premiums. Further, Broker received substantial sums directly from loan proceeds, such as broker fees and insurance premiums. As the Commission properly concluded, these items are considered terms of a loan transaction.

Given a broker's legal duty to its customers, the specific inclusion of brokers in the scope of the Act, and the way Broker operated here, we discern no error in the Commission's finding on this issue.

2.

We next review the Commission's determination that Respondents' practices were predatory and unfair. Whether lending practices are predatory and unfair is a question for the fact finder. *Hargraves.*

In finding Broker arranged predatory and unfair loans for Complainants, the Commission applied the *Hargraves* definition of "predatory lending practices." The *Hargraves* Court stated predatory lending practices are indicated by loans with unreasonably high interest rates and loans based on the value of the asset securing the loan rather than the borrower's capacity to repay it. The Court also recognized predatory lending practices include "loan servicing procedures in which excessive fees are charged." *140 F. Supp. 2d at 21.*

The Commission also noted the New Jersey Superior Court's decision in *Assocs. Home Equity Servs., Inc. v. Troup, 343 N.J. Super. 254, 778 A.2d 529 (N.J. Super. 2001)*. The *Troup* Court explained the term "predatory lenders" refers to those lenders who target certain populations for credit on unfair or onerous terms. Characteristically, predatory loans do not fit the borrower either because the borrower's needs are not met or because the terms are so onerous there is a strong likelihood the borrower will be unable to repay the loan. *Id.*

In determining what lending practices are predatory and unfair, the Commission also accepted as credible Complainants' experts opinions as to what constitutes a predatory loan. Complainants' first expert testified there are a number of loan features which are characteristic of a predatory loan. They include high interest rates, paying off a low interest mortgage with a high interest mortgage, payment of points, yield spread premiums, high broker fees, undisclosed fees, balloon payments, pre-payment penalties, arbitration clauses and fraud. A predatory and unfair loan may include any combination of these characteristics. *Id. at 275*a. *See also In re Barker* (Pennsylvania's Credit Services Act (CSA) and Unfair Trade Practices and Consumer Protection Law (UTP-CPL) prohibit loan brokers from making false or misleading representations or engaging in deceptive or fraudulent conduct).

Complainants' second expert testified that, even assuming a borrower is an enhanced credit risk, the difference in interest rates between a subprime and prime market loan is usually no greater than three percentage points. Anything higher than a three-point difference is indicative of a predatory loan. This expert also testified predatory loan practices include, among other things: flipping (successive refinancing of the same loan); hiding critical terms, establishing loan terms the borrower cannot meet; packing (including unnecessary products such as insurance policies); charging improper fees for items outside the settlement sheet; creation of false documents; and failing to advise borrowers of their recission rights.

The Commission examined the terms of Complainants' loans and their experiences with Respondents in light of the foregoing. We briefly review the Commission's findings regarding Complainants Taylor and Poindexter.

Taylor. Taylor contacted Broker in October 2000 in order to obtain a refinancing loan of $10,000.00 to make some emergency home repairs (leaky roof, doors and windows, plumbing repair). In 2000, she owed $7,300.00 on her home. Her home mortgage had a 3% interest rate with a monthly payment of $110.90. *Id.* Taylor's sole income source was social security disability.

Broker arranged a 30-year mortgage loan for Taylor with Delta Funding Corporation (Delta) in the amount of $20,500.00 with a 13.09% interest rate. Taylor was not given an opportunity to review any of the documents before signing them. Taylor was told to sign the documents.

The Commission found Taylor's loan transaction had several predatory characteristics. Taylor was charged $4,276.60 in total settlement costs, or approximately 20% of the loan. Two days after Taylor signed the loan documents, her uncle reviewed them and advised her to cancel the loan. Taylor called Aaron McGlawn, a Broker employee, and stated she did not want the loan. He did not advise Taylor she could legally rescind the loan within a three-day period; rather, he told Taylor she could cancel the loan if she had the money to pay the people Broker already paid.

At closing, Reginald McGlawn informed Taylor she owed an additional $1,200.00 fee because of where she lived. Anthony McGlawn cashed the check and gave Taylor the money. He then asked Taylor for the $1,200.00 fee. Taylor paid the fee out of the cash; but she was not given a receipt. This fee was not reflected on the settlement sheet.

Complainants' second expert reviewed Taylor's loan transaction. He noted several predatory characteristics. First, Taylor's 13.09% interest rate was substantially above the three-point spread between sub-prime and prime loans. The Commission noted Broker arranged a loan for Taylor at twice the amount she requested and increased her interest rate from 3% to 13.09%. Such loans are considered to be deceptive and detrimental. *In re Barker*. In addition, Taylor's loan included an additional undisclosed $1,200.00 broker fee.

The Commission found Broker engaged in predatory brokering activities on Taylor's behalf. These Broker actions resulted in a predatory and unfair refinancing loan. This finding is supported by substantial evidence.

B. Intentional Discrimination

The second element of a reverse redlining claim is a showing that the defendant either intentionally targeted on the basis of race or that there was a disparate impact on the basis of race. *Hargraves*. Here, the Commission determined Broker intentionally targeted African Americans and African American neighborhoods. The Commission also found ample evidence of disparate impact.

However, Broker contends the record lacks convincing evidence demonstrating either (1) that Broker intentionally targeted a protected class or (2) that policies and practices had a disparate impact on the basis of race. Rather, Broker maintains its mission is to provide an opportunity for people with poor credit to obtain funds to get out of debt and keep their homes. Broker claims several of the Complainants first went to other mortgage brokers who turned them down.

"Although evidence of intent is not necessary to show discriminatory impact, it can support such a finding." *Hargraves, 140 F. Supp. 2d at 21*. In reverse redlining cases, evidence of the defendant's advertising efforts in African American communities is sufficient to show intentional targeting on the basis of race. *Id.*

The Commission reviewed Broker's advertisements. On its website, Broker states "it is one of the first African American owned and operated Mortgage and Insurance Financial Services in Philadelphia and the surrounding area." Broker's website also states "our primary focus is to assist financially challenged customers in purchasing and or refinancing their existing mortgage, as well as providing various types of insurance."

In addition, Anthony McGlawn, Broker's co-founder and insurance specialist, testified Broker engaged in extensive advertising on radio and television, in the newspapers and in the yellow pages. Several of these sources are oriented toward African American audiences and readers. Reginald McGlawn also testified the majority of Broker's customers are African Americans.

Moreover, Complainants testified they contacted Broker as a result of its advertisements. Taylor contacted Broker after viewing one of its television commercials. Poindexter called Broker after listening to one of its radio commercials. Nearly all of the eight similarly situated Complainants also contacted Broker in response to one of its radio, television and newspaper advertisements.

Complainants also testified the decision to contact Broker was influenced by the fact that it was an African American company. For example, both Taylor and Poindexter testified this fact played a role in their decisions to use Broker's services.

The record also indicates Broker's business activities have a disparate impact on African American neighborhoods. This can be established by statistical evidence. *Hargraves*. The Commission accepted the testimony of Radcliffe Davis, a Commission investigator (Investigator). In response to Taylor and Poindexter's complaints, Investigator visited Broker's office and reviewed 100 customer loan applications for things such as refinancing, debt consolidation and home improvement. Of those 100 applications, 66 identified the race of the applicant. *Id.* Of those 66 applicants, 65 were African American.

In addition, Complainants' second expert testified he prepared a document mapping the 11 properties involved in this matter. Nine of these properties were in areas that have at least a 90% African American population. The other two areas have a 50-75% African American population.

Considering the foregoing, the Commission's conclusion regarding intentional discrimination is supported by substantial evidence and is in accord with applicable law. *Hargraves*. Complainants also established by statistical evidence that Broker's business activities had a disparate impact on African Americans and African American neighborhoods. *Id.*

In sum, Complainants met their burden of establishing a prima facie reverse redlining claim against Broker. *Id.*

C. *Rebuttal*

"Once a prima facie case is established, a rebuttable presumption of discrimination arises." *DeFelice, 782 A.2d at 591.* "The burden then shifts to the defendant to show some legitimate, nondiscriminatory reason for its action." *Id.* In predatory lending cases, the financial institution may avoid liability by showing its lending practices were legitimate. *Hargraves.*

Respondents contend Complainants did not prove Broker's business activities were discriminatory because they did not establish Broker made loans to non-African Americans on more preferable terms. This argument was rejected in *Hargraves*. Citing *Contract Buyers League v. F & F Investment, 300 F. Supp. 210 (N.D. Ill. 1969)*, the *Hargaves* Court recognized that injustice cannot be permitted merely because it is visited exclusively upon African Americans. We adopt this reasoning now.

Respondents also argue that any mortgage broker which arranges sub-prime loans could be considered a predator. We disagree. The interest rates of Complainants' loans are far in excess of the three-point difference usually separating prime and sub-prime loans. In addition, Broker's high broker fees, undisclosed fees and padded closing costs benefited Broker, not Complainants. These types of loans do not serve the borrower's wants or needs. *See In re Barker* (broker's motivation for arranging this type of loan was not to serve borrower's interest, "but to serve its own interest of obtaining a handsome broker's fee.") 251 B.R. at 260. "Such self-dealing constitutes a flagrant violation of the Broker's fiduciary duties to the [borrower]." *Id.*

Respondents further argue Broker had no legal obligation to ensure Complainants could repay their loans.

Whether or not a broker must ensure a client's ability to repay a loan, a broker cannot ignore circumstances suggesting an inability to repay. Indeed, one of the clearest indicators of a predatory and unfair loan is one which exceeds the borrower's needs and repayment capacity. *Hargraves; Troup.*

On several occasions, Broker arranged loans in excess of the amounts Complainants sought. Moreover, Broker discouraged several Complainants from canceling their loans within the three-day recission period. Broker also submitted falsified documents with Complainants' loan applications indicating Complainants possessed greater income or assets than they really did. Broker's disregard of Complainants' ability to repay their loans strongly supports the Commission's decision to reject the legitimate practice defense.

Respondents also assert they did not target African Americans or African American neighborhoods. Rather, Respondents claim Complainants, who are poor credit risks, came to Broker after being turned down by other brokers.

As discussed above, nearly all Complainants contacted Broker in response to one of its radio, television or newspaper advertisements targeting individuals with poor credit. Further, Broker concentrated its advertising efforts in the African American media. The Commission did not err in concluding Broker intentionally targeted African Americans for sub-prime mortgage loans.

NOTES AND QUESTIONS

1. Two other acts prohibit intentional discrimination within the context of credit and mortgage transactions. First, Section 1691 of the Equal Credit Opportunity Act (ECOA) states, in relevant part, that

> (a) It shall be unlawful for any creditor to discriminate against any applicant, with respect to any aspect of a credit transaction—
>
> (1) on the basis of race, color, religion, national origin, sex or marital status, or age (provided the applicant has the capacity to contract);
>
> (2) because all or part of the applicant's income derives from any public assistance program.

15 U.S.C. §1691 (2006).

The scope of ECOA is limited, as Tania Davenport notes, because it applies only to "the granting of credit, and the act does not directly address any other predatory lending abuses." Tania Davenport, *An American Nightmare: Predatory Lending in the Subprime Home Mortgage Industry,* 36 Suff. L. Rev. 531, 551 (2003). The other primary act is the Home Ownership and Equity Protection Act (HOEPA), which requires that additional protections for lending be extended for loans based on equity in a home. In particular, the rather complex provisions of the Act, which were best summarized by the Court in *Cooper v. First Gov't Mort. & Investment Corp.*, 238 F.Supp. 2d 50, 54-55 (2002), the Act applies only to a specific category of "high cost" loans, which the Court in *Cooper* defined as

> 1) a consumer credit transaction
> 2) with a creditor
> 3) that is secured by the consumer's principal dwelling
> 4) and is a second or subordinate residential mortgage, not a residential mortgage transaction, a reverse mortgage transaction, or a transaction under an open credit plan
> 5) and that satisfies either of the following two tests:
> (a) the annual percentage rate ("APR") of interest for the loan transaction exceeds certain levels; or

> (b) the total "points and fees" payable by the borrower at or before closing will exceed the greater of (i) 8% of the total loan amount; or (ii) $400.00.

Id. at 55-54, citing (15 U.S.C. §1602(aa)).

As these provisions indicate, HOEPA has a limited scope. In particular, HOEPA does not apply to residential mortgage transactions, a reverse mortgage transaction, or a transaction under an open credit plan. 12 C.F.R. 226.32 (i)-(ii).

2. How did the Court utilize the federal statutes to sustain in its claim under the Pennsylvania Human Rights Act? States such as Pennsylvania and North Carolina have been at the forefront of action against predatory lending activities. *See* Therese G. Franzén and Leslie M. Howell, *State and Local Predatory Lending Issues and Developments,* 59 Bus. Law. 1179 (2004) (surveying the laws of 23 states as to the state of predatory lending laws within the relevant jurisdiction).

3. What were the types of practices alleged by the complainants? Can you think of other types of practices that might be relevant here?

The other major set of practices that seeks to alleviate lending practices that unduly impact neighborhoods of color are those statutes that seek to create transparency as to the lending practices of lending institutions: the Community Reinvestment Act (CRA), 12 U.S.C. §§2901-2908 (2006); and the Home Mortgage Disclosure Act (HMDA), §§2801-2811(2006).

The CRA "is intended to encourage depository institutions to help meet the credit needs of the communities in which they operate, including low- and moderate-income neighborhoods, consistent with safe and sound banking operations. It was enacted by Congress in 1977 (12 U.S.C. §2901) and is implemented by Regulations 12 CFR parts 25, 228, 345, and 563e. Federal Financial Institutions Examining Council, Background and Purpose, *available at* http://www.ffiec.gov/CRA/history.htm (last visited June 14, 2009).

The CRA was designed as a civil rights initiative and thus hoped to end the practice of redlining by encouraging banks to improve their lending practices to the formerly redlined neighborhoods. Marsico, *supra,* at 14. The Act has significant limits, however. First, the CRA is "not a directive to undertake any particular program or to provide credit to any particular individual." *Lee v. Board of Governors of the Federal Reserve System,* 118 F.3d 905, 913 (2nd Cir. 1997). Instead, the CRA requires only that the Federal agencies produce written evaluations that contain both a public section and a confidential section. 12 U.S.C. §2906(a)(2). The evaluations assign one of four possible ratings: (1) outstanding record of meeting community credit needs; (2) satisfactory record of meeting community credit needs; (3) needs to improve record of meeting community credit needs; and (4) substantial noncompliance in meeting community credit needs. 12 U.S.C.

§2906(b)(2)(A-D). "The agencies' only enforcement authority is to examine banks for CRA performance and to take account of these evaluations in considering whether to grant certain bank expansion applications." Richard D. Marsico, *Democratizing Capital: The History, Law and Reform of the Community Reinvestment Act* 31 (2005). Second, the CRA covers only "insured depository institutions," that is, "any bank or saving associations" whose deposits are insured by the Federal Deposit Insurance Corporation. 12 U.S.C. §2902(2). This limited coverage was a problem during the recent financial crisis, as neither nondepository institutions such as mortgage brokers nor nondepository affiliates of covered institutions were exempt from the CRA. Raymond H. Brescia, *Part of The Disease or Part of the Cure: The Financial Crisis and the Community Reinvestment Act,* 60 S. C. L. Rev. 618, 629 (2009).

Community Reinvestment Act

12 U.S.C. §2901 (2006)

Section 2901. Congressional Findings and Statement of Purpose

(a) The Congress finds that—

(1) regulated financial institutions are required by law to demonstrate that their deposit facilities serve the convenience and needs of the communities in which they are chartered to do business;

(2) the convenience and needs of communities include the need for credit services as well as deposit services; and

(3) regulated financial institutions have continuing and affirmative obligation to help meet the credit needs of the local communities in which they are chartered.

(b) It is the purpose of this chapter to require each appropriate Federal financial supervisory agency to use its authority when examining financial institutions, to encourage such institutions to help meet the credit needs of the local communities in which they are chartered consistent with the safe and sound operation of such institutions.

Section 2903. Financial Institutions; Evaluation

(a) In general. In connection with its examination of a financial institution, the appropriate Federal financial supervisory agency shall—

(1) assess the institution's record of meeting the credit needs of its entire community, including low- and moderate-income neighborhoods, consistent with the safe and sound operation of such institution; and

(2) take such record into account in its evaluation of an application for a deposit facility by such institution.

NOTES AND QUESTIONS

1. The CRA designates four federal agencies to evaluate financial institutions: (1) the Comptroller of the Currency (for national banks); (2) the Board of Governors of the Federal Reserve System (for state-chartered banks that are members of the Federal Reserve System and bank holding companies); (3) the Federal Deposit Insurance Corporation (for state-chartered banks and savings banks that are not members of the Federal Reserve System and the deposits of which are insured by the Corporation); and (4) the Director of the Office of Thrift Supervision (for savings associations, the deposits of which are insured by the Federal Deposit Insurance Corporation, and savings and loan holding companies). *See* 12 U.S.C. §2902(1)(A-D).

2. Courts ruled that the CRA does not create a private right of action because the CRA was not intended to protect individuals from discriminatory practices. *Hicks v. Resolution Trust Corp.*, 970 F.2d 378, 382 (7th Cir. 1992); *Lee*, 118 F.3d at 913; *Powell v. American General Finance, Inc.*, 310 F. Supp. 2d 481, 485-86 (N.D.N.Y. 2004); *Exchange Bank v. Director of the Office of Thrift Supervision*, 29 F. Supp. 2d 1272, 1276 (N.D. Okla. 1998).

3. Do you think that there should be a private right of action, as is available under the FHA? Would that make it easier to enforce these issues?

4. During the recent mortgage crisis, some authors have argued that the CRA's requirements forced banks to adopt relaxed lending standards, thus worsening the housing crisis. John Carney, The Phony Time-Gap Alibi for the Community Reinvestment Act, *available at* http://www.businessinsider.com/the-phony-time-gap-alibi-for-the-community-reinvestment-act-2009-6 (last visited July 1, 2009). These critics suggest, in particular, that these standards resulted in banks issuing no-down-payment loans with 100-percent loan-to-value ratios, *id.*, and this has sparked a debate as to whether these standards are the cause of the current mortgage crisis, *id.* Supporters of the CRA argue that if the CRA was responsible for the mortgage crisis, the market would have collapsed in a different way. Barry Ritholz, CRA Thought Experiment, *available at* http://www.ritholtz.com/blog/2009/06/cra-thought-experiment/(last visited July 1, 2009).

5. Given its limitations, the CRA may need revision as a result of the ongoing mortgage crisis. Raymond Brescia has suggested that the Act be revised in the following manner: (1) broadening the CRA to all financial institutions and banking institutions; (2) permitting state enforcement of CRA claims; (3) subjecting the relevant agencies that conduct review of banks under the CRA to judicial review under the Administrative Procedure Act, and (4) allowing citizen review of bank submissions under the CRA. Brescia, *supra*, at 662-75.

The final relevant statute is the Home Mortgage Disclosure Act (HMDA). Carol Necole Brown notes that Congress enacted the HMDA to provide public loan data that could be used to aid in "(1) in discerning lending patterns that are discriminatory; (2) in verifying whether finical institutions covered by the legislation are serving their communities' housing needs; and (3) public officials as they attempt to distribute investments from the public sector in an effort to attract private investments to areas in need." Brown, *supra* at 19. Again, the HMDA is not to be used in intentional discrimination, so like in the CRA, there is no private right of action to enforce the statute. Brescia, *supra* at 629.

Recently, however, states have begun to use HDMA data to aid in equitable actions that seek to prevent foreclosure of homes in potentially redlined or reverse redlined homes.

M & T Mortgage Corp. v. Foy

858 N.Y.S.2d 567 (2008)

Equity abhors discrimination.

Equity will not enforce discriminatory practices.

This court holds, for reasons set forth below, that a mortgage granted to a minority buyer for the purchase of property in a minority area which carries an interest rate that exceeds nine percent creates a rebuttable presumption of discriminatory practice.

This court further holds that the lender who has brought this proceeding to foreclose the mortgage must demonstrate by a fair preponderance of the evidence that the mortgage was not the product of unlawful discrimination. If the lender is unable to do so, the foreclosure proceeding will be dismissed and the lender left to its remedies at law.

Major Jahn K. Foy, a reserve officer, was engaged on active duty when foreclosure proceedings were initiated against her property, 517 Rogers Avenue in Brooklyn, which is located within a minority neighborhood. The 30-year note and mortgage dated July of 2000 carried an interest rate of 9 1/2%. . . .

. . . .[A]dditional research suggested that the defendant may have been the victim of a process called "reverse redlining." Accordingly, on December 6, 2007, this court informed the parties that it intended to continue the hearing and placed the burden on the defendant to demonstrate that she was a victim of discriminatory lending.

Thus, the court now modifies that decision so as to place the burden of proof upon the plaintiff to demonstrate that the loan in question is not a "higher priced loan" which is the product of discriminatory practices. In so doing this court is mindful of the effect of discrimination upon the larger population. Research has revealed that when minorities subjected to discrimination represent a very small percentage of the population, the cost of discrimination falls mainly upon the minority; however, when they represent a larger segment of society, the cost of discrimination falls upon both the minorities and the majority as currently evidenced by the worldwide subprime mortgage meltdown.

In shifting the burden of proof this court will use the Home Mortgage Disclosure Act (HMDA) definition of "higher priced loan" to determine whether the loan is one that may require [further investigation for possible discriminatory practices. [Under the HDMA] a loan is deemed "'higher priced' . . . [if its] rate spread . . . [for a first tier loan] is three percentage points above the Treasury security of comparable maturity . . . . [Moreover,] [t]hough the price data [in and of itself does not] support definitive conclusions [with respect to the issue of unlawful discrimination, it provides] a useful screen, previously unavailable, to identify lenders, products, applicants, and geographic markets where price differences among racial or other groups are sufficiently large to warrant further investigation." (*Frequently Asked Questions About the New HMDA Data,* Price Data on "Higher-Priced Loans" [Federal Reserve Bank Apr. 2006]; *see also Proposed Rules, Regulation Z, 73 Fed Reg 1673.*)

This is to be distinguished from the Home Ownership and Equity Protection Act which targets high cost loans and imposes substantive restrictions and special preclosing disclosures on particularly high-cost refinancing and home equity loans where the "APR at consummation will exceed the yield on Treasury securities of comparable maturity by more than 8 percentage points for first-lien loans" *Board of Governors of the Federal Reserve System, Proposal to Amend Regulation Z 73 FR 1677 n.23*. Regulation Z implements the federal Truth in Lending Act and the Home Ownership and Equity Protection Act in order to protect consumers in the mortgage market from unfair, abusive or deceptive lending and services practices. (*See also Banking Law 6-l* [which has comparable standards and restrictions].)

The mortgage in the instant matter and indeed most 30-year mortgages written after the year 2000, which call for an interest rate of nine percent, would constitute "higher priced loans" under these criteria. Thus, this court holds that an interest rate exceeding nine percent evidences the existence of a higher priced loan and creates a rebuttable presumption of discrimination. (*See also McGlawn v. Pennsylvania Human Relations Commn., 891 A2d 757 [Pa. Commonwealth, 2006]* [Pennsylvania Human Relations Commission relied upon expert testimony indicating that an interest rate three percent beyond that which exists in the general market is predatory and thus discriminatory].)

Equity, which abhors unconscionable and unjust results, mandates a shift in the burden of proof to the plaintiff lender to demonstrate that the loan is not discriminatory. Indeed, our decisional law has long since recognized that a litigant "seeking affirmative judicial action in equity . . . may not succeed if [the litigant] is asking [for] an inequitable or unconscionable result." *Monaghan v. May, 242 App Div 64, 66, 273 NYS 475 [2d Dept. 1934].*). . . .

Indeed, in our current climate where—this court takes judicial notice—there are substantial amounts of undefended foreclosure proceedings in minority neighborhoods, the placement of the burden of proof upon the borrower who is very much in a distaff position when it comes to protecting his or her rights, renders illusory the possibility of meaningful legal redress. (*See e.g. EquiCredit Corp. of N.Y. v Turcios, 300 AD2d 344, 752 NYS2d 684 [2d Dept 2002]* [counterclaims alleging reverse redlining practices in claimed violation of the Equal Credit Opportunity Act and the Fair Housing Act dismissed for failure to show that mortgagors qualified for the loans in question as required pursuant to these statutes].)

The courts are not merely automatons mindlessly processing paper motions in mortgage foreclosure actions most of which proceed on default. Where, as here, there is a presumably discriminatory rate, the court must order a hearing in a litigated action or an inquest where there is a default. This presumption may be rebutted by proof that the mortgage was given for nondiscriminatory economic reasons.

NOTES AND QUESTIONS

1. How does the Court invoke the HMDA data in this case? How does the Court distinguish for HOEPA?

2. How does the Court construe its position in equity? What type of relief will that lead to for the homeowner? What would have been the result had the Court had not found in equity that the homeowner could challenge the discriminatory rate? Why do you think that the Court determined it was an unconscionable result?

5.2.4 Takings and Urban Design: A Right to Your Community?

Yale Rabin has described practices such as discriminatory housing patterns, expulsive zoning, and urban renewal as "a web-like pattern of interacting public practices that serve to reproduce and reinforce the disadvantages of blacks. Urban renewal, public housing site selection, school segregation, highway route selection, and code enforcement are a few of the other frequently encountered cords of the web." Rabin, *supra*, at 102-03. The question of "urban renewal"—"the use of federal funds [by] local cities to plan, acquire, clear, and re-develop designated areas of urban renewal[,]" Rutherford H. Platt, Land Use and Society: Geography, Law, and Public Policy 326 (2004)—has prompted a significant controversy over the scope of government authority to "take" these properties under the Fifth Amendment. The key issue in this area has been whether large-scale appropriation by the government actor constitutes a sufficient public use under the Fifth Amendment, particularly when the individual property is not blighted and will be sold to another private party. In *Berman v. Parker*, 348 U.S. 26 (1954), the Supreme Court upheld the congressional enactment of the District of Columbia Redevelopment Act of 1945, which authorized the condemnation of properties within "blighted areas" of Washington D.C. In doing so, Justice Douglas, the author of the opinion, stated that judicial review of a legislature's stated "public purpose" under the Fifth Amendment was a narrow one, and that removal of a blighted area served a legitimate public use:

> Public safety, public health, morality, peace and quiet, law and order—these are some of the more conspicuous examples of the traditional application of the police power to municipal affairs. Yet they merely illustrate the scope of the power and do not delimit it. See Noble State Bank v. Haskell, 219 U.S. 104, 111, 31 S.Ct. 186, 188, 55 L.Ed. 112. Miserable and disreputable housing conditions may do more than spread disease and crime and immorality. They may also suffocate the spirit by reducing the people who live there to the status of cattle. They may indeed make living an almost insufferable burden. They may also be an ugly sore, a blight on the community which robs it of charm, which makes it a place from which men turn. The misery of housing may despoil a community as an open sewer may ruin a river.
>
> We do not sit to determine whether a particular housing project is or is not desirable. The concept of the public welfare is broad and inclusive. See Day-Brite Lighting, Inc. v. State of Missouri, 342 U.S. 421, 424, 72 S.Ct. 405, 407, 96 L.Ed. 469. The values it represents are spiritual as well as physical, aesthetic as well as monetary. It is within the power of the legislature to determine that the community should be beautiful as well as healthy, spacious as well as clean, well-balanced as well as carefully patrolled. In the present case, the Congress and its authorized agencies have made determinations that take into account a wide variety of values. It is not for us to reappraise them. If those who govern the District of Columbia decide that the Nation's Capital should be beautiful as well as sanitary, there is nothing in the Fifth Amendment that stands in the way.
>
> Once the object is within the authority of Congress, the right to realize it through the exercise of eminent domain is clear. For the power of eminent domain is merely the means to the end. See Luxton v. North River Bridge Co., 153 U.S. 525, 529-530, 14 S.Ct. 891, 892, 38 L.Ed. 808; United States v. Gettysburg Electric R. Co., 160 U.S. 668, 679, 16 S.Ct. 427, 429, 40 L.Ed. 576. Once the object is within the authority of Congress, the means by which it will be attained is also for Congress to determine. Here one of the means chosen is the use of private enterprise for redevelopment of the area. Appellants argue that this makes the project a taking from one businessman for the benefit of another businessman. But the means of executing the project are for Congress and Congress alone to determine, once the public purpose has been established. See Luxton v. North River Bridge Co., supra; cf. Highland v. Russell Car Co., 279 U.S. 253, 49 S.Ct. 314, 73 L.Ed. 688. The public end may be as well or better served through an agency of private enterprise than through a department of government—or so the Congress might conclude. We cannot say that public ownership is the sole method of promoting the public purposes of community redevelopment projects. What we have said also disposes of any contention concerning the fact that certain property owners in the area may be permitted to repurchase their properties for redevelopment in harmony with the overall plan. That, too, is a legitimate means which Congress and its agencies may adopt, if they choose.

Berman, 348 U.S. at 33-34.

Berman's broad interpretation of "public use" under the Fifth Amendment remained a controversial holding, and, in 2005, the Supreme Court revisited it in *Kelo v. City of New London*, 545 U.S. 469 (2005). The majority opinion of *Kelo*, authored by Justice Stevens and joined by Justices Kennedy, Souter, Breyer, and Ginsburg, upheld *Berman*'s broad construction of "public use," emphasizing that "[f]or more than a century, our public use jurisprudence has wisely eschewed rigid formulas and intrusive scrutiny in favor of affording legislatures broad latitude in determining what public needs justify the use of the takings power." *Id.* at 483. Justice Kennedy, concurring in the majority opinion, contended the majority's adoption of a rational-basis review under the Fifth Amendment could be limited when judicial scrutiny indicated that a taking was undertaken to clearly favor a particular private party, with only incidental or pretextual benefits. *Id.* at 491.

The majority's holding in *Kelo* prompted vigorous dissents. Justice O'Connor, joined by Chief Justice Rehnquist, Justice Scalia, and Justice Thomas, argued that *public use* should be defined narrowly to those circumstances in which the legislatively enumerated public purpose sought to eliminate a harmful use. *Id.* at 501. O'Connor contended that the urban renewal taking undertaken in *Berman* could be supported because the "extraordinary, pre[-]condemnation use of the targeted property inflicted affirmative harm on society—in *Berman* through blight resulting from extreme poverty . . ." *Id.* at 500. Justice Thomas, in a separate opinion, argued even more vehemently against the majority's opinion on two bases. First, Thomas would define "public use" even more narrowly than O'Connor, arguing that the constitutional text of the Fifth Amendment means "that the government may take property only if it actually uses or gives the public a legal right to use the property." *Id.* at 521. Second, Thomas specifically invoked the contested history of urban renewal, stating that

> [t]he consequences of today's decision are not difficult to predict, and promise to be harmful. So-called "urban renewal" programs provide some compensation for the properties they take, but no compensation is possible for the subjective value of these lands to the individuals displaced and the indignity inflicted by uprooting them from their homes. Allowing the government to take property solely for public purposes is bad enough, but extending the concept of public purpose to encompass any economically beneficial goal guarantees that these losses will fall disproportionately on poor communities. Those communities are not only systematically less likely to put their lands to the highest and best social use, but are also the least politically powerful. If ever there were justification for intrusive judicial review of constitutional provisions that protect "discrete and insular minorities," *United States v. Carolene Products Co.*, 304 U.S. 144, 152, n. 4, 58 S.Ct. 778, 82 L.Ed. 1234 (1938), surely that principle would apply with great force to the powerless groups and individuals the Public Use Clause protects. The deferential standard this Court has adopted for the Public Use Clause is therefore deeply perverse. It encourages "those citizens with disproportionate influence and power in the political process, including large corporations and development firms," to victimize the weak. . . .

> Those incentives have made the legacy of this Court's "public purpose" test an unhappy one. In the 1950's, no doubt emboldened in part by the expansive understanding of "public use" this Court adopted in *Berman,* cities "rushed to draw plans" for downtown development. B. Frieden & L. Sagalayn, *Downtown, Inc. How America Rebuilds Cities,* 17 (1989). "Of all the families displaced by urban renewal from 1949 through 1963, 63 percent of those whose race was known were nonwhite, and of these families, 56 percent of nonwhites and 38 percent of whites had incomes low enough to qualify for public housing, which, however, was seldom available to them." *Id.,* at 28, 75 S.Ct. 98. Public works projects in the 1950's and 1960's destroyed predominantly minority communities in St. Paul, Minnesota, and Baltimore, Maryland. *Id.,* at 28-29, 75 S.Ct. 98. In 1981, urban planners in Detroit, Michigan, uprooted the largely "lower-income and elderly" Poletown neighborhood for the benefit of the General Motors Corporation. J. Wylie, Poletown: Community Betrayed 58 (1989). Urban renewal projects have long been associated with the displacement of blacks; "[i]n cities across the country, urban renewal came to be known as 'Negro removal.'" Pritchett, *The "Public Menace" of Blight: Urban Renewal and the Private Uses of Eminent Domain, 21 Yale L. & Pol'y Rev. 1, 47 (2003).* Over 97 percent of the individuals forcibly removed from their homes by the "slum-clearance" project upheld by this Court in *Berman* were black. 348 U.S., at 30, 75 S.Ct. 98. Regrettably, the predictable consequence of the Court's decision will be to exacerbate these effects.

Id. at 521-22.

NOTES AND QUESTIONS

1. Thirty-nine states enacted legislation or passed ballot measures during 2005-2007 in response to the *Kelo* decision. According to the National Conference of State Legislatures, the laws and ballot measures generally fall into the following categories:

- Restricting the use of eminent domain for economic development, enhancing tax revenue, or transferring private property to another private entity (or primarily for those purposes).
- Defining what constitutes public use.
- Establishing additional criteria for designating blighted areas subject to eminent domain.
- Strengthening public notice, public hearing, and landowner negotiation criteria, and requiring local government approval before condemning property.
- Placing a moratorium on the use of eminent domain for a specified period and establishing a task force to study the issue and report findings to the legislature.

National Conference of State Legislatures, http://www.ncsl.org/default.aspx?tabid=13252 (last visited July 27, 2009).

For further information on state response to *Kelo,* see Anastasia C. Sheffler-Wood, Comment, *Where Do We Go from Here? States Revise Eminent*

Domain Legislation in Response to Kelo, 79 Temp. L. Rev. 617 (2006); Michelle B. Mudd, *Was the Big Sky Really Falling? Examining Montana's Response to Kelo v. City of New London*, 69 Mont. L. Rev. 79 (2008); Kenneth H. Hemler, Note, *Michigan's Proposed Constitutional Amendment in Response to Kelo: Adequate Protection against Eminent Domain Abuse or False Hope to Private Property Owners*, 84 U. Det. Mercy L. Rev. 187 (2006-07); Anthony B. Seitz, Comment, *The Property Rights Protection Act: An Overview of Pennsylvania's Response to Kelo v. City of New London*, 18 Widener L. Rev. 205 (2008-09); Joyce Ehimwenma Iyamu, Note, *What is in a Name? Public Use in Texas after Kelo v. New London*, 37 St. B. Tex. Envtl. L.J. 30 (2006-07); Carolyn A. Pearce, Note, *Forcing under Redevelopment to Proceed Building by Building: North Carolina's Flawed Policy Response to Kelo v. City of New London*, 85 N.C. L. Rev. 1784 (2006-07); Molly G. Bronmiller, Comment, *Is This the Start of a Silent Spring? Kelo v. City of New London's Effect on Environmental Reforms*, 56 Cath. U. L. Rev. 1107 (2006-07).

2. The Supreme Court of Ohio in *City of Norwood v. Horney*, 853 N.E.2d 1115 (2006), held that Ohio's state constitution required any taking to be examined under a heightened scrutiny so as to ensure searching review of transfers of private property to other private entities. *Id.* at 1140. Speaking specifically about the issue of urban renewal, the Supreme Court of Ohio noted

> Our understanding of the individual's fundamental rights in property, as guaranteed by the Ohio Constitution and our consistent holdings throughout the past two centuries that a genuine public use must be present before the state invokes its right to take, is better reflected by *Hathcock*'s holdings that economic development by itself is not a sufficient public use to satisfy a taking. Although economic benefit can be considered as a factor among others in determining whether there is a sufficient public use and benefit in a taking, it cannot serve as the sole basis for finding such benefit.

Id. at 1141.

3. Could a court undertake an analysis that fairly accounts for the "subjective value of the condemned lands" or "indignity inflicted by uprooting them from their homes"? *See, e.g., Cornerstone Group XXII, L.L.C. v. Wheat Ridge Urban Renewal Authority*, 151 P.3d 601 (Colo. App. 2006) (analyzing trial court's use of "subjective values" in consideration of preliminary injunction). Are communities that are primarily minority or poor potentially subject to unfair subjective determinations of blight? *See* Sheila R. Foster, *The City as an Ecological Space: Social Capital and Urban Land Use*, 82 Notre Dame L. Rev. 527 (2006-07) (examining how choices about physical space can have impact on social networks of urban commons).

4. Additional state provisions addressing zoning and fair housing issues may be found in "statutory and constitutional recognition of a regional 'general welfare' for which all localities in a geographic region bear responsibility." Richard Thompson Ford, *The Boundaries of Race: Political*

Geography in Legal Analysis, 107 HARV. L. REV. 1841, 1898 (1993-94). In *Southern Burlington County N.A.A.C.P. v. Township of Mount Laurel*, plaintiffs representing minority group poor sought a decision "attack[ing] the system of land use regulation by defendant . . . on the ground that low and moderate income families [were] . . . unlawfully excluded from the municipality." 336 A.2d 713, 716 (N.J. 1975). The court held that "every such municipality must, by its land use regulations, presumptively make realistically possible an appropriate variety and choice of housing[,] . . . [and] cannot foreclose the opportunity of the classes of people mentioned for low and moderate income housing and in its regulations must affirmatively afford that opportunity." *Id.* at 724. As a result, Mount Laurel's exclusionary zoning was disallowed. Ford, *supra*, at 1898. *Mount Laurel* thus provides precedent "for important new remedies to local government and housing inequalities[,]" *id.* at 1897, and has since been codified by legislatures into state fair housing provisions, *id.* at 1899. For additional information, see Bernard K. Ham, *Exclusionary Zoning and Racial Segregation: A Reconsideration of the Mount Laurel Doctrine*, 7 SETON HALL CONST. L.J. 577 (1996-97); John M. Payne, *Title VIII and Mount Laurel: Is Affordable Housing Fair Housing*, 6 YALE L. & POL'Y REV. 361 (1988); Bruce L. Ackerman, *The Mount Laurel Decision: Expanding the Boundaries of Zoning Reform*, 1976 U. ILL. L.F. 1 (1976); Paula A. Franzese, *Mount Laurel III: The New Jersey Supreme Court's Judicious Retreat*, 18 SETON HALL L. REV. 30 (1988).

6 CONTEMPORARY COMMON LAW PROPERTY

In this chapter we shift our focus from statutes, such as the Fair Housing Act (FHA), to the common law and explore the relationship between time-honored common-law property doctrines and race in the modern courtroom. Although the majority of the cases in this chapter are more recent when compared to those covered in prior chapters, the issues confronted by the courts and the implications of their decisions have deep roots. Whether on its face or hidden in its subtext, each case in this chapter raises questions about the intersection of race and property in contemporary society.

6.1 FIRST POSSESSION AND OWNERSHIP

Many property casebooks begin with former Chief Justice Marshall's famous, or perhaps infamous, decision in *Johnson v. M'Intosh,* 21 U.S. (8 Wheat.) 543 (1823). In *Johnson,* Chief Justice Marshall's opinion concluded that a Native American tribe lacked the power to convey title to real property because title to that same real property had vested in the United States by virtue of the discovery rule. Although Justice Marshall recognized Native Americans as prior possessors of the land, prior possession merely gave Native Americans a right of "occupancy" without legal authority to convey title to the land to the detriment of the United States. During the course of his opinion, Chief Justice Marshall struggled with basic questions in the law of property—what is the definition of "possession" and what protection is to be afforded prior possessors? The material in this section involves questions regarding possession and ownership a mere 170 years later.

Great Property Cases: Johnson v. M'Intosh and the South Dakota Fossil Cases

*Dana G. Jim, 46 St. Louis L.J. 791 (2002)**

Every autumn in American law schools, future attorneys begin their introduction to the study of law by focusing on the four primary concepts of the American legal system: Contracts, Civil Procedure, Torts, and Property. Of the many cases these students will read to start their legal journey, the case of *Johnson v. M'Intosh* is special because it brings up issues of wealth, power and politics. This case gives students a glimpse into America's past and gives students and teachers alike the opportunity to analyze the premises that guide Supreme Court decisions.

In *Johnson,* we learned that Indians have rights of occupancy and use of the land under the concept of Indian title. In addition, the case stood for the principle that the federal government had the "exclusive right to extinguish" the Indian title. In other words, the federal government must approve the sale of Indian land. This concept of federal supremacy over the conveyance of Indian lands was codified in the early years of the federal government through the Nonintercourse Acts. Enacted in the early 1790s, these laws rendered void any land sale by Indians if the sale was not made according to "the authority of the United States," or "treaty or convention entered into pursuant to the constitution. . . ."

These statutes were only the tip of the iceberg. Today, there are numerous federal statutes and regulations that govern transactions that occur on Indian land. For example, federal law mandates that a federal government official, the Secretary of the Interior, make the final decision to grant the following leases on Indian land: farming and grazing leases, mineral leases and oil and gas leases. Another statute is 25 U.S.C. 483, which governs conveyances of land. It states the following in part:

> 483. Sale of land by individual Indian owners
>
> The Secretary of the Interior . . . is authorized in his discretion, and upon application of the Indian owners, . . . to approve conveyances, with respect to lands or interests in lands held by individual Indians . . . .

The reason for citing to these various statutes is to reinforce the most important concept of *Johnson*: the Sovereign controls Indian land conveyances. There is no better example of illustrating the way this principle of the Johnson case has been applied to the present day than by the story of "Sue," the Tyrannosaurus Rex fossil found in South Dakota in the early 1990s.

Black Hills Institute of Geological Research v. South Dakota School of Mines and Technology

12 F.3d 737 (8th Cir. 1993)

MAGILL, Circuit Judge.

Black Hills Institute of Geological Research and Black Hills Museum of Natural History Foundation (collectively, "Black Hills") appeal the district court's judgment in favor of the United States. The district court found that the United States holds title to a valuable Tyrannosaurus rex skeleton ("the fossil" or "Sue") in trust for Maurice Williams ("Williams"), an individual Indian who is the beneficial owner of trust land on which Black Hills discovered the fossil.

This case is before us for the third time. The factual background is uncomplicated. Black Hills collects and restores fossils for display in museums. In August 1990, Black Hills was excavating fossils in western South Dakota. Sue Hendrickson, a researcher working on the project, discovered Sue on Williams' ranch while on break. Since 1969, the United States has held this ranch land in trust for the sole use and benefit of Williams, an Indian. Two days after the discovery, Black Hills scientists began excavating Sue, the most complete and valuable Tyrannosaurus rex skeleton known to man, from Williams' land. At some point during the excavation, Black Hills purported to purchase from Williams the right to excavate Sue for $5000. After excavation, Black Hills moved the ten tons of bones to Hill City, South Dakota, where scientists began the laborious process of restoring the fossil.

In May 1992, however, federal officers seized Sue and moved her to the South Dakota School of Mines and Technology ("School of Mines"). The United States attorney for South Dakota ordered the seizure on the ground that Black Hills' removal of Sue from Williams' land violated federal criminal statutes relating to federal lands. Black Hills then brought suit in district court to quiet title to Sue. . . .

We now reach the merits of the case. We must first decide precisely what issue is before us. Initially, Black Hills sued the government to quiet title to Sue. Black Hills' second amended complaint abandoned the quiet title action and sought an order requiring the government to return the fossil. Black Hills argues that the district court erred because it determined ownership, an issue Black Hills claims that it did not raise in the second amended complaint. According to Black Hills, the district court "only had jurisdiction to determine whether [Black Hills] or the Department of Justice was entitled to possession of the fossil."

In the second amended complaint, however, Black Hills stated that it "paid Williams $5000 in exchange for Sue. [Black Hills] scientists wrote a check to Williams on August 27, 1990, which he accepted and cashed in full payment for Sue." Thus, Black Hills alleged that it owned the fossil outright, not that it leased it or had some possessory interest that did not amount to full ownership. In light of this allegation, we can only construe its request that the district court order the "United States to return the fossil to [Black Hills]" as a claim for permanent possession of Sue. Determining whether Black Hills is entitled to permanent possession necessarily requires determining which party actually owns the fossil. Thus, we must determine whether the transaction between Williams and Black Hills transferred title of Sue to Black Hills.

The ownership issue depends on our construction of several statutes governing Indian trust land. Sue Hendrickson discovered the fossil on land to which the United States holds legal title in trust for Williams, an individual Indian. Under the trust instrument, the United States will hold the land "in trust for the sole use and benefit of" Williams until the trust relationship expires on September 23, 1994. The United States acquired the land pursuant to the Indian Reorganization Act of 1934 ("the IRA"), the trust patent to Williams pursuant to a provision of the General Allotment Act of 1887 ("the GAA"). Until the trust expires in 1994, Williams is a beneficial owner of the land, retaining certain judicially-recognized rights but lacking the absolute right to dispose of the land as he pleases.

Other provisions of the IRA reflect the limits of Williams' interest in his trust land. Section four of the IRA, subject to several exceptions not relevant here, prohibits the "sale, devise, gift, exchange, or other transfer of restricted" Indian trust lands. On application of Indian owners, however, the Secretary has discretion "to remove restrictions against alienation, and to approve conveyances, with respect to lands or interests in lands held by individual Indians under [the IRA]." These statutes and regulations establish a scheme by which beneficial owners of Indian land such as Williams may alienate all or part of their interest before their trust instruments expire. Outside of the permitted transactions not applicable here, the only way such owners may alienate an interest in their trust land is by securing the prior approval of the Secretary. An attempted sale of an interest in Indian trust land in violation of this requirement is void and does not transfer title.

Here, Black Hills claims that it purchased the right to excavate Sue from Williams for $5000. Williams did not apply to the Secretary for prior approval of this transaction nor did the Secretary ever approve it. All parties agree that the fossil is now personal property because it has been severed from the land. In *Starr v. Campbell*, 208 U.S. 527, 534 . . . (1908), however, the Supreme Court held that timber from Indian trust land that the beneficial owner sold was subject to the trust patent's restraint on alienation even though the timber became personal property after the purchaser severed it from the land.

Thus, the relevant inquiry for purposes of assessing the validity of the transaction is whether the fossil was personal property or land before Black Hills excavated it. If it was land within the meaning of the relevant statutes and regulations, the transaction between Williams and Black Hills is void and the United States holds Sue in trust for Williams because the trust continued in Sue when she became personalty.

Whether the fossil was "land" within the meaning of both 25 U.S.C. §464 and 25 U.S.C. §483 is a matter of federal law. Because Congress has provided no definition of "land" applicable to these statutes, however, we may refer to state property law for guidance. South Dakota law denominates two classes of property: "[r]eal or immovable" property and "[p]ersonal or movable" property. S.D. Codified Laws Ann. §43-1-2. "Real or immovable property consists of: (1) Land; (2) That which is affixed to land; (3) That which is incidental or appurtenant to land; (4) That which is immovable by law. Every kind of property that is not real is personal." "Land," in turn, "is the solid material of the earth, whatever may be the ingredients of which it is composed, whether soil, rock, or other substance."

We hold that the fossil was "land" within the meaning of §464 and §483. Sue Hendrickson found the fossil embedded in the land. Under South Dakota law, the fossil was an "ingredient" comprising part of the "solid material of the earth." It was a component part of Williams' land, just like the soil, the rocks, and whatever other naturally-occurring materials make up the earth of the ranch. Black Hills makes several arguments to the contrary, none of which we find persuasive. That the fossil once was a dinosaur which walked on the surface of the earth and that part of the fossil was protruding from the ground when Hendrickson discovered it are irrelevant. The salient point is that the fossil had for millions of years been an "ingredient" of the earth that the United States holds in trust for Williams. The case very well might be different had someone found the fossil elsewhere and buried it in Williams' land or somehow inadvertently left it there. Here, however, a Tyrannosaurus rex died some 65 million years ago on what is now Indian trust land and its fossilized remains gradually became incorporated into that land. Although it is movable, personal property now, at the time Hendrickson discovered the fossil it was part of Williams' land and thus is subject to §464 and §483. As in *Starr,* where an Indian sold timber constituting 15/16 of the value of the land, we would render the statutory restraint on alienation here essentially meaningless if Williams could transfer the right to excavate a priceless fossil derived from otherwise nondescript land without the Secretary's permission. Because he did not seek the Secretary's approval, we hold that Williams' attempted sale to Black Hills is void and that the United States holds Sue in trust for Williams pursuant to the trust patent. . . .

Black Hills next argues in effect that holding Williams' sale invalid is bad policy. It asserts that Williams was competent to sell the fossil even if it was an interest in land and that finding the sale invalid would undermine the current legislative trend favoring tribal self-determination. These points are matters of policy for Congress to consider, not federal courts. The current statutory scheme reflects Congress's desire to protect beneficial owners of Indian trust land like Williams regarding disposition of interests in such land. Congress may very well determine that the historic practice of shielding beneficial owners from their own improvident decisions, unscrupulous offerors, and whatever other evils the enacting Congresses contemplated decades ago is no longer wise.[1] Until it does, however, we are bound to apply the statutes and regulations forbidding such owners from alienating trust land without the Secretary's approval. . . .

We also reject Black Hills' claim that the district court's decision violated its due process rights because the government seized the fossil without a pre-deprivation hearing and because Black Hills added value to Sue that it will be unable to recoup. Because we find that Black Hills has no interest in Sue, we reject its claim that the lack of a pre-deprivation hearing violated its rights. Moreover, although it is unfortunate that Black Hills spent a great deal of time and resources adding value to a fossil it does not own, concluding that Black Hills' transaction with Williams is void does not deprive Black Hills of due process where it had no interest in the fossil and it could have taken any number of steps to protect itself in the first place. At the very least, for instance, that the fossil was embedded in land located within the boundaries of the Cheyenne River Sioux Indian Reservation should have alerted Black Hills to the possibility that the federal government had some interest in Sue. Because it did not, however, we hold that the United States holds Sue in trust for Williams pursuant to the trust patent.

For the foregoing reasons, we affirm the judgment of the district court that the United States holds Sue in trust for Williams pursuant to the trust patent.

NOTES AND QUESTIONS

1. How many parties in *Black Hills* have an ownership claim to Sue? Do you agree with the court's conclusion that the United States holds Sue in trust for Williams? Does the answer depend on the definition of "possession" or what we mean by being first? Who was the first possessor?

2. Is the court's statutory construction persuasive? Do you think that the ordinary definition of "land" includes dinosaur bones?

3. What made Sue a celebrity and, as the case suggests, a source of controversy? Sue was a 90% complete skeleton of a Tyrannosaurus Rex, which made her very valuable. *See* Phillip Zonkel, "Sue-per Sized Awesome T. Rex Fossil Gets Presented in its Full Glory at Natural History Museum," *L.A. Daily News*, Nov. 29, 2000, at L6. In the autumn of 1997, Sotheby's

1. Congress has already eliminated many of the protections earlier statutes provided for Indians. Section 483 itself, for instance, allows Indians to apply to the Secretary for removal of alienation restrictions. Thus, the statutes reflect the trend toward Indian self-determination. Although it has diminished the practice of protecting Indians, however, Congress has not completely eliminated it. Williams was free to request that the government end the trust or that he be allowed to alienate his land, but he did not. Because he did not, the vestiges of protection that remain still apply.

auctioned Sue and the Chicago Field Museum paid approximately $8.4 million for the South Dakota "land." Sue resides in the museum today. *See* Larry McShane, "Museum Pays $ 8.4 Million for T-Rex: 65-Million-Year-Old Fossil to Go on Display in Chicago in 2000," *Wash. Post,* Oct. 5, 1997, at A10. Adding to her notoriety, Sue has been the subject of two books: *Tyrannosaurus Sue: The Extraordinary Saga of the Largest, Most Fought Over T. Rex Ever Found,* by Steve Fiffer (W.H. Freeman and Co. 2000), and *Rex Appeal: The Amazing Story of Sue, the Dinosaur That Changed Science, the Law, and My Life,* by Peter L. Larson and Kristin Donnan (Invisible Cities Press 2002). For more on Sue's odyssey, see Patrick K. Duffy & Lois A. Lofgren, *Jurassic Farce: A Critical Analysis of the Government's Seizure of "Sue [TM]," A Sixty-Five-Million-Year-Old Tyrannosaurus Rex Fossil,* 39 S.D. L. Rev. 478 (1994). For images of Sue, visit http://www.fieldmuseum.org/sue/#photo-gallery-displaying-sue (last visited August 31, 2010)

4. Native American tribes and Native Hawaiians have a statutory right to the return of human remains and "funerary objects" unearthed on tribal or federal lands by virtue of the Native American Graves Protection and Repatriation Act, 25 U.S.C. §§3001-3013, 18 U.S.C. §1170. Section §3002 of the Act assigns ownership of the discovered remains or objects in the following order: (1) the lineal descendents of the decedent; (2) the tribe owning the land on which the discovery was made; (3) the tribe having "the closest cultural affiliation with such remains or objects and which, upon notice, states a claim for such remains or objects." In the event that the cultural affiliation is ambiguous or the remains and objects are unclaimed, the statute sets guidelines to distribute the remains or objects. For cases construing the Act, see *Yankton Sioux Tribe v. U.S. Army Corps of Engineers,* 209 F. Supp. 2d 1008 (S.D. 2002) (operation of the notice provisions of the Act); *Kickapoo Traditional Tribe of Texas v. Chacon,* 46 F. Supp. 2d 644 (W.D. Tex. 1999) (construing the phrase "human remains" under the Act).

5. Congress recognized that prior possession of land entitled Native Alaskans to compensation by passing the Alaska Native Claims Settlement Act, 43 U.S.C. §§1601-1629 (2000). In exchange for the termination of "aboriginal title" to Alaskan lands, the Act established 13 corporations, which were associated with Alaskan geography, to manage almost $1 billion dollars for the benefit of the native shareholders of the corporations. For a discussion of the history of the Act, *see United States v. Atlantic Ritchfield Co.,* 435 F. Supp. 1009 (D.C. Alaska 1977).

6.2 THE LAW OF GIFTS

As you know from your casebook, the elements required to show that a valid inter vivos gift has been made are easily listed — intent, delivery, and acceptance. Although the elements are quickly summarized, the cases in your book undoubtedly reveal that they are more complicated than they appear on first blush. For example, the evidence must show that the donor had a present intent to transfer ownership to the donee. If the donor intends to transfer ownership in the future, the donor has failed to make a valid gift. Furthermore, courts recognize various types of delivery and showing that one of the forms of delivery occurred can be fact-sensitive. For its part, acceptance is often the easiest element to show because it is a presumption. After all, few people decline gifts. However, the presumption of acceptance can be rebutted by appropriate evidence. To add another wrinkle to the law of gifts, courts often craft decisions around unstated notions of fairness, which can leave one with the impression that the law of gifts is haphazard.

As your experiences will likely confirm, most gifts are given unconditionally. The donee of a Christmas present, for example, usually does not have to satisfy any requirements to keep the present. Some gifts, however, come with strings attached, and such conditional gifts can be recognized by courts. Judicial decisions might turn on whether the condition is a condition precedent or a condition subsequent that is required to make the gift effective. Among the most commonly encountered conditional gifts are engagement rings, and a wealth of jurisprudence has grown up around which party is entitled to the ring in the event that the happy day is canceled. The next case involves a conditional gift that conjures up a troubling past, which presents an obstacle for the court in its attempt to determine the appropriate remedy.

United Daughters of the Confederacy v. Vanderbilt University

174 S.W.3d 98 (Tenn. Ct. App. 2005)

William C. Koch, JR., P.J., M.S.

In 1867, George Peabody, an American merchant and financier living in London, donated one million dollars to establish a fund for the improvement of education in the South in the aftermath of the Civil War. . . . [In 1909 the Tennessee General Assembly incorporated Peabody College.] The construction of the Peabody College's campus provided the Tennessee Division of the United Daughters of the Confederacy ("Tennessee U.D.C.") with the perfect opportunity to implement a project it had been contemplating for some time. Since 1902, the Tennessee U.D.C. had been discussing the idea of raising funds for the construction of a women's dormitory for the use of descendants of Confederate soldiers at a college or university in Tennessee. Accordingly, following the announcement of Peabody College's decision to move to a new campus, the Tennessee U.D.C. and Peabody

College began to discuss underwriting the construction of a dormitory on Peabody College's new campus. . . .

[The court describes three contracts between Peabody College and the Tennessee U.D.C. for the construction of a women's dormitory at Peabody College. In 1913, the first contract required the college to permit women descendents of Confederate soldiers to reside in the dorm without paying rent. However, fundraising problems prior to construction led to the execution of a second contract between the parties in 1927. The second contract specified that both parties wanted to build a "Confederate Memorial Hall" building on Peabody's campus. By the time that the money had been raised to construct the dormitory, both parties wanted to build a larger women's dormitory. As a result, the parties entered into a third contract in 1933 for the construction of a larger women's dormitory. The third contract allowed Peabody to use the money already acquired to build a larger women's dormitory so long as the first two floors were used for the purposes identified in the 1913 and 1927 contracts. Furthermore, the third contract required the college to place a plaque on the new building that identified it as "Confederate Memorial Hall."]

From 1935 until the late 1970's, women descendants of Confederate soldiers nominated by the Tennessee U.D.C. and accepted by Peabody College lived in Confederate Memorial Hall rent-free. However, by the late 1970's, Peabody College found itself in increasingly dire financial straits. In the spring of 1978, the trustees of the college decided to lease two dormitories, including Confederate Memorial Hall, to Vanderbilt as a way to raise revenue. By that time, only a few students nominated by the Tennessee U.D.C. were living in Confederate Memorial Hall, but Confederate Memorial Hall still housed various artifacts placed there by the Tennessee U.D.C., including Confederate portraits, furniture, and scrapbooks. . . .

On April 28, 1979, the trustees of Vanderbilt and Peabody College entered into an agreement effectuating the merger. Under the terms of the merger agreement, Vanderbilt succeeded to all of Peabody's legal obligations. . . .

E. Gordon Gee became the new chancellor of Vanderbilt in July 2000. In conversations with Vanderbilt students, faculty, and alumni over the next two years, the name of Confederate Memorial Hall was repeatedly identified as a major impediment to the progress of the university. In June 2002, Chancellor Gee discussed the matter with the executive committee of the Vanderbilt board of trust, and the executive committee decided that Chancellor Gee would handle the issue as an administrative matter. Chancellor Gee, without consulting the Tennessee U.D.C., then decided to change the name of "Confederate Memorial Hall" to "Memorial Hall," and his decision was made public in the fall of 2002. . . .

On October 10, 2002, Chancellor Gee drafted a memorandum to the full Vanderbilt board of trust explaining his decision to rename the building. Chancellor Gee stated that former, current, and prospective students, faculty, and staff had identified the presence on the Vanderbilt campus of a building named "Confederate Memorial Hall" as a barrier to achieving an inclusive and welcoming environment that is essential for a world-class university. He also noted that some individuals had refused to live or attend events in the building; that the building was originally named "Confederate Memorial Hall" to commemorate values that do not reflect those of a university dedicated to educating all and meeting the aspirations of the broader society; and that assigning students to live in a dormitory so named implied an endorsement, if not a celebration, of a system that many people find offensive. Finally, Chancellor Gee observed that having a building on the campus named "Confederate Memorial Hall" strongly reinforced the worst stereotypes held by many people that Vanderbilt is an institution trapped in a long-distant past.

The Vanderbilt board of trust supported Chancellor Gee's decision to rename Confederate Memorial Hall. Since then, Vanderbilt has changed its maps, website, and correspondence to reflect the building's new name of "Memorial Hall." Vanderbilt has not yet removed the name "Confederate Memorial Hall" from the pediment on the front of the building but has indicated its unequivocal intention to do so. The 1989 plaque describing the history of the building and the contributions of the Tennessee U.D.C. remains in place by the entrance of the building. . . .

On October 17, 2002, the Tennessee U.D.C. filed suit against Vanderbilt for breach of contract in the Chancery Court for Davidson County. . . .

The trial court heard the parties' summary judgment motions on September 22, 2003, and filed a memorandum opinion on September 30, 2003. The memorandum opinion, as well as the final order filed on October 9, 2003, granted Vanderbilt's motion for summary judgment and denied the Tennessee U.D.C.'s motion for partial summary judgment. The Tennessee U.D.C. appealed. . . .

In order to determine whether it is Vanderbilt or the Tennessee U.D.C. that is entitled to a judgment as a matter of law, we must first determine the precise nature of the legal relationship formed between the Tennessee U.D.C. and Peabody College by the 1913, 1927, and 1933 agreements. Although all three agreements use the word "contract," they do not purport to establish a typical commercial arrangement in which one party provides certain goods or services in return for a sum to be paid by the other party. Instead, the agreements indicate that the $50,000 to be raised by the Tennessee U.D.C. was to be transferred to Peabody College as a gift. . . .

Donors often seek to impose conditions on gifts to charitable organizations. In the case of *inter vivos* transfers, the conditions are generally embodied in a gift agreement or a deed of conveyance. . . . In the case of transfers to take place on the death of the donor, the conditions are generally contained in the terms of the donor's will.

A conditional gift is enforceable according to the terms of the document or documents that created the gift. If the recipient fails or ceases to comply with the conditions, the donor's remedy is limited to recovery of the gift. Because noncompliance results in a forfeiture of the gift, the conditions must be created by express terms or by clear implication and are construed strictly. . . .

Taking all three contracts together, the gift from the Tennessee U.D.C. to Peabody College was subject to three specific conditions. First, Peabody College was required to use the gift to construct a dormitory on its campus conforming to plans and specifications approved by the Tennessee U.D.C. Second, Peabody College was required to allow women descendants of Confederate soldiers nominated by the Tennessee U.D.C. and accepted by Peabody College to live on the first and second floors of the dormitory without paying rent and paying all other dormitory expenses on an estimated cost basis. Third, Peabody College was required to place on the dormitory an inscription naming it "Confederate Memorial." The contracts do not specify the duration of these conditions. In such circumstances, the court must determine whether a duration can be inferred from the nature and circumstances of the transaction. Given the nature of the project and the content of the conditions, we conclude that these conditions were not meant to bind Peabody College forever but instead were to be limited to the life of the building itself. Thus, as long as the building stands, these three conditions apply to the gift. . . .

In its complaint, the Tennessee U.D.C. claimed that Vanderbilt had already violated the condition requiring an inscription on the building naming it "Confederate Memorial" by publicly and privately announcing its intention to rename the building "Memorial Hall" and that Vanderbilt planned to violate the condition further by removing or altering the inscription on the pediment. In its answer, Vanderbilt admitted its plans to rename the building "Memorial Hall" and to remove the word "Confederate" from the inscription on the pediment but denied that these actions would violate the conditions of the gift as reflected in the agreements between the parties. In its summary judgment papers and its brief on appeal, Vanderbilt argues that the Tennessee U.D.C. cannot succeed on its claim against Vanderbilt as a matter of law because the undisputed evidence in the record shows that Vanderbilt and Peabody College substantially performed their obligations under the contracts, that the Tennessee U.D.C. has already received full consideration for its original contribution. . . . We find no merit in these arguments.

Vanderbilt's claim that the placement of a plaque by the entrance to the building describing the contributions of the Tennessee U.D.C. to the original construction constitutes substantial performance with the inscription condition cannot be taken seriously. The determination of whether a party has substantially performed depends on what it was the parties bargained for in their agreement. Here, the 1933 contract expressly and unambiguously required Peabody College to place an inscription on the building naming it "Confederate Memorial," and we have already concluded that the parties intended the inscription to remain until the building was torn down. Peabody College complied with the condition by placing a large inscription in stone on the pediment of the building reading "Confederate Memorial Hall." Peabody College did so in conformity with Peabody College's own 1934 construction drawings which show these words in large incised lettering on the pediment of the building.

Vanderbilt continued to comply fully with this condition from its 1979 merger with Peabody College until 2002 when it announced its plans to remove the word "Confederate" from the building's pediment. It is doubtful that a party such as Vanderbilt that has wilfully changed course after over twenty years of compliance with the literal terms of an agreement could ever rely on the doctrine of substantial performance. Even if it could, no reasonable fact-finder could conclude that replacing a name written in stone in large letters on the pediment of a building with a plaque by the entrance constitutes substantial performance of a requirement to do the former.

Vanderbilt's argument that it should be excused from complying with the inscription condition contained in the 1933 contract because the Tennessee U.D.C. has already received enough value for its original contribution to the construction of the building is likewise without merit. The courts must interpret contracts as they are written, and will not make new contracts for parties who have spoken for themselves. The courts do not concern themselves with the wisdom or folly of a contract, and are not at liberty to relieve parties from contractual obligations simply because these obligations later prove to be burdensome or unwise.

The same is true of conditions contained in a gift agreement. By entering into the 1913, 1927, and 1933 contracts, Peabody College necessarily agreed that the value of the gift it was receiving was worth the value of full performance of the conditions of the gift. In short, Vanderbilt's unilateral assessment that Peabody College gave away too much in the 1913, 1927, and 1933 agreements does not constitute a legal defense that would excuse Vanderbilt from complying with the conditions of the original gift. . . .

In summary, we have determined that the undisputed facts establish that the Tennessee U.D.C. gave a monetary gift to Vanderbilt's predecessor-in-interest subject to conditions and that Vanderbilt's predecessor-in-interest accepted the gift as well as the conditions that accompanied it. It is further undisputed that Vanderbilt now declines to abide by the conditions attached to the gift. Thus, because Vanderbilt has presented no legal basis for permitting it to keep the gift while refusing to honor the conditions attached to it, Vanderbilt must now either return the present value of the gift to the Tennessee U.D.C. or reverse its present course and agree to abide by the conditions originally placed on the gift.

Accordingly, we reverse the summary judgment entered in favor of Vanderbilt not because the record reveals disputed issues of material fact but rather because Vanderbilt has failed to demonstrate that it is entitled to a judgment as a matter of law. We have also determined that, if Vanderbilt insists on changing the name of Confederate Memorial Hall, the Tennessee U.D.C. has demonstrated that it is entitled to a judgment as a matter of law on its motion for partial summary judgment. We remand the case with directions to calculate the present value of the Tennessee U.D.C.'s gift to Peabody College, to enter a judgment in favor of the Tennessee U.D.C. in that amount, and to make whatever further orders may be required.

NOTES AND QUESTIONS

1. Do you think that Vanderbilt fulfilled the conditions of the gift? Why or why not? Is the remedy ordered by the court fair? How would you calculate the value of the Tennessee U.D.C.'s gift to Peabody for purposes of the remedy ordered by the court?

2. What should Vanderbilt do under these circumstances? What if the Vanderbilt community refused to use the building at all because of the name of the building and the history associated with that name?

3. Judge William B. Cain wrote a concurrence to explain what he thought was Vanderbilt University's "misperception that somehow the dormitory is a memorial to the institution of slavery or, indeed, to the Confederate government." Judge Cain referred to a portion of the plaque's language to respond to the "misperception":

> The inscription thereon reads: "Constructed in 1935 by George Peabody College for Teachers, in part, with funds raised at personal sacrifice during the Great Depression, by Tennessee women of the United Daughters of the Confederacy, in memory of their fathers and brothers who fought in the war between North and South, 1861-65." While in the longer aftermath of history few will doubt that the outcome of the great war was a blessing to North and South alike, the word "confederate" has many meanings to many people. To those diminished few who would gladly fight the war again, it has an almost mystic significance. To the descendants of slaves whose "250 years of unrequited toil" built a cotton empire and nourished it with blood, toil, tears and sweat until the Thirteenth Amendment to the United States Constitution swept the institution of slavery into the annals of history, it is a demeaning reminder of indignities and persecution. To others, it represents a remote chapter in history of little relevance to the global issues facing the world today. To the parties to this bilateral contract, its meaning under the record in this case cannot be clouded by any reasonable doubt. The plaque installed by Vanderbilt in 1989 said it all.

Judge Cain continues:

> It is to the memory of these men that Confederate Memorial Hall was built and, to that end and at great personal sacrifice in the midst of the Great Depression, that the United

Daughters of the Confederacy raised and contributed to Peabody College more than one-third of the total cost of the construction of the dormitory.

What was Judge Cain's purpose in writing the concurrence? Do you think he successfully changed the minds of many observers about the meaning of the name "Confederate Memorial Hall"?

4. Ongoing controversies continue to exist over the naming of buildings and parks. *See* Ann M. Bartow, *Trademarks of Privilege: Naming Rights and the Physical Public Domain*, 40 U.C. Davis L. Rev. 919 (2007).

6.3 ADVERSE POSSESSION

From Justice Marshall's opinion in *Johnson v. M'Intosh* to the decision in *Black Hills*, the notion of "first in time" lies at the foundation of much of property law. However, adverse possession vests title in an individual who was unquestionably later in time if that individual fulfills certain requirements. These requirements generally include an open, notorious, continuous, and exclusive use of the disputed land in a manner that is adverse to the true owner for a statutory period of time. If the adverse possessor's acts satisfy these elements, the true owner of the real property at issue is barred from bringing an action for ejectment against the adverse possessor and a new title vests in the adverse possessor that dates from the original date of entry. Because it permits a trespasser to acquire title to real property, adverse possession seemingly rewards a wrongdoer. But as a theoretical matter, adverse possession represents the just deserts for an individual who has made a productive use of the real property for a pre-determined time period while the true owner did not make productive use of the land. In the alternative, adverse possession punishes the lazy true owner who neglects to remove a trespasser for a long time.

Nome 2000 v. Fagerstrom

799 P.2d 304 (Alaska 1990)

Matthews, Chief Justice.

This appeal involves a dispute over a tract of land measuring approximately seven and one-half acres, overlooking the Nome River (hereinafter the disputed parcel). Record title to a tract of land known as mineral survey 1161, which includes the disputed parcel, is held by Nome 2000.

On July 24, 1987, Nome 2000 filed suit to eject Charles and Peggy Fagerstrom from the disputed parcel. The Fagerstroms counterclaimed that through their use of the parcel they had acquired title by adverse possession. . . .

The disputed parcel is located in a rural area known as Osborn. During the warmer seasons, property in Osborn is suitable for homesites and subsistence and recreational activities. During the colder seasons, little or no use is made of Osborn property.

Charles Fagerstrom's earliest recollection of the disputed parcel is his family's use of it around 1944 or 1945. At that time, he and his family used an abandoned boy scout cabin present on the parcel as a subsistence base camp during summer months. Around 1947 or 1948, they moved their summer campsite to an area south of the disputed parcel. However, Charles and his family continued to make seasonal use of the disputed parcel for subsistence and recreation.

In 1963, Charles and Peggy Fagerstrom were married and, in 1966, they brought a small quantity of building materials to the north end of the disputed parcel. They intended to build a cabin.

In 1970 or 1971, the Fagerstroms used four cornerposts to stake off a twelve acre, rectangular parcel for purposes of a Native Allotment application. . . .

Also around 1970, the Fagerstroms built a picnic area on the north end of the disputed parcel. The area included a gravel pit, beachwood blocks as chairs, firewood and a 50-gallon barrel for use as a stove.

About mid-July 1974, the Fagerstroms placed a camper trailer on the north end of the disputed parcel. The trailer was leveled on blocks and remained in place through late September. Thereafter, until 1978, the Fagerstroms parked their camper trailer on the north end of the disputed parcel from early June through September. The camper was equipped with food, bedding, a stove and other household items.

About the same time that the Fagerstroms began parking the trailer on the disputed parcel, they built an outhouse and a fish rack on the north end of the parcel. Both fixtures remained through the time of trial in their original locations. The Fagerstroms also planted some spruce trees, not indigenous to the Osborn area, in 1975-76.

During the summer of 1977, the Fagerstroms built a reindeer shelter on the north end of the disputed parcel. The shelter was about 8x8 feet wide, and tall enough for Charles Fagerstrom to stand in. Around the shelter, the Fagerstroms constructed a pen which was 75 feet in diameter and 5 feet high. The shelter and pen housed a reindeer for about six weeks and the pen remained in place until the summer of 1978.

During their testimony, the Fagerstroms estimated that they were personally present on the disputed parcel from 1974 through 1978, "every other weekend or so" and "[a] couple times during the week . . . if the weather was good." When present they used the north end of the parcel as a base camp while using the entire parcel for subsistence and recreational purposes. Their activities included gathering berries, catching and drying fish and picnicking. Their children played on the parcel. The Fagerstroms also kept the property clean, picking up litter left by others.

While so using the disputed parcel, the Fagerstroms walked along various paths which traverse the entire parcel. The paths were present prior to the Fagerstroms' use of the parcel and, according to Peggy Fagerstrom, were free for use by others in connection with picking berries and fishing. On one occasion, however, Charles Fagerstrom excluded campers from the land. They were burning the Fagerstroms' firewood.

Nome 2000 placed into evidence the deposition testimony of Dr. Steven McNabb, an expert in anthropology, who stated that the Fagerstroms' use of the disputed parcel was consistent with the traditional Native Alaskan system of land use. According to McNabb, unlike the non-Native system, the traditional Native system does not recognize exclusive ownership of land. Instead, customary use of land, such as the Fagerstroms' use of the disputed parcel, establishes only a first priority claim to the land's resources. The claim is not exclusive and is not a matter of ownership, but is more in the nature of a stewardship. That is, other members of the claimant's social group may share in the resources of the land without obtaining permission, so long as the resources are not abused or destroyed. McNabb explained that Charles' exclusion of the campers from the land was a response to the campers' use of the Fagerstroms' personal property (their firewood), not a response to an invasion of a perceived real property interest.[2]

Nevertheless, several persons from the community testified that the Fagerstroms' use of the property from 1974 through 1977 was consistent with that of an owner of the property. For example, one Nome resident testified that since 1974 "[the Fagerstroms] cared for [the disputed parcel] as if they owned it. They made improvements on it as if they owned it. It was my belief that they did own it."

During the summer of 1978, the Fagerstroms put a cabin on the north end of the disputed parcel. Nome 2000 admits that from the time that the cabin was so placed until the time that Nome 2000 filed this suit, the Fagerstroms adversely possessed the north end of the disputed parcel. Nome 2000 filed its complaint on July 24, 1987.

The Fagerstroms' claim of title by adverse possession is governed by AS 09.10.030, which provides for a ten-year limitations period for actions to recover real property. Thus, if the Fagerstroms adversely possessed the disputed parcel, or any portion thereof, for ten consecutive years, then they have acquired title to that property. Because the Fagerstroms' use of the parcel increased over the years, and because Nome 2000 filed its complaint on July 24, 1987, the relevant period is July 24, 1977 through July 24, 1987.

2. However, Charles Fagerstrom testified that when he excluded the campers he felt that they were "on our property." He also testified that during the mid to late 70s he would have "frown[ed]" upon people camping on "my property."

We recently described the elements of adverse possession as follows: "In order to acquire title by adverse possession, the claimant must prove, by clear and convincing evidence, . . . that for the statutory period 'his use of the land was continuous, open and notorious, exclusive and hostile to the true owner.'" *Smith v. Krebs*, 768 P.2d 124, 125 (Alaska 1989). The first three conditions — continuity, notoriety and exclusivity — describe the physical requirements of the doctrine. The fourth condition, hostility, is often imprecisely described as the "intent" requirement.

On appeal, Nome 2000 argues that as a matter of law the physical requirements are not met absent "significant physical improvements" or "substantial activity" on the land. Thus, according to Nome 2000, only when the Fagerstroms placed a cabin on the disputed parcel in the summer of 1978 did their possession become adverse. For the prior year, so the argument goes, the Fagerstroms' physical use of the property was insufficient because they did not construct "significant structure[s]" and their use was only seasonal. Nome 2000 also argues that the Fagerstroms' use of the disputed parcel was not exclusive because "[o]thers were free to pick the berries, use the paths and fish in the area." We reject these arguments.

Whether a claimant's physical acts upon the land are sufficiently continuous, notorious and exclusive does not necessarily depend on the existence of significant improvements, substantial activity or absolute exclusivity. Indeed, this area of law is not susceptible to fixed standards because the quality and quantity of acts required for adverse possession depend on the *character* of the land in question. Thus, the conditions of continuity and exclusivity require only that the land be used for the statutory period as an average owner of similar property would use it. Where, as in the present case, the land is rural, a lesser exercise of dominion and control may be reasonable.

The character of the land in question is also relevant to the notoriety requirement. Use consistent with ownership which gives visible evidence of the claimant's possession, such that the reasonably diligent owner "could see that a hostile flag was being flown over his property," is sufficient. Where physical visibility is established, community repute is also relevant evidence that the true owner was put on notice.

Applying the foregoing principles to this case, we hold that the jury could reasonably conclude that the Fagerstroms established, by clear and convincing evidence, continuous, notorious and exclusive possession for ten years prior to the date Nome 2000 filed suit. We point out that we are concerned only with the first year, the summer of 1977 through the summer of 1978, as Nome 2000 admits that the requirements of adverse possession were met from the summer of 1978 through the summer of 1987.

The disputed parcel is located in a rural area suitable as a seasonal homesite for subsistence and recreational activities. This is exactly how the Fagerstroms used it during the year in question. On the premises throughout the entire year were an outhouse, a fish rack, a large reindeer pen (which, for six weeks, housed a reindeer), a picnic area, a small quantity of building materials and some trees not indigenous to the area. During the warmer season, for about 13 weeks, the Fagerstroms also placed a camper trailer on blocks on the disputed parcel. The Fagerstroms and their children visited the property several times during the warmer season to fish, gather berries, clean the premises, and play. In total, their conduct and improvements went well beyond "mere casual and occasional trespasses" and instead "evince[d] a purpose to exercise exclusive dominion over the property." See *Peters v. Juneau-Douglas Girl Scout Council,* 519 P.2d at 826, 830 (Alaska 1974). That others were free to pick berries and fish is consistent with the conduct of a hospitable landowner, and undermines neither the continuity nor exclusivity of their possession.

With respect to the notoriety requirement, a quick investigation of the premises, especially during the season which it was best suited for use, would have been sufficient to place a reasonably diligent landowner on notice that someone may have been exercising dominion and control over at least the northern portion of the property. Upon such notice, further inquiry would indicate that members of the community regarded the Fagerstroms as the owners. Continuous, exclusive, and notorious possession were thus established.

Nome 2000 also argues that the Fagerstroms did not establish hostility. It claims that "the Fagerstroms were required to prove that they intended to claim the property as their own." According to Nome 2000, this intent was lacking as the Fagerstroms thought of themselves not as owners but as stewards pursuant to the traditional system of Native Alaskan land usage. We reject this argument and hold that all of the elements of adverse possession were met.

What the Fagerstroms believed or intended has nothing to do with the question whether their possession was hostile. Hostility is instead determined by application of an *objective* test which simply asks whether the possessor "acted toward the land as if he owned it," without the permission of one with legal authority to give possession. *Hubbard v. Curtis,* 684 P.2d 842, 848 (Alaska 1984). As indicated, the Fagerstroms' actions toward the property were consistent with ownership of it, and Nome 2000 offers no proof that the Fagerstroms so acted with anyone's permission. That the Fagerstroms' objective manifestations of ownership may have been accompanied by what was described as a traditional Native Alaskan mind-set is irrelevant. To hold otherwise would be inconsistent with precedent and patently unfair.

Having concluded that the Fagerstroms established the elements of adverse possession, we turn to the question whether they were entitled to the entire disputed parcel. Specifically, the question presented is whether the jury could reasonably conclude that the Fagerstroms adversely possessed the southerly portion of the disputed parcel.

Absent color of title, only property actually possessed may be acquired by adverse possession. Here, from the summer of 1977 through the summer of 1978, the Fagerstroms' only activity on the southerly portion of the land included use of the pre-existing trails in connection with subsistence and recreational activities, and picking up litter. They claim that these activities, together with their placement of the cornerposts, constituted actual possession of the southerly portion of the parcel. Nome 2000 argues that this activity did not constitute actual possession and, at most, entitled the Fagerstroms to an easement by prescription across the southerly portion of the disputed parcel.

Nome 2000 is correct. The Fagerstroms' use of the trails and picking up of litter, although perhaps indicative of adverse use, would not provide the reasonably diligent owner with visible evidence of another's exercise of dominion and control. To this, the cornerposts add virtually nothing. Two of the four posts are located well to the west of the disputed parcel. Of the two that were allegedly placed on the parcel in 1970, the one located on the southerly portion of the parcel disappeared at an unknown time. The Fagerstroms maintain that because the disappearing stake was securely in place in 1970, we should infer that it remained for a "significant period." Even if we draw this inference, we fail to see how two posts on a rectangular parcel of property can, as the Fagerstroms put it, constitute "[t]he objective act of taking physical possession" of the parcel. The two posts simply do not serve to mark off the boundaries of the disputed parcel and, therefore, do not evince an exercise of dominion and control over the entire parcel. Thus, we conclude that the superior court erred in its denial of Nome 2000's motion for a directed verdict as to the southerly portion. This case is remanded to the trial court, with instructions to determine the extent of the Fagerstroms' acquisition in a manner consistent with this opinion.

NOTES AND QUESTIONS

1. What arguments did the true owner in Nome make to show that the Fagerstroms' possession of the disputed land failed to satisfy Alaska's requirements for adverse possession? Does the definition of "possession" differ by culture? Race? For another case involving adverse possession in Alaska, see *Vezey v. Green*, 35 P.3d 14 (Alaska 2001).

2. Native Americans have initiated a number of suits seeking return of their lands that have been defended by the assertion of adverse possession. See, e.g., *Mohegan Tribe v. Connecticut*, 638 F.2d 612, 614-15 n.3 (1980) (listing cases and stating that "[t]o date, the Indians have been largely successful in their legal battles regarding their claims to the eastern lands. Defenses based upon state adverse possession laws and state statutes of limitation have been consistently rejected.") However, not all defenses of adverse possession have failed. In *Catawba Indian Tribe v. South Carolina*, 978

F.2d 1334 (4th Cir. 1992), the Catawba Indian Tribe sought to reacquire some 144,000 acres of land alleged to have been set aside for it by two treaties from the 1760s. *Id.* at 1337. In response, South Carolina moved to dismiss the claim based on the 1959 Division of Catawba Assets Act, which terminated the tribe's "special federal status" and subjected it to all state laws. *Id.* A lower court decision found that the tribe's claim exceeded South Carolina's statutory limit to recover dispossessed lands by eight years. *Id.* at 1337-38. The Fourth Circuit agreed and concluded that the tribe had lost much of its land by adverse possession. *Id.* at 1339-45 (the court found that the statute of limitations had not been satisfied for some of the disputed lands because of tacking problems).

One of the persistent problems associated with many cases of adverse possession is whether or not successive adverse possessors may add the time of prior occupants to their own times of possession to satisfy the statutory period for adverse possession. For example, imagine that a person takes up residence in an unoccupied building in an urban center but then abandons the premises after another person moves into the same unoccupied building. Is an individual claiming title to the unoccupied property by adverse possessor entitled to add the time of prior occupants to meet the statutory period required to gain title? The answer depends on whether or not the adverse possessors were in privity with one another. As the next case shows, the privity question becomes thorny if the relationship between the adverse possessors is ambiguous.

East 13th Street Homesteaders' Coalition v. Lower East Side Coalition Housing Development

230 A.D.2d 622 (N.Y. App. Div. 1996)

Elliot Wilk, J.

The petitioners are occupants of 537, 539, 541, and 545 East 13th Street, who brought this suit to prevent the City from removing them from these buildings to implement a Federally subsidized plan to rehabilitate the buildings and create low-income housing units. The narrow issue presently on appeal is whether the petitioners should be granted a preliminary injunction barring their eviction pending trial on the issue of whether legal title to the property passed to them through adverse possession. . . .

Considering that the petitioners claim the apartment buildings upon a theory of adverse possession, they must show that they are likely to prove, by clear and convincing evidence that for a period of ten years they actually possessed the subject property at issue, and that their possession was open and notorious, exclusive, continuous, hostile, and under claim of right.

Our review of the record reveals that petitioners are not likely to prove ten years of actual, continuous, open and notorious possession of the subject buildings (between 1984 and 1994, the period here in question). Since petitioners' claim of right is not supported by a written instrument, they must show actual, not constructive, possession to establish the requisite temporal element. The record contains documentary and photographic evidence that the City sealed the buildings numerous times during the claimed period, and that the occupants had to break these seals, sometimes with a sledgehammer, to reenter the buildings.

The petitioners argue that there was a chain of possession of coalition members in all of the buildings during the requisite period to support the requirement of continuous ownership, but the record does not reveal that such successive possession was continued by an unbroken chain of privity such that it could be tacked for adverse possession purposes. In fact, there is no evidence of privity between successive occupants of the apartments, nor is there evidence of any intended transfers. In addition, some of the apartments were vacant for some period, such that the vacating occupant and the new occupant apparently had no contact at all.

In sharp distinction, the claimant in *Ray v Beacon Hudson Mtn. Corp.* (88 N.Y.2d 154), the case relied upon in the dissent, was the same person who had occupied the property there in issue from 1963 through 1988, a period of twenty-five years. Such is not the case here, where we are presented with an oft-interrupted number of unrelated occupants.

Since petitioners have failed to demonstrate ten years of continuous possession of the subject property, a condition precedent to a claim for adverse possession, the likely success of which is evaluated on this motion, and respondents have countered with proof which persuasively weighs against the petitioners' claims, the motion for a preliminary injunction [is] denied.

Dissent By: Kupferman

In the recent case of *Ray v Beacon Hudson Mtn. Corp.* (88 N.Y.2d 154, 156), Judge Titone, speaking for a unanimous Court, stated: "In determining whether the common-law requirement of 'continuity of possession' has been met in an adverse possession claim to an estate in land, a court should consider not only the adverse possessor's physical presence on the land but also the claimant's other acts of dominion and control over the premises that would appropriately be undertaken by owners of properties of similar character, condition and location. Thus, we conclude that plaintiffs' occupancy of the summer cottage in a now-defunct resort town for one month during the summer, coupled with their regular efforts taken to secure and improve the premises and to eject trespassers during their absences for the 10-year statutory period while all neighboring structures collapsed due to vandalism or abandonment, satisfied the element of continuous actual possession."

This statement is, mutatis mutandis, substantially analogous to our current situation.

Further on in his opinion, Judge Titone states "[P]laintiffs' installation of utilities and over-all preservation of the cottage, a permanent and substantial structure, in a veritable ghost town, for the duration of the statutory period demonstrates continuous, actual occupation of land by improvement." (*supra,* at 161.)

In the case at bar, there is no doubt that the plaintiffs made improvements and attempted to preserve the buildings involved in an area that could be considered the equivalent of a "ghost town." Moreover, as in the *Ray* case, where the occupation was for only one month during the summer, we have intermittent occupation by various people who are a part of a cohesive group.

In 1977 and 1978, by in rem proceedings, the City acquired title to the four buildings in question. As the IAS Court found at the hearing it conducted, by the early 1980's the buildings had become a "neighborhood hazard, housing drug activity, litter and trash." The City having defaulted on its obligation to maintain order and ensure tranquility, the plaintiffs moved into the vacant buildings.

The City now indicates that it is prepared to gut the buildings and rehabilitate the neighborhood with private funds and Federal tax credits after having failed to do so for many years. This may be a consummation to be wished but not necessarily a firm result. In the interim, the preliminary injunctive relief granted by the IAS Court should be continued, preventing a warrant of eviction, until such time as there can be a definitive conclusion as to the claim that the plaintiffs have adverse possession.

NOTES AND QUESTIONS

1. In what way does the dissenting opinion differ from that of the majority? Did the majority and dissent agree that privity existed between the occupants? Do you think privity existed between the occupants of the apartment building? Why or why not?

2. Do the consequences of the court's decision fall equally on all adverse possessors or more harshly on individuals residing in crowded urban centers?

3. Without specificity, the dissent suggests that the occupants "made improvements to the property." Is it important to improve property for purposes of adverse possession? If so, what type of improvements might support a claim of adverse possession? The same court that decided *East 13th Street Homesteaders' Coalition* commented on this question in *Paulino v. Wright,* 210 A.D. 171 (1994). In *Paulino,* a group of homeless persons occupied an abandoned property owned by the City of New York and were evicted from the premises by police officers. *Id.* at 171-72. As part of a

lawsuit that centered on the availability of self-help under these circumstances, the evicted occupants claimed that they had obtained title to the property by adverse possession. *Id.* at 171. Addressing the claim of adverse possession, the court observed that

> [d]uring their occupancy, plaintiffs claim that certain repairs were made to the building including: the installation of a circuit breaker box, electrical wiring, and pipes; the construction and demolition of walls, ceilings, windows and floors; and the installation of plumbing and bathroom fixtures. It is important to note that there is no proof that any of these repairs were done by competent or licensed electricians or plumbers, or that they meet minimal safety levels and, although we recognize plaintiffs' desire to remain in this building, the potential for injury or death to the occupants due to poor and improper construction or hazardous conditions must be of greater concern. *Id.* at 171-72.

Given the court's discussion, what obstacles do occupants in these situations encounter in their attempts to satisfy the elements of adverse possession? Is adverse possession a meaningful remedy under these circumstances?

6.4 ESTATES AND FUTURE INTERESTS

One of the most challenging areas in many property courses is the material on possessory estates and future interests. Studying this material is difficult, much like learning a new language. Once finished, however, an attorney possesses the tools to help a client distribute his/her property in a manner that comports with the client's wishes. As a result, the subjects of estates and future interests often arise in conjunction with the disposition of property by will. Although the context of the estates and future interests in a wills setting is different from a typical conveyance of real property, the complicated nomenclature retains its meaning. With that in mind, consider the following case.

Hermitage Methodist Homes of Virginia v. The Miller School of Albemarle County, Seven Hills School Inc., and Dominion Trust Co.

387 S.E.2d 740 (Va. 1990)

COMPTON, Justice.

In 1956, Jack Adams, a resident of Lynchburg, executed his will establishing the trust in question. In 1964, the testator executed a codicil to the will. In 1968, Adams died testate. The will and codicil, drafted by a Lynchburg attorney, were duly probated.

Article IV of the codicil provides that the residuum of Adams' estate be held in trust and the income therefrom be distributed pursuant to clause (a). The clause provides, in part:

> So long as Prince Edward School Foundation, Prince Edward Co., Va., admits to any school, operated or supported by it, only members of the White Race . . . my said Trustee shall pay the net income . . . to the Trustees (or other governing body) of such Foundation, to be expended by them . . . for the benefit of any of said schools.

The clause further provides:

> In the event that the said Foundation should cease to operate for one year, or should at any time permit to matriculate in any of the schools operated or supported by it any person who is not a member of the White Race, no further payment of income shall be made to the said Foundation; but all income accruing after such date shall be paid to the Trustees of the Miller School . . . so long as said School admits only members of the White Race; said income shall be expended . . . for the payment of the expenses of maintaining and operating said School. . . .

The clause further provides for successive gifts over first to Seven Hills School, Inc., located in Lynchburg, and then to Hampden-Sydney College, in the event of the occurrence of the same contingencies. The final beneficiary of the successive gifts over is Hermitage Methodist Homes of Virginia, Inc., without the limitation of the described contingencies. . . .

In 1987, appellee Dominion Trust Company filed the present suit naming as parties defendant the income beneficiaries and the Attorney General of Virginia. Asserting that it was the successor trustee of the Adams Trust, the trustee alleged that it had paid over the income to Prince Edward School Foundation since the creation of the trust. It stated that "a determinable event" as described in Article IV may have occurred with respect to the school administered by the Foundation. (Counsel represented at the bar of this Court that subsequent to creation of the trust each educational beneficiary had enrolled black students in its schools.)

The trustee sought advice and guidance on "whether the determinative event or contingency [was] legal, valid and enforceable." Therefore, the trustee asserted, it was "uncertain as to the proper income beneficiary of said trust" and asked the court to construe and interpret the will to determine the rights of the parties. . . .

These assignments of error present the following issues on appeal. First, are the discriminatory provisions of Article IV valid, or are they unconstitutional and invalid? Second, if such provisions are invalid, is the primary educational bequest of the trust nevertheless valid, or must it fail, requiring future income to be paid to Hermitage? [An omitted third assignment of error involved the applicability of the doctrine of cy pres.]

Because of the view we take of the second issue, based on principles of real property law, we will agree with Prince Edward, Seven Hills School, and the Miller School on the first issue for purposes of this decision. Whether the discriminatory provisions are valid or void, the result is the same, as we will demonstrate below. Thus, we will assume, without deciding, that the trial court correctly ruled that the racially discriminatory provisions are unconstitutional and void. This brings us to the second issue, that is, whether the educational trust is otherwise valid.

Asserting that the restrictive language provides for an illegal condition subsequent, Prince Edward relies on *Meek v. Fox,* 118 Va. 774, 88 S.E. 161 (1916), to sustain the trial court's ruling that the racially discriminatory condition is void, but the gift is valid. . . .

The principle of striking the offending condition subsequent and thereby creating an absolute estate, as applied in *Meek,* does not control this case because the provision at issue here is not a condition subsequent. Rather, this provision is a special limitation. Further, the estate in personalty created here is defeasible subject to an executory limitation.

Professor Minor explains that "special limitations are created by such words as 'while,' 'during,' 'as long as,' 'until,' etc. Thus, a grant to A *until* Z returns from abroad; to a woman *while* she remains a widow, or *during* widowhood . . . , to D and his heirs *as long as* Y has heirs of his body . . . , all these are special limitations and not conditions subsequent." 1 Minor on Real Property §525 at 690 (Ribble ed. 1928). "Limitations differ from conditions subsequent in this: A limitation marks the *utmost time of continuance* of an estate; a condition marks some event, which, if it happens in the course of that time, is to *defeat the estate.*" Id., quoted in *Meek, 118 Va. at 778, 88 S.E. at 162.*

In the granting clauses of Adams' will, he repeatedly specified that each educational beneficiary's right to receive income extended only "so long as" the beneficiary complied with the restrictive provision. But, if an educational beneficiary violated the restrictive provision by the matriculation of a black student, that beneficiary's interest would terminate, and the gift would devolve to successive educational beneficiaries who had not violated the provision. Further, Adams makes his intent clear in clause (b) that the creation of the educational beneficiaries' rights to receive income "shall be determinable" upon the happening of the contingency and that "all rights" of those institutions, successively to receive income from the trust "shall automatically terminate." Clearly this is language of limitation and not condition.

Meek makes clear that if the provision in that case had been a limitation, although equally offensive to the public policy against restraints on marriage, the Court could not have found it void. "Hence, while an estate limited 'to A in fee, but if he attempts to alien his estate then to B in fee,' would give A an absolute estate and in fee, free from condition, because the condition is an unreasonable restraint of alienation and void, yet a limitation 'to A until he attempts to alien, and then to B,' would be a perfectly good limitation, and upon A's attempt his estate would cease and go over to B." 118 Va. at 779-80, 88 S.E. at 162-63. Although it did not address the issue of what happens when a gift subject to a special limitation offends constitutional considerations, the essential nature of a limitation as described by the Court in *Meek* points to the decision of the issue in this case.

In the words of Minor, a limitation marks the utmost time of continuance of the estate. And, a limitation cannot be altered to extend "beyond that period without violating the terms of the devise." *Id.* at 779, 88 S.E. at 162. If a condition subsequent is unlawful, a court can merely excise the offending language and leave the remaining estate intact. But, where a gift or estate subject to a limitation is unlawful, in order to cure the defect the court must terminate the entire gift or estate.

Therefore, unlike in *Meek*, the interests of the educational charities fail completely. And, this is not because we give effect to an invalid trust provision. Rather, we strike the entire gift to Prince Edward and the gifts to the other educational beneficiaries because the offending language cannot be stricken from the provision without changing the essential nature and quality of the estate.

It necessarily follows from the foregoing that, while the gifts to all the beneficiaries of Adams' charitable educational trust must fail, the executory interest of Hermitage survives. Adams did not place any unconstitutional limitations upon Hermitage's interest. And, as all prior estates have been declared invalid, Hermitage has the only valid, remaining interest. The trial court erred in holding to the contrary.

Because we find that the provision is a limitation, the same final result would be reached if we found that the trust's provisions were constitutional, as we have said earlier. By the natural operation of this limitation, if it were valid, upon the matriculation of a black student into Prince Edward, the school's interest terminated. And, because as counsel have represented, the educational institutions have all admitted black students, their respective interests in the trust proceeds can never vest into possession. Hermitage would be the ultimate beneficiary since no limitations are placed on its interest.

For these reasons . . . we will enter final judgment here ordering the trustee to pay all retained trust income and future trust income to Hermitage.

NOTES AND QUESTIONS

1. How does the placement of the racial restriction within the granting clause affect the court's decision? Is the court's analysis of the distinction between a limitation and a condition subsequent persuasive? For an argument in favor of eliminating the distinction between limitations and conditions, see Gerald Korngold, *For Unifying Servitudes and Defeasible Fees:*

Property Law's Functional Equivalents, 66 Tex. L. Rev. 533 (1988). For more on the *Hermitage Methodist Homes* case, see Jonathan L. Entin, *Defeasible Fees, State Action, and the Legacy of Massive Resistance*, 34 Wm. & Mary L. Rev. 769 (1993).

2. The Supreme Court faced a similar issue in *Evans v. Newton*, 382 U.S. 296 (1966). In *Evans*, former United States Senator A.O. Bacon of Georgia devised a parcel of real property in trust to his hometown of Macon, Georgia, for use as a park for white people only. Although the park was segregated for some period of time, the city eventually decided that it could not operate the park on a segregated basis and African-Americans used the park thereafter. The Supreme Court characterized the park as "public" because the city maintained the park in fulfillment of its role as trustee under the senator's will. As a result, the Court decided that the Fourteenth Amendment applied to the public park regardless of titleholder. However, the Court's decision left one important issue unresolved — if the city could not maintain a segregated public park in accordance with the senator's will, then who gets title to the property? The Supreme Court of Georgia tackled that issue in *Evans v. Abney*, 165 S.E.2d 160 (1968). The court reasoned that the Supreme Court's decision had made it impossible to give effect to the senator's will as it pertained to the park; therefore, the land reverted to the senator's heirs by operation of law. Following the decision in Georgia's highest court, the case again made its way to the Supreme Court in *Evans v. Abney*, 396 U.S. 435 (1970). In this iteration of the case, a group of African-American residents of Macon contended that terminating the trust violated their due process and equal protection rights under the Fourteenth Amendment. The Supreme Court upheld Georgia's ruling and asserted that Georgia's interpretation of Georgia law did not amount to state action for constitutional purposes. The Court distinguished *Shelley v. Kraemer*, 334 U.S. 1 (1948), because Georgia's ruling that the property should return to the senator's heirs caused all citizens to lose a park whereas only some citizens suffered the harm of *Shelley*'s racially discriminatory private covenants.

3. *Tinnin v. First United Bank of Mississippi*, 502 So.2d 659 (Miss. 1987), provides an alternative solution to the problem of racially restrictive provisions in trusts as compared to the holdings in *Hermitage*, *Evans v. Newton*, and *Evans v. Abney*. In *Tinnin*, a testator established a testamentary charitable trust to "make loans to students of a state college or university of and operated by the state of Mississippi, who are found worthy and who are of the Caucassion [sic] race." *Id.* at 661. The trustee, the First United Bank of Mississippi, administered the trust without regard to the racial restriction, which spurred the four heirs of the settlor to file suit to terminate the trust and receive the assets of the trust post-termination. *Id.* at 662. The assets of the trust amounted to almost $300,000. *Id.* The trial court dismissed the complaint and the Tinnins appealed. *Id.*

Because all parties conceded that the racial restriction was unenforceable, the issue before the Supreme Court of Mississippi was whether to reconstruct the trust for the benefit of all students or to terminate the trust and distribute its corpus to the Tinnin heirs based on the intent of the testator. *Id.* at 667. The question boiled down to whether the testator would have preferred to have the trust benefit students without regard to race or whether the racial restriction was so important that the testator would have preferred to end the trust in the absence of the racial restriction. *Id.* at 668. Although the lower courts dismissed the Tinnins' complaint on the basis of documentary evidence, the Supreme Court of Mississippi ruled that the documentary evidence was ambiguous regarding the intent of the testator. *Id.* at 669. As a result, the court remanded the case with an order to accept extrinsic evidence of the testator's intent such as the nature of the relationship between the heirs and the testator and the importance of helping students attend college as against the conviction to limit the assistance by race. *Id.* at 669-70. On remand, the trial court concluded that the heirs were not close to the testator and that the primary intent of the testator to provide help to students attending college outweighed the intent to discriminate by race. *Tinnin v. First United Bank of Mississippi,* 570 So.2d 1193, 1194 (Miss. 1990). As a result, the trial court modified to the trust to permit the assets to benefit college students regardless of race. *Id.* The Tinnins appealed and the case again made its way to the Supreme Court of Mississippi. The Supreme Court of Mississippi upheld the modification of the trust. *Id.* at 1196.

6.5 CONCURRENT OWNERSHIP—PARTITION

The previous material on possessory estates and future interests parses property interests in chronological fashion—Party A has an interest that denotes present possession of property, while Party B has a future interest that may or may not result in possession of that same property. On the other hand, concurrent interests—tenancies in common, joint tenancies, and tenancies by the entirety—describe interests held by different parties in the same piece of property at the same time. Each of the concurrent owners not only has a right to use the property, but also owes duties to each of the other co-owners. Concurrent owners might reach an agreement regarding how to use the property, but what happens if the parties disagree about how to use the property? For tenants in common and joint tenants, one answer to this question is to partition the real property. A partition action severs concurrent interests into individual interests; an individual owner can use her property free from the obligations owed to her former co-owners.

As a general matter, the co-owner seeking to partition the property need not provide a justification for the partition, which means that the partition seeker may ignore the hardship imposed on other co-owners as a result of the termination of the concurrent estate. Upon receiving a request for partition, a court may physically divide the property among the interest holders according to their proportionate shares, which is labeled a *partition in kind*, or the property can be sold and the proceeds split in the same manner, which is a *partition by sale*. The choice between a partition in kind and a partition by sale can be critical for the holders of concurrent interests. A partition in kind severs the concurrent interests, but the individual interest holder obtains some portion of the real property post-severance. Conversely, a partition by sale leaves the interest holder with only money. Consider this distinction in conjunction with the following material.

Chuck v. Gomes

532 P.2d 657 (Haw. 1975)

KOBAYASHI, Justice.

This is an appeal from the decree of the trial court ordering a sale of realty at public auction rather than a partition of the real estate. We affirm.

The real estate is owned equally by nine individuals as tenants in common, each owning an undivided one-ninth (1/9th) interest in fee. An action for partition of the realty or sale thereof was filed by three of the owners against the other owners.

The issues are: (1) whether or not evidence adduced at the trial made it appear "that a partition cannot be made without great prejudice to the owners", and (2) whether or not the trial court was correct in requiring the sale of the realty at public auction.

The relevant statutes are HRS §668-1, which provides in part:

> *Suits for partition.* When two or more persons hold or are in possession of real property as joint tenants or as tenants in common, in which one or more of them have an estate in fee, or a life estate in possession, a suit in equity may be brought by any one or more of them in the circuit court of the circuit in which the property is situated, for a partition of the property, according to the respective rights of the parties interested therein, and *for a sale* of the same or a part thereof *if it appears that a partition cannot be made without great prejudice to the owners* [emphasis added];

and HRS §668-7(6) which provides:

> *Powers of the court.* The court shall have power:
>
> (6) to divide and allot portions of the premises to some or all of the parties and order a sale of the remainder, or to sell the whole, where for any reason partition in kind would be *impracticable* in whole or in part *or be greatly prejudicial* to the parties interested . . . . (Emphasis added.)

The trial court issued an "Order for Commissioner to Investigate and Report to the Court Re Feasibility of Partition of Property" which provided, *inter alia*, as follows:

> 1. The Court hereby appoints John W. J. Lum, as Commissioner in partition, to investigate and report to the Court as to the feasibility and practicality of the partition of the property described in the Complaint filed herein for a (1) one-ninth (1/9th) interest in favor of Antone S. Teixeira, and a (2) eighth-ninth (8/9th) interest in favor of a proposed purchaser *or in any other division* and to prepare a plan for such division into lots or *as to the non-feasibility and impracticality of any physical partition of said property*." (Emphasis added.)

The trial court's order was premised on the fact that there was constant bickering and disagreement among the nine owners and upon the further fact that, of the nine persons who owned the fee as tenants in common, only defendant Antone S. Teixeira initially refused to agree to sell the real estate to a proposed purchaser. Mr. Antone Teixeira sought to have his share by way of partition of the realty, or in the alternative, be given the right to purchase the entire property in question.

The filed report of the Commissioner, a registered civil engineer and a land surveyor, gives the following relevant facts:

> 1. The total area of the property is 178,325 square feet and a one-ninth parcel would be composed of 19,814 square feet; . . .
>
> 7. It is feasible and practical to partition the property into two separate parcels — one parcel would contain 19,814 square feet and the other parcel would contain 158,511 square feet;
>
> 8. An exhibit map "A" shows the 19,814 square foot parcel as Parcel A and an alternate Parcel B. Parcel A is contiguous to land owned by defendant Antone S. Teixeira and Marjory Ann Teixeira. Further, Parcel A has the same general topography as the remaining 158,511 square foot parcel. In addition, Parcel A can be consolidated with Antone and Marjory Teixeira's land into a parcel acceptable to the City's Planning Department;
>
> 9. Parcel B would lengthen and enlarge Antone and Marjory Teixeira's land. This addition would be in more level land but would be encumbered by a 30-foot right-of-way (2,733 square feet) to the 158,511 square foot parcel. Parcel B would separate the remainder into two parcels and its acceptability to the City's Planning Department would be in doubt;
>
> 10. In conclusion, the Commissioner recommended only the partition in kind creating Parcel A, as shown on Exhibit A, and the eight-ninths (8/9ths) portion.

At the trial the Commissioner, in answer to a question whether or not it was *possible* to subdivide the realty into nine separate parcels, stated that it was *possible* to so subdivide but *difficult*.

Mr. Ray W. Hambleton, a licensed real estate appraiser, testified to the effect that the realty is worth more if partition is not had. He further testified that Parcels A and B are worth less separated from the whole of the realty and that Parcel B is worth more than Parcel A. . . .

The trial court, in its decree of sale of the realty, held that a partition of the real property into nine individual parcels was not feasible.

The appellants do not contest the trial court's finding of the lack of feasibility. However, they contend that the record herein fails to show that a partition of the realty into nine individual parcels or any other form of partition would be with great prejudice to the owners. We disagree with appellants' contention. The totality of the proceeding shows that a partition of the realty into nine individual parcels or any other form of partition would be with great prejudice to the owners.

In the instant case Antone Teixeira refused to accept Parcel A or Parcel B in satisfaction of his one-ninth (1/9th) undivided interest in the realty. And neither Antone Teixeira nor the other appellants urged upon the court or adduced evidence regarding a different form of partition of the realty that would be feasible or practical, that is, a partition that would be without great prejudice to the owners.

In addition, the Commissioner, after receipt of the order of the trial court directing him to determine the feasibility of a partition of the realty not only into one one-ninth (1/9th) parcel and one eight-ninths (8/9ths) parcel but also a partition of the realty "in any other division", concluded that only a partition of the realty into Parcel A or Parcel B and one eight-ninths (8/9ths) parcel was feasible and practical. Implicit in the Commissioner's conclusion is that any other form of partition of the realty was not feasible or practical and that any other form of partition would be with great prejudice to the owners.

The testimony of the appraiser is also relevant in denying the contention of the appellants.

We are of the opinion that implicit in the trial court's finding that a partition of the realty into nine individual parcels is not feasible, is the trial court's conclusion that partition of the realty into nine individual parcels cannot be made without great prejudice to the owners.

The record of the case sustains the trial court in its decree of public sale of the realty in question. Under the provisions of HRS §668-7(6) the trial court is empowered to order the sale of the realty in question "where for any reason partition in kind would *be impracticable* in whole or in part *or be greatly prejudicial* to the parties interested".

In our opinion the words "not feasible" in the context of the trial court's finding are synonymous with the word "impracticable". See *People v. Poly*, 40 N.Y.S. 990, 992, 17 Misc. 162, 164, 11 N.Cr. 346 (1896); Webster's Third New International Dictionary (unabridged, 1966).

The other issues raised by the appellants are without merit.

Dissent By: Richardson

The partition statute allows partition by judicial sale where actual division is shown to be *impracticable or greatly prejudicial* to the interested parties. Absent a showing of great prejudice to the owners resulting from an actual division of the property, it must then be determined if such division is impracticable. In so ascertaining whether partition in kind is impracticable, I believe the focus should be placed on whether physical division of the subject property is feasible and practical, that is, whether the property is susceptible of partition in kind. If such actual division is indeed found to be practicable, as in the case at bar where the Commissioner so recommended, then HRS Section 668-7(6) precludes the trial court from ordering a judicial sale, but rather authorizes the court to effect partition in kind of the realty.

In the instant case the Commissioner's finding that partition in kind was feasible and practical offered evidence of practicability sufficient to obviate the necessity of partition by judicial sale. I therefore conclude that the trial court erred in ordering partition by sale in light of the Commissioner's Report and in the absence of any showing of great prejudice to the owners. I would thus reverse. . . .

It is especially important to restate this preference for partition in kind so that in Hawaii we preserve the right of the individual joint tenant or tenant in common to hold onto his parcel of land where he opposes any forced sale of such property. Indeed, there are interests other than financial expediency which I recognize as essential to our Hawaiian way of life. Foremost is the individual's right to retain ancestral land in order to perpetuate the concept of the family homestead. Such right is derived from our proud cultural heritage wherein it was believed that:

> . . . [T]he one guarantee of survival [was] land . . [which was] in short supply either because of the density of population or because of the large holdings of exploiting gentry landholders . . . .
>
> . . . Because peasants depend for their survival on specific plots of land, ownership is their goal and once land is owned it must be *preserved and passed on intact* to the children. All this makes for the *great emphasis* on the *survival of the particular family line which owns the particular plot of land.* Thus peasants stress the unity and continuity of the family—large number of children, particularly sons who will work the plots of land, inherit them, and perhaps add to them. (Emphasis supplied.)

Undoubtedly there will be circumstances which justify the invocation of partition by judicial sale under HRS §§668-1 and 668-7(6). In the situation where the statutory grounds are met the preference for actual division of property must yield to partition by judicial sale.

But let us recognize that such preference for partition in kind should not be so easily disregarded. "Mindful of our Hawaiian heritage," we must not lose sight of the cultural traditions which attach fundamental importance to keeping ancestral land in a particular family line.

As the prior case suggests, real property is commonly handed down from generation to generation, thereby remaining in a family. An action for partition by sale threatens to eliminate the possibility of keeping real property within the family because, if successful, the land will be sold and the proceeds of the sale will be divided among the interest holders. The deleterious effect of partition is exemplified by the experience of African-American farm owners in the United States. In his book, *Gridlock Economy* (Basic Books 2008), Professor Michael Heller observes that

> [f]ollowing the Civil War, black Americans began acquiring land in earnest. By 1920, almost 1 million black families owned farms; they formed an integral part of the southern rural economy up through the 1930s and 1940s. But today, black families own fewer than 19,000 farms nationwide — a drop of 98 percent in less than a century. (By contrast, white-operated farms dropped by about 50 percent, from about 5.5 million to 2.4 million.) Partial explanations include consolidation of inefficient small farms and intense racial discrimination in farm lending. But there is more . . . .

Id. at 122.

The following selection from Professor Thomas Mitchell describes what Professor Heller refers to as "more"; the case that follows, *McNeely v. Bone*, represents one of the legal challenges filed to prevent the loss of land by partition.

From Reconstruction to Deconstruction: Undermining Black Landownership, Political Independence, and Community Through Partition Sales of Tenancies in Common

Thomas W. Mitchell, 95 Nw. U. L. Rev. 505 (2001)*

As we enter a new millennium, the pattern of landownership in the rural African American community represents the mirror opposite of the trend in black land acquisition one hundred years ago at the dawn of the twentieth century. A remarkable history of land acquisition has given way to extraordinary levels of land loss in the past half century. Today, the most current census of agriculture reveals that African American owner-operators of farms — whether full or part owners — own at most little more than two million acres of land in the United States. Despite hard-fought struggles to retain their land, many African Americans have lost land involuntarily.

Even the USDA has acknowledged that for many farmers, "especially minority and limited-resource farmers," land loss has been involuntary. This Article focuses on one of the primary causes of involuntary black land loss in recent times — partition sales of black-owned land held under tenancies in common. A partition sale can be viewed as a "private" forced sale of land held under a concurrent ownership arrangement,

*Reprinted by special permission of Northwestern School of Law, *Journal of Criminal Law and Criminology*.

typically a tenancy in common. The combined effect of two sets of legal rules contributes to the loss of black-owned rural land as a result of partition actions. First, like many other poor Americans, rural African American landowners have tended not to make wills; at the owner's death, state intestacy laws enable a broad class of heirs to acquire an interest in real property of the decedent. Interests in property transferred by intestacy from one generation to another become highly fragmented, splintering the fee into hundreds and even thousands of interests. A tenancy in common so splintered is commonly referred to as fractionated heir property or just heir property.

Second, the resulting tenancies in common are governed by common ownership rules that fail to distribute rights and responsibilities fairly among the tenants in common. Any tenant in common, whether a cotenant holding a minute interest or a substantial interest, may force a sale of the land, thereby ending the tenancy in common. Any cotenant may sell her interest to someone outside of the family or ownership group, bringing a stranger into the circle of cotenants, without seeking the consent of the other cotenants. Despite these broad powers, there are no corresponding obligations to contribute to the ongoing costs of maintaining the property.

Opportunistic lawyers and land speculators have taken advantage of these legal rules in order to force sales of black-owned land. Many times, family members know—or learn from an outsider—that they own an interest in a tenancy in common and decide to cash out. Although some of these people seek legal assistance, many of these people do not want the entire land sold. Many of these family members exit the tenancy in common by selling their interest to nonfamily members. They often do not know the financial pressure this may place on other cotenants who may wish to remain on the land or to preserve it for the family. Unbeknownst to the family member, the buyer often takes the interest with the underlying motive of seeking a partition sale. Even the partition actions initiated by family members who seek a sale of the property tend to be brought by "heirs who are physically removed from the land." . . .

The tenancy in common represents a potentially unstable form of landownership because alienability is unrestricted and the partition remedy is weighted toward dissolution. A tenancy in common with a large number of cotenants is even more unstable simply because the problems of free-riding and exit are multiplied. Because of the low incidence of estate planning among poor, rural African Americans, much of the black-owned land base in the South has been traditionally transferred from one generation to another under state intestacy laws. Property acquired under the intestacy laws is commonly referred to as "heir property."

Although a tenancy in common created by volition and a tenancy in common created by operation of the laws of intestacy may be governed by the same set of property laws, these two methods of formation yield ownership arrangements that are vastly different in character. A tenancy in common created consensually resembles a closely held corporation: there tends to be a small number of co-owners, each member of the ownership structure knows the other owners, and the owners are likely to live within close proximity of one another. A tenancy in common created under the laws of intestacy, by contrast, bundles together groups of people who may possess little actual connection to one another and perhaps lack even knowledge of one another's identity.

As time passes, not only does the number of interests increase in a tenancy in common created by operation of law, but divergences also appear in the size of individual ownership interests, especially after any in the first generation of heirs with children or lineal heirs die and their interests pass to their descendants. When the property comes to be held by owners from multiple generations, the common owners are likely to value the land differently and conflicts are more likely to arise. Further, as the number of interests increase, the owners are more likely to live in scattered locations. Decisions regarding the disposition of the property that may have been fairly simple to coordinate when all of the tenants in common resided, for example, in Sumpter County, Alabama, become more difficult if some common owners live in Demopolis, Alabama, others in Albany, Georgia, and still others in Chicago, Illinois. And as the number of interests increases, it becomes difficult to locate and keep track of the owners: problems arise with the unlocatable heir and with unknown heirs. Moreover, heir property often lacks record title. Because of these characteristics of heir property, economic development of a significant proportion of land owned by African Americans has been stifled. Owners have difficulty obtaining financing and co-owners may not be able to agree on the most appropriate use of the land.

Consider the case study of an African American estate in Mississippi conducted by the Emergency Land Fund. A certain African American named John Brown purchased eighty acres of land in Rankin County, Mississippi, in 1887. After he died intestate in 1935, the land continued to be passed down by intestacy. By the time an heir holding more than fifty percent of the interest in the land filed for a partition in kind of the property in 1978, there were sixty-seven heirs who held an interest in the property, with the smallest interest holder owning a 1/19440th interest in the land. As in many other cases, the desire of the majority interest holder to secure a physical partition of the land was frustrated when the court decided to order a sale of the property after a few of the other heirs holding a minority interest objected to the proposed division of the property. The fractionated heir property problem within rural African American communities manifested by the John Brown estate is typical; a 1984 study estimated that forty-one percent of black-owned land in the southeastern states is heir property.

If heir property tends to be highly fractionated and fractionation increases the risk of partition, then this pattern of family wealth transmission directly contributes to black land loss.

McNeely v. Bone

698 S.W.2d 512 (Ark. 1985)

NEWBERN, Justice.

This appeal results from an order to sell real estate and divide the proceeds. The appellants contend the land, of which they are part owners, could have been partitioned in kind, and they contend the partition statutes are unconstitutionally applied in this case. We find no merit in either point, and thus we affirm.

1. CONSTITUTIONALITY

The appellants, descendants of John B. Blanton, have inherited various undivided interests in 160 acres of land which Blanton obtained by patent in 1904. The appellees have purchased the undivided interests of twelve other Blanton descendants. Ark. Stat. Ann. §34-1801 permits any person owning an interest in land in common with others to seek a partition of the land. The appellees have obtained an order partitioning the land and for sale of it because the court found it could not be partitioned in kind.

For their argument that partition in this case should not be permitted because it is unconstitutional, harsh and unreasonable, the appellants have cited the Fifth and Fourteenth Amendments to the U. S. Constitution, a newspaper article, and, in their reply brief, C. Kelly, Stemming the Loss of Black Owned Farmland Through Partition Actions—A Partial Solution, 1985 Arkansas Law Notes.

The appellants make no argument connecting any of the evidence abstracted to any particular allegation of violation of the Fifth or Fourteenth Amendments. The argument, rather, is that the Arkansas statutes permitting partition of land are being abused in a manner that is causing black persons to have to sell their inherited ancestral lands. No evidence to that effect was introduced at the trial. Nor was there any allegation or evidence produced that the appellants had not had sufficient notice or were discriminated against because of their race or otherwise.

The facts in this case may be close to the scenario addressed in the Arkansas Law Notes article, i.e., a white speculator buying black owned land for less than its value by using the partition device, but there is no evidence to show it. Even if there were, the cited article suggests legislative solutions which would permit persons desirous of holding on to ancestral land to fend off partition speculators. It does not suggest that §34-1801 or the Arkansas partition statutes, generally, are unconstitutional.

2. Partition in Kind

The appellants contend it was error for the court to find that the land could not be partitioned in kind. The land consists of four forty-acre tracts. They contend that they were willing to accept one forty-acre tract (25%) even though they owned 28.6% of the land. The problem with that argument is that it ignores the disparity in value of the forty-acre tracts. In kind division must take account of the quality as well as the quantity of the land being divided. Ark. Stat. Ann. §34-1818 (Repl. 1962).

The only testimony in the record on the question of the possibility of an in kind division came from an expert witness presented by the appellees. He testified he could not think of a way to achieve a fair in kind division. The appellants asked that the court divide the property in kind giving them either of two designated forty-acre tracts. The court refused to do it on the ground that the only evidence presented was that no such division could be fairly made. The fact that the appellants were willing to take a tract which was less than their 28.6% of the total acreage is not compelling, as there was no evidence presented to show that such a division would be fair in terms of the comparative values of the forty-acre tracts. The only evidence before the court was to the contrary.

Section 34-1801 provides a party seeking partition may ask for division of the land ". . . and for a sale thereof if it shall appear that partition cannot be made without great prejudice to the owners. . . ." Section 34-1815 provides that when partition has been adjudged the court may appoint commissioners to make the partition according to the interests of the owners. It further provides the court may order a sale without appointing commissioners ". . . if the court determines from the evidence presented that there is no necessity for the appointment of commissioners." Considered together these statutes confer upon the chancellor the authority to decide whether partition in kind is feasible. That is a question of fact, the answer to which depends on evidence of the nature of the land and the nature of the interests of the owners. Factual determinations made by the court trying a case without a jury will not be overturned unless they are clearly erroneous or clearly against the preponderance of the evidence.

Affirmed.

NOTES AND QUESTIONS

1. Do you agree with the majority or dissenting opinion in *Chuck*? Should cultural traditions play a role in a court's decision to partition real property by sale, as the dissent in *Chuck* suggests? If so, why did the majority fail to account for such traditions in its decision? If not, why not?

2. Is the purchase of a share of a tenancy in common "opportunistic," as Professor Mitchell suggests, or is it simply a result of market forces?

3. According to the court in *McNeely*, the plaintiffs failed to offer evidence of their assertions regarding the purchases of shares of tenancies in common by land speculators. Assume that the plaintiffs had presented evidence regarding the nature of the transactions. Do you think that the court would have reached the opposite conclusion?

4. What legal changes might be instituted to guard against the land losses mentioned by the court in *McNeely* and discussed by Professor Mitchell? Should courts initiate such changes or wait for the legislature to act? What are the pros and cons of either approach? For more on the effects of partition on African-Americans and some proposed remedies, see Phyliss Craig-Taylor, *Through the Colored Looking Glass: A View of Judicial Partition, Family Land Loss, and Rule Setting*, 78 Wash. U. L. Q. 737 (2000).

5. As Professor Mitchell points out and as *McNeely* indicates, one of the common mechanisms by which interest fractionation occurs is intestate succession or devise. Some cases of fractionation pit family members against one another in actions for partition. In *Black v. Stimpson*, 602 So.2d 368 (Ala. 1992), four of Elizabeth Phelon's heirs took a one-quarter interest in an eighty-acre parcel of land as tenants in common upon her death. *Id.* at 369. Two of those heirs conveyed their interests to the Stimpsons while the interests of the other two heirs remained on the Phelon side of the family. *Id.* Because they did not think that the land could be equitably divided in kind, the Stimpsons requested a partition by sale. *Id.* The Phelons argued that the property could be equitably partitioned in kind by dividing the property in half and granting one-half to the Stimpsons and the other to the Phelons. *Id.* After losing in the trial court, the Phelons appealed, but the Supreme Court of Alabama found that the facts justified a partition by sale. *Id.* at 370. The court highlighted evidence that the land could not be equitably divided in kind because of flooding problems associated with some of the property along with other topographical issues. *Id.* at 369. Furthermore, the court noted that "one of the largest Phelon heirs . . . advised the court the she was not interested in receiving title to a portion of the property, but preferred that the property be sold and that she receive her share of the proceeds. Some other defendants also expressed an interest in having the land sold for division." *Id.* at 369-70. Interestingly, two Phelon heirs resided on the property at the time of partition action. *Id.* at 370. However, the residential use of the property by the two Phelon heirs did not provide a ground to overturn the order for partition by sale and the court upheld the sale of the property. *Id.*

6. The Public Broadcasting System (PBS) television channel sponsored the making of a film by Charlene Gilbert, titled "Homecoming . . . Sometimes I Am Haunted by Memories of Red Dirt and Clay," depicting the experiences of African-American farmers who lost land; information about the film can be found at *http://www.pbs.org/itvs/homecoming/film1.html* (last visited August 31, 2010).

6.6 LANDLORD-TENANT RELATIONS

From constructive eviction to retaliatory eviction, modern landlord-tenant law provides a tenant with an array of protections from a landlord's acts or failure to act that were unknown to the thirteenth-century tenant in England. This expansion of tenant protections reflects an increase in the duties placed upon landlords to maintain leased premises. One of the most important, and most recent, additions to landlord-tenant law is the implied warranty of habitability, which traces its origins to *Pines v. Perssion*, 111 N.W. 2d 409 (1961). In *Pines*, four University of Wisconsin students agreed to lease a house from a landlord for the academic year. *Id.* at 409. Shortly after taking possession of the house, the students discovered that the premises suffered from electrical, plumbing, and heating defects; therefore, the students vacated the premises. *Id.* The students brought suit seeking to recover sums paid to the landlord prior to taking possession of the premises, and the case eventually found its way onto the docket of the Supreme Court of Wisconsin. Although the Supreme Court of Wisconsin observed that the law in Wisconsin did not recognize an implied warranty of habitability, the court asserted that "the frame of reference in which the old common-law rule operated has changed." *Id.* at 412. According to the court,

> [l]egislation and administrative rules, such as the safeplace statute, building codes, and health regulations, all impose certain duties on a property owner with respect to the condition of his premises. Thus, the legislature has made a policy judgment— that it is socially (and politically) desirable to impose these duties on a property owner— which has rendered the old common-law rule obsolete. To follow the old rule of no implied warranty of habitability in leases would, in our opinion, be inconsistent with the current legislative policy concerning housing standards. The need and social desirability of adequate housing for people in this era of rapid population increases is too important to be rebuffed by that obnoxious legal cliche, *caveat emptor*. Permitting landlords to rent "tumble-down" houses is at least a contributing cause of such problems as urban blight, juvenile delinquency, and high property taxes for conscientious landowners.

Id. at 413.

Despite the pro-tenant result in *Pines*, the implied warranty of habitability did not gain widespread acceptance as it applied to post-possession defects until *Javins v. First National Realty Corp.*, 428 F. 2d 1071 (D.C. Cir. 1970).

The implied warranty of habitability imposes added costs on landlords that they would not incur in its absence. Although the implied warranty of habitability is a benefit to tenants, it may come at the expense of increased rental payments as landlords attempt to defray the added expense. While reading the next case, consider the following question: Under what conditions should a court impose a new duty on landlords?

Chapman v. Silber

97 N.Y.2d 9 (2001)

CIPARICK, J.

I.

Chapman v. Silber

In August 1994, plaintiffs James and Sallie Chapman rented the second floor apartment at 443 Myrtle Avenue in Albany from Dennis Silber, Jay Silber and Gertrude Silber. On September 23, 1994, shortly after the Chapmans moved into the apartment, Dennis and Gertrude conveyed their interests in the property to Jay and his wife, Judith Harrington. All four were named as defendants and will be collectively referred to as the "landlord."

The two-year lease between the parties states that "[t]he tenant must maintain the apartment" and that "[t]he tenant agrees, at tenant's own cost to make all repairs to the apartment . . . whenever the need results from the tenant's acts or neglect." The lease further provides "[t]he tenant agrees to allow the landlord to enter the leased premises at any reasonable hour to repair, inspect, install or work . . . and to perform such other work that the landlord may decide is necessary."

The facts as stated herein are taken from the parties' affidavits and deposition testimony. The Chapmans moved into the apartment with their three children, including one-year-old Jaquan. Before they moved in, Dennis Silber painted the apartment. Mrs. Chapman noted that the apartment had been "redone" but that the window sills appeared old and the paint on the second floor porch was chipped and peeling. In spring 1995, the Chapmans observed that the condition of the paint on their porch had deteriorated. As the weather got warmer and the family began to open their windows more frequently, Mrs. Chapman also noticed that the paint in the window tracks was chipped and peeling and that the window sills held an accumulation of paint chips and dust. Mrs. Chapman claims that by July 1995, the condition of the paint in both areas had worsened.

Mrs. Chapman first complained about peeling paint in April or May 1995, when she told defendant Jay Silber that there were large "chunks" of peeling paint on the front porch. She again complained to him about the porch in July 1995 at which time he promised he would take care of the situation. He did so by paying James Chapman $300 to paint the porch.

In addition to these complaints, Mrs. Chapman claims that Dennis Silber, Jay Silber and Judith Harrington all were in the upstairs apartment during her tenancy and each saw the condition of the paint. Dennis came to the apartment to repair a jammed window one week after the Chapmans moved in. Jay Silber and Judith Harrington came to the apartment in

October or November 1994 to take over day-to-day responsibility for the apartment and to collect the rent.

While admitting his presence in the apartment at various times, Dennis Silber denied seeing chipped or peeling paint despite the fact that he and his wife resided in that apartment prior to the Chapman tenancy. He also painted the apartment before the Chapmans rented it and claims that the front porch was scuffed, but not peeling, at the time the Chapmans moved in. Dennis knew that the building was old and was aware of the hazards of lead paint.

Jay Silber admitted visiting the apartment on several occasions while the Chapmans were living there in order to make repairs. Jay was aware that the house was built in the early 1900s but claimed not to be aware of the dangers of lead-based paint. He did admit the possibility that chipped or peeling paint could have been present in the apartment.

Judith Harrington was aware that lead paint was dangerous. She recalled receiving a call from Sallie Chapman in summer 1995 in which Mrs. Chapman requested that something be done about chipping paint on the upstairs porch. When asked who was responsible for maintenance in the Chapman apartment, Ms. Harrington responded, "Dennis [Silber], from the point at which we rented to [the Chapmans] until he was no longer part of the partnership, then my husband Jay [Silber]." Ms. Harrington also admitted that her husband would visit the property "when something needed to be fixed."

Gertrude Silber never visited the property during the Chapman tenancy and had no knowledge of day-to-day operations. She knew, however, that lead was dangerous.

About a month after moving in, a blood test performed as part of a routine physical examination indicated that Jaquan had a moderately elevated level of lead in his blood. A second test performed about two months later showed that the condition persisted. On August 15, 1995, Jaquan's blood lead level tested so high that he had to be re-tested two days later. The August 17th test showed the same high blood lead level. The City of Albany inspected the premises and detected the presence of lead paint. On August 21, 1995, another test revealed even higher levels of lead in Jaquan's blood and he was hospitalized. The family moved out of the apartment by September 1995.

James and Sallie Chapman commenced this action, in their individual capacities and as parents of Jaquan, alleging claims for common-law negligence, statutory violations evidencing negligence per se, breach of warranty and nuisance. Dennis Silber moved for summary judgment dismissing the complaint against him on the grounds that he conveyed his interest in the premises prior to the injury and that he did not have actual or constructive notice of a lead-based paint condition. The other defendants cross-moved on notice grounds as well. Supreme Court denied all defendants' motions finding issues of fact as to notice. The Appellate

Division reversed and granted summary judgment dismissing the complaint. We granted leave to appeal and now reverse.

Stover v. Robilotto

On February 1, 1993, Carlisa Stover, then eight months pregnant, and her five-year-old son moved into the first floor apartment of the two-family home at 22 Judson Street in Albany. Her landlord was James O'Connor. Carlisa Stover did not enter into a written lease with Mr. O'Connor but was a month-to-month tenant. The apartment had been re-painted when Ms. Stover moved in. In the year and a half she resided there, she complained to her landlord several times about her bedroom door and toilet. Each time she reported a problem, it was repaired. She never complained about the condition of paint.

Ms. Stover's younger son, Everton Lewis, was born on March 19, 1993. At about 15 months, when Everton began to walk, both Ms. Stover and her niece observed Everton on the stairway between the upstairs and downstairs apartments removing material from holes in the wall and placing it in his mouth. In September 1994, Everton's blood lead level was so high he had to be hospitalized. When the child was discharged, Ms. Stover and her family moved into a friend's apartment and never again resided at 22 Judson Street.

Although James O'Connor did not personally perform the repairs in Ms. Stover's apartment, he had been there twice to assess the problem with the door. He claimed not to have seen chipping paint inside the apartment. Mr. O'Connor also testified at his deposition that he knew lead paint was dangerous to children. Mr. O'Connor claimed, however, that he was not aware either that Ms. Stover had a young child when she moved in or that she was pregnant at the time. Mr. O'Connor testified, however, that he later learned of the older child when the boy visited his grocery store.

Carlisa Stover commenced this action, in her individual capacity and as mother of Everton Lewis, against her landlord, alleging the same causes of action as the Chapmans. Supreme Court granted defendant's motion for summary judgment, concluding that defendant did not have notice of a hazardous lead paint condition. The Appellate Division affirmed. We granted leave to appeal and now affirm.

II.

Our analysis begins with an examination of premises liability generally, and the duty imposed on landlords to maintain premises in reasonably safe condition. Historically, landlords could not be held liable for injuries caused by dangerous conditions on their premises when possession had been transferred. Courts opined that conveyance of possession by lease was similar in effect to conveyance of title. In time, this Court relaxed the doctrine, imposing a duty to remedy dangerous conditions on a landlord who had contractually assumed the responsibility to make repairs. Thus, a landlord may be found liable for failure to repair a dangerous condition, of which it has notice, on leased premises if the landlord assumes a duty to make repairs and reserves the right to enter in order to inspect or to make such repairs. . . .

New York State has not enacted . . . legislation that imposes a duty on landlords to test for or abate lead-based paint hazards absent official notification of a problem. We recognize, moreover, that absent explicit legislative authorization we should not hastily impose a new duty since doing so "requires a weighing of policy interests, a responsibility that rests with Federal, State and local legislative bodies" (Juarez, supra, 88 NY2d, at 641). The absence of a statutory scheme, however, is not fatal to this type of action. Where certain requisites are satisfied, a landlord still may be liable for negligence under traditional common-law principles.

III.

The decisions of the Appellate Division in *Chapman* and *Stover* focused primarily on the issue of notice. This was an appropriate inquiry since, without notice of a specific dangerous condition, an out-of-possession landlord cannot be faulted for failing to repair it. The Appellate Division concluded as a matter of law that neither landlord knew, or should have known, of the existence of a hazardous lead paint condition. We disagree in *Chapman,* and agree in *Stover.*

In granting summary judgment to the defendants, the Appellate Division applied the following notice principle: The fact that a landlord is aware of the presence of chipped or peeling paint in an old apartment does not raise an issue of fact as to the landlord's notice of lead in the paint. That rule leaves plaintiffs in an impossible situation. Defendant-landlords cannot be held liable for a hazardous lead paint condition unless they are actually aware that lead is present in chipping paint. Yet because lead in paint is undetectable to the senses, a landlord cannot actually know of its presence without testing. Thus, applying the Appellate Division principle, landlords who deliberately refrain from testing for lead can shield themselves from liability.

We conclude that only in *Chapman* is there a triable issue of fact as to whether the landlord knew or should have known of a hazardous condition on its premises. Notwithstanding the Appellate Division holding that the lease did not impose a duty on the landlord to make repairs, Ms. Harrington's uncontroverted testimony reveals that the landlord assumed that duty. Moreover, only in *Chapman* was the landlord aware that, due to its age, the premises probably contained lead paint and, that ingestion of lead paint chips posed a health hazard to young children. The landlord further admitted awareness that young children lived in the apartment and that there had been complaints about chipped and peeling paint. Under these circumstances, a jury could reasonably infer that the landlord, at the least, *should have known* of the hazardous lead paint condition.

In so holding, we are mindful of our own prior admonitions regarding the creation of a new duty where none existed before. We decline to impose a new duty on landlords to test for the existence of lead in leased properties based solely upon the "general knowledge" of the dangers of lead-based paints in older homes. We have never held, as the Supreme Court of Wisconsin did in *Antwaun A. ex rel. Muwonge v Heritage Mut. Ins. Co.*, 228 Wis. 2d 44, 62, 596 NW2d 456, 464, that general knowledge of a particular type of risk creates a duty to test for, or remedy, it. We hold only that a landlord who actually knows of the existence of many conditions indicating a lead paint hazard to young children may, in the minds of the jury, also be charged constructively with notice of the hazard. . . .

Applying the foregoing principle, defendants in *Chapman*—aware of the age of the building, the presence of chipped and peeling paint, the dangers of lead paint to children, and the presence of young children in the apartment—may have an obligation to take precautions to provide a reasonably safe environment for plaintiffs. Although plaintiffs in *Chapman* could not show that the landlord actually knew that lead was present in the chipped and peeling paint in their apartment, they did raise an issue as to the landlord's knowledge of a high degree of risk that there was a lead paint danger in the apartment sufficient to trigger its duty to address the condition. For that reason, the question as to whether the landlord in *Chapman* should have known of a lead paint condition should be presented to the trier of fact, precluding summary judgment. Plaintiffs have yet to establish the other elements of their negligence cause of action, including a negligent breach of the landlord's duty and a legally sufficient causal nexus between the alleged breach and the claimed damages.

By contrast, in *Stover,* there is no record evidence that the landlord was on actual or constructive notice of a chipped or peeling paint condition inside the apartment. The landlord had entered to make repairs to the bedroom door and toilet and had repaired holes in a stairway wall—a common area of the building never identified as a source of lead contamination. The evidence is insufficient to raise an issue of fact as to whether the landlord in *Stover* should have known of a lead paint condition.

Accordingly, the order of the Appellate Division in *Chapman* should be reversed, with costs, and defendants' motions for summary judgment denied and the order of the Appellate Division in *Stover* should be affirmed, without costs.

NOTES AND QUESTIONS

1. Which of the common law protections for tenants is the focus of *Chapman*? What is the reason for the differing results in *Chapman* and *Stover*?

2. Spurred by the evolution of the lease from a conveyance to a contract, new duties have been placed on landlords over time. Why is the court reluctant to place a new duty on landlords under the circumstances in *Chapman*?

3. According to a survey conducted from 1999-2002, "non-Hispanic blacks and Mexican Americans had higher percentages of elevated blood lead levels (1.4% and 1.5%, respectively) than non-Hispanic whites (0.5%). Among subpopulations, non-Hispanic blacks aged 1-5 years and aged [greater than] 60 years had the highest prevalence of elevated blood lead levels (3.1% and 3.4%, respectively)." Blood Lead Levels, 1999-2002, Centers for Disease Control and Prevention, Morbidity and Mortality Weekly Report, vol. 54, issue 20, May 27, 2005. Should data such as this affect the duties owed by landlords to tenants?

4. Some states have enacted statutes that address the issue of lead paint in residences and the risk such paint imposes upon children. See, e.g., Mass. Gen. Laws Ann. ch. 111, §197 (2007) (banning lead paint in locations where children under the age of six reside); MGL §333.5475a (2007) (creating a presumption of actual knowledge of the presence of lead-based paint and imposing a penalty of no more than 93 days in prison or a fine of up to $5,000, or both as a penalty for a violation); Cal. Health and Safety Code §124160 (2007) (developing a program for children at high risk of lead poisoning); 410 ILCS 55/701 (2007) (requiring lead blood level tests for children prior to attending a day care facility).

5. The Consumer Product Safety Commission banned the use of lead paint for residential purposes in 1978. See 16 C.F.R. 1301.1 (2004). Congress enacted the Lead Contamination Act of 1988 in an effort to combat the problem of lead poisoning. Part of the Act directed the Centers for Disease Control (CDC) to create programs aimed at eliminating lead poisoning in children across the nation. One such program, Healthy People 2010, pairs the CDC with the Environmental Protection Agency and the United States Department of Housing and Urban Development in an effort to reach this goal. According to Healthy People 2010, the federal agencies will "identify and control lead paint hazards, identification and care for children with elevated blood lead levels, surveillance of elevated blood lead levels in children to monitor progress, and research to further improve childhood lead poisoning prevention methods." For more on the program, see *http://www.cdc.gov/nceh/lead/about/program.htm* (last visited August 31, 2010).

6.7 EASEMENTS

An *easement* is a non-possessory interest in land that allows the holder to use land in the possession of another. Although it seems straightforward, the legal definition of an easement masks a clash between traditional activities and property rights that often occurs with the growth of society. Individuals or groups might use a parcel of real property to perform traditional ceremonies or as a place for gathering resources. As societal expansion captures such parcels of real property, the legal owners of the land might seek to curtail access to the land by virtue of the right to exclude that we addressed in Chapter 1. However, strict enforcement of the right to exclude would mean that the prior users of the land would be unable to continue their traditional activities. The challenge for courts in these cases is to balance the right of an individual or group to continue customary activities with the right to exclude that accompanies private ownership of real property. In that sense, these cases hark back to the problem of prior possession that we encountered in the first section of this chapter.

Because the United States acquired much of its land from other countries, issues regarding the rights of prior users of the land became an important legal issue as ownership of those lands changed hands. The following materials illustrate the difficult property law issues faced by courts as they attempted to balance the rights of prior users under a different legal regime with those of current possessors. The first selection describes the problems encountered by prior users of land ceded to the United States from Mexico under the Treaty of Guadalupe Hidalgo; the case that follows the passage illustrates how one court weighed the balance between prior usage and present possession.

Chicana/Chicano Land Tenure in the Agrarian Domain: On the Edge of a "Naked Knife"

Guadalupe T. Luna, 4 Mich. J. Race & L. 39, 40-137 (1998)*

As early as 1885, the federal courts evinced clear awareness of their dubious record in deciding disputes between Mexican landowners and American settlers in the Southwest. In *United States v. San Jacinto Tin Company*, the court poignantly addressed the subject as follows:

> Those familiar with the notorious public history of land titles in this state need not be told that our people coming from the states east of the Rocky Mountains very generally denied the validity of Spanish grants . . . and, determining the rights of the holders for themselves, selected tracts of land wherever it suited their purpose, without regard to the claims and actual occupation of holders under Mexican grants. . . . Many of the older, best-authenticated, and most-desirable grants in the state were thus, more or less, covered by trespassing settlers. When the claims of Mexican grantees came to be presented for confirmation, these settlers aided the United States; the most formidable opposition usually coming from them, first, to

> the confirmation of the grants, on every imaginable ground, of which the most frequent was fraud in some form at some stage of the proceedings. When confirmed, and the officers of the government came to the location, the contest became still more vigorous and acrimonious; the trespassing settlers, or adverse claimants . . . would seek to move the location . . . in opposition to confirmation. . . . Charges of fraud are easily made, and they were by no means sparingly made by incensed defeated parties, and these reckless charges by disappointed trespassing and opposing claimants, in many instances, as in this case, involved the officers of the government, as well as the claimants under the grant. . . .

Prior to the U.S.-Mexico War, the Mexican government awarded and recognized private and communally held grants of property throughout its territories. After the Conquest, the United States annexed the former Mexican territories through the Treaty of Guadalupe Hidalgo ("Treaty"). In establishing new national geographic borders, the Treaty also obligated the United States to provide grantees in the annexed areas citizenship status and to protect their fee interests. Notwithstanding the promises contained in the Treaty, grantees of Mexican descent and their successors in title experienced the loss of the very property interests the Treaty pledged to protect.

Scholars outside of legal academia have long investigated the issue of Chicana/Chicano property dispossession. Three theories regarding the origins of Chicana/Chicano alienation from their property interests emerge from these scholars' work. Two of these theories attribute alienation to differences between Anglo-American and Mexican property law, while the third relies on cultural differences.

The first theory places responsibility for property dispossession on the substantive differences between United States common law and Mexican civil law. Adherents of this theory contend "not so much that Americans ran roughshod over the legal rights of Mexican landowners [but rather] that different traditions of property rights came into conflict." Such an argument is difficult to reconcile with the Treaty, international law, constitutional provisions, and subsequent congressional legislation obligating the United States to protect the property rights of those remaining in the annexed territories. Thus, by relying on conflict between the different property traditions, the first theory does not completely explain Chicana/Chicano land alienation.

A second theory argues that the procedural differences between the systems led to the loss of property. Characterizing Anglo-Saxon law approvingly as "exact, clear, and precise," while criticizing Mexican legal institutions as employing "loose and careless methods," proponents of this theory assert that "the defects in the Spanish and Mexican records and titles," rather than the unfair treatment of Mexican grantees, resulted in alienation. American courts, however, did not always share this view. In Davis v. California Powder Works, for example, the court declared that "the Mexicans of the Spanish race, like their progenitors, were a formal people, and their officials were usually formal and careful in the administration of their public affairs." Thus, the second theory does not adequately link Chicana/Chicano land dispossession to differences in procedural administration of the laws.

The last theory asserts that the cultural differences between the United States and Mexico produced dispossession of Mexican grantees' property interests. This theory posits that "the original holders being Mexicans were improvident and really squandered [their land] for riotous living." As one author has noted, while early Anglo-Americans pejoratively characterized the Mexican population as "indolent, ignorant, and backward, Americans of the late nineteenth century re-imagined the Californios as unhurried [and] untroubled." This theory is grounded in part on the same demeaning ethnic stereotypes that shaped court decisions in the nineteenth and early twentieth centuries. Moreover, evidence from historical texts demonstrates the industry of Mexican grantees' land use practices. Cultural biases alone cannot justify any theory. The lack of evidentiary support further demonstrates that this theory fails as a sufficient explanation for Chicana/Chicano alienation. . . .

With the Treaty of Guadalupe Hidalgo, the United States formally established a legal relationship with the population of Mexican descent. Although annexing the former Mexican provinces, the United States "acquired no right of the soil included in this grant; nothing but the political powers, jurisdiction, and sovereignty, under a special stipulation that the owners of property should be protected in the enjoyment thereof." Treaties, like federal law, are "the supreme Law of the Land" under the Constitution. Treaties are deemed legal contracts between their signatories and The Constitution directs judges to give them effect. In *Ely's Administrator v. United States* the Court verified that, notwithstanding the Conquest, Mexican grantees should have been protected "in harmony with the rules of international law, as well as with the terms of the treaties of cession, the change of sovereignty should work no change in respect to rights and titles; that which was good before should be good after . . . ." Nonetheless, "that which was good before" did not protect grantees from shifting and elusive norms within the new legal regime.

As provided under the Land Acts, five different laws obligated the United States to protect grantees and their property rights. In addition to the Treaty and the Constitution, Mexico's colonization laws and its customary practices were to govern the land grant adjudication process, while international law and the laws of the United States would also protect grantees as citizens and forever foreign subjects. Thus, the United States pledged to protect the rights of Mexican grantees in the grantees' newly adopted nation.

Instead, grantees faced prohibitive burdens of proof, shifting rules and standards that deviated from long-established American legal norms, and selective application of the law. Legal actors disregarded the fact that

Mexican land was not part of the public domain, thereby promoting biased actions that ran counter to the express obligations of the Treaty. By these means, the United States openly made available land that supposedly "had been so completely severed from the public domain of Mexico, so perfectly vested in the grantee by a legal title in fee, that no right of property in the land passed to the United States." Courts enhanced the wealth of the dominant population by awarding it title to land that rightfully belonged to grantees or, more rarely, awarding invalid grants to non-Mexican petitioners that should have reverted to the public domain. Hence, the treatment of Mexican grantees violated not only the Treaty and the Constitution but also the pledges made by both President Polk and the Senate.

Lobato v. Taylor

71 P.3d 938 (Colo. 2002)

Chief Justice Mullarkey delivered the Opinion of the Court.

The history of this property rights controversy began before Colorado's statehood, at a time when southern Colorado was part of Mexico; at a time when all of the parties' lands were part of the one million acre Sangre de Cristo grant, an 1844 Mexican land grant. Here, we determine access rights of the owners of farmlands in Costilla County to a mountainous parcel of land now known as the Taylor Ranch. As successors in title to the original settlers in the region, the landowners exercised rights to enter and use the Taylor Ranch property for over one hundred years until Jack Taylor fenced the land in 1960 and forcibly excluded them. These rights, they assert, derive from Mexican law, prescription, and an express or implied grant, and were impermissibly denied when the mountain land was fenced. . . .

In 1844, the governor of New Mexico granted two Mexican nationals a one million-acre land grant, located mainly in present-day southern Colorado (Sangre de Cristo grant), for the purpose of settlement. The original grantees died during the war between the United States and Mexico. The land was not settled in earnest until after the cessation of the war, and Charles (Carlos) Beaubien then owned the grant.

In 1863, Beaubien gave established settlers deeds to their vara strips. That same year, Beaubien executed and recorded a Spanish language document that purports to grant rights of access to common lands to settlers on the Sangre de Cristo grant (Beaubien Document). In relevant part, this document guarantees that "all the inhabitants will have enjoyment of benefits of pastures, water, firewood and timber, always taking care that one does not injure another."

A year later, Beaubien died. Pursuant to a prior oral agreement, his heirs sold his interest in the Sangre de Cristo grant to William Gilpin, who was Colorado's first territorial governor. The sales agreement (Gilpin agreement) stated that Gilpin agreed to provide vara strip deeds to settlers who had not yet received them. The agreement further stated that Gilpin took the land on condition that certain "settlement rights before then conceded . . . to the residents of the settlements . . . shall be confirmed by said William Gilpin as made by him."

In 1960, Jack Taylor, a North Carolina lumberman, purchased roughly 77,000 acres of the Sangre de Cristo grant (mountain tract) from a successor in interest to William Gilpin. Taylor's deed indicated that he took the land subject to "claims of the local people by prescription or otherwise to right to pasture, wood, and lumber and so-called settlement rights in, to, and upon said land."

Despite the language in Taylor's deed, he denied the local landowners access to his land and began to fence the property. Taylor then filed a Torrens title action in the United States District Court for the District of Colorado to perfect his title (Torrens action). The district court found that the local landowners did not have any rights to the mountain tract; the Tenth Circuit Court of Appeals affirmed. . . .

The landowners claim rights to graze livestock, gather firewood and timber, hunt, fish, and recreate. Before discussing the sources of the settlement rights, we characterize the claimed rights in order to determine the rules of law that govern them.

The parties, at various points in the voluminous briefing of this twenty-one year-old litigation, agree that the rights at issue are most appropriately characterized as profits à prendre. A profit à prendre — in modern parlance, a profit — "is an easement that confers the right to enter and remove timber, minerals, oil, gas, game, or other substances from land in the possession of another." Restatement (Third) of Property: Servitudes §1.2(2)(1998) [hereinafter Restatement]. Thus, a profit is a type of easement.

This court has described an easement as "a right conferred by grant, prescription or necessity authorizing one to do or maintain something on the land of another which, although a benefit to the land of the former, may be a burden on the land of the latter." Lazy Dog Ranch v. Telluray Ranch Corp., 965 P.2d 1229, 1234 (Colo.1998).

An easement can be in gross or appurtenant. An easement in gross does not belong to an individual by virtue of her ownership of land, but rather is a personal right to use another's property. An easement appurtenant, on the other hand, runs with the land. It is meant to benefit the property, or an owner by virtue of her property ownership. An easement is presumed to be appurtenant, rather than in gross.

In this case, the landowners allege that the settlement rights were to be used in connection with their land. They argue that the firewood was used to heat their homes, the timber to frame their adobe houses, and the grazing necessary to the viability of their farms. The landowners also assert that the settlement rights were granted to their predecessors in title by virtue of their interest in their vara strips and were in fact a necessary incentive for settlement in the area.

We conclude that the rights the landowners are claiming are best characterized as easements appurtenant to the land. We reach this conclusion from the evidence that under Mexican custom access to common land was given to surrounding landowners, the evidence that this access was used to benefit the use of the land, and the presumption in favor of appurtenant easements.

Having established the nature of the rights at issue, we now turn to the sources of these rights. [The court rejected the claim that Mexican law granted rights to the landowners because the land had been ceded to the United States prior to the creation of any such rights.]

As evidence of a grant of rights from Carlos Beaubien, the landowners rely primarily on the Beaubien Document. The document was written by Beaubien in 1863, one year before his death.

One English translation of the document reads, in part:

> It has been decided that the lands of the Rito Seco remain uncultivated for the benefit of the community members (gente) of the plazas of San Luis, San Pablo and Los Ballejos and for the other inhabitants of these plazas for pasturing cattle by the payment of a fee per head, etc. and that the water of the said Rito remains partitioned among the inhabitants of the same plaza of San Luis and those from the other side of the vega who hold lands almost adjacent to it as their own lands, that are not irrigated with the waters of the Rio Culebra. The vega, after the measurement of three acres from it in front of the chapel, to which they have been donated, will remain for the benefit of the inhabitants of this plaza and those of the Culebra as far as above the plaza of Los Ballejos . . . . Those below the road as far as the narrows will have the right to enjoy the same benefit . . . . *[No one may] place any obstacle or obstruction to anyone in the enjoyment of his legitimate rights* . . . . Likewise, each one should take scrupulous care in the use of water without causing damage with it to his neighbors nor to anyone. According to the corresponding rule, *all the inhabitants will have enjoyment of benefits of pastures, water, firewood and timber, always taking care that one does not injure another*. . . .

We agree [with the lower court] that the Beaubien Document does not meet the formal requirements for an express grant of rights. However, we find that the document, when taken together with the other unique facts of this case, establishes a prescriptive easement, an easement by estoppel, and an easement from prior use. . . .

An easement by prescription is established when the prescriptive use is: 1) open or notorious, 2) continued without effective interruption for the prescriptive period, and 3) the use was either a) adverse or b) pursuant to an attempted, but ineffective grant.

A court can imply an easement created by estoppel when 1) the owner of the servient estate "permitted another to use that land under circumstances in which it was reasonable to foresee that the user would substantially change position believing that the permission would not be revoked," 2) the user substantially changed position in reasonable reliance on that belief, and 3) injustice can be avoided only by establishment of a servitude. Restatement §2.10. Whether reliance is justified depends upon the nature of the transaction, including the sophistication of the parties. . . .

An easement implied from prior use is created when 1) the servient and dominant estates were once under common ownership, 2) the rights alleged were exercised prior to the severance of the estate, 3) the use was not merely temporary, 4) the continuation of this use was reasonably necessary to the enjoyment of the parcel, and 5) a contrary intention is neither expressed nor implied. . . .

Prescriptive Easement

Because Taylor's deed indicates that Taylor's ownership of the land is subject to the landowners' prescriptive rights, we begin with an application of the law of prescriptive easements. The court of appeals in this case concluded that the landowners failed to prove a prescriptive easement claim because their use was not adverse. The court erred in this respect.

Although adversity is a necessary requisite for adverse possession claims, it is not required for a prescriptive easement. Courts often find prescriptive easements even when the owner of the servient estate allows the use. Significantly, the Restatement articulates that a prescriptive use is either:

> (1) a use that is adverse to the owner of the land or the interest in land against which the servitude is claimed, or
>
> (2) a use that is made pursuant to the terms of an intended but imperfectly created servitude, or the enjoyment of the benefit of an intended but imperfectly created servitude. . . .

Having established that adversity is not required when a grant has been imperfectly attempted, we turn to the facts of the current case.

First, the use must be open and notorious. There is no doubt that the landowners' use was well known to Taylor and his predecessors in title. The trial court noted that Taylor's predecessors in title not only knew of the landowners' access, but they even went so far as to direct the location of grazing. Most significantly, Taylor and his predecessors in title had express notice of the landowners' claims of right from the language of their deeds. The use was open and notorious.

Second, the use must continue without effective interruption for the prescriptive period. In Colorado, the statutory period is eighteen years. §38-41-101, 10 C.R.S. (2001). Here, the trial court explicitly found that the landowners and their predecessors in title "grazed cattle and sheep, harvested timber, gathered firewood, fished, hunted and recreated on the land of the defendant from the 1800s to the date the land was acquired by the defendant, in 1960." The trial court also found that this access was never denied. This more than satisfies the statutory time period.

Third, the access must either be adverse or pursuant to an intended, but imperfectly executed, grant. Here, the access was permissive, rather than adverse. However, there is ample evidence of an intended grant of these rights. The Beaubien Document, although imperfect as an express grant, evidences Beaubien's intent to grant rights to the landowners' predecessors in title. Moreover, the express language in the deeds of conveyance for the Taylor Ranch, from Gilpin ultimately to Taylor, indicate an intention that the rights burden the land.

Thus, the landowners have established a prescriptive claim.

Easement by Estoppel

The landowners have also established every element of an easement by estoppel. First, Taylor's predecessors in title "permitted [the settlers] to use [the] land under circumstances in which it was reasonable to foresee that the [settlers] would substantially change position believing that the permission would not be revoked." Restatement, supra, §2.10. The settlers' reliance was reasonable because rights were expected, intended, and necessary. It was expected because of the Mexican settlement system discussed above. Also discussed above, this settlement system, combined with the actual practices and the deeds associated with the Taylor Ranch, show that rights were intended.

The rights were also necessary. The plaintiffs' expert, Dr. Marianne Stoller, testified that access to wood was necessary to heat homes, access to timber was necessary to build homes, and access to grazing was necessary for maintaining livestock. Moreover, Beaubien included each of these resources in a lease to the United States for the first military post in Colorado. The trial court found that during the 1850s Beaubien executed a lease to the United States government for the maintenance of Fort Massachusetts on grant land. In this lease Beaubien granted the army the right to "pasture, cut grass, timber and collect firewood" on Beaubien's land. We can safely assume that the United States was more sophisticated in its dealings with Beaubien than were the landowners' predecessors in title and that it insisted on putting Beaubien's promises into writing. Under these circumstances, it is reasonable to foresee that that a settler would substantially change position believing that the permission would not be revoked.

The second element, that the user substantially change position in reasonable reliance on the belief, is easily found. The landowners' predecessors in title settled Beaubien's grant for him. They moved onto the land and established permanent farms.

The third element, the avoidance of injustice, is also undeniably present. The original Sangre de Cristo grant was given on the condition that it be settled. Indeed, under Mexican law, the grant would have been revoked if settlement did not succeed. The settlers, then, fulfilled the condition of the grant that made Beaubien fee owner of one million acres of land.

Beaubien attracted settlers to the area by convincing them that he would provide them with the rights they needed for survival. Beaubien knew that families would rely on his promises and leave their homes to travel hundreds of miles on foot or horseback to establish new homes.

A condition of the conveyance of Beaubien's land, from Gilpin down to Taylor, was that the owner honor these rights. Although these promised rights were exercised for over one hundred years, although these rights were necessary to the settlers' very existence, and although Taylor had ample notice of these rights, Taylor fenced his land over forty years ago. It is an understatement to say that this is an injustice.

The landowners have established each element of an easement by estoppel.

Easement from Prior Use

Lastly, every element of an easement from prior use has been shown. First, both Taylor's and the landowners' lands were originally under the common ownership of Beaubien who owned the entire Sangre de Cristo grant before settlement.

Second, the rights were exercised prior to the severance of the estate. As discussed above, many of the rights the landowners claim were needed and expected for life in the San Luis Valley. This necessity existed from the first days of settlement—indicating that these rights were exercised prior to severance of title.

The third and fourth prongs—that the use was not merely temporary and is reasonably necessary to the enjoyment of the land—are also easily established. The trial court's findings of fact establish that the rights were exercised from the time of settlement until Taylor came on the scene. Moreover, as discussed above, the rights were reasonably necessary.

Lastly, no contrary intention is expressed or implied; thus, the fifth element is present. Custom, expectation, practice, and language in the documents and deeds surrounding the Taylor ranch property indicate not only that a contrary intention did not exist, but that the parties affirmatively intended for these rights to exist.

All five elements of an easement from prior use have been established.

Accordingly, we hold that the landowners have implied rights in Taylor's land for the access detailed in the Beaubien Document—pasture, firewood, and timber. These easements should be limited to reasonable use—the grazing access is limited to a reasonable number of livestock given the size of the vara strips; the firewood limited to that needed for each residence; and the timber limited to that needed to construct and maintain residence and farm buildings located on the vara strips.

NOTES AND QUESTIONS

1. What role does custom play in *Lobato*? Do you agree with the court's characterization of the property interests as easements appurtenant to the land? Why or why not?

2. What limitations, if any, are imposed upon the holders of the interests in *Lobato*? If such limitations exist, how will they be enforced? What is the likelihood of future litigation? The history of the Treaty of Guadalupe Hidalgo has received a large amount of scholarly attention. For more on Mexican-American land loss associated with the 1848 Treaty of Guadalupe Hidalgo and more generally, see George A. Martinez, *Legal Indeterminacy, Judicial Discretion, and the Mexican-American Litigation Experience: 1930-1980*, 27 U.C. DAVIS L. REV. 555, 566 (1994); Rebecca Tsosie, *Sacred Obligations: Intercultural Justice and the Discourse of Treaty Rights*, 47 UCLA L. REV. 1615 (2000); Tomas Almaguer, RACIAL FAULT LINES: THE HISTORICAL ORIGINS OF WHITE SUPREMACY IN CALIFORNIA 65-87 (1994); Griswold del Castillo, THE TREATY OF GUADALUPE HIDALGO: A LEGACY OF CONFLICT 87-108 (1992).

3. The custom of grazing cattle on public lands not only advanced the development of the West, but also led to violent clashes between landowners and so-called free grazers who did not own land in the area but still grazed their animals in the area. For more on the historical development of western grazing rights and custom, see Frank J. Falen and Karen Budd-Falen, *The Right to Graze Livestock on the Federal Lands: The Historical Development of Western Grazing Rights*, 30 IDAHO L. REV. 505 (1993); Marc Stimpert, *Counterpoint: Opportunities Lost and Opportunities Gained: Separating Truth from Myth in the Western Ranching Debate*, 36 ENVTL. L. 481, 488-95 (2006). The clash between landowners and free grazers resulted in at least one legal case that made it to the Supreme Court. In *Buford v. Houtz*, 133 U.S. 320 (1890), a group of cattle-owning landowners sought an injunction that prevented non-landowning sheep ranchers from crossing their private properties to reach the public lands for grazing purposes. Denying relief to the cattle ranchers, the Supreme Court observed that "there is an implied license, growing out of the custom of nearly a hundred years, that the public lands of the United States, especially those in which the native grasses are adapted to the growth and fattening of domestic animals, shall be free to the people who seek to use them where they are left open and unenclosed, and no act of government forbids this use." *Id.* at 620. Furthermore, it became a custom for persons to make a business or pursuit of gathering herds of cattle or sheep, and raising them and fattening them for market upon these unenclosed lands of the government of the United States. Of course the instances became numerous in which persons purchasing land from the United States put only a small part of it in cultivation, and permitted the balance to remain unenclosed and in no way separated from the lands owned by the United States. All the neighbors who had settled near one of these prairies or on it, and all the people who had cattle that they wished to graze upon the public lands, permitted them to run at large over the whole region, fattening upon the public lands of the United States, and upon the unenclosed lands of the private individual, without let or hindrance. The owner of a piece of land, who

had built a house or enclosed twenty or forty acres of it, had the benefit of this universal custom, as well as the party who owned no land. Everybody used the open unenclosed country, which produced nutritious grasses, as a public common on which their horses, cattle, hogs, and sheep could run and graze. *Id.* at 327-28.

In addition to the actions of landowners like Mr. Taylor in *Lobato*, the development of land as society changes and grows often threatens traditional practices. New buildings and roads may cut off access to resources traditionally available to individuals engaging in traditional practices. The next case considers the rights of a Native American tribe to cross land that their ancestors have been crossing for generations. As you read, consider how the law of easements reconciles the rights of those who have been crossing the land with the landowner.

United States v. Platt

730 F.Supp. 318 (D. Ariz. 1990)

CARROLL, District Judge.

The Zuni Indians, as a part of their religion, make a regular periodic pilgrimage at the time of the summer solstice, on foot or horseback, from their reservation in northwest New Mexico to the mountain area the tribe calls Kohlu/wala:wa which is located in northeast Arizona. It is believed by the Zuni Indians that Kohlu/wala:wa is their place of origin, the basis for their religious life, and the home of their dead.[1]

There is historical evidence that the Zuni pilgrimage was occurring as early as 1540 A.D. . . . The pilgrimage has been largely uncontested until recent times.

In 1985 defendant, Earl Platt, declared his intention of preventing the Zuni Indians from crossing his land on their pilgrimage. Earl Platt and the estate of Buena Platt (defendant), own or lease from the United States or the state of Arizona land in Apache County over which the Zuni Indians cross on their pilgrimage to Kohlu/wala:wa. On June 12, 1985 the United States on behalf of the Zuni Tribe instituted this action claiming a prescriptive easement by adverse possession across the Platt land. . . .

1. These lands were lost to the Zuni Tribe as a result of an executive order in 1877, however, 1984 legislation, Public Law 98-408 §4 (98 Stat. 1533), allowed the Tribe to acquire lands in Arizona for religious purposes. The legislation also allowed the Zuni Indians to acquire a permanent right of ingress and egress to Kohlu/wala:wa for traditional religious pilgrimages and ceremonies. As a part of the purchase of Kohlu/wala:wa, from Seven Springs Ranch Inc. the Zuni Tribe was granted a right of ingress and egress to the mountain connecting with an existing roadway from Hunt, Arizona. Exhibit 430, paragraph 6(d). This point of access is on the west side of the mountain and would not enable the pilgrimage to have access to the area in the traditional manner.

Findings of Fact

The evidence presented at trial shows that the Zuni Indians have gone on their quadrennial pilgrimage, approximately every four years . . . since, at least, the early twentieth century. There was direct evidence presented at trial, in the form of motion picture documentation, of the pilgrimage occurring in 1924. . . . Furthermore, John Niiha, the Zuni Dance priest, testified that he has been on 11 pilgrimages since his first in approximately 1949. Another Zuni religious leader, Mecalite Wytsallaci, the Zuni Rain Priest of the North for the last 39 years, who is ninety-nine years old, testified that he went on a pilgrimage when he was a young man but has not participated in the pilgrimage since he has been the Rain Priest. Wytsallaci's testimony, indicates that he participated in a pilgrimage sometime prior to 1940. Since 1976 the Apache County Sheriff's office has set up a road block, north of St. Johns, on Highway 666, at the request of the Zuni Tribe, so as ensure the safety and privacy of the pilgrims as they cross the highway going to and coming from Kohlu/wala:wa on their pilgrimage.

Eighty Tribe members are selected to participate in the pilgrimage. However, due to age, health and other considerations not all actually go along. The pilgrimage party generally consists of forty to sixty Zuni Indians and twenty to forty horses. . . . The Zuni pilgrimage begins at the Zuni Reservation, in Northwestern New Mexico, and follows a fairly direct path to Kohlu/wala:wa in Apache County, Arizona. . . . The pilgrimage generally crosses the defendant's land . . .

The total trek is 110 miles in length. It takes four days for the pilgrims to travel to Kohlu/wala:wa and return back to the reservation. The pilgrimage crosses approximately 18-20 miles of land owned or leased by the defendant Earl Platt.

The path or route used by the Zuni Indians, on their religious pilgrimage has been consistent and relatively unchanged. . . . The plaintiffs concede that topographical changes may necessarily alter the route. However, man made obstacles will not cause the Zuni pilgrims to deviate from their customary path. This is evidenced by the fact the pilgrims cut or take down fences in their way.

The pathway used by the pilgrims is approximately fifty feet wide. . . . The Zuni Indians use of the route in question is limited to a path or a place crossed enroute to Kohlu/wala:wa. Other than the path itself there are no points or landmarks of religious significance to the Zuni Indians on the defendant's land and the pilgrims do not camp on the defendant's land but they do stop for lunch on Platt land. . . .

The use of the property, by the Zuni Indians, along the pilgrimage route has been open visible and known to the community. Several witnesses who have been long time residents of the St. Johns area, which is in close proximity to the land in question, testified that they knew of the

Zuni pilgrimage and that it was generally known throughout the community.

The Zuni Tribe, and the people going on the pilgrimage, believed that they had a right to cross the lands traversed by their established route. There has been no showing that they sought to cross lands under permission or by authority of other persons.

Conclusions of Law

The Arizona statute defining adverse possession provides:

> "Adverse possession" means an actual and visible appropriation of the land, commenced and continued under a claim of right inconsistent with and hostile to the claim of another.

A.R.S. §12-521. The Arizona statutes further provide that:

> A. A person who has a cause of action for recovery of any lands, tenements or hereditaments from a person having peaceable and adverse possession thereof, cultivating, using and enjoying such property, shall commence an action therefor within ten years after the cause of action accrues, and not afterward.

A.R.S. §12-526.

The Arizona statutes follow the generally held rule that in order for one to acquire right to property purely by adverse possession, such possession must be actual, open and notorious, hostile, under a claim of right, continuous for the statutory period of 10 years, and exclusive. Whittemore v. Amator, 148 Ariz. 200, 202, 713 P.2d 1258 (App.1985) See also LaRue v. Kosich, 66 Ariz. 299, 187 P.2d 642 (1947).

The Arizona Courts place the burden of proof on the party claiming the right to use another's land. LaRue, 66 Ariz. at 303, 187 P.2d 642. Once the prima facie elements of prescription are met, the law presumes the use to be under a claim of right and not permissive. Gusheroski v. Lewis, 64 Ariz. 192, 198, 167 P.2d 390 (1946). The burden of proving permissive use then falls upon the landowner. Brown v. Ware, 129 Ariz. 249, 251, 630 P.2d 545 (App. 1981).

The proof necessary to establish a prescriptive easement to use land is not the same as that to establish a claim of title by adverse possession. Etz v. Mamerow, 72 Ariz 228, 232, 233 P.2d 442 (1951). "[I]t is only the use to which the premises are put which must be shown to be adverse, open and notorious. To the extent that the use is established, it, of course, is hostile to the title of the servient estate." Id. at 233, 233 P.2d 442. Therefore, although the plaintiffs in this case must prove all the elements essential to title by prescription, . . . their burden of proof must be measured in terms of the right to the use they claim, i.e. a very limited periodic use.

ELEMENTS ESTABLISHING AN EASEMENT

As stated above the plaintiffs must have proven, at trial, every element essential to adverse possession to establish a prescriptive easement over the pilgrimage route in question. Arizona case law does not provide a clear delineation as to the requirements of each element of adverse possession and often two or more requirements are analyzed in conjunction with each other.

The requirements of establishing actual possession and continuous possession are similar and inseparable and therefore they shall be considered together. Neither actual occupancy nor cultivation nor residence is necessary to constitute actual possession, and what acts may or may not constitute possession are necessarily varied and depend on the circumstances surrounding the case. . . .

Neither A.R.S. §12-521, subsec. A(1) nor §12-521, subsec. A(2) sets any specific time requirement for physical bodily presence which must be complied with in order for a claimant to claim the continuous possession required to perfect title by adverse possession. "Possession" as used in §12-521, subsec. A is not synonymous with the physical bodily presence of the adverse claimant. Continuous bodily presence is not required. . . .

The Zuni tribe has had actual possession of the route used for the religious pilgrimage for a short period of time every four years. They have had actual possession of the land in the sense that they have not recognized any other claim to the land at the time of the pilgrimage, as evidenced by their lack of deviation from the established route and disregard for fences or any other man made obstacle that blocks their course of travel. This Court also finds that the Zuni Tribe continually used a portion of the defendant's land for a short period of time every four years at least since 1924 and very probably for a period of time spanning many hundreds of years prior to that year.

Therefore, the plaintiffs have established the "actual" and "continuous" possession elements of their claim for adverse possession. Furthermore this "actual" possession has been continuous for over ten years which is required for a claim of a prescriptive right. *Whittemore,* 148 Ariz. at 202, 713 P.2d 1258 (App. 1985).

The open and notorious element of adverse possession requires that the acts of ownership must be of the character so as to indicate to the community in which the land is situated that it is in the exclusive possession and enjoyment of the claimant. 2 *C.J.S.* Adverse Possession §50 at 714 (1972). There must be physical facts which openly evince and give notice of an intent to hold the land in hostile dominion and indicate to a prudent owner that an adverse claim is being asserted. *Conwell v. Allen,* 21 Ariz. App. 383, 384-385, 519 P.2d 872 (1974). However, an owner's actual knowledge of the adverse possession is equivalent to, and disposes with the necessity of open and notorious possession. *2 C.J.S.* Adverse Possession §51 at 718

(1972). Furthermore, presumption of notice or fact of notice upon the part of the title owner would arise to bar his right. *Tenney v. Luplow*, 103 Ariz. 363, 367, 442 P.2d 107 (1968). Presumption of notice may arise when there is shown, under all facts and circumstances, a concurrence of the elements of adverse possession and the facts of use, possession and enjoyment indicating on the part of the claimant an intent to repudiate title and interest of the land owner. Id. at 368, 442 P.2d 107.

The Zuni Tribe has not attempted to hide their pilgrimage or the route they were taking, although they do regard it as a personal and private activity. It was known generally throughout the community that the Zuni Indians took a pilgrimage every few years. It was also common knowledge in the community, generally, what route or over which lands the pilgrimage took place. Mrs. Hinkson, a resident of the St. John's area since 1938 and an owner of a ranch which the Zuni Indians cross on their pilgrimage, testified it was generally understood that the Zuni Tribe had set a precedent of crossing the land of ranchers that could not be changed even if owners of the land objected to such crossings or use of their property. The Zuni tribe also cut, tore down or placed gates in, fences on the property owned or leased by defendant and others.

This Court draws the reasonable inference, from all the facts and circumstances, that Earl Platt, the defendant in this case, was aware that a pilgrimage occurred, that it occurred approximately every four years and that the pilgrimage went across his property. . . .

Consequently, the Zuni Tribe's open and notorious use of Platt land and the inference that Earl Platt knew of such use satisfies and/or obviates the "open and notorious" element of an adverse possession.

It is contended by the plaintiffs that the Zuni's use of the Platt lands also fulfills the requirement of the "hostile" and "claim of right" elements of adverse possession. "Hostile" as applied to possession of realty does not connote ill will or evil intent, but merely a showing that the one in possession of the land claims exclusive rights thereto and denies by word or act the owner's title. . . . Similarly a "claim of right" is:

> [N]othing more than the intention of the party in possession to appropriate and use the land as his own to the exclusion of others irrespective of any semblance or shadow of actual title or right.

Tenney, 103 Ariz. at 366, 442 P.2d 107 (1968).

The record reflects, as discussed earlier, the Zuni pilgrims, at the time of their pilgrimage, claim exclusive right to the path they cross to Kohlu/wala:wa. The claim of right to temporary and periodic use of the defendant's land is evidenced by the cutting or pulling down of fences and the lack of deviation from the route. In recent years the Zuni Indians, with the aid of the Bureau of Land Management, placed gates in fences which impeded the pilgrimage route of the Zuni Indians. . . . The use, by the pilgrims, of the defendant's land is "hostile" to Earl Platt's title. Also there was no evidence presented at trial which would indicate that the Zuni tribe sought permission to cross the land of Earl Platt. The evidence clearly illustrated that the Zuni Indians never sought permission to cross lands on their pilgrimage but rather it was believed said crossing was a matter of right.

The record leaves no doubt that the "hostile" and "claim of right" elements of adverse possession has been satisfied by the plaintiffs.

Insofar as the exclusivity of possession is required, in the context of the claim asserted here, it is reasonable to conclude that if people are occupying a tract of land at a particular time, another person or other people, cannot simultaneously occupy the same space. Therefore, the Zuni's participating in the quadrennial pilgrimage have exclusive possession of the land upon which they cross enroute to Kohlu/wala:wa when they are crossing that land.

The Zuni Indian's use and possession of the Platt land has been actual, open and notorious, continuous and uninterrupted for at least 65 years and under a claim of right. Such use was known by the surrounding community.

It is clear from the record that the plaintiffs have established that the Zuni Indians meet the standards of adverse possession, set forth in A.R.S. §12-521 and the applicable case law for purposes of the limited use sought. The Zuni Tribe is entitled to a prescriptive easement over the land of the defendant for the purposes of their quadrennial pilgrimage. The defendant presented no evidence and has not otherwise proven that the Zuni Indians' use of the land in question was permissive or otherwise.

SCOPE OF THE EASEMENT

Since the plaintiffs have established the Zuni Indians' right to a prescriptive easement this Court must determine the scope of that easement.

The scope of a prescriptive easement is determined by the use through which it is acquired. *Stamatis v. Johnson*, . . . 224 P.2d 201 (1950). Those using the land of another for the prescriptive period may acquire the right to continue such use, but do not acquire the right to make other uses of it. *Id.*

The Governor of the Zuni Tribe, Robert E. Lewis, testified that his tribe did not use the path or route across the defendant's land for any other purpose than the quadrennial pilgrimage. The testimony presented at trial showed that the path used by the pilgrims was approximately 50 feet wide, not one mile, as asserted by the plaintiffs. Furthermore, there has been no evidence the Zuni pilgrims have built fires on the Platt ranch, nor has it been established that the pilgrims use water from the water sources or wells on the Platt property.

In reaching its decision, the Court does not base its ruling on any religious or 1st Amendment rights to the land in question. . . . The evidence of the religious purposes of the Zuni pilgrimage was admissable only to the extent it demonstrated when and how the land in question was used.

Applying the above stated law this Court can only grant an easement for the use of defendant's land to the extent the use claimed has been proven or established at trial. Accordingly,

IT IS ORDERED that the Zuni Tribe is granted an easement over the land owned by Earl Platt and the estate of Buena Platt, for 25 feet in either direction, of the route established by the October 27, 1987 Bureau of Land Management Survey, Exhibit 307.3, for the purposes of ingress to and egress from Kohlu/wala:wa by no more than 60 persons on foot or horseback.

IT IS FURTHER ORDERED that the Zuni Tribe shall use gates along the pilgrimage route already in existence and shall not construct gates in or alter existing fence lines without first obtaining leave of this Court.

IT IS FURTHER ORDERED the easement granted by this Court is limited to a 2 day period (one day each direction), during the summer solstice, once every four years to commence in 1993 and to continue on at 4 year intervals.

IT IS FURTHER ORDERED that the rights granted by this easement do not include the right to use defendant's water sources, nor does it include the right to light fires on the lands of the defendant.

IT IS FURTHER ORDERED that the Zuni Indian Tribe will be liable for any damage that occurs on defendant's property that is a result of the pilgrimage.

IT IS FURTHER ORDERED that the Zuni Tribe notify the defendant when the pilgrimage is going to occur at least 14 days prior to its commencement.

NOTES

1. The right of access may be created explicitly as well. Conservation easements, which preserve the right to access (often in the community in general) and limit development, are increasingly popular. *See, e.g.*, Lawrence R. Kueter and Christopher S. Jensen, *Conservation Easements: An Underdeveloped Tool to Protect Cultural Resources*, 83 Denver U. L. Rev. 1057 (2006). How long such easements should last has become controversial. Sometimes, commentators argue, they may even become a detriment to the community they were designed to protect. *See* Nancy A. McLaughlin, *Rethinking the Perpetual Nature of Conservation Easements*, 29 Harv. Environmental L. Rev. 421 (2006). The debate over the perpetuity of conservation easements illustrates some of the competing views on whether property rights should be construed broadly or narrowly. *Contrast* Susan F. French, *Perpetual Trusts, Conservation Servitudes, and the Problem of the Future*, 27 Cardozo L. Rev. 2523 (2006) and Carol N. Brown, *A Time to Preserve: A Call for*

Formal Private-Party Rights in Perpetual Conservation Easements, 40 GA. L. REV. 85 (2005).

Platt protected a limited right of access, based on a traditional concept of easement by prescription. Other cases have been even more explicit in protecting native rights to access. The next case, decided while the movement for native Hawaiian rights was gathering steam, recognizes such a right.

Public Access Shoreline Hawaii v. Hawaii County Planning Commission Nansay Hawaii

903 P.2d 1246 (Haw. 1995)

KLEIN, Justice.

We issued a writ of certiorari to review the decision of the Intermediate Court of Appeals (ICA) in this case, which concerns a challenge by Public Access Shoreline Hawaii (PASH) to the Hawaii County Planning Commission's (HPC) decision denying them standing to participate in a contested case hearing on an application by Nansay Hawaii, Inc. (Nansay) for a Special Management Area (SMA) use permit. . . .

The HPC received a SMA use permit application from Nansay for a resort development on the Big Island. Nansay sought approval of its plans to develop a community complex including: two resort hotels with over 1,000 rooms; 330 multiple family residential units; 380 single family homes; a golf course; a health club; restaurants; retail shops; an artisan village; a child care center; and other infrastructure and improvements over a 450 acre shoreline area in the ahupua'a[3] of Kohanaiki on the Big Island. On September 28, 1990, the HPC held a public hearing on Nansay's permit application, as required by the agency's rules. At the public hearing, many parties presented testimony, including . . . the coordinator of PASH. Various individuals and groups orally requested contested case hearings.

On November 8, 1990, after further testimony and discussion, the HPC determined that PASH['s] . . . interests were "not clearly distinguishable from that of the general public" and, therefore, that they did not have standing to participate in a contested case. The HPC then voted to deny the contested case requests and to grant Nansay a SMA use permit.

PASH . . . sought review in circuit court of both agency decisions (denial of . . . contested case requests and issuance of the SMA use permit)

3. An "ahupua'a" is a land division usually extending from the mountains to the sea along rational lines, such as ridges or other natural characteristics. In re Boundaries of Pulehunui, 4 Haw. 239, 241 (1879) (acknowledging that these "rational" lines may also be based upon tradition, culture, or other factors).

pursuant to HRS §§91-14 and 205A-6 (1985). The circuit court determined that the HPC erred in finding that PASH . . . did not have interests that were distinguishable from the general public. Accordingly, the court remanded the case with instructions for the HPC to grant PASH . . . a contested case hearing pursuant to its rules.

Nansay and the HPC appealed, and the ICA affirmed in part, holding that PASH was entitled to contested case hearing procedures. *PASH I*, slip op. at 12. The ICA's conclusion was based on its determination that the HPC "disregarded the rules regarding the gathering rights of native Hawaiians and its obligation to preserve and protect those rights." *Id.* In other words, the ICA determined that PASH's "interest in the proceeding was clearly distinguishable from that of the general public[.]" *Id.* . . .

The HPC and Nansay subsequently applied for a writ of certiorari, which we granted on May 7, 1993.

Nansay argues that the HPC has no obligation . . . to consider, much less require, protection of traditional and customary Hawaiian rights. In any event, the HPC contends that it did not disregard protection of gathering rights because the SMA permit contains a condition requiring establishment of a program for preserving and maintaining the anchialline ponds on the development site. Nansay and the HPC also contend that PASH failed to establish a prima facie claim of native Hawaiian gathering rights—specifically, Nansay claims that the evidence only shows shrimp gathering at the ponds as far back as the late 1920s. . . .

In addition to the requirements of the Coastal Zone Management Act, the HPC is obligated to protect customary and traditional rights to the extent feasible under the Hawaii Constitution and relevant statutes. Article XII, section 7 of the Hawaii Constitution (1978) provides:

> The State reaffirms and shall protect all rights, customarily and traditionally exercised for subsistence, cultural and religious purposes and possessed by ahupua'a tenants who are descendants of native Hawaiians who inhabited the Hawaiian Islands prior to 1778, subject to the right of the State to regulate such rights.

HRS §1-1 (Supp.1992) provides:

> The common law of England, as ascertained by English and American decisions, is declared to be the common law of the State of Hawaii in all cases, except as otherwise expressly provided by the Constitution or laws of the United States, or by the laws of the State, or fixed by Hawaiian judicial precedent, or established by Hawaiian usage; provided that no person shall be subject to criminal proceedings except as provided by the written laws of the United States or of the State.

In order to determine whether the HPC must protect traditional and customary rights of the nature asserted in this case, we shall first review our analysis of gathering rights in Kalipi and Pele. . . . Finally, we will provide the HPC with some specific, although not necessarily exhaustive, guidelines to aid its future deliberations in the event that Nansay elects to pursue its challenges to the legitimacy of PASH's claims.

1. Kalipi v. Hawaiian Trust Co.: Judicial Recognition of Traditional Hawaiian Gathering Rights Based Upon Residency in a Particular Ahupua'a

Kalipi involved an individual's attempt to gain access to private property on the island of Moloka "in order to exercise purportedly traditional Hawaiian gathering rights." The court prefaced its consideration of Kalipi's claims with a discussion of the State's obligation to preserve and enforce traditional Hawaiian gathering rights under article XII, section 7 of the Hawaii Constitution:

> We recognize that permitting access to private property for the purpose of gathering natural products may indeed conflict with the exclusivity traditionally associated with fee simple ownership of land. But any argument for the extinguishing of traditional rights based simply upon the possible inconsistency of purported native rights with our modern system of land tenure must fail.

The court then began its analysis of Kalipi's asserted gathering rights by interpreting HRS §7-1 (1985)[4] so as to essentially "conform these traditional rights born of a culture which knew little of the rigid exclusivity associated with the private ownership of land, with a modern system of land tenure in which the right to exclude is perceived to be an integral part of fee simple title." Accordingly, the court fashioned a rule permitting "lawful occupants of an ahupua'a . . . [to] enter undeveloped lands within the [ahupua'a] to gather those items enumerated in the statute [HRS §7-1]."

The requirement that these rights be exercised on undeveloped land is not, of course, found within the statute. However, if this limitation were not imposed, there would be nothing to prevent residents from going anywhere within the ahupua'a, including fully developed property, to gather the enumerated items. In the context of our current culture this

4. HRS §7-1, which has not undergone significant change since the 1851 enactment that amended an earlier version of the statute, provides:

> Building materials, water, etc.; landlords' title subject to tenants' use. Where the landlords have obtained, or may hereafter obtain, allodial titles to their lands, the people on each of their lands shall not be deprived of the right to take firewood, house-timber, aho cord, thatch, or ki leaf, from the land on which they live, for their own private use, but they shall not have a right to take such articles to sell for profit. The people shall also have a right to drinking water, and running water, and the right of way. The springs of water, running water, and roads shall be free to all, on all lands granted in fee simple; provided that this shall not be applicable to wells and watercourses, which individuals have made for their own use.

The term "landlord" appears to be a loose translation of "konohiki" from the Hawaiian language versions of these acts. The word "konohiki" is defined as "[h]eadman of an ahupua'a land division under the chief."

result would so conflict with understandings of property, and potentially lead to such disruption, that we could not consider it anything short of absurd and therefore other than that which was intended by the statute's framers. Moreover, it would conflict with our understanding of the traditional Hawaiian way of life in which cooperation and non-interference with the well-being of other residents were integral parts of the culture.

Similarly the requirement that the rights be utilized to practice native customs represents, we believe, a reasonable interpretation of the Act as applied to our current context. The gathering rights of §7-1 were necessary to insure the survival of those who, in 1851, sought to live in accordance with the ancient ways. They thus remain, to the extent provided in the statute, available to those who wish to continue those ways.

Because Kalipi did not actually reside within the subject ahupua'a, the court held that he was not entitled to exercise HRS §7-1 gathering rights there. Id. at 9, 656 P.2d at 750. Nevertheless, the court specifically refused to decide the ultimate scope of traditional gathering rights under HRS §1-1 because there was "an *insufficient basis* to find that such rights would, or should, accrue to persons who did not actually reside within the [ahupua'a] in which such rights are claimed." Id. at 12, 656 P.2d at 752 (emphasis added). In other words, Kalipi did not foreclose the possibility of establishing, in future cases, traditional Hawaiian gathering and access rights in one ahupua'a that have been customarily held by residents of another ahupua'a.

2. *Pele Defense Fund v. Paty: Judicial Recognition of Traditional Access and Gathering Rights Based Upon Custom*

Pele involved, inter alia, the assertion of customarily and traditionally exercised subsistence, cultural, and religious practices in the Wao Kele O Puna Natural Area Reserve on the Big Island. For the purposes of summary judgment, we held that there was a sufficient basis to find that gathering rights can be claimed by persons who do not reside in the particular ahupua'a where they seek to exercise those rights. We specifically held that "native Hawaiian rights protected by article XII, §7 may extend beyond the ahupua'a in which a native Hawaiian resides." In so holding, we explicated the discussion of gathering rights in Kalipi by recognizing that a claim based on practiced customs raises different issues than assertions premised on mere land ownership.

> Unlike Kalipi, [Pele Defense Fund] members assert native Hawaiian rights based on the traditional access and gathering patterns of native Hawaiians in the Puna region. Because Kalipi based his claims entirely on land ownership, rather than on the practiced customs of Hawaiians on Molokai, the issue facing us is somewhat different from the issue in Kalipi. Pele, 73 Haw. At 618-19, 837 P.2d at 1271.

Although we later mentioned "other requirements of Kalipi" with approval—implicitly referring to the "undeveloped lands" and "no actual harm" requirements of Kalipi, our holding in Pele was not intended to foreclose argument regarding those requirements in future, unrelated cases involving assertions of customary and traditional rights under HRS §1-1. In Kalipi, we foresaw that "[t]he precise nature and scope of the rights retained by §1-1 would, of course, depend upon the particular circumstances of each case." Pele, 73 Haw. At 619, 837 P.2d at 1271 (quoting Kalipi, 66 Haw. at 12, 656 P.2d at 752). . . .

Nansay argues that the recognition of rights exercised by persons who do not actually reside in the subject ahupua'a "represents such a departure from existing law . . . [that *Pele*] should be overruled or strictly limited to its specific facts." Nansay contends further that *Pele* is inconsistent with the fundamental nature of Hawaiian land tenure, which allegedly recognizes only three classes: government, landlord, and tenant.

We decline Nansay's invitation to overrule *Pele;* on the contrary, we reaffirm it and expressly deem the rules of law posited therein to be applicable here. In *Pele,* we held that article XII, section 7, which, inter alia, obligates the State to protect customary and traditional rights normally associated with tenancy in an ahupua'a, may also apply to the exercise of rights beyond the physical boundaries of that particular ahupua'a. Therefore, we hold that common law rights ordinarily associated with tenancy do not limit customary rights existing under the laws of this state. . . .

For the purposes of this opinion, we choose not to scrutinize the various gradations in property use that fall between the terms "undeveloped" and "fully developed." Nevertheless, we refuse the temptation to place undue emphasis on non-Hawaiian principles of land ownership in the context of evaluating deliberations on development permit applications. Such an approach would reflect an unjustifiable lack of respect for gathering activities as an acceptable cultural usage in pre-modern Hawaii,[5] which can also be successfully incorporated in the context of our current culture. Contrary to the suggestion in *Kalipi* that there would be nothing to prevent the *unreasonable* exercise of these rights, article XII, section 7 accords an ample legal basis for regulatory efforts by the State. In other words, the State is authorized to impose appropriate regulations to govern the exercise of native Hawaiian rights in conjunction with permits issued for the development of land previously undeveloped or not yet fully developed.

Depending on the circumstances of each case, once land has reached the point of "full development" it may be inconsistent to allow or enforce the practice of traditional Hawaiian gathering rights on such property. However, legitimate customary and traditional practices must be protected to the extent feasible in accordance with article XII, section 7. Although access is only *guaranteed* in connection with undeveloped lands, and article

5. In accordance with HRS §5-7.5(b), we are authorized to "give consideration to the 'Aloha Spirit'." The Aloha Spirit "was the working philosophy of native Hawaiians . . . 'Aloha' is the essence of relationships in which each person is important to every other person for collective existence." HRS §5-7.5(a).

XII, section 7 does not *require* the preservation of such lands, the State does not have the unfettered discretion to regulate the rights of ahupua'a tenants out of existence.

Thus, to the extent feasible, we hold that the HPC must protect the reasonable exercise of customary or traditional rights that are established by PASH on remand.

NOTES AND QUESTIONS

1. Does custom play the same role in *PASH* as it did in *Lobato*? What is the court protecting in each of the cases? Why would a court protect customary practices? Is the extinction of custom a natural consequence of development? For a similar case regarding an easement based on ancient Hawaiian custom, see *Palama v. Sheehan*, 440 P.2d 95, 97-98 (Haw. 1968) (finding a right of way through an owner's land for access to the ocean based upon a traditional route used by ahupua'a tenants).

2. Do you think that the court's protection of customary practices along a sliding scale of development in *PASH* is meaningful? How would you apply the courts' decisions? Do these opinions create or reduce further litigation?

3. How would you identify a customary practice worthy of legal protection? In his Commentaries on the Laws of England, William Blackstone identified various factors that can be used to identify customs that cannot be superseded by written law. According to Blackstone, a custom is a practice that has occurred for such a long time "that the memory of man runneth not to the contrary. So that, if any one can shew [sic] the beginning of it, it is no good custom." The practice must be continuous and "[a]ny interruption would cause a temporary ceasing: the revival gives it a new beginning, which will be within time of memory, and thereupon the custom will be void. But this must be understood with regard to an interruption of the *right*; for an interruption of *possession* only, for ten or twenty years, will not destroy the custom." The practice must also have been reasonable, specific in scope, and consistent with other customs. Finally, the alleged custom "must be compulsory; and not left to the option of every man, whether he will use them or no. Therefore a custom, that all the inhabitants shall be rated toward the maintenance of a bridge, will be good; but a custom, that every main is to contribute thereto at his own pleasure, is idle and absurd, and indeed no custom at all." 1 William Blackstone, COMMENTARIES ON THE LAWS OF ENGLAND 77-78 (Christian et. al ed. 1859). Did the grazing activities in *Lobato* or the Hawaiian practices in *PASH* satisfy Blackstone's definition?

4. Customary practices do not always receive the protection of the courts. Although the Alaska Native Claims Settlement Act compensated Native Alaskans for the loss of title, the Act also terminated "any aboriginal

hunting and fishing rights that may exist." 43 U.S.C. §1603(b). In *Native Village of Eyak v. Trawler Diane Marine*, 154 F.3d 1090 (9th Cir. 1998), five native Alaskan villages sought to enjoin federal regulations that limited hunting and fishing on native lands that they possessed based on 7,000 years of practice and "unextinguished aboriginal title." *Id.* at 1091. The Ninth Circuit Court of Appeals dismissed "the argument that the Native Villages are entitled to exclusive use of the outer continental shelf (OCS) because they have hunted and fished in the sea for thousands of years prior to the founding of the United States. While we respect the history of the Native Villages and appreciate the importance of the OCS to them, the Supreme Court was likewise cognizant of the history of the coastal states. . . . This did not, however, convince the Court to put the ocean and its resources at the disposal of the states. Whatever interests the states might have had in the OCS and marginal sea prior to statehood were lost upon ascension to the Union. The Constitution allotted to the federal government jurisdiction over foreign commerce, foreign affairs, and national defense so that as attributes of these external sovereign powers, it has paramount rights in the contested areas of the sea. This principle applies with equal force to *all* entities claiming rights to the ocean: whether they be the Native Villages, the State of Oregon, or the Township of Parsippany. "National interests, national responsibilities, national concerns are involved" in all these cases. The Native Villages' claim to complete control over the OCS is contrary to these national interests and inconsistent with their position as a subordinate entity within our constitutional scheme. We therefore hold that the Native Villages are barred from asserting exclusive rights to the use and occupancy of the OCS based on unextinguished aboriginal title." *Id.* at 1096-97.

5. In some states, family members have a statutorily created easement to visit gravesites of deceased family members that are located on private property. Virginia created one of the most comprehensive statutory easements that permit family members to visit burial grounds. According to Va. Code Ann. §57.27.1 (1993), "family members and descendants of deceased persons buried there" as well as genealogical researchers have a right to visit burial grounds so long as they provide "reasonable notice to the owners of record or to the occupant of property or both." Under that section, access to the burial site(s) must be "reasonable and limited to the purposes of visiting graves, maintaining the gravesite or cemetery, or conducting genealogical research." Why would Virginia limit access to the graves? What factors would a court examine to determine whether or not a private property owner has provided family members with "reasonable" access to the gravesites?

The issue of family access to gravesites in Virginia has arisen in a setting of historical interest—access to Thomas Jefferson's gravesite by the descendents of Sally Hemings, who was one of Jefferson's slaves. One of the nagging questions surrounding Thomas Jefferson is whether or not he and

Sally Hemings had children together. Several committees have studied the results of DNA tests as well as circumstantial evidence associated with the historical record and have reached differing conclusions. Some scholars conclude that it is likely that Jefferson and Hemings had children, while others question the blood relationship between the descendants of Hemings and Jefferson. The DNA evidence identifies a genetic connection between Hemings' children and the Jefferson family, but cannot identify Thomas Jefferson as the father of those children. Based on the ambiguous scientific results, the Monticello Association, which owns the Jefferson family cemetery (in which Jefferson is buried), voted against offering membership to the Hemings descendants. If the Hemings descendants seek access to Jefferson's gravesite, does Va. Code Ann. §57.27.1 grant them access to the gravesite? What factors would you examine to decide whether or not to grant access to the cemetery to the Hemings descendants? For more on the issue involving the Hemings descendants and the Jefferson cemetery, see Dan Barry, "Atop a Hallowed Mountain, Small Steps Toward Healing," *N.Y. Times*, March 31, 2008. For more on the relationship between Hemings and Jefferson and the various studies that have reviewed the question of Jefferson's paternity of Hemings' children, see *http://www.monticello.org/plantation/hemingscontro/hemings-jefferson_contro.html* (last visited August 31, 2010).

6.8 COVENANTS RUNNING WITH THE LAND

As we described in Chapter 4, *Shelley v. Kraemer*, 334 U.S. 1 (1948), held that the Fourteenth Amendment of the United States Constitution barred courts from enforcing racially restrictive covenants. In addition to *Shelley*, two federal civil rights statutes feature prominently in the effort to eradicate racial discrimination in housing. The first of those statutes is Section 1982 of the Civil Rights Act of 1866, 42 U.S.C. §1982, which states that

> [a]ll citizens of the United States shall have the same right, in every State and Territory, as is enjoyed by white citizens thereof to inherit, purchase, lease, sell, hold, and convey real and personal property.

Similar to the result in *Shelley*, the Supreme Court rejected an argument that the prohibitions contained in §1982 did not reach purely private acts in *Jones v. Alfred H. Mayer Co.*, 392 U.S. 409 (1968).

The most recent addition to the fight against racial discrimination in housing is the FHA, which was one of the primary topics addressed in Chapter 5. Section 3604(a) of the FHA, 42 U.S.C.A. §3601 et. seq., prohibits housing discrimination based on race, color, religion, sex, familial status, or national origin. Furthermore, section 3604(c) makes it illegal "to make, print, or publish . . . any notice, statement, or advertisement . . . that indicates any preference" on the basis of race, color, religion, sex, handicap, familial status, or national origin. As you read the next case, consider the following question: Does the protection offered by *Shelley*, Section 1982 of the Civil Rights Act of 1866, and the FHA mean that covenants cannot be used to discriminate on the basis of race?

Regency Homes Association v. Egermayer

498 N.W.2d 783 (Neb. 1993)

FAHRNBRUCH, Justice.

The sole issue raised by the Egermayers on appeal is whether the trial court erred in finding the Declaration of March 19, 1968 (Declaration), to be a valid covenant running with the land as it applies to the obligation of a property owner to pay dues to a social club open to the public and owned by a private individual.

For reasons hereinafter discussed, we believe the Egermayers have mischaracterized the nature of the obligation imposed by the covenant. The issue may more accurately be described as whether the trial court erred in finding the Declaration to be a valid covenant running with the land as it applies to the obligation of a property owner to pay money to a homeowners' association that operates a recreational facility. . . .

The Regency subdivision, a large multiuse development with residential, commercial, and recreational areas, was developed in Omaha in the late 1960s by Regency, Inc., and United of Omaha. Regency, Inc., apparently was or is a wholly owned subsidiary of United of Omaha. The plaintiff, RHA, was incorporated in the State of Nebraska on March 15, 1968.

In the Declaration, Regency, Inc., set forth the general and specific covenants governing the subdivision, and five individuals described as "all of the owners other than Regency, Inc.," accepted and agreed to the Declaration. At issue in this lawsuit is §4 of the Declaration, requiring property owners to be members of RHA. That section provides:

> 4. *Association:* The involved property is . . . included in membership in [RHA] subject to all and each of the following conditions and other terms:
>
> a. [RHA] will have the right, in general, without any part of its net earnings inuring to the private benefit of its members, to promote and sustain their social welfare and otherwise provide for their health, pleasure, recreation, safety, and other nonprofitable interests by acquiring, maintaining, operating, contributing to the acquisition, maintenance, or operation of, or otherwise *making available for use any one or more area entrances or entry structures, boat docks, golf courses, lakes, parks, swimming pools, tennis courts, and any other recreational equipment,* facilities, grounds, or structures, by providing weed and other actual or potential nuisance abatement or control, security service, and other community services, by exercising architectural

> control and securing compliance with or enforcement of applicable covenants, easements, restrictions, and similar limitations, *by fixing and collecting or abating dues or other charges for financing its operations* . . . .
>
> b . . . [E]very lot will be automatically included in membership in [RHA] as a benefit or burden running with and charge upon the ownership of each such lot . . .
>
> c. Dues or other charges for each lot included in membership fixed by [RHA] in the manner set out in its Articles of Incorporation or its By-Laws, as from time to time amended, will each constitute until abated or paid a lien upon and charge against such lot in favor of [RHA] . . . .

Section 5 of the Declaration provides for enforcement of covenants, easements, and other terms of the Declaration through legal and equitable proceedings, and entitles RHA to "fix a reasonable charge for such action as a lien upon and charge against such lot in favor of [RHA]." The parties have stipulated that the Declaration was recorded at pages 103 through 116 of book 461 of the Miscellaneous Records of the Register of Deeds of Douglas County, Nebraska. . . .

Generally, in the United States the three essential requirements for a covenant of any type to run with land are (1) the grantor and the grantee intend that the covenant run with the land, as determined from the instruments of record; (2) the covenant must "touch and concern" the land with which it runs; and (3) the party claiming the benefit of the covenant and the party who bears the burden of the covenant must be in privity of estate.

The Egermayers do not dispute that the first and third of these requirements are met. Moreover, the recorded instruments in the record support that the grantor, Regency, Inc., and the five original grantees intended the covenants contained in the Declaration to run with the land and that the Egermayers and RHA are in privity of estate. Rather, the Egermayers argue that the covenant in question does not "touch and concern" the land. Therefore, we limit our analysis to that issue.

The "touch and concern" requirement of a real covenant is one with which many jurisdictions have struggled. The New York Court of Appeals has held that a covenant which runs with the land must affect the legal relations — the advantages and the burdens — of the parties to the covenant, as owners of particular parcels of land and not merely as members of the community in general, such as taxpayers or owners of other land. That method of approach has the merit of realism. The test is based on the effect of the covenant rather than on technical distinctions. Does the covenant impose, on the one hand, a burden upon an interest in land, which on the other hand increases the value of a different interest in the same or related land? . . .

[F]or the purpose of analysis, we adopt the New York Court of Appeals' rule that the touch and concern requirement of a real covenant is met when the covenant affects the legal relations — the advantages and the burdens — of the parties to the covenant, as owners of particular parcels of land and not merely as members of the community in general, such as taxpayers or owners of other land. The covenant must impose, on the one hand, a burden upon an interest in land, which on the other hand increases the value of a different interest in the same or related land. . . .

This brings us to the ultimate question of whether RLTC enhances the value of individual properties in the Regency subdivision. George Egermayer testified that in his opinion, RLTC adds no value whatsoever to his property because the facility is located across four lanes of traffic from the residential area, it is not centrally located, it is next to a commercial area, and it is open to the public. Another homeowner in the Regency subdivision testified that in his opinion, mandatory membership in the RHA definitely enhanced the property values in the area and that property values would be adversely affected if membership in RHA were to be voluntary rather than mandatory. Two of the original developers of the Regency subdivision, neither of whom lives in Regency, also testified that the absence of mandatory dues to RHA would be detrimental to property owners and that property values would be lowered.

Whether membership in RHA benefits individual Regency homeowners is a material issue of fact in determining whether the covenant requiring membership touches and concerns the land. The only evidence that membership in RHA does not benefit individual property owners was offered by the party seeking to avoid payment of the mandatory dues. After considering all the testimony on this issue, we agree with the California Court of Appeals that "the maintenance of a well-kept clubhouse, recreational area and swimming pool . . . enhance[s] the value of each home therein. . . . [T]he so-called 'burden' of maintaining membership in this association would in reality be an asset to each and every property owner in the use of his land." Anthony v. Brea Glenbrook Club, 58 Cal.App.3d 506, 511, 130 Cal.Rptr. 32, 34 (1976).

Apart from the social amenities offered by RLTC, we find that membership in RHA provides numerous other benefits to property owners. There was testimony that RHA dues pay for maintenance of a 1-acre park within the subdivision, as well as the green areas at the 96th Street entrance to the subdivision. George Egermayer concedes that maintenance of the common areas of the subdivisions, parks, drives, and trees adds value to his property. We can only conclude that maintenance of the green areas owned by RHA and paid for through part of the annual $225 assessment contributes some of this added value.

Dues also paid for the services of a private security patrol for the residential neighborhood until sometime after the subdivision was annexed by the city of Omaha. Financial statements entered into evidence reflect that as much as $17,128 per year was spent for security patrol through the fiscal year ending May 31, 1985. Private security service is an asset which enhances the value of individual properties.

The bylaws of RHA provide for an architectural control committee and authorize the expenditure of funds by that committee. The architectural review committee reviews and approves all new construction, as well as additions or modifications to existing structures, to ensure that the external designs of all buildings and structures are in harmony with the "surroundings, topography, and other relevant architectural factors of concern." A former president of RHA testified that while he was president the committee met from time to time and incurred certain expenses, including payments to experts to advise the committee. Again, this is a function of RHA which benefits all property owners in Regency by protecting against unsightly or inappropriate building in the subdivision.

Upon a de novo review of the record, we conclude that the covenant requiring membership in the RHA enhances the value of individual properties in the Regency subdivision so as to meet the "touch and concern" requirement of a real covenant running with the land. RHA is entitled to foreclose its lien upon the Egermayer property to enforce payment of the RHA dues and other charges required by the covenant.

NOTES AND QUESTIONS

1. Do subdivisions target specific buyers by offering various community amenities to be made available upon purchase? If so, is it possible that the imposition of fees for recreational facilities with the aid of running covenants is a screening device designed to exclude those deemed undesirable? What types of community amenities might serve to screen out some buyers? If not, what other reasons exist for the inclusion of such covenants? Does the suggestion that such covenants mask discriminatory motives conflate discrimination with culture? For more on the potential of facially non-discriminatory covenants to achieve discriminatory ends, see Lior J. Strahilevitz, *Exclusionary Amenities in Residential Communities*, 92 VA. L. REV. 437 (2006).

2. *Shelley v. Kraemer*, of course, made racially discriminatory restrictive covenants unenforceable by courts. But what effect does the inclusion of a racially restrictive covenant have on other restrictions contained in a deed today? In *Corner v. Mills*, 650 N.E.2d 712 (Ind. 1995), the deed to a parcel of real property restricted the land to residential use. *Id.* at 714. Furthermore, one of the covenants specified that "no persons of any race other than the white race shall use or occupy any building or any lot, except that this covenant shall not prevent occupancy by domestic servants of a different race domiciled with an owner or tenant." *Id.* Because the landowner believed that the land would be most profitable if put to a commercial use, the landowner sought declaratory relief to have the burden of the covenants removed. *Id.* Neighboring landowners sought to have the covenants enforced to prevent commercial development. *Id.* According to the landowner seeking to eliminate all of the covenants, the mere presence of the racial restriction "poison[ed]" all of the covenants;

therefore, the court should remove all restrictions on the use of the land. *Id.* at 715. Although the court ruled that the racial restrictions were unenforceable, it did not eliminate the remaining covenants that burdened the land. The court observed that illegal covenants could be redacted if doing so did not "affect the intent or symmetry of the remaining covenants." *Id.* As a result, the court redacted the unconstitutional racial provision and enforced the residential requirements of the covenant. *Id.*

3. As *Regency Homes* demonstrates, the touch and concern requirement for the burden of an affirmative real covenant to run with the land has, to say the least, caused interpretive difficulty. Do any of the definitions described by the court provide meaningful guidance to the courts in their efforts to apply the requirement to the facts of cases before them? If not, what purpose might the retention of the touch and concern requirement serve? For one possible answer to this question, see Susan French, *Servitudes Reform and the New Restatement of Property: Creation Doctrines and Structural Simplification*, 73 CORNELL L. REV. 928 (1988) (suggesting that the touch and concern requirement permits courts to strike down covenants based on public policy). For opposing views on the necessity of retaining the touch and concern requirement, compare Richard A. Epstein, *Notice and Freedom of Contract in the Law of Servitudes*, 55 S. CAL. L. REV. 1353 (1982) (arguing in favor of eliminating the touch and concern requirement on contractual and economic grounds); Gregory S. Alexander, *Freedom, Coercion, and the Law of Servitudes*, 73 CORNELL L. REV. 883 (1988) (arguing in favor of retaining the status quo to counter acts done in bad faith).

6.9 THE COMMUNITY'S INTEREST IN CHARITABLE TRUSTS

One issue we have dealt with several times in this book is the rights of non-owners of property. We have studied the interests of non-owners in easement cases, such as the right to access property to participate in traditional religious ceremonies, for beach access, and to visit people buried on private property, as well as the right of tenants to receive guests at their homes. Although most of this book is focused on cases involving race and ethnicity, we conclude this chapter with a case that apportions rights between the community and a charitable trust, because it relates to the theme of non-owners. It involves the Hershey Trust, a charitable trust established by Milton Hershey in 1909 to provide a school for orphans. The Trust owns a controlling share of the Hershey Chocolate Company. In 2002 the Trust began discussions about selling its controlling share — in part to diversify its holdings — to other candy companies. The controlling share would have brought a premium price; it would also have very likely resulted in the closing of the Hershey operations in Hershey, Pennsylvania and the relocation of those jobs offshore. So when the announcement came that the Hershey Trust planned to sell its controlling share to the Cadbury Company, the Pennsylvania Attorney General sought an injunction in the local court (before a judge who was elected by the local community). The Attorney General has standing to challenge the actions of charitable trusts.

The local judge granted the Attorney General's request for a temporary restraining order. Then, on appeal, the Pennsylvania Commonwealth Court refused to overturn the temporary restraining order. The trial court's opinion is excerpted below. In reading it, keep in mind that to prevail in a temporary restraining order, the Attorney General did not need to show final success on the merits. For a temporary (as opposed to a permanent) injunction, a claimant need only show that there is substantially likelihood of success on the merits and the threat of irreparable harm. Although the Attorney General's legal theory was, perhaps, suspect, the trial court saw the enormity of the harm and granted the injunction. See if you can pick out the Attorney General's legal theory; and then try to square it with what you know about property law.

In Re: Milton Hershey School Trust

(Court of Common Pleas of Dauphin County, Pennsylvania, Sept. 10, 2002)

Warren G. Morgan, Senior Judge

The Hershey Trust Company and the Board of Managers of the Milton Hershey School (the Board of the Trust Company is also the Board of Managers) propose to sell the controlling interest in the Hershey Foods Corporation now held in trust for the School. On August 19, 2002, on the Petition of the Attorney General of the Commonwealth we issued a Citation directing the Trust Company and the Managers to show cause why information regarding the sale process should not be disclosed to this Court and the Attorney General and why a hearing should not be held on any proposed sale. On August 23, 2002, the Attorney General filed a Petition for an *ex parte* injunction against the same respondents upon which we deferred consideration until a hearing on September 3, 2002. . . .

The issue herein discussed is whether the proof available to this Court supports the injunctive relief granted. We should here note that prior to the hearing on the injunction we advised counsel for both the petitioner and the respondents that we do not view our role in this matter, commencing with this proceeding, as "a passive instrument of the parties" [Wyzanski, *A Trial Judge's Freedom and Responsibility*, 65 Harvard L. Rev.

1292 (quoting Edmund Burke)]; that the public interest in the controversy and this Court's inherent plenary powers of supervision over trusts may lead us to add to our consideration of the issues such facts not offered by the parties as might aid our determination; and we particularly referenced, but did not thus limit, judicial notice of adjudicative facts disclosed in the records of this Court in prior proceedings involving the Milton Hershey School Trust wherein the respondents here were the moving parties.

Findings of Fact

In 1909 Milton S. Hershey and Catherine, his wife, by deed of trust endowed for the benefit of orphan children an institution now known as the Milton Hershey School. In 1918, after Catherine's death, Mr. Hershey added to the trust (hereafter referred to as the School Trust) most of his fortune including the controlling shares of stock of the Hershey Chocolate Company (now Hershey Foods Corporation). The Hershey Trust Company, then owned by Mr. Hershey, was and still is the trustee of the School Trust and, as directed in the trust deed, the members of the Board of Directors of the Hershey Trust Company also serve as the Board of Managers of the School.

By his Will, Mr. Hershey gave the stock of the Hershey Trust Company to the School Trust. Accordingly, there now exists a unique arrangement for the election and composition of the Directors/Managers. During Mr. Hershey's entire lifetime and thereafter until the 1980's the Directors/Managers all resided in Derry Township (where the community of Hershey is located) or nearby. The present membership of the Directors/Managers includes only four who live near Hershey. . . . The Deed of Trust directs that the Milton Hershey School shall be located in Derry Township, Pennsylvania, and gives preference to children born in the Pennsylvania counties of Dauphin (where Derry Township is located) and Lebanon and Lancaster which adjoin Dauphin County. . . . Moreover, in the area in close proximity to his chocolate factory he created a community, now known as Hershey, including banks, a department store, community center, hotel, sports facilities, theatre, hospital, utility companies, transportation, and homes for himself and for many of his employees. Milton Hershey's charitable interests were narrowly restricted. He was concerned for children and for his community.

Shares of Hershey Foods Corporation amounting to a controlling interest in the Corporation have comprised the corpus of the School Trust from 1918 until the present date. At the request of the present Directors/Managers, the Hershey Foods Corporation is soliciting bids for the acquisition of the Corporation which would include purchase of the shares of stock held in the School Trust representing 77% of the voting power of all outstanding shares of the Hershey Foods Corporation. . . .

Discussion

At the outset we would state that the Attorney General's Petition for a Citation raises issues of the effect on public interests of a sale by the School Trust of its controlling shares in Hershey Foods Corporation and is broad enough to also raise issues of abuse of discretion by the Directors/Managers in initiating the process.

That the Attorney General has standing in this proceeding is the law of this Commonwealth. The responsibility for public supervision of charitable trusts traditionally has been delegated to the Attorney General to be performed as an exercise of his *parens patriae* powers. . . . Our Supreme Court in *In re Pruner's Estate*, . . . 136 A.2d 107, 110 (1957), explained this interest: "[I]n every proceeding which affects a charitable trust, whether the action concerns invalidation, administration, termination or enforcement, the attorney general must be made a party of record because the public as the real party in interest in the trust is otherwise not properly represented." Property given to a charity is in a measure public property, *McKee Estate*, . . . 108 A.2d 214 (1954), and the beneficiary of charitable trusts is the general public to whom the social and economic benefits of the trusts accrue. *In re Pruner's Estate, supra*. We conclude therefore that the Attorney General has the authority to inquire whether an exercise of a trustee's power, even if authorized under the trust instrument, is inimical to the public interest. . . .

The rules relating to preliminary injunctions are stated in a number of ways but an acceptable version of the governing general principles is set forth in 15 *Standard Pennsylvania Practice* §83.18:

1. the relief is necessary to prevent irreparable harm;
2. the relief will restore the status quo;
3. there is greater injury in denying than granting; and
4. the right to relief is clear.

In their Answer to the petition for injunctive relief, the Directors/Managers suggest that they cannot be charged as causing any harm relative to the sale process because (1) the Hershey Foods Corporation is conducting the process, not they and (2) there is yet no proposed sale. The sale process according to them is just an "exploration" of "options" regarding a diversification policy. This explanation is more than disingenuous; it is an affront to the intelligence. They admit in their Answer that they requested the sale process. Are we to believe that having induced prospective purchasers to develop financing, tour plants, and obtain confidential information from Hershey Foods Corporation that is it just as likely that they won't sell as it is that they will? If, as they argued at hearing, horrific fluctuations in stock price causing potential for losses to the School Fund will follow from any delay in the sale process, what, pray tell, will the market reaction be and that of prospective bidders if this process is just a "look see"? The testimony of their own witness, an officer of UBS Warburg AG, the investment bankers representing the Directors/Managers, confirms that the process is far beyond that.

The Attorney General has sufficiently carried his burden of proving the potential harm that he seeks to prevent, namely, the adverse economic and social impact against the public interest if a sale of Hershey Foods Corporation takes place, particularly in its effect on employees of the Corporation and the community of Derry Township. The persuasive thrust of the testimony of Richard A. Zimmerman, a former CEO and Chairman of the Board of Hershey Foods Corporation with years of experience in mergers and acquisitions, was that a sale of the controlling interest in Hershey Foods Corporation creates a likelihood that there will be reduction in the work force and that relocations of plant operations and closing of duplicate facilities will be matters of probable immediate consideration by the acquiring company. We would add that this Court is not required to be blind and deaf to that which has been commonplace information to the public during the recent past period of numerous mergers and acquisitions of public companies.

. . . There are also other issues that await consideration. Granted, the deed of trust gives the trustee discretionary powers of investment and a court will not ordinarily interfere with what appears to be an act within that discretion. The rule is, however, a general rule, not an absolute.

Mr. Hershey maintained the controlling interest in his chocolate business as essentially the sole asset of the corpus of the School Trust from 1918 when he made the gift until he died in 1945. His deed of trust provides that the corpus cannot be used for the operating expenses of the School. The trust was administered by a small trust company owned by Mr. Hershey, and located where its directors, comprised until recent years of local citizens and officers of his company, could conveniently both manage the School and monitor the condition of the business that sustained the School. The trust company is located in a small town built by Mr. Hershey around his manufacturing facilities and the entire fortune earned from that business by Mr. Hershey he dedicated to the School he located in that town and to its residents. The symbiotic relationship among the School, the community, and the Company is common knowledge. The business was not, during Mr. Hershey's life, is not now, nor foreseeably in financial difficulty, and the School, according to statements by officers of the Directors/Managers has ample funds in its accumulated income to carry out its purposes. The proposal by the Directors/Managers is for the sale of all of the shares of Hershey Foods Corporation. There is no suggestion of a sale of such number of shares as would still reserve control of the Corporation nor explanation why, if any need for funds exists for which a sale is necessary, it could not be met while still keeping control. The question certainly occurs as to whether an immediate premium share price obtained in losing control is a reasonable trade-off for permanently retaining it.

. . . The only explanation given by the Director/Managers for the proposed sale is that they have a duty to diversify their investment portfolio. Their consultant who recommends this divesting of the asset that has sustained the School for most of its years was unaware that the law of Pennsylvania for long years, until 1999, was that a trustee had no obligation to diversify the trust corpus. . . .

If we deny the injunction, the experts in mergers and acquisitions called by both parties agreed that the sale of the Hershey Foods Corporation will be consummated within a short time; a few weeks, possibly only days. The opportunity to act against the potential harm that concerns the Attorney General will have passed as well as the immediate occasion for inquiry into issues having to do with the performance by the Trustees of their fiduciary duties.

Weighing the probative value of the testimony by an employee of the investment banking firm advising the Directors/Managers against that of an independent witness with as much or more expertise, we are persuaded by the latter that a delay in the sale process will not discourage prospective bidders at this stage from going forward in the sale process. Further, we do not find compelling the argument that any order delaying the process will cause significant fluctuations in Hershey Foods Corporation stock that will result in possible loss to the School fund. Guessing about the price of the stock of Hershey Foods Corporation in the ensuing weeks will be for the gambler, not for this Court.

The Directors/Managers argue at length that the Attorney General has failed to establish that he has the required right to relief. The arguments are without merit. . . . [T]he Directors/Managers argue that the law of Pennsylvania establishes that the duty of a trustee is to administer the trust solely for the benefit of the beneficiaries of the trust, quoting in support the statement under Comment p. of §1701(1) of the Restatement, Trusts which reads, "The trustee is under a duty to the beneficiary in administering the trust not to be guided by the interest of any third person." We are familiar with these rules but do not construe them to mean that as long as the act of a trustee is an exercise of a power given in the trust instrument and purports to serve the trust, the trustee can act with impunity and without regard for adverse effects on others. We know of no case that employs the rules advanced by the Directors/Managers in the context of an Attorney General asserting his duty to see that the public interest is not harmed by an act of a trustee that may otherwise be lawful and purports to be in furtherance of the trust. Few such issues are likely to arise and rarely one with the aspects of the case before us. How many trusts enjoy holding a controlling interest in one of this nation's largest, historically profitable, and best-known corporations? The duties of a trustee and the Attorney General are concomitant in so far as assuring that the benefits of a charitable trust are delivered in accordance with the Settlor's intent; but because the socio-economic benefits of a charitable trust extend beyond the designated beneficiaries to the public itself, although ordinarily compatible with each other, the Attorney General has an added responsibility of assuring that compatibility. . . .

We hereby Order . . . that that pending disposition of the citation issued by the Court on August 19, 2002, and/or further order of this Court, the Board of Managers of the Milton Hershey School and the Hershey Trust Company as Trustee of the Milton S. and Catherine S. Hershey Trust . . . shall not enter into any agreement or other understanding that would or could commit the respondents to a sale or other disposition of any or all of the shares of Hershey Foods Corporation held as corpus of the Trust . . . .

NOTES AND QUESTIONS

1. What is the standard for preliminary injunctive relief?
2. How does the Pennsylvania Attorney General's interest in the community enter into the preliminary injunction calculus? What is the legal basis for asserting the Attorney General's interest?

The Attorney General's theory looks like a stretch, doesn't it? On appeal, the Commonwealth Court affirmed the preliminary injunction, but it seemed to think that the legal theory was—at least—suspect. The court concluded that "Because we cannot conclude that no reasonable grounds exist to support Judge Morgan's order, we must affirm his grant of the preliminary injunction." 807 A.2d 324, 327 (Pa. Cmwlth., 2002). That was less than a resounding endorsement of the trial court's decision. A dissenting judge focused on the question of whether the Attorney General was acting for the public and within the terms of the trust document:

> [F]or the Attorney General to properly exercise *parens patriae* powers, his concern must be on behalf of the public and tied to the express desires of the Trust settlor. *See Commonwealth v. Barnes Foundation,* . . . 159 A.2d 500, 503 (1960) (in case involving art collection held by charitable foundation, "essential element of public charity is the right of public visitation for correction of abuses and enforcement of founders' will"). The Deed of Trust specifically gives the Trust Company, with approval by the School, sole and exclusive authority over the management of investments, including the sale of stock. Paragraph 5 of the Trust provides:
>
>> The funds of the principal in the trust estate and the unexpended income of the property held in trust, not immediately needed for the purposes of the School, shall be vested, and the Trustee at all times by and with the authority and approval of the Managers shall have full power and authority to invest all or any part thereof in any securities which the Trustee and the Managers together may consider safe . . .

807 A.2d at 338.

3. Although the trial court's legal theory may not have been accepted on appeal from a permanent (rather than preliminary) injunction, the *Hershey Trust* case still raises serious questions about scope of the *parens patriae* doctrine. Christopher Gadsden asked, do trustees "now owe duties to the public at large? Traditionally, trustees understood that their duty was to manage prudently the assets of the trust for the benefit of the named beneficiaries or class of beneficiaries. . . ." *The Hershey Power Play*, Trusts and Estates (November 11, 2002).

Gadsden worries that "the attorney general's position implies that the trustee of a charitable trust also must take into account the consequences of a trust action on all segments of the public at large. This duty potentially has no bounds. Should the trustee consider impact on the local community, the statewide population or the nation as a whole? If a sale of the controlling interest in the company did lead to job reductions in Hershey, would additional employment opportunities be created in some other state? Must the trustee of a charitable trust prepare a form of environmental impact statement for every major action?"

4. There are some other cases that read the *parens patriae* doctrine rather broadly (even if not as broadly as the trial court in *Hershey Trust*). In *Commonwealth v. Barnes Foundation*, 159 A.2d 500 (1960), for instance, the Attorney General opened up the Barnes Foundation's art collection to the public, in spite of explicit directions by the settlor of the trust that admissions be quite limited.

5. For more on the *Hershey Trust* case, see Robert H. Sitkoff and Jonathan Klick, *Agency Costs, Charitable Trusts, and Corporate Control: Evidence from Hershey's Kiss-Off*, 108 Columbia L. Rev. 749 (2008); Mark Sidel, *The Struggle for Hershey: Community Accountability, and the Law of Modern American Philanthropy*, 65 U. Pitt. L. Rev. 1 (2003).

7 RACE, ETHNICITY, AND CULTURE IN INTERNATIONAL AND COMPARATIVE PROPERTY

Although we have discussed domestic property conflicts within the United States, racial, ethnic, and cultural conflicts over tangible and intangible property are experienced in many different ways throughout the world. Such conflicts include the demand of indigenous communities to have their understanding of property recognized, the long-term challenge of shifting concentrations of land ownership in multi-racial societies, and the return of displaced ethnic or racial groups after dispossession of land occurred during a conflict.

Studying these property conflicts from an international perspective provides three benefits. First, these issues present significant challenges to any property system. For instance, different conceptions of property held by indigenous or religious populations may not fit comfortably within the context of secular land systems. Furthermore, using property to ameliorate existing social inequities may undermine the rights of other private property owners, creating significant uncertainties as to the boundaries of a given property right. Questions regarding these issues are asked with varying intensity in the international context. Second, by studying these issues in different contexts, students are able to see that the solutions to property dilemmas proposed by domestic property law are not the *only* solutions available to governing bodies. Finally, studying these solutions from an international perspective shows how diverse national and regional governing institutions have used flexible property concepts to resolve ethnic and racial conflicts.

This chapter surveys a number of cases addressing racial, ethnic, and cultural conflicts over tangible and intangible property. Initially, this chapter examines the increasing recognition of the traditional rights of indigenous communities and the ensuing controversies created by such recognition. The chapter next examines different land reform measures that seek to alleviate social tensions by re-allocating ownership of land. To conclude, this chapter examines ways in which post-conflict societies resolve significant ethnic tensions over the way property is allocated.

This chapter analyzes these issues from two perspectives. First, the cases and materials included allow students to evaluate how different national regimes address conflicts within a comparative framework. Second, this chapter also examines how different international treaty frameworks address these particular issues.

These materials are intended to prompt such questions as the following:

1. What are the responsibilities of a society to provide support for alternative notions of ownership within mainstream legal traditions?
2. How can re-allocation of land resolve or exacerbate social conflict between racial or ethnic groups?
3. What are the ways in which ethnic conflict can disrupt property ownership? What are the ways in which international treaty frameworks have sought to address these issues?

7.1 EMERGING PROPERTY RIGHTS IN INTERNATIONAL AND COMPARATIVE PERSPECTIVE: TRADITIONAL KNOWLEDGE

As we have discussed throughout this text, a key issue in property law is the emergence of property rights — that is, the recognition of the existence of the property right in question, as well as the right of an individual and community to claim that right. Recently, in both national and international law, we have seen the emergence of property claims based on communal membership in specific indigenous or ethnic communities. These groups have increasingly called for the right to control access to their traditional knowledge and cultural expression. Traditional knowledge differs from other types of intellectual property because (1) it may be owned in common and (2) it may not be original; instead, it constantly evolves over time in response to the surrounding cultural environment. *Information Note on Traditional Knowledge,* prepared by the International Bureau of WIPO, in cooperation with the Government of the Sultanate of Oman, August 2001. WIPO Doc. WIPO/IPTK/MCT/02/INT.3, *available at http://www.wipo.int/arab/en/meetings/2002/muscat_forum_ip/pdf/iptk_mct02_i3.pdf* (last visited on September 3, 2010).

Nations and international institutions have turned to two different mechanisms to protect traditional knowledge. First, traditional knowledge claims can be addressed by existing intellectual property mechanisms, such as protecting traditional geographical names through trademarks and geographical indications or protecting contemporary adaptations of traditional knowledge materials, through copyright. *See* Wend B. Wendland, *Intellectual Property and the Protection of Traditional Knowledge and Cultural Expressions, in* ART AND CULTURAL HERITAGE: LAW, POLICY AND PRACTICE 327, 332 (Barbara Hoffman ed., 2006). Second, traditional knowledge can be preserved in a *sui generis* manner that protects indigenous creations outside of typical intellectual property norms. *Id.* at 333-39. These protective mechanisms can be found in national legal traditions as well as in new international norms. National legal traditions have come to embrace the positive creation of indigenous rights in traditional knowledge, and since 2000, the World Intellectual Property Organization (WIPO) has considered adopting a framework for two types of traditional knowledge. These categories are the following:

- **Traditional cultural expression or folklore**, which has currently been defined as any form, whether tangible, intangible, or a combination thereof, in which traditional cultural knowledge is expressed, appears, or is manifested, and passed generation to generation, or tangible expressions, such as masks, or dances, that are products of: (1) creative individual or communal activity; (2) authentic cultural heritage, and (3) maintained by indigenous and traditional peoples and communities, or individuals who have responsibility for maintaining that tradition. World Intellectual Property Organization, WIPO Intergovernmental Committee on Intellectual Property and Genetic Resources, Traditional Knowledge and Folklore, Rep., 16th Sess., May 3-May 7, 2010, WIPO/GRTKF/IC/16/4 (March 22, 2010) (*http://www.wipo.int/edocs/mdocs/tk/en/wipo_grtkf_ic_17/wipo_grtkf_ic_17_4_prov.pdf*) (last visited September 3, 2010).
- **Traditional knowledge**, which has currently been defined as the "content or substance resulting from intellectual activity in a traditional context, and includes the know-how, skills, innovations, practices and learning that form part of traditional knowledge systems, and knowledge embodying traditional lifestyles, of indigenous local communities, or contained in codified knowledge systems passed between generations." World Intellectual Property Organization, WIPO Intergovernmental Committee on Intellectual Property and Genetic Resources, Traditional Knowledge and Folklore, Rep., 16th Sess., May 3-May 7, 2010, WIPO/GRTKF/IC/16/5

(March 22, 2010) (*http://www.wipo.int/edocs/mdocs/tk/en/wipo_grtkf_ic_16/wipo_grtkf_ic_16_5.pdf*) (last visited September 3, 2010). WIPO's efforts draw on previous treaties in this area. For instance, Article 8(j) of the Convention on Biological Diversity (known informally as the Biodiversity Convention) states that each contracting party shall "respect, preserve and maintain knowledge, innovations and practices of indigenous and local communities embodying traditional lifestyles . . . and promote their wider application[.]" *See* Convention on Biological Diversity, art. 8(j), *opened for signature* June 5, 1992, 1760 U.N.T.S. 149 (191 parties, 168 of which are signatories—including the United States). For more information, *see, e.g.*, Weerawit Weeraworawit, *Formulating an International Legal Protection for Genetic Resources, Traditional Knowledge and Folklore: Challenges for the Intellectual Property System*, 11 CARDOZO J. INT'L & COMP. L. 769 (2003); David G. Victor, *The Global Conflict over Genetic Resources*, 97 AM. SOC'Y INT'L L. PROC. 29 (2003).

While reading the following, consider the following question: What type of protections does the Federal Court of Australia take in this case?

Bulun Bulun and Anor v. R & T Textiles Pty. Ltd.

(1998) 157 A.L.R. 193 (Australia)

These proceedings arise out of the importation and sale in Australia of printed clothing fabric which infringed the copyright of the first applicant Mr Bulun Bulun, in the artistic work known as "Magpie Geese and Water Lilies at the Waterhole" ("the artistic work").

The proceedings were commenced on 27 February 1996 by Mr Bulun Bulun[.] Both applicants are leading Aboriginal artists. The respondents were at that time, R & T Textiles Pty Ltd ("the respondent") and its three directors. Mr Bulun Bulun sued as the legal owner of the copyright pursuant to the Copyright Act 1968 (Cth) for remedies for the infringement, for contraventions of sections of PtV of the Trade Practices Act 1974 (Cth) dealing with misleading or deceptive conduct, and for nuisance. . . . These proceedings represent another step by Aboriginal people to have communal title in their traditional ritual knowledge, and in particular in their artwork, recognised and protected by the Australian legal system. The inadequacies of statutory remedies under the Copyright Act as a means of protecting communal ownership have been noted in earlier decisions of this Court: see Yumbulul v Reserve Bank of Australia (1991) 21 IPR 481 at 490 and Milpurrurru v Indofurn Pty Ltd (1994) 54 FCR 240 at 247. . . .

Mr Bulun Bulun's Claim

As soon as the proceedings were served the respondent admitted infringement of Mr Bulun Bulun's copyright in the artistic work, and pleaded that the infringement had occurred in ignorance of the copyright. The respondent immediately withdrew the offending fabric from sale. At that time approximately 7,600 metres of the fabric had been imported and approximately 4,231 metres sold in Australia. . . .

The High Court's decision in Mabo v The State of Queensland [No 2] (1992) 175 CLR 1 shows that customary indigenous law has a role to play within the Australian legal system. Indeed the conclusion that native title survived the Crown's acquisition of sovereignty was dependent upon the Court's acceptance of antecedent traditional laws and customs acknowledged and observed by the indigenous inhabitants of the land claimed. Whilst Mason CJ observed in Walker v New South Wales (1994) 182 CLR 45 at 49-59, that it is not possible to use evidence about indigenous customs and traditions to operate as "customary law" in opposition to or alongside Australian law, (see also Coe v The Commonwealth (1993) 118 ALR 193 at 200, and Wik Peoples v Queensland (1996) 187 CLR 1 at 214 per Kirby J) Australian courts cannot treat as irrelevant the rights, interests and obligations of Aboriginal people embodied within customary law. Evidence of customary law may be used as a basis for the foundation of rights recognised within the Australian legal system. Native title is a clear example. In Milpurrurru v Indofurn the Court took into account the effect of the unauthorised reproduction of artistic works under customary Aboriginal laws in quantifying the damage suffered. In my opinion the evidence about Ganalbingu law and customs is admissible.

The amended application in this case alleges that the Ganalbingu people are the traditional Aboriginal owners of Ganalbingu country who have the right to permit and control the production and reproduction of the artistic work under the law and custom of the Ganalbingu people. It is pleaded that the traditional owners of Ganalbingu country comprise:

(i) Members of the Ganalbingu people;
(ii) The Yolngu people (Aboriginal people of Arnhem Land) who are the children of the women of the Ganalbingu people;
(iii) The Yolngu people who stand in a relationship of mother's-mother to the members of the Ganalbingu people under Ganalbingu law and custom;
(iv) Such other Yolngu people who are recognised by the applicants according to Ganalbingu law and custom as being traditional Aboriginal owners of Ganalbingu country.

The amended statement of claim pleads that the Ganalbingu people are the traditional Aboriginal owners of the corpus of ritual knowledge from which the artistic work is derived, including the subject matter of the artistic work and the artistic work itself.

Mr Bulun Bulun is the most senior person of the "bottom" Ganalbingu and is second in line to Mr Milpurrurru of the Ganalbingu people generally.

Djulibinyamurr is the site of a waterhole complex situated close to the eastern side of the Arafura Swamp between the Glyde and Goyder river systems and the Woolen River. Djulibinyamurr, along with another waterhole site, Ngalyindi, are the two most important sites on Ganalbingu country for the Ganalbingu people. Mr Bulun Bulun describes Djulibinyamurr as the ral'kal for the lineage of the bottom Ganalbingu people. In his affidavit evidence Mr Bulun Bulun says:

> "Ral'kal translates to mean the principal totemic or clan well for my lineage. Ral'kal is the well spring, life force and spiritual and totemic repository for my lineage of the Ganalbingu people. It is the place from where my lineage of the Ganalbingu people are created and emerge. It is the equivalent of my 'warro' or soul.
>
> Djulibinyamurr is the place where not only my human ancestors were created but according to our custom and law emerged, it is also the place from which our creator ancestor emerged. Barnda, or Gumang (long neck tortoise) first emerged from inside the earth at Djulibinyamurr and came out to walk across the earth from there. It was Barnda that caused the natural features at Djulibinyamurr to be shaped into the form that they are now.
>
> Barnda not only created the place we call Djulibinuyamurr but it populated the country as well. Barnda gave the place its name, created the people who follow him and named those people. Barnda gave us our language and law. Barnda gave to my ancestors the country and the ceremony and paintings associated with the country. My ancestors had a responsibility given to them by Barnda to perform the ceremony and to do the paintings which were granted to them. This is a part of the continuing responsibility of the traditional Aboriginal owners handed down from generation to generation. Djulibinyamurr is then our life source and the source of our continuing totemic or sacred responsibility. The continuity of our traditions and ways including our traditional Aboriginal ownership depends upon us respecting and honouring the things entrusted to us by Barnda.
>
> Djulibinyamurr is my ral'kal, it is the hole or well from which I derive my life and power. It is the place from which my people and my creator emerged. Damage to Djulibinyamurr will cause injury and death to the people who are its owners. Damage to a ral'kal is the worst thing that could happen to a Yolngu person. It is the ultimate act of destruction under our law and custom — it upsets the whole religious, political and legal balance underpinning Yolngu society. It destroy (sic) the relationship and the maintenance of the trust established between the creator ancestor and their human descendants and also between traditional Aboriginal owners. This relationship controls all aspects of society and life, for example ownership of country, relations with other clans, marriage and ceremonial life and its attributes. If the life source is damaged or interfered with in any way the power and stability derived from it and the power and stability which has continued from the time of creation is diminished and may collapse.
>
> In the same way my creator ancestor formed the natural landscape and granted it to my human ancestors who in turn handed it to me. My creator ancestor passed on to me the elements for the artworks I produce for sale and ceremony. Barnda not only creates the people and landscape, but our designs and artworks originate from the

> creative acts of Barnda. They honour and deliberate the deeds of Barnda. This way the spirit and rule of Barnda is kept alive in the land. The land and the legacy of Barnda go hand in hand. Land is given to Yolngu people along with responsibility for all of the Madayin (corpus of ritual knowledge) associated with the land. In fact for Yolngu, the ownership of land has with it the corresponding obligations to create and foster the artworks, designs, songs and other aspects of ritual and ceremony that go with the land. If the rituals and ceremonies attached to land ownership are not fulfilled, that is if responsibilities in respect of Madayin are not maintained then traditional Aboriginal ownership rights lapse. Paintings, for example, are a manifestation of our ancestral past. They were first made, in my case by Barnda. Barnda handed the painting to my human ancestors. They have been handed from generation to generation ever since . . . .
>
> Unauthorised reproduction of 'at the Waterhole' threatens the whole system and ways that underpin the stability and continuance of Yolngu society. It interferes with the relationship between people, their creator ancestors and the land given to the people by their creator ancestor. It interferes with our custom and ritual, and threaten our rights as traditional Aboriginal owners of the land and impedes in the carrying out of the obligations that go with this ownership and which require us to tell and remember the story of Barnda, as it has been passed down and respected over countless generations." . . .

Why the Claim Is Confined to One for Recognition of an Equitable Interest

The submissions of counsel for the applicants reflected a wide ranging search for a way in which the communal interests of the traditional Aboriginal owners in cultural artworks might be recognised under Australian law. . . . That the claim was ultimately confined to one for recognition of an equitable interest in the legal copyright of Mr Bulun Bulun is an acknowledgment that no other possible avenue had emerged from the researches of counsel. Whilst it is superficially attractive to postulate that the common law should recognise communal title, it would be contrary to established legal principle for the common law to do so. There seems no reason to doubt that customary Aboriginal laws relating to the ownership of artistic works survived the introduction of the common law of England in 1788. The Aboriginal peoples did not cease to observe their sui generis system of rights and obligations upon the acquisition of sovereignty of Australia by the Crown. The question however is whether those Aboriginal laws can create binding obligations on persons outside the relevant Aboriginal community, either through recognition of those laws by the common law, or by their capacity to found equitable rights in rem.

In Mabo Deane and Gaudron JJ, after analysing the effects of the introduction of the common law of England into Australia in 1788 said, at 79 "The common law so introduced was adjusted in accordance with the principle that, in settled colonies, only so much of it was introduced as was 'reasonably applicable to the circumstances of the colony'. This left room for the continued operation of some local laws or customs among the native people and even the incorporation of some of those laws and customs as part of the common law."

In 1788 there may have been scope for the continued operation of a system of indigenous collective ownership in artistic works. At that time the common law of England gave the author of an artistic work property in unpublished compositions which lasted in perpetuity: Mansell v Valley Printing Company [1908] 1 Ch 567 and Laddie Prescott and Vitoria, "The Modern Law of Copyright" 1980 para4.64. That property was lost upon publication of the artistic work. Exhibition for sale or sale constituted publication: Britain v Hanks Bros and Co (1902) 86 LT 765. This property interest was separate from the right recognised in equity to restrain a breach of confidence, a right which continues and was invoked in Foster v Mountford and Rigby Ltd (1976) 14 ALR 71. The common law of England did not protect an author of an artistic work after publication. If the common law had not been amended in the meantime by statute, an interesting question would arise as to whether Aboriginal laws and customs could be incorporated into the common law. However, the common law has since been subsumed by statute. The common law right until first publication was abolished when the law of copyright was codified by the Copyright Act of 1911 in the United Kingdom. That Act, subject to some modifications, became the law in Australia by s8 of the Copyright Act 1912 (Cth). Copyright is now entirely a creature of statute: McKeough and Stewart, Intellectual Property in Australia 1991 at para504, Copinger and Skone James on Copyright, 13th ed Para1-43. The exclusive domain of the Copyright Act 1968 in Australia is expressed in s8 (subject only to the qualification in s8A) namely that "copyright does not subsist otherwise than by virtue of this Act".

S35(2) of the Copyright Act 1968 provides that the author of an artistic work is the owner of the copyright which subsists by virtue of the Act. That provision effectively precludes any notion of group ownership in an artistic work, unless the artistic work is a "work of joint ownership" within the meaning of s10(1) of the Act. A "work of joint authorship" means a work that has been produced by the collaboration of two or more authors and in which the contribution of each author is not separate from the contribution of the other author or the contributions of the other authors. In this case no evidence was led to suggest that anyone other than Mr Bulun Bulun was the creative author of the artistic work. A person who supplies an artistic idea to an artist who then executes the work is not, on that ground alone, a joint author with the artist: Kenrick & Co v Lawrence & Co (1890) 25 QBD 99. Joint authorship envisages the contribution of skill and labour to the production of the work itself: Fylde Microsystems Ltd v Kay Radio Systems Ltd (1998) 39 IPR 481 at 486.

In Coe v The Commonwealth (1993) 118 ALR 193 at 200 Mason CJ rejected the proposition that Aboriginal people are entitled to rights and interests other than those created or recognised by the laws of the Commonwealth, its States and the common law. See also Walker v New South Wales at 45-50 and Kirby J in Wik Peoples v Queensland at 214. To conclude that the Ganalbingu people were communal owners of the copyright in the existing work would ignore the provisions of s8 of the Copyright Act, and involve the creation of rights in indigenous peoples which are not otherwise recognised by the legal system of Australia.

Do the Circumstances in Which the Artistic Work Was Created Give Rise to Equitable Interests in the Ganalbingu People?

The statement of claim alleges "on the reduction to material form of a part of the ritual knowledge of the Ganalbingu people associated with Djulibinyamurr by the creation of the artistic work, the First Applicant held the copyright subsisting in the artistic work as a fiduciary and/or alternatively on trust, for the second applicant and the people he represents".

* * *

It is contended that the customs and traditions regulating this use of the corpus of ritual knowledge places Mr Bulun Bulun as the author of the artistic work in the position of a fiduciary, and, moreover, make Mr Bulun Bulun a trustee for the artwork, either pursuant to some form of express trust, or pursuant to a constructive trust in favour of the Ganalbingu people. The right to control the production and reproduction of the corpus of ritual knowledge relating to Djulibinyamurr is said to arise by virtue of the strong ties which continue to exist between the Ganalbingu people and their land.

Was There an Express Trust?

The possibility that an express trust was created in respect of the artistic work or the copyright subsisting in it was not at the forefront of the applicants' submissions. In my opinion that possibility can be dismissed on the evidence in this case. The existence of an express trust depends on the intention of the creator. No formal or technical words constituting an expression of intention are necessary to create an express trust. Any apt expression of intention will suffice: Registrar, Accident Compensation Tribunal v Commissioner of Taxation (1993) 178 CLR 145 at 166. What is important is that intention to create a trust be manifest in some form or another. There must be an intention on the part of the putative creator to divest himself or herself the beneficial interest, and to become a trustee of the property for another party: Garrett v L'Estrange (1911) 13 CLR 430. An intention to create a trust may be inferred even where the creator has not in words expressed such an intention: see Jacobs' Law of Trusts, 6th Ed Para 309. The intention to create a trust may be inferred from conduct: Gissing v Gissing [1971] AC 886 at 900, 906, and A-One Accessory Imports Pty Ltd v Off Road Imports Pty Ltd (1996) 143 ALR 543 at 557. A trust created in such circumstances remains an express trust based on the actual intention of the creator as inferred from his or her conduct: Bahr v Nicolay [No 2] (1988) 164 CLR 604 at 618-619.

In the present case it is suggested that it should be inferred that by creating the artistic work with the permission of those of the Ganalbingu people who had the right to control the corpus of ritual knowledge associated with Djulibinyamurr Mr Bulun Bulun intended to hold the copyright subsisting in the artistic work for the benefit of the Ganalbingu people. The artwork, when completed, was sold by Mr Bulun Bulun to the Maningrida Arts and Crafts Centre. It is not suggested that he did not receive and retain the sale price for his own use. Moreover, the evidence indicates that on many occasions paintings which incorporate to a greater or lesser degree parts of the ritual knowledge of the Ganalbingu people are produced by Ganalbingu artists for commercial sale for the benefit of the artist concerned.

On the evidence there is no suggestion that ownership and use of the artistic work itself should be treated separately from ownership in the copyright to the artistic work. The evidence was directed to uses made of the artwork itself that were permissible or impermissible under Ganalbingu law and customs. Notions of copyright ownership have not developed under Ganalbingu law. If it were possible to infer an express trust, on the evidence the subject matter of the trust would be the artistic work itself and all the rights that attach to its creation under the Australian legal system. . . .

Did Mr Bulun Bulun Hold the Copyright as a Fiduciary?

. . . The existence of a fiduciary relationship is said to arise out of the nature of ownership of artistic works amongst the Ganalbingu people.

The factors and relationships giving rise to a fiduciary duty are nowhere exhaustively defined: Mabo [No 2], at 200 per Toohey J, Hospital Products v USSC (1984) 156 CLR 41 at 68, 96-97, PD Finn, Fiduciary Obligations (1977) p1, and News Ltd v ARL at 564. It has been said that the term "fiduciary relationship", defies definition: Breen v Williams at 106 per Gaudron and McHugh JJ, see also Gibbs CJ in Hospital Products v USSC at 69. For this reason the fiduciary concept has developed incrementally throughout the case law which itself provides guidance as to the traditional parameters of the concept. The essential characteristics of fiduciary relationships were referred to by Mason J in Hospital Products at 96-97:

> "The critical feature of [fiduciary] relationships is that the fiduciary undertakes or agrees to act for or on behalf of or in the interests of another person in the exercise of a power or discretion which will affect the interests of that other person in a legal or practical sense. The relationship between the parties is therefore one which gives the fiduciary a special opportunity to exercise the power or discretion to the detriment of that other person who is accordingly vulnerable to abuse by the fiduciary of his

> position . . . It is partly because the fiduciary's exercise of the power or discretion can adversely affect the interests of the person to whom the duty is owed and because the latter is at the mercy of the former that the fiduciary comes under a duty to exercise his power or discretion in the interests of the person to whom it is owed".

. . . The Court was not referred to any authority in support of the imposition of equitable principles to govern relations amongst members of a tribal group. However, the application of the principles of equity in this situation is not unknown to the common law as it has been applied outside of this country. Amongst tribal communities of African countries tribal property is regarded as being held on "trust" by the customary head of a tribal group: see SKB Asante "Fiduciary Principles in Anglo-American Law and The Customary Law of Ghana" (1965) 14 International & Comparative Law Quarterly 1144 at p1145. This principle received judicial recognition in Kwan v Nyieni (1959) 1 GLR 67 at 72-73 where the Court of Appeal of Ghana held that members of the tribal group were entitled to initiate proceedings for the purpose of preserving family property in the event of the failure of the head of the tribal group to do so. The head of the tribal group is regarded as a fiduciary: SKB Asante, at p1149.

The relationship between Mr Bulun Bulun as the author and legal title holder of the artistic work and the Ganalbingu people is unique. The "transaction" between them out of which fiduciary relationship is said to arise is the use with permission by Mr Bulun Bulun of ritual knowledge of the Ganalbingu people, and the embodiment of that knowledge within the artistic work. That use has been permitted in accordance with the law and customs of the Ganalbingu people.

The grant of permission by the djungayi and other appropriate representatives of the Ganalbingu people for the creation of the artistic work is predicated on the trust and confidence which those granting permission have in the artist. The evidence indicates that if those who must give permission do not have trust and confidence in someone seeking permission, permission will not be granted.

The law and customs of the Banalbingu people require that the use of the ritual knowledge and the artistic work be in accordance with the requirements of law and custom, and that the author of the artistic work do whatever is necessary to prevent any misuse. The artist is required to act in relation to the artwork in the interests of the Ganalbingu people to preserve the integrity of their culture, and ritual knowledge.

This is not to say that the artist must act entirely in the interests of the Ganalbingu people. The evidence shows that an artist is entitled to consider and pursue his own interests, for example by selling the artwork, but the artist is not permitted to shed the overriding obligation to act to preserve the integrity of the Ganalbingu culture where action for that purpose is required.

In my opinion, the nature of the relationship between Mr Bulun Bulun and the Ganalbingu people was a fiduciary one which gives rise to fiduciary obligations owed by Mr Bulun Bulun.

The conclusion that in all the circumstances Mr Bulun Bulun owes fiduciary obligations to the Ganalbingu people does not treat the law and custom of the Ganalbingu people as part of the Australian legal system. Rather, it treats the law and custom of the Ganalbingu people as part of the factual matrix which characterises the relationship as one of mutual trust and confidence. It is that relationship which the Australian legal system recognises as giving rise to the fiduciary relationship, and to the obligations which arise out of it. . . .

The Fiduciary Obligation

Having regard to the evidence of the law and customs of the Ganalbingu people under which Mr Bulun Bulun was permitted to create the artistic work, I consider that equity imposes on him obligations as a fiduciary not to exploit the artistic work in a way that is contrary to the laws and custom of the Ganalbingu people, and, in the event of infringement by a third party, to take reasonable and appropriate action to restrain and remedy infringement of the copyright in the artistic work.

Whilst the nature of the relationship between Mr Bulun Bulun and the Ganalbingi people is such that Mr Bulun Bulun falls under fiduciary obligations to protect the ritual knowledge which he has been permitted to use, the existence of those obligations does not, without more, vest an equitable interest in the ownership of the copyright in the Ganalbingu people. Their primary right, in the event of a breach of obligation by the fiduciary is a right in personam to bring action against the fiduciary to enforce the obligation.

In the present case Mr Bulun Bulun has successfully taken action against the respondent to obtain remedies in respect of the infringement. There is no suggestion by Mr Milpurrurru and those whom he seeks to represent that Mr Bulun Bulun should have done anything more. In these circumstances there is no occasion for the intervention of equity to provide any additional remedy to the beneficiaries of the fiduciary relationship. . . .

NOTES AND QUESTIONS

1. What is the type of knowledge that is being claimed here?
2. What type of mechanisms to protect this knowledge did the Australian Federal Court adopt in *Bulun Bulun?* Did the Australian Federal Court seek to find a traditional knowledge right in available sources of law, or did it seek to craft a *sui generis* right?

3. Why did the Australian Federal Court hold that the work of Mr. Bulun Bulun could not be addressed under Australia's copyright law? Do you find that court's reasoning persuasive?

4. Why did the Australian Federal Court reject the application of express trust doctrine to Mr. Bulun Bulun's work?

5. Why did the Australian Federal Court find that Mr. Bulun Bulun had a fiduciary duty to the Ganalbingu peoples? What is the scope of Mr. Bulun Bulun's fiduciary obligations?

6. How is membership within a particular group defined in *Bulun Bulun*?

7. Why would the protection of indigenous rights in tangible and intangible property be problematic?

7.2 REFORMING PROPERTY DISTRIBUTION: RESOLVING RACIAL, ETHNIC, AND SOCIAL INEQUITIES THROUGH LAND ALLOCATION

In many countries, troubling wealth inequities exist over the use and ownership of land. These inequities often are exacerbated by existing racial, ethnic, and social tensions. A number of countries facing significant racial, ethnic, and social conflicts over land have turned to a variety of innovative techniques to ameliorate the tension, with varying degrees of success. These techniques include land redistribution, restitution, and granting of expansive squatters' rights.

7.2.1 Land Redistribution: The Social Function Doctrine

A number of Latin American countries facing significant disparities in land ownership have adopted policies that attempt to draw a proper balance between the needs of landless individuals and dominant private property owners. The predominant example of this type of policy is the social function doctrine. Thomas T. Ankerson and Thomas Ruppert have identified two obligations under the social function doctrine: (1) the landowner must fulfill some continuing societal goal or risk expropriation of his or her land; and (2) the state has a corresponding obligation to expropriate land that is not fulfilling its social function. Thomas T. Ankerson and Thomas Ruppert, *Tierra Y Libertad: The Social Function Doctrine and Land Reform in Latin America,* 19 Tul. Envtl. L. J. 69, 99 (2006). Mexico first incorporated the social function doctrine in Article 27 of its 1917 Constitution.

As recently as 1988, Brazil incorporated the social function doctrine into its revised constitution. Three examples of the Brazilian use of the social function doctrine follow.

Constituição Federal [Constitution] [C.F.] art. 182-85 (Braz.)

Article 182. The urban development policy carried out by the municipal government, according to general guidelines set forth in the law, is aimed at ordaining the full development of the social functions of the city and ensuring the well-being of its inhabitants.

Paragraph 1—The master plan, approved by the City Council, which is compulsory for cities of over twenty thousand inhabitants, is the basic tool of the urban development and expansion policy.

Paragraph 2—Urban property performs its social function when it meets the fundamental requirements for the ordainment of the city as set forth in the master plan.

Paragraph 3—Expropriation of urban property shall be made against prior and fair compensation in cash.

Paragraph 4—The municipal government may, by means of a specific law, for an area included in the master plan, demand, according to federal law, that the owner of unbuilt, underused or unused urban soil provide for adequate use thereof, subject, successively, to: I—compulsory parceling or construction; II—rates of urban property and land tax that are progressive in time; III—expropriation with payment in public debt bonds issued with the prior approval of the Federal Senate, redeemable within up to ten years, in equal and successive annual installments, ensuring the real value of the compensation and the legal interest.

Article 183. An individual who possesses an urban area of up to two hundred and fifty square meters, for five years, without interruption or opposition, using it as his or as his family's home, shall acquire domain of it, provided that he does not own any other urban or rural property.

Paragraph 1—The deed of domain and concession of use shall be granted to the man or woman, or both, regardless of their marital status.

Paragraph 2—This right shall not be recognized for the same holder more than once.

Paragraph 3—Public real estate shall not be acquired by prescription.

Article 184. It is within the power of the Union to expropriate on account of social interest, for purposes of agrarian reform, the rural property which is not performing its social function, against prior and fair compensation in agrarian debt bonds with a clause providing for maintenance of the real value, redeemable within a period of up to twenty years computed as from the second year of issue, and the use of which shall be defined in the law.

Paragraph 1 — Useful and necessary improvements shall be compensated in cash.

Paragraph 2 — The decree declaring the property as being of social interest for agrarian reform purposes empowers the Union to start expropriation action.

Paragraph 3 — It is incumbent upon a supplementary law to establish special summary adversary proceeding for expropriation action.

Paragraph 4 — The budget shall determine each year the total volume of agrarian debt bonds, as well as the total amount of funds to meet the agrarian reform programme in the fiscal year.

Paragraph 5 — The transactions of transfer of property expropriated for agrarian reform purposes are exempt from federal, state and municipal taxes.

Article 185. Expropriation of the following for agrarian reform purposes is not permitted: I — small and medium-size rural property, as defined by law, provided its owner does not own other property; II — productive property. Sole paragraph — The law shall guarantee special treatment for the productive property and shall establish rules for the fulfillment of the requirements regarding its social function.

Article 186. The social function is met when the rural property complies simultaneously with, according to the criteria and standards prescribed by law, the following requirements:

I — rational and adequate use;

II — adequate use of available natural resources and preservation of the environment;

III — compliance with the provisions that regulate labour relations;

IV — exploitation that favours the well-being of the owners and labourers.

NOTES AND QUESTIONS

1. State use of the social function doctrine can be very disruptive to individualized private property ownership. Any coercive distribution of land through land reform necessarily weakens private property rights. "A very skewed wealth distribution creates social conditions that may weaken the security of property rights. At the same time, however, aggressive land redistribution also weakens property rights, leading to the loss of incentives that provide socially beneficial economic behavior." *See* Lee J. Alston, Gary D. Libecap & Bernando Mueller, TITLES, CONFLICT AND LAND USE: THE DEVELOPMENT OF PROPERTY RIGHTS AND LAND REFORM ON THE BRAZILIAN AMAZON FRONTIER 31 (2003). For instance, in November 2006, Roberto Requaio, governor of the Brazilian state of Parana, decreed appropriation under the social function clauses of the Brazilian Constitution of an experimental agricultural site maintained by Sygenta, a biotechnology company located

in Switzerland. Biotechnology opponents occupied the site, claiming their occupation was justified because genetically modified soybean crops were impacting a national park located next to the site. Mary Ann Liebert, *Sygenta Land in Brazil to Be Expropriated,* 26 BIOTECHNOLOGY LAW REPORT 126 (2007). Do you think that the state should be able to appropriate property in the manner contemplated by the social function doctrine? Do you think that the limits announced in Articles 185 and 186 provide sufficient limits on the use of that doctrine?

2. Articles 182 and 183 also provide for the use of the social function doctrine within the urban context. Article 182 provides for its use within the context of urban planning and ties the social function of property to participation in the master plan process associated with zoning practices. To return to a previous topic, would the social function process be useful within context of the environmental justice movement? *See, e.g.,* Ngai Pindell, *Finding a Right to the City: Exploring Property and Community in Brazil and in the United States,* 39 VAND. J. TRANSNAT'L L. 435, 464 (2006) (suggesting the usefulness of the social doctrine process to inclusionary zoning practices in the United States).

3. Article 183 provides that an urban dweller can obtain ownership of the land through occupation, similar to an adverse possession claim, within the domestic context. Do you see any differences from adverse possession?

7.2.2 Land Reform in South Africa: Restitution, Redistribution, and Land Tenure Reform

In South Africa, differential land access based on race was enshrined in the legal order. This began with the Native Lands Act of 1913, which set aside seven percent of the land for blacks, who comprised 75 percent of the population at that time, as well as imposed significant restrictions on land transactions (sale and lease) outside of the reserves. Lauren G. Robinson, *Rationales for Rural Land Redistribution in South Africa,* 23 BROOK. J. INT'L L. 465, 472-74 (1997). South Africa further systematically dispossessed black, "coloured," and Indian citizens under the Group Areas Act of 1950, which forcibly removed these individuals from land owned by whites, and the Prevention of Illegal Squatting Act of 1951, which evicted non-formal land possessors from inhabited lands. Sam Rugege, *Land Reform in South Africa: An Overview,* 32 INT'L J. LEGAL INFORMATION 283, 285 (2004).

In the post-apartheid era, South Africa has used land reform to underscore a transitional process that seeks to redress significant inequities premised on race and ethnic division. *See* Aeyal M. Gross, *The Constitution, Reconciliation and Transitional Justice: Lessons from South Africa and Israel,* 40 STAN. J. INT'L L. 47, 85-92 (2004).

Article 25 of the South African Constitution sought to redress the significant inequities in land that resulted from the historic legacy of apartheid. Article 25 states that

1. No one may be deprived of property except in terms of law of general application, and no law may permit arbitrary deprivation of property.
2. Property may be expropriated only in terms of law of general application—
   a. for a public purpose or in the public interest; and
   b. subject to compensation, the amount of which and the time and manner of payment of which have either been agreed to by those affected or decided or approved by a court.
3. The amount of the compensation and the time and manner of payment must be just and equitable, reflecting an equitable balance between the public interest and the interests of those affected, having regard to all relevant circumstances, including—
   a. the current use of the property;
   b. the history of the acquisition and use of the property;
   c. the market value of the property;
   d. the extent of direct state investment and subsidy in the acquisition and beneficial capital improvement of the property; and
   e. the purpose of the expropriation.
4. For the purposes of this section—
   a. the public interest includes the nation's commitment to land reform, and to reforms to bring about equitable access to all South Africa's natural resources; and
   b. property is not limited to land.
5. The state must take reasonable legislative and other measures, within its available resources, to foster conditions which enable citizens to gain access to land on an equitable basis.
6. A person or community whose tenure of land is legally insecure as a result of past racially discriminatory laws or practices is entitled, to the extent provided by an Act of Parliament, either to tenure which is legally secure or to comparable redress.
7. A person or community dispossessed of property after 19 June 1913 as a result of past racially discriminatory laws or practices is entitled, to the extent provided by an Act of Parliament, either to restitution of that property or to equitable redress.
8. No provision of this section may impede the state from taking legislative and other measures to achieve land, water and related reform, in order to redress the results of past racial discrimination, provided that any departure from the provisions of this section is in accordance with the provisions of section 36(1).

The first three provisions of Article 25 affirm and protect individualized property ownership; however, Article 25 also provides for three additional property reforms. First, Article 25(5) provides that the state can acquire and re-distribute land to citizens that have no land or inadequate access to land. Rugege, *supra*, at 295. Second, Article 25(6) seeks to protect a person or community whose right to occupied land is insecure because of racially discriminatory laws or practices. *Id.* at 289-304. Third, Article 25(7) provides that a person dispossessed of land as a result of past discriminatory laws or practices is entitled to restitution.

As you read the next case, consider the following question: How do these reforms work in practice?

The Minister of Land Affairs of the Republic of S. Africa v. Slamdien

1999 (1) BCLR 413, para 26 (LCC)

This matter concerns the ambit of the right to restitution in respect of the loss of land rights as a result of past racially discriminatory laws or practices. . . .

The claim was referred to the Land Claims Court by the third respondent in terms of section 14(1) of the Restitution of Land Rights Act. I will refer to it as "the Restitution Act". The applicants seek declaratory relief to the effect that the first and second respondents are precluded from claiming restitution because they were not "dispossessed of a right in land . . . as a result of past racially discriminatory laws or practices" as required by section 2(1)(a) of the Restitution Act. Only the first and second respondents have opposed the application. . . .

The Facts

The parties have prepared an agreed statement of facts. The first respondent purchased a property in Surrey Estate, Cape Town on 16 April 1955. I will refer to it as "the property". On 5 July 1957, the area in which the property fell was declared a group area for the "coloured group" in terms of section 3 of the Group Areas Act with effect from 6 July 1960. On 5 December 1960, transfer of the property was registered in favour of the first respondent. He is described in the deed of transfer as a member of the "coloured group".

On 7 July 1966, the Secretary for Coloured Affairs wrote to the Secretary for Public Works, [requesting that land be appropriated for the construction of a new primary school.].

[On 10 February 1969, the Secretary for Public Works directed the Secretary for Agricultural Credit and Land Tenure to appropriate a tract of land, which included the property, for the construction of the school.]

The property was purchased by the State from the first respondent on 16 March 1970. The Surrey Primary School was subsequently erected on the consolidated erf formed by the property and adjoining properties purchased or expropriated for this purpose. The second respondent, who is the first respondent's father, was one of the occupants of the property who had to vacate it pursuant to the sale. The State entered into the sale agreement, not in terms of any statutory power, but in terms of its common-law prerogative power to contract.

On 1 July 1995 the respondents lodged a claim for restitution of the property with the Regional Land Claims Commissioner: Western and Northern Cape in terms of section 10 of the Restitution Act. On 15 October 1998, the claim was referred to this Court.

Applicable constitutional and statutory provisions

The following are the main provisions relevant to the decision of this matter. The first is section 25(7) of the Constitution of the Republic of South Africa. I will refer to it as "the Constitution", unless I wish to distinguish it from the "interim Constitution", in which event I will refer to the former as "the 1996 Constitution" and the latter as "the 1993 Constitution". Section 25(7) of the Constitution reads:

> "A person or community dispossessed of property after 19 June 1913 as a result of past racially discriminatory laws or practices is entitled, to the extent provided by an Act of Parliament, either to restitution of that property or to equitable redress."

The Act of Parliament which determines the extent of the rights conferred by section 25(7) of the Constitution is the Restitution Act, as amended. The most important amending Act for present purposes is the Land Restitution and Reform Laws Amendment Act 63 of 1997, the latter Act having amended the Restitution Act with a view, amongst others, to aligning it with the 1996 Constitution. Section 2(1)(a) of the Restitution Act is based on section 25(7) of the Constitution and reads

> "(1) A person shall be entitled to restitution of a right in land if
>
> (a) he or she is a person or community dispossessed of a right in land after 19 June 1913 as a result of past racially discriminatory laws or practices or a direct descendant of such a person;"

A number of the terms in section 2(1)(a) are defined in section 1 of the Restitution Act. Of these the only ones which impact on this matter are the following:

> " 'racially discriminatory laws' include laws made by any sphere of government and subordinate legislation;

> 'racially discriminatory practices' means racially discriminatory practices, acts or omissions, direct or indirect, by—
>
> (a) any department of state or administration in the national, provincial or local sphere of government;
>
> (b) any other functionary or institution which exercised a public power or performed a public function in terms of any legislation;".

There are other qualifying criteria for entitlement to restitution in section 2 of the Restitution Act, but these are not in dispute for purposes of this application. The applicants did not dispute that the way in which the first and second respondents lost their rights in land (if any, in the case of second respondent) was a "dispossession" as that term is referred to in section 2(1)(a) of the Restitution Act or that such dispossession occurred after 19 June 1913. The applicants did dispute second respondent's assertion that his occupation of the property was based on a "right in land" as that term is defined in the Restitution Act. However, on the view I take of the matter, it is not necessary for me to decide this issue and I will assume in favour of the second respondent that his claim does not fail on this basis. What must be decided then in this application is whether the dispossession in this case was "as a result of past racially discriminatory laws or practices" as contemplated by section 2(1)(a) of the Restitution Act.

The parties' contentions

. . . On the basis of these contentions, it seems to me, on a generous interpretation of the respondents' opposing affidavits, that the following points emerge for decision:

(i) Was the Group Areas Act of 1950 a "racially discriminatory law" as that phrase is referred to in section 2(1)(a), and defined in section 1, of the Restitution Act?

(ii) Was the building of a racially exclusive coloured primary school a "racially discriminatory practice" as that phrase is referred to in section 2(1)(a), and defined in section 1, of the Restitution Act?

(iii) Was the dispossession of the property "as a result of" the law referred to in (i) or the practice referred to in (ii)?

Method of interpretation

What method should be used in interpreting section 2(1)(a)? The approach to the interpretation of constitutional and statutory provisions in our law is not harmonious. . . .

[After reviewing relevant cases and constitutional provisions, the court adopted a purposive approach to interpret Section 2(1)(a).]

The purposive approach as elucidated in the decisions of the Constitutional Court and this Court requires that one must:

(i) in general terms, ascertain the meaning of the provision to be interpreted by an analysis of its purpose and, in doing so;
(ii) have regard to the context of the provision in the sense of its historical origins;
(iii) have regard to its context in the sense of the statute as a whole, the subject matter and broad objects of the statute and the values which underlie it;
(iv) have regard to its immediate context in the sense of the particular part of the statute in which the provision appears or those provisions with which it is interrelated;
(v) have regard to the precise wording of the provision; and
(vi) where a constitutional right is concerned, as is the case here, adopt a generous rather than a legalistic perspective aimed at securing for individuals the full benefit of the protection which the right confers.

With reference to the last of these guidelines, the observation needs to be made that the adoption of a purposive approach will not always mean the adoption of a wide or literal interpretation of the words concerned. It may well be that, upon a proper analysis of the purpose of the provision, a meaning which is narrower than the ordinary, literal meaning of the provision is arrived at. The goal is to ascertain the proper ambit of the provision. . . .

A further observation which needs to be made in relation to the Constitutional Court decisions is that a purposive approach still allows reference to the maxims and presumptions of statutory interpretation. . . .

Purposive analysis

Applying the purposive method to the interpretation of section 2(1)(a) of the Restitution Act, one must start with the historical origin of the Restitution Act in general and of that section in particular. That origin is so notorious that I may take judicial notice of it. It is the policy of previous governments which sought to divide up the country spatially along racial and ethnic lines. That policy was central to the broader policy of governing the country on the basis of racial separation. The policy of racial zoning was extended throughout the rural and urban areas of the entire country. It was implemented via a complex matrix of statutes regulating the ownership and occupation of land on a racial basis with clear boundary delineations between the different racial zones, either in the statutes themselves or in the proclamations of such zones in terms of those statutes. Where it so happened that the owners or occupants of an area racially zoned were of the wrong race group, the law contained an arsenal to ensure that such persons could be deprived of any rights to the land which they might enjoy and coerced into moving to the correct racial zone. The consequences of the implementation of this policy are also notorious in all senses of that word. The places to which people were removed were in many instances desolate, undeveloped and far from proper amenities and sources of employment. Because the area zoned for the white racial group was an extra-ordinarily large portion of the overall area of the country, it was the other race groups who inevitably bore the brunt of the policy of racial zoning. The discriminatory component of forced removals was a source of enormous psychological harm on its own. Family life was disrupted. The education of children was interrupted. The economic and financial impact was often devastating. The estrangement which it caused between the different race groups is something which will haunt this country for generations. . . .

The whole issue of land restitution became part of the debate around property rights which preceded the adoption of the 1993 Constitution. As a result, a fresh approach to restitution was adopted in sections 121 to 123, read with section 8(3)(b), of the 1993 Constitution. Those provisions regulated in detail the basis upon which restitution could be claimed and the remedies which were available. Section 122 provided for the establishment of the Commission on the Restitution of Land Rights.

The most important provision for present purposes was section 121 which read:

> "121 Claims
>
> (1) An Act of Parliament shall provide for matters relating to the restitution of land rights, as envisaged in this section and in sections 122 and 123.
>
> (2) A person or a community shall be entitled to claim restitution of a right in land from the state if—
>
> > (a) such person or community was dispossessed of such right at any time after a date to be fixed by the Act referred to in subsection (1); and
> >
> > (b) such dispossession was effected under or for the purpose of furthering the object of a law which would have been inconsistent with the prohibition of racial discrimination contained in section 8(2), had that section been in operation at the time of such dispossession.
>
> (3) The date fixed by virtue of subsection (2)(a) shall not be a date earlier than 19 June 1913.
>
> . . ."
>
> [my emphasis].

. . . The test for determining whether or not a person qualifies to claim restitution as set out in section 121(2) was incorporated in section 2(1)(a) of the Restitution Act (as it then read) by cross-reference. Section 121 to 123 of the 1993 Constitution read with the Restitution Act made a number of important changes to the land restitution regime. . . . For the first time, claims could also be submitted in respect of land, both rural and urban, which, at the time of the claim is privately owned. Claims were no longer circumscribed to narrow categories of land. The range of remedies available was broadened to include compensation, a broader category of alternative state-owned land and "alternative relief". The regime became far more rights based than discretionary. The institutions created to oversee the process, including this Court, were given wider and more independent powers. The range of persons entitled to claim was expanded to include communities and direct descendants.

Where the new restitution regime did not signal a substantial departure from the old regime was in the range of laws which would give rise to a restitution claim. . . .

The history of the Restitution Act and section 2(1)(a), as set out above, strongly points to its underlying purpose being to address dispossessions of land rights which were the result of a particular class of racially discriminatory laws and practices, namely those that sought specifically to achieve the (then) ideal of spatial apartheid, with each racial and ethnic group being confined to its particular racial zone. These would then be those laws and practices which discriminated against persons on the basis of race in the exercise of rights in land in order to bring about that racial zoning. It does not, in my view, include any racially discriminatory law or practice whatsoever, regardless of the particular area of human activity where the discrimination had its impact. It was that particular class of laws which gave rise to the phenomenon of forced removals with their associated awful consequences. It is that phenomenon which the land restitution regime seeks to address.

Apart from the historical origin, I must also consider the statutory context of the provision in question. Section 2(1)(a) of the Restitution Act essentially gives the content to a constitutional right contained in the Bill of Rights. Important themes or values which underlie both the 1993 and 1996 Constitutions are the desirability of reconciliation, reconstruction and the healing of past injustices, along with the need to put the country's unjust past behind us. Recognition of the latter need requires acknowledgement of the fact that not every past injustice is capable of being remedied. An interpretation of section 2(1)(a) which most effectively promotes these values or themes is therefore to be preferred. . . .

* * *

Is the Group Areas Act a racially discriminatory law?

Applying the above analysis to the first of the three questions referred to in paragraph above, it seems to me that the Group Areas Act of 1950 is plainly the type of law which is contemplated by section 2(1)(a) of the Restitution Act. It was central to the racial zoning of primarily urban areas of South Africa. It incorporated the concept of a "disqualified person".

This included, for example, "in relating to immovable property, land or premises in any group area, a person who is not a member of the group specified in the relevant proclamation". The definition of "group" began "either the white group, the coloured group or the native group referred to in section two . . .". Section 2 then contained detailed descriptions of the different groups. Section 4 prohibited the occupation of a proclaimed group area by a disqualified person (except with a permit). Section 5 prohibited the acquisition of land in a proclaimed group area by a disqualified person (except with a permit). It was also one of the laws which caused people to be relocated against their will. Together with its successor, the Group Areas Act of 1966, it caused enormous social upheaval and the types of infringement of human rights which accompanied forced removals. On a purposive interpretation, this Act falls squarely within the notion of a "racially discriminatory law" as contemplated by section 2(1)(a) of the Restitution Act. That, however, is not the end of the enquiry, as it is still a requirement that the dispossession of their rights in land was "as a result of" the Group Areas Act of 1950.

Was the establishment of the school a racially discriminatory practice?

Although the matter was not canvassed in argument, the only law which provided for the establishment of a racially exclusive school at the time appears to have been the Coloured Persons Education Act of 1963. That Act allowed the Minister of Coloured Affairs to "establish, erect and maintain" a primary school. A primary school was specifically defined as "a school for the education of Coloured persons up to and including the sixth standard". There was no suggestion that the decision to establish the school in this case was unlawful. We must therefore proceed on the basis that there was a decision of the Minister of Coloured Affairs to establish the primary school in question. It is this decision which must be tested for compliance with the term "racially discriminatory practice", for it was after this decision that the dispossession complained of, took place.

If regard is had to the definition of "racially discriminatory practice" it would seem to me that such a decision would qualify as a "practice" or "act . . . by . . . [a] functionary . . . which exercised a public power or performed a public function in terms of any legislation". However, on a purposive interpretation of the term "racially discriminatory practice" along the lines which I have suggested, the discriminatory component of the practice was not directed at the exercise of land rights, either directly or indirectly. The discrimination was directed at the school's prospective pupils who would have to be educated separately from other race groups. It would also have discriminated against any persons who wished to be educated at a school in the area but who were not of the right race group. That, in my view, is not the type of racially discriminatory practice which is contemplated by section 2(1)(a). If it is to be interpreted in accordance with its underlying purpose, it must be interpreted restrictively so as to exclude the type of racially discriminatory practice here referred to. . . .

Was the dispossession as a result of the Group Areas Act?

The words "as a result of" in section 2(1)(a) of the Restitution Act represent a departure from the "under or for the purposes of furthering the objects of . . ." formulation of the 1993 Constitution. They must also be interpreted purposively in accordance with the analysis referred to . . . above. The same considerations would apply in so far as the historical origins and the statutory context are concerned as I have identified in relation to the other phrases in section 2(1)(a). As far as the particular words are concerned, "result" is defined in the New Shorter Oxford English Dictionary under note 4 as "[t]he effect, consequence, issue, or outcome of some action, process, or design".

. . . It is clear from these cases and the dictionary definition of "result", as well as a proper consideration of the purpose of section 2(1)(a) of the Restitution Act, that the use of the words "as a result of" contemplates a causal connection being established between the dispossession complained of and a racially discriminatory law or practice. . . .

* * *

Turning to the facts of this case, the only evidence regarding any causal impact of the Group Areas Act is that the area in which the school was later to be established was proclaimed a coloured group area with effect from 6 July 1960 in terms of that Act. Whether it was a necessary condition for a coloured school to be established that it should be in a coloured group area was not dealt with at all in the papers or in argument. I have not been able to find any express provision to this effect in the Coloured Persons Education Act. It may well be that the effect of the prohibition on occupation of a group area by a disqualified person prevented a school for disqualified persons from being established there as a matter of law. If this is so, it would have meant that a coloured school could only be established in a coloured area. Certainly, this is likely to have been so as a matter of practical reality.

Applying the law regarding causation, the result is clear whether one simply applies the principles of statutory interpretation or whether one follows the two-stage enquiry. Starting with the former, one would usually be able to trace the establishment of racially exclusive institutions back, one way or another, to an original statute which provided for the racial zoning of the area in which the institution is established. If that was accepted as a basis for a valid claim, it would give rise to the same difficulties as those identified above in relation to a broad and literal interpretation of a racially discriminatory practice, including the potential multiplicity of historical valuation based claims. For this reason, on the facts of this particular matter, and on a purposive analysis of section 2(1)(a), it cannot be said that the dispossession was "as a result of" the Group Areas Act of 1950.

NOTES AND QUESTIONS

1. At the start of this text, we posited that the start of possession in property can be dispossession. How is the term "dispossession" defined within the context of South Africa's Restitution Act? Is this a plausible definition?

2. Why did the Court take "judicial notice" of the discriminatory consequences of the Group Areas Act? What were the elements of "restitution" for these and other acts as contemplated by the Court in *Slamdien*?

3. What constitutional approach did the court use in *Slamdien*? Do you think that another test, such as a plain meaning or an originalist test, would have created a different outcome in this case?

4. How does the court use this approach in interpreting Section 2(1)(a) of the Restitution Act? In *Slamdien*, the court appears to establish a two-part test to determine whether a violation of the Restitution Act has occurred. First, the court must determine whether the disputed act is a racially discriminatory law or a racially discriminatory practice. Second, the court must determine whether the dispossession occurred as a result of either one of those actions. Why did the court find that the Group Areas Act was a racially discriminatory law? Why did the court find that the establishment of a racially exclusive school on the disputed plot of land was *not* a racially discriminatory practice? Do you think the court's argument was persuasive as to the second instance?

5. Was the court's requirement of *causality* in *Slamdien* an important limiting principle under Section 2(1)(a) of the Restitution Act? Do you think such a requirement fits within the overall purpose of the Restitution Act as described in *Slamdien*?

Another key reform in the constitution of South Africa was Article 26, which guaranteed the right of housing to South African citizens. Article 26 states that

1. Everyone has the right to have access to adequate housing.
2. The state must take reasonable legislative and other measures, within its available resources, to achieve the progressive realisation of this right.

3. No one may be evicted from their home, or have their home demolished, without an order of court made after considering all the relevant circumstances. No legislation may permit arbitrary evictions.

The Constitutional Court of South Africa addressed the impact of Article 26 in 2004 in *Port Elizabeth Municipality v. Various Occupiers*, excerpted below.

Port Elizabeth Municipality v. Various Occupiers

2004 (12) BCLR 1268, 2006 SACLR LEXIS 25 (2004)

The applicant in this matter is the Port Elizabeth Municipality (the Municipality). The respondents are some 68 people, including 23 children, who occupy twenty-nine shacks they have erected on privately owned land (the property) within the Municipality. Responding to a petition signed by 1600 people in the neighbourhood, including the owners of the property, the Municipality sought an eviction order against the occupiers in the South Eastern Cape Local Division of the High Court (High Court).

[* * *]

The Municipality submitted that it was aware of its obligation to provide housing and had for that reason embarked on a comprehensive housing development programme. It contended that if alternative land was made available to the occupiers, they would effectively be "queue-jumping"; by occupying private land and, when asked to vacate it, demanding that they be provided with alternative accommodation, they would be disrupting the housing programme and forcing the Municipality to grant them preferential treatment.

The High Court held that the occupiers were unlawfully occupying the property and that it was in the public interest that their unlawful occupation be terminated. [* * *]

The whole case turns on the interpretation to be given to various provisions in the Constitution, as well as to the statute adopted to give effect to a provision of the Constitution.

I. The Constitutional and Statutory Context

The Prevention of Illegal Squatting Act 52 of 1951

In the pre-democratic era the response of the law to a situation like the present would have been simple and drastic. In terms of the Prevention of Illegal Squatting Act 52 of 1951 (PISA), the only question for decision would have been whether the occupation of the land was unlawful.

Once it was determined that the occupiers had no permission to be on the land, they not only faced summary eviction, they were liable for criminal prosecution. Expulsion from land of people referred to as squatters was accordingly accomplished through the criminal and not the civil courts, and as a matter of public rather than of private law. The process was deliberately made as swift as possible: conviction followed by eviction. Thus, even if they had been born on the land and spent their whole lives there, persons from whom permission to remain on land had been withdrawn by new owners were treated as criminals and subjected to summary eviction.

[* * *]

PISA was an integral part of a cluster of statutes that gave a legal/administrative imprimatur to the usurpation and forced removal of black people from land and compelled them to live in racially designated locations. For all black people, and for Africans in particular, dispossession was nine-tenths of the law. Residential segregation was the cornerstone of the apartheid policy. This policy was aimed at creating separate "countries" for Africans within South Africa. Africans were precluded from owning and occupying land outside the areas reserved for them by these statutes. The Native Urban Areas Consolidation Act 25 of 1945, was premised on the notion of Africans living in rural reserves and coming to the towns only as migrant workers on temporary sojourn. Through a combination of spatial apartheid, permit systems and the creation of criminal offences the Act strictly controlled the limited rights that Africans had to reside in urban areas. People living outside of what were defined as native locations were regarded as squatters and, under PISA, were expelled from the land on which they lived.

[* * *]

Differentiation on the basis of race was accordingly not only a source of grave assaults on the dignity of black people. It resulted in the creation of large, well-established and affluent white urban areas co-existing side by side with crammed pockets of impoverished and insecure black ones. The principles of ownership in the Roman-Dutch law then gave legitimation in an apparently neutral and impartial way to the consequences of manifestly racist and partial laws and policies. In this setting of State-induced inequality the nominally race-free PISA targeted black shack-dwellers with dramatically harsh effect. As Van der Walt has pointed out:

> "The 'normality' assumption that the owner was entitled to possession unless the occupier could raise and prove a valid defence, usually based on agreement with the owner, formed part of Roman-Dutch law and was deemed unexceptional in early South African law, and it still forms the point of departure in private law.

> However, it had disastrous results for non-owners under . . . apartheid land law: the strong position of ownership and the (legislatively intensified) weak position of black non-ownership rights of occupation made it easier for the architects of apartheid to effect the evictions and removals required to establish the separation of land holdings along race lines."

[* * *]

The Prevention of Illegal Eviction from and Unlawful Occupation of Land Act 19 of 1998 (PIE)

The Prevention of Illegal Eviction from and Unlawful Occupation of Land Act 19 of 1998 (PIE) was adopted with the manifest objective of overcoming the above abuses and ensuring that evictions in future took place in a manner consistent with the values of the new constitutional dispensation. Its provisions have to be interpreted against this background.

PIE not only repealed PISA but in a sense inverted it: squatting was decriminalised and the eviction process was made subject to a number of requirements, some necessary to comply with certain demands of the Bill of Rights. The overlay between public and private law continued, but in reverse fashion, with the name, character, tone and context of the statute being turned around. Thus the first part of the title of the new law emphasised a shift in thrust from prevention of illegal squatting to prevention of illegal eviction. The former objective of reinforcing common-law remedies while reducing common-law protections, was reversed so as to temper common-law remedies with strong procedural and substantive protections; and the overall objective of facilitating the displacement and relocation of poor and landless black people for ideological purposes was replaced by acknowledgment of the necessitous quest for homes of victims of past racist policies. While awaiting access to new housing development programmes, such homeless people had to be treated with dignity and respect.

[* * *]

The broad constitutional matrix for the interpretation of PIE

In this context PIE cannot simply be looked at as a legislative mechanism designed to restore common-law property rights by freeing them of racist and authoritarian provisions, though that is one of its aspects. Nor is it just a means of promoting judicial philanthropy in favour of the poor, though compassion is built into its very structure. PIE has to be understood, and its governing concepts of justice and equity have to be applied, within a defined and carefully calibrated constitutional matrix.

As with all determination about the reach of constitutionally protected rights, the starting and ending point of the analysis must be to affirm the values of human dignity, equality and freedom. One of the provisions of the Bill of Rights that has to be interpreted with these values in mind, is section 25, which reads:

> "Property
>
> (1) No one may be deprived of property except in terms of law of general application, and no law may permit arbitrary deprivation of property."

[* * *]

The blatant disregard manifested by racist statutes for property rights in the past makes it all the more important that property rights be fully respected in the new dispensation, both by the state and by private persons. Yet such rights have to be understood in the context of the need for the orderly opening-up or restoration of secure property rights for those denied access to or deprived of them in the past.

[* * *]

The preamble to the Constitution indicates that one of the purposes of its adoption was to establish a society based, not only on 'democratic values' and 'fundamental human rights' but also on 'social justice'. Moreover the Bill of Rights places positive obligations on the State in regard to various social and economic rights. Van der Walt (1997) aptly explains the tensions that exist within section 25:

> '[T]he meaning of section 25 has to be determined, in each specific case, within an interpretative framework that takes due cognisance of the inevitable tensions which characterise the operation of the property clause. . . .

[* * *]

The transformatory public-law view of the Constitution referred to by Van der Walt is further underlined by section 26, which reads:

> "Housing
>
> (1) Everyone has the right to have access to adequate housing.
>
> (2) The State must take reasonable legislative and other measures, within its available resources, to achieve the progressive realisation of this right.
>
> (3) No one may be evicted from their home, or have their home demolished, without an order of court made after considering all the relevant circumstances. No legislation may permit arbitrary evictions."

Section 26(3) evinces special constitutional regard for a person's place of abode. It acknowledges that a home is more than just a shelter from the elements. It is a zone of personal intimacy and family security. Often it will be the only relatively secure space of privacy and tranquillity in what (for poor people in particular) is a turbulent and hostile world. Forced removal is a shock for any family, the more so for one that has established itself on a site that has become its familiar habitat. As the United Nations Housing Rights Programme report points out:

> "To live in a place, and to have established one's own personal habitat with peace, security and dignity, should be considered neither a luxury, a privilege nor purely the good fortune of those who can afford a decent home. Rather, the requisite imperative of housing for personal security, privacy, health, safety, protection from the elements and many other attributes of a shared humanity, has led the international community to recognise adequate housing as a basic and fundamental human right."

[* * *]

It is not only the dignity of the poor that is assailed when homeless people are driven from pillar to post in a desperate quest for a place where they and their families can rest their heads. Our society as a whole is demeaned when State action intensifies rather than mitigates their marginalisation. The integrity of the rights-based vision of the Constitution is punctured when governmental action augments rather than reduces denial of the claims of the desperately poor to the basic elements of a decent existence. Hence the need for special judicial control of a process that is both socially stressful and potentially conflictual.

Much of this case accordingly turns on establishing an appropriate constitutional relationship between section 25, dealing with property rights, and section 26, concerned with housing rights. The Constitution recognises that land rights and the right of access to housing and of not being arbitrarily evicted, are closely intertwined. The stronger the right to land, the greater the prospect of a secure home. Thus, the need to strengthen the precarious position of people living in informal settlements is recognised by section 25 in a number of ways. Land reform is facilitated [* * *] and the State is required to foster conditions enabling citizens to gain access to land on an equitable basis; persons or communities with legally insecure tenure because of discriminatory laws are entitled to secure tenure or other redress; and persons dispossessed of property by racially discriminatory laws are entitled to restitution or other redress. Furthermore, sections 25 and 26 create a broad overlap between land rights and socio-economic rights, emphasising the duty on the State to seek to satisfy both, as this Court said in Grootboom.

[* * *]

II. The Structure of PIE

[* * *]

Section 6, the governing provision in the present matter, reads:

> "6. Eviction at instance of organ of State.—
>
> (1) An organ of State may institute proceedings for the eviction of an unlawful occupier from land which falls within its area of jurisdiction, except where the unlawful occupier is a mortgagor and the land in question is sold in a sale of execution pursuant to a mortgage, and the court may grant such an order if it is just and equitable to do so, after considering all the relevant circumstances, and if—
>
> (a) the consent of that organ of State is required for the erection of a building or structure on that land or for the occupation of the land, and the unlawful occupier is occupying a building or structure on that land without such consent having been obtained; or
>
> (b) it is in the public interest to grant such an order.
>
> (2) For the purposes of this section, "public interest" includes the interest of the health and safety of those occupying the land and the public in general.
>
> (3) In deciding whether it is just and equitable to grant an order for eviction, the court must have regard to—
>
> (a) the circumstances under which the unlawful occupier occupied the land and erected the building or structure;
>
> (b) the period the unlawful occupier and his or her family have resided on the land in question; and
>
> (c) the availability to the unlawful occupier of suitable alternative accommodation or land."

Simply put, the ordinary prerequisites for the Municipality to be in a position to apply for an eviction order are that the occupation is unlawful and the structures are either unauthorised, or unhealthy or unsafe. Contrary to the pre-constitutional position, however, the mere establishment of these facts does not require the court to make an eviction order. In terms of section 6, they merely trigger the court's discretion. If they are proved, the court then may (not must) grant an eviction order if it is just and equitable to do so. In making its decision it must take account of all relevant circumstances, including the manner in which occupation was effected, its duration and the availability of suitable alternative accommodation or land.

[* * *]

[The court reviewed various factors and concluded by examining the meaning of just and equitable.—Eds.]

"Just and equitable"

[* * *]

The phrase "just and equitable" makes it plain that the criteria to be applied are not purely of the technical kind that flow ordinarily from the provisions of land law. The emphasis on justice and equity underlines the central philosophical and strategic objective of PIE. Rather than envisage the foundational values of the rule of law and the achievement of equality as being distinct from and in tension with each other, PIE treats these values as interactive, complementary and mutually reinforcing. The necessary reconciliation can only be attempted by a close analysis of the actual specifics of each case.

The court is thus called upon to go beyond its normal functions, and to engage in active judicial management according to equitable principles of an ongoing, stressful and law-governed social process. This has major implications for the manner in which it must deal with the issues before it, how it should approach questions of evidence, the procedures it may adopt, the way in which it exercises its powers and the orders it might make. The Constitution and PIE require that in addition to considering the lawfulness of the occupation the court must have regard to the interests and circumstances of the occupier and pay due regard to broader considerations of fairness and other constitutional values, so as to produce a just and equitable result.

Thus, PIE expressly requires the court to infuse elements of grace and compassion into the formal structures of the law. It is called upon to balance competing interests in a principled way and promote the constitutional vision of a caring society based on good neighbourliness and shared concern. The Constitution and PIE confirm that we are not islands unto ourselves. The spirit of ubuntu, part of the deep cultural heritage of the majority of the population, suffuses the whole constitutional order.[1] It combines individual rights with a communitarian philosophy.

It is a unifying motif of the Bill of Rights, which is nothing if not a structured, institutionalised and operational declaration in our evolving new society of the need for human interdependence, respect and concern. . . .

[* * *]

1. As Mokgoro J has explained: "Generally, ubuntu translates as 'humaneness'. In its most fundamental sense it translates as personhood and 'morality'. Metaphorically, it expresses itself in umuntu ngumuntu ngabantu, describing the significance of group solidarity on survival issues so central to the survival of communities. While it envelops the key values of group solidarity, compassion, respect, human dignity, conformity to basic norms and collective unity, in its fundamental sense it denotes humanity and morality. Its spirit emphasises a respect for human dignity, marking a shift from confrontation to conciliation. In South Africa ubuntu has become a notion with particular resonance in the building of a democracy. It is part of our rainbow heritage, though it might have operated and still operates differently in diverse community settings. In the Western cultural heritage, respect and the value for life, manifested in the all-embracing concepts of 'humanity' and 'menswaardigheid', are also highly priced. It is values like these that (s 39(1)(a)) requires to be promoted. They give meaning and texture to the principles of a society based on freedom and equality." (Footnotes omitted.) See S v Makwanyane and Another 1995 (3) SA 391 (CC); 1995 (6) BCLR (CC) at para 308.

IV. Should the Decision of the SCA Be Overturned?

It is necessary now to consider whether the application for leave to appeal should be granted. In considering this question it is important to identify the relevant facts of this case to which the legal principles identified above must be applied. The Municipality launched motion proceedings to seek the eviction of the occupiers. Many of the facts it alleged in its founding affidavits were disputed by the occupiers in response. Accordingly we must accept those facts asserted by the applicant that remain undenied by the respondent, together with the facts as alleged by the respondents.

The occupiers have built shacks on privately owned land in the suburb of Lorraine, in Port Elizabeth. It is clear that the shacks were erected without the necessary approval from the Municipality. Accordingly, the requirement of section 6(1)(a) of the Act is met. The occupiers assert that eight of the respondent families have resided on the land for eight years (as at August 2000 when the answering affidavits were signed), three of them for four years and only one family for two years. They aver that most of them moved to the land in Lorraine after having been evicted from land in Glenroy, Port Elizabeth. They also state that they are willing to move again but want to do so only if they are provided with a piece of land upon which to live "without fear of further eviction" until they are provided with housing in terms of the Municipality's housing scheme. In this short tale, the hard realities of urbanisation and homelessness in South Africa are captured.

[* * *]

The occupiers claim that when they moved onto the land they were given permission to do so by a woman whom they assumed to be the owner. The Municipality, in reply, filed affidavits on behalf of all the owners of the erven concerned indicating that the current occupiers do not have permission to reside on the land. These specific and emphatic denials must be accepted to establish that the occupiers, even if they were once given permission to occupy the land by an owner, no longer have permission to do so. However, the owners do not assert that they require the land for their own personal use at this stage.

It is clear from the Municipality's affidavits that the land is vacant land, upon which some trees and bushes are growing, but that it is not being used by the owners at present for any productive purpose. The Municipality wishes the occupiers to move because firstly, it has received a petition signed by 1600 members of the public requesting the Municipality to move the occupiers, and secondly because it asserts that the conditions in which the occupiers are occupying the land constitute a health risk because of the absence of toilet facilities. . . .

The occupiers deny that their occupation of the land creates a health risk. They state that they use pit latrines which are hygienic. They also state that they obtain water on a daily basis from a gentleman at the nearby Riding Club, though this allegation, in turn is denied by the Municipality. . . .

In determining whether the Municipality is entitled to obtain the eviction of the occupiers, the three criteria mentioned in section 6 of the Act must be considered: the circumstances under which the unlawful occupier occupied the land and erected the structures; the period the occupier has resided on the land, and the availability of suitable alternative land. [It] is clear from what has been said above that the occupiers moved onto the land with what they considered to be the permission of the owner and that they have been there for a long period of time. Eight children are attending local schools in the area and several of the adults have work nearby.

The Municipality, in its founding affidavit, pointed to two possible sites as suitable alternative land: the first was Walmer, which the occupiers reject as being overcrowded and unsafe; the second is Greenbushes, which the occupiers reject as being too far away for them to go to their work and for their children to school in the Lorraine area. It is quite clear that the Municipality has not entered into any discussions with the respondents, who are a relatively small group of people (only 68), to identify their particular circumstances or needs. The occupiers do mention two areas, Seaview and Fairview, as potentially suitable alternative land, but the Municipality does not address these suggestions in their reply.

* * *

These paragraphs capture the nub of the Municipality's case. It asserts that having established a four peg housing programme, it need do no more to accommodate individually homeless families such as the occupiers than offer them registration in that housing programme which, it admits, may not provide housing for the occupiers for some years. It is not accurate, however, on the facts before us to define the occupiers as "queue jumpers". They are a community who are homeless, who have been evicted once, and who found land to occupy with what they considered to be the permission of the owner where they have been residing for eight years. This is a considerable period of time. The Municipality now seeks to evict them without any discussion with them, or consideration of their request that they be provided with security of tenure on a suitable piece of land pending their accommodation in the housing programme.

In considering whether it is "just and equitable" to make an eviction order in terms of section 6 of the Act, the responsibilities that municipalities, unlike owners, bear in terms of section 26 of the Constitution are relevant. As Grootboom (supra) indicates, municipalities have a major function to perform with regard to the fulfilment of the rights of all to have access to adequate housing. Municipalities, therefore, have a duty systematically to improve access to housing for all within their area.

* * *

To sum up: in the light of the lengthy period during which the occupiers have lived on the land in question, the fact that there is no evidence that either the Municipality or the owners of the land need to evict the occupiers in order to put the land to some other productive use, the absence of any significant attempts by the Municipality to listen to and consider the problems of this particular group of occupiers, and the fact that this is a relatively small group of people who appear to be genuinely homeless and in need, I am not persuaded that it is just and equitable to order the eviction of the occupiers.

[* * *]

NOTES AND QUESTIONS

1. Bernadette Atuahene has written extensively on land reform in post-apartheid South Africa. Her scholarly work has usefully supplied two key insights in this area. First, Atuahene contends that "past property theft" can cause significant instabilities in nascent democracies, particularly where there is pre-existing racial or ethnic conflict. *See* Bernadette Atuahene, *Things Fall Apart: The Illegitimacy of Property Rights in the Context of Past Property Theft,* 51 Ariz. L. Rev. 829 (2009). She states "past property theft" occurs when "a society has a generalized belief that one group would not own their property if it were not for the past systematic and uncompensated confiscation from another group." *Id.* at 835. Second, Atuahene emphasizes that nascent democracies, so as to resolve these disputes over "past property theft," should utilize a "transformative conception" of property law. Bernadette Atuahene, *Property Rights and the Demands of Transformation,* Mich. J. Int'l Law 6-8 (forthcoming 2010). A transformative conception seeks to mediate between two potential extremes, the classical conception of property that affords absolute protection to deed holders, and unmediated conception of property, in which pre-existing property rights are subject to group-based expropriation with little or no compensation to owners (Atuahene's given example is the current situation in Zimbabwe, in which white farmers have been significantly displaced by the government). *Id.* at 8.

Does the holding in *Port Elizabeth* signal acceptance of transformative notion of property law? Does it accord with the decision of *Slamdien*?

2. We began this casebook by analyzing the origins of property right in dispossession, rather than possession. How does the Court address this particular question in *Port Elizabeth*? How does the Court use the works of Van Der Walt to discuss the question of dispossession as opposed to others' possession?

3. What is the concept of *ubuntu*? How does the Court incorporate *ubuntu* in its opinion?

4. How does the Court view the guarantee of housing articulated in Article 26 in light of other constitutional provisions? What are the strategies that the municipal government could use to be responsive to this decision? How does the Court view Section 25 and Section 26 as intertwined?

7.3 PROTECTING THE PROPERTY RIGHTS: RESTITUTION IN POST-CONFLICT SOCIETIES

Post-conflict property restitution — that is, the restitution of property to owners or tenants dispossessed of their property as the result of an ongoing ethnic conflict — has become an additional remedy. Paolo Sergio Pinheiro, in a report drafted on behest of the United Nations, defines *restitution* as the right "to an equitable remedy, or a form of restorative justice, by which persons, who suffer loss or injury are returned as far as possible to their original pre-loss or pre-injury position." *Housing and Property Restitution in the Context of the Return of Refugees and Internally Displaced Persons*, U.N. Econ. & Soc. Council [ECOSOC], Sub-Comm'n on the Promotion and Prot. of Human Rights, ¶4, U.N. Doc. E/CN.4/Sub.2/2005/17/Add.1 (June 28, 2005) (*http://www.unhcr.org.ua/img/uploads/docs/PinheiroPrinciples.pdf*) (last visited September 3, 2010). This report, referred commonly to as the Pinheiro Principles, outlines the basic human rights enjoyed by individuals as to their property during conflicts. For example, Section Two provides that

> 2.1 All refugees and displaced persons have the right to have restored to them any housing, land and/or property of which they were arbitrarily or unlawfully deprived, or to be compensated for any housing, land and/or property that is factually impossible to restore as determined by an independent, impartial tribunal.
>
> 2.2 States shall demonstrably prioritize the right to restitution as the preferred remedy for displacement and as a key element of restorative justice. The right to restitution exists as a distinct right, and is prejudiced neither by the actual return nor non-return of refugees and displaced persons entitled to housing, land and property restitution.

We examine conflicts in two countries — Bosnia-Herzegovina and Guatemala — to understand the how the right of return has been developed within the international context.

7.3.1 *Bosnia-Herzegovina*

The Republic of Bosnia-Herzegovina was engulfed in an internal war after the country's 1992 declaration of independence from the former Yugoslavia. Lynn Hastings, *Implementation of the Property Legislation in Bosnia*

Herzegovina, 37 STAN. J. INT'L L. 221, 221 (2001). Ethnic cleansing was common among each of Bosnia-Herzegovina's three primary ethnic groups: Croats, Serbs, and Muslim Bosniaks. *Id.* Soldiers or local authorities from each ethnic group often forcibly evicted from their homes members of the minority ethnic groups in their region; the evicted minorities were then replaced with residents of the majority ethnic group. *Id.* By the end of the war in 1995, Bosnia-Herzegovina had been divided into two separate "entities": the predominately Bosniak and Croat Federation of Bosnia-Herzegovina ("Federation") and the predominately Serbian Republika Srpska ("RS"). *Id.* at 222.

Property in the former Yugoslavia was both privately and socially owned. *Id.* at 225. Municipalities or state-owned companies usually controlled socially owned property. *Id.* The registered owner could allocate "occupancy rights" to employees. *Id.* The occupancy right holder did not acquire ownership through this right but still had a possessory interest that was greater than a lease: the registered owner granted the occupancy right for an indefinite period, there were restrictions on the termination of the occupancy right, and the occupancy right was inheritable. *Id.* at 225-26.

During the internal war, each ethnic group established its own administration that oversaw the redistribution of both privately and socially owned property. *Id.* at 226. These administrations relied on new or existing housing regulations that retroactively legalized the property redistribution along ethnic lines. *Id.* at 226. The Human Rights Commission, established under the Dayton Accord peace agreement that ended the war, denounced the property laws, declaring that they violated the European Convention for the Protection of Human Rights and Fundamental Freedoms. *Id.* at 228.

In 1996 the Federation and RS agreed to amend their property laws, *id.*, but after the entities failed to do so, the Office of the High Representative (OHR), created by the Dayton Accord to oversee civilian implementation of the peace agreement, *id.* at 224, drafted amending legislation, *id.* at 228, versions of which were adopted by the Federation and RS after intensive negotiations with the OHR and the U.N. High Commissioner for Refugees the Federation, *id.* at 230. The draft legislation voided wartime laws, gave prewar occupants a right of return, and required municipalities to provide accommodations for residents forced to vacate because of another's right of return. *Id.* at 228-29. The RS property legislation differed from the Federation legislation in three key ways: first, current occupants could not be evicted unless they were able to return to their prewar residence; second, there was no process for initiating evictions; and third, the law allowed appeals to delay implementation of decisions. *Id.* These differences all but ensured that current occupants would not be evicted from their residences. *Id.*

Indifference, noncooperation, and obstruction by Bosnian authorities hampered the legislation of both entities. *Id.* at 230. The international community responded to the obstruction in an ad hoc manner by providing conditional incentives to encourage implementation of the legislation. *Id.* at

233. These efforts proved inefficient and resulted in a system in which municipalities would comply only if they wanted the support of the international community. *Id.* at 233-34. One of the primary impediments preventing displaced persons from reclaiming their property was the eviction process. *Id.* at 239. For the returnee to claim possession, the current occupier had to be evicted. *Id.* Police officers were often required to remove the occupier from the residence; however, this meant that the officers would have to remove a member of their own ethnic group so that a returnee, generally of another ethnic group, could move back. *Id.* Many police officers were unwilling to enforce these evictions. *Id.* Even when the police were willing to cooperate, protestors often hindered the process. *Id.* The following case deals with a Bosniak who was forcibly evicted and sought to reclaim possession of his home in Republika Srpska.

Human Rights Chamber of Bosnia and Herzegovina, "M.J." v. Republicka Srpska

Decision on Admissibility of Nov. 7, 1997, Case CH/96/28 (1997)

I. Introduction

1. The applicant is a citizen of Bosnia and Herzegovina of Bosniak descent. He and his family were forcibly evicted from their apartment in Banja Luka in September 1995 by a Serbian refugee, Mr. K.V. The applicant instituted proceedings before the Court of First Instance in Banja Luka, which ordered the eviction of Mr. K.V. Several attempts were made to execute its decision but without results because the police did not take any action to assist court officials. The case concerns non-enforcement of the court decision and raises issues under . . . Article 8 of the European Convention for the Protection of Human Rights and Fundamental Freedoms (hereinafter "the Convention") and Article 1 of Protocol No. 1 to the Convention.

II. Proceedings Before the Chamber

2. This case was referred to the Chamber by decision of the Human Rights Ombudsperson for Bosnia and Herzegovina (hereinafter "the Ombudsperson") dated 20 November 1996, taken under Article V paragraph 5 of the Human Rights Agreement (hereinafter "the Agreement") set out in Annex 6 to the General Framework Agreement for Peace in Bosnia and Herzegovina. . . .

III. Establishment of the Facts

6. The facts of the case as they appear from the parties' submissions and the documents in the case file are not generally in dispute and may be summarised as follows.

7. The applicant has held an occupancy right over an apartment in Banja Luka since 1966. He occupied the apartment as his home together with his wife and daughter. On 19 September 1995 he, his wife and daughter were forcibly evicted from the apartment by three armed persons. According to the applicant they were reserve police from Drvar. The applicant subsequently found out that a Mr KECMAN Veljko (Mr K.V.) had moved into the apartment on the night in question. The applicant's wife died on 14 October 1995.

8. On 12 October 1995 the applicant instituted proceedings against Mr K.V. in the Court of First Instance in Banja Luka, seeking his eviction from the apartment on the basis of disturbance of possession. He alleged in the application to the Court that he had been forcibly evicted from the apartment by Mr K.V. without legal ground. The Court scheduled a hearing in the case for 19 December 1995. Mr K.V. did not appear. The applicant gave oral evidence as to the circumstances of his eviction. The Court gave its decision on the same day. It appears from the decision that the applicant stated that he heard knocking on the door at about 20.00 hours on the evening in question. He had asked the persons outside to identify themselves and they had stated that they were police. They had attempted to break in he had called the public security station Mejdan for assistance and two policemen from there had arrived at the apartment. They had entered the apartment first followed by the three reserve police from Drvar, who had been at the door. The police from the Mejdan station had questioned him and left. The three police from Drvar had then given him five minutes to leave the apartment together with his wife and daughter. The Court stated in its decision that it found the applicant's allegations and oral statements to be truthful. It found that the applicant had been disturbed in his possession of the apartment and ordered Mr K.V. to vacate the apartment immediately, and at the latest within eight days, and also to refrain from similar disturbances.

9. Mr K.V. did not comply with the order of the Court. On 24 January 1996 the Court issued a Decision on Execution in which Mr K.V. was ordered to vacate the apartment and place it at the disposal of the applicant, free of all persons and his things, together with all belongings of the applicant. Mr K.V. did not comply with this decision and on 12 February 1996 the Court issued an Executory Conclusion. This stated that it was decided to carry out the Decision on Execution of the judgement on 11 March 1996 and that the execution would be carried out by an official assisted by organs of public security and military police, delivering into the applicant's possession the apartment free of all persons and things. On 11 March 1996 the court official and police went to the apartment. Mr K.V. was at the apartment with ten to twenty other people. They adopted a threatening attitude and refused to leave. The eviction was not carried out. Further Executory Conclusions in similar terms were issued by the Court in which the eviction was scheduled for 29 April 1996, 23 May 1996, 19 July 1996, 9 September 1996, 14 October 1996 and 22 November 1996. According to the applicant a

similar situation arose on each of these occasions, namely that a group of people assembled to oppose the eviction and that in the face of threats, insults and obstruction from these people and inaction on the part of the police, the eviction was not carried out.

10. On the last two occasions on which the eviction was scheduled, i.e. 14 October and 22 November 1996, the court official and the police stated that the eviction could not be carried out because the person in the apartment was not Mr K.V. but a Mr Marinko RUJEVIĆ. The court official and the police informed the applicant's representative that they could not carry out the eviction because Mr K.V. was no longer in the apartment and it would be necessary to bring proceedings against Mr Rujević.

11. On or about 23 December 1996 the applicant instituted proceedings against Mr Rujević in the Court of First Instance in Banja Luka seeking to recover possession of the apartment from Mr Rujević. He also sought, as a provisional measure, an order for immediate possession of the apartment and its contents. In his application to the Court he set out details of the events which had occurred from the time of his forcible eviction onwards and suggested that it was more that obvious that Mr Rujević had moved illegally into the apartment on the basis of an agreement with Mr K.V., with the intention or preventing the execution of the lawful order of the court. According to the applicant's representative numerous oral requests were made to the Court to schedule a hearing. A hearing was fixed for 31 March 1997 but was postponed on the ground that the respondent was undergoing medical treatment abroad. On 8 May 1997 a request for the matter to be treated urgently was submitted to the Court by the applicant's lawyer. A further hearing was scheduled for 18 September 1997. According to the applicant Mr Rujević claimed that he had not received the application to the court. The applicant's lawyer has objected to the judge in these proceedings. It appears that no decision has been taken on the merits of the case or on the application for provisional measures and that the proceedings are still pending.

IV. Final Submissions of the Parties

A. The applicant

12. The applicant submits that his rights under Article 8 of the European Convention on Human Rights and Article 1 of Protocol No. 1 to the Convention have been violated by reason of his inability to recover possession of his apartment.

B. The respondent party

13. The respondent Party submits that the applicant has not exhausted all effective remedies at his disposal since the Court proceedings for recovery of

the apartment are still pending and that the Chamber should declare the application inadmissible under Article VIII paragraph 2 (a) of the Agreement.

C. *The Ombudsperson*

14. The Ombudsperson submits that the Chamber should find that there have been violations of Articles 6 and 8 of the Convention and of Article 1 of Protocol No. 1 to the Convention.

V. Opinion of the Chamber

A. *Admissibility*

15. Before considering the merits of the case the Chamber must decide whether to accept the case taking into account the admissibility criteria set out in Article VIII paragraph 2 of the Annex 6 Agreement.

16. The respondent Party has suggested that the Chamber should not deal with the case whilst proceedings are still pending before the courts of the Republika Srpska, in particular whilst the proceedings instituted by the applicant against Mr Rujević, the second unlawful occupant of his apartment, are still pending. The Chamber has considered this argument in the light of paragraph 2 (a) of Article VIII of the Agreement, which, so far as relevant, provides as follows:

> "The Chamber shall decide which applications to accept . . . . In so doing the Chamber shall take into account the following criteria:
>
> (a) Whether effective remedies exist, and the applicant has demonstrated that they have been exhausted . . . ."

17. In relation to the rule concerning exhaustion of domestic remedies in Article 26 of the European Convention on Human Rights, the European Court of Human Rights has, in the case of Akdivar v. Turkey, stated as follows:

> "Under Article 26 normal recourse should be had by an applicant to remedies which are available and sufficient to afford redress in respect of the breaches alleged. The existence of the remedies in question must be sufficiently certain not only in theory but in practice, failing which they will lack the requisite accessibility and effectiveness . . ." (Akdivar v. Turkey, Judgement of 16 September 1996, para. 66).

The Court also stated that in applying the rule it is necessary to "take realistic account not only of the existence of formal remedies in the legal system of the Contracting Party concerned but also of the general legal and political context in which they operate as well as the personal circumstances of the applicants." These principles should also be taken into account, in the Chamber's opinion, in the application of the criterion concerning exhaustion of remedies in Article VIII paragraph 2 (a) of the Agreement.

18. The Chamber notes that in the present case the applicant obtained a judgement against Mr K.V. giving him the right to re-obtain possession of the apartment and that he made repeated attempts to enforce the judgement without success. The applicant has thus had "normal recourse" to the court remedy available to him to restore possession of the apartment whilst it was in the hands of Mr K.V., but the remedy in question has proved to be ineffective in practice. In so far as the applicant's complaint relates to the failure of the authorities to enforce the judgement in the period up to Mr K.V.'s apparent departure from the apartment no effective remedy is now available to him.

19. In so far as the applicant's complaint relates to his continuing inability to obtain possession of his apartment, now apparently occupied by Mr Rujević, he has instituted civil proceedings against Mr Rujević and those proceedings are still pending. However there appears to be no reason why this remedy should be any more effective in practice against Mr Rujević than it was against Mr K.V. In the Chamber's opinion it is not therefore established with sufficient certainty that any effective remedy is in practice available to the applicant. The Chamber therefore finds that there is no obstacle to the admissibility of the application under Article VIII paragraph 2 (a) of the Agreement. . . .

B. The merits

21. Under Article XI of the Agreement the Chamber must, in the present decision, address the question whether the facts found indicate a breach by the respondent Party of its obligations under the Agreement. In terms of Article I of the Agreement the Parties are obliged to "secure to all persons within their jurisdiction the highest level of internationally recognized human rights and fundamental freedoms" including the rights and freedoms provided for in the Convention. The Chamber will therefore consider whether the applicant's exclusion from his apartment has involved a breach by the respondent Party of his rights under the Articles of the Convention which have been invoked in the proceedings.

1. Article 8 of the Convention

22. The Chamber has first considered the case in the light of Article 8 of the Convention, which provides as follows:

> "1. Everyone has the right to respect for his private and family life, his home and his correspondence.
>
> 2. There shall be no interference by a public authority with the exercise of this right except such as is in accordance with the law and is necessary in a democratic society in the interests of national security, public safety or the economic well-being of the country, for the prevention of disorder or crime, for the protection of health or morals, or for the protection of the rights and freedoms of others."

23. The question which arises is whether the failure of the authorities to enforce the judgement in question against Mr K.V., and the applicant's continued exclusion from the apartment since Mr K.V. moved out, involved a violation of the applicant's right to respect for his "home." The Chamber has already found that the applicant, together with his wife and daughter, occupied the apartment in question as their home before they were turned out by Mr K.V. It also follows from the findings of the Banja Luka Court of First Instance that the initial eviction of the applicant and his family and their continued exclusion from the house thereafter by Mr K.V. were unlawful. In the Chamber's opinion the facts of the case therefore reveal an unlawful interference on the part of Mr K.V. with the applicant's right to respect for his home, which continued at least until the time when he moved out of the apartment in about October 1996. After Mr K.V. moved out he was replaced by Mr Rujević. It has not been suggested that he had any right to occupy the apartment and in the Chamber's opinion it is established that his occupation of the apartment also amounted to an unlawful interference with the applicant's right to respect for his home, which has continued to the present time.

24. According to the applicant members of the police of the respondent Party participated in his initial unlawful eviction, which occurred before the Agreement came into force. On the evidence before it the Chamber does not, however, consider it established that the police or other public authorities of the respondent Party have taken an active role in maintaining the applicant's continued exclusion from the apartment since 14 December 1995. It is suggested however, by the applicant and the Ombudsperson, that the respondent Party is responsible for the applicant's continued exclusion because the police were passive and failed to give necessary assistance to the court officials in carrying out the eviction of Mr K.V. The police appear to have taken the attitude that they were justified by considerations of public safety in not taking an active role.

25. The European Court of Human Rights has held that, although the object of Article 8 is essentially that of protecting the individual against arbitrary interference by public authorities, it may also give rise to positive obligations, which are inherent in an effective respect for the rights which it guarantees, and that in this context, as in others, a fair balance must be struck between the general interest and the interests of the people concerned (see e.g. Marckx v. Belgium, 1979 Series A No. 31, para. 31; Airey v. Ireland, 1979 Series A No. 32, para. 32; X & Y v. Netherlands, Series A No. 91, paras. 23 et *seq;* Velosa Barreto v. Portugal, 1995 Series A No. 334, para. 23). Furthermore in considering whether a fair balance has been struck in relation to the positive obligations flowing from the first paragraph of Article 8, the aims mentioned in the second paragraph also have a certain relevance (Lopez Ostra v. Spain, 1994 Series A No. 303C, para. 51).

26. In the Chamber's opinion the obligation effectively to secure respect for a person's home implies that there must be effective machinery

for protecting it against unlawful interference of the kind which the applicant has suffered. In particular there must be effective machinery for obtaining and enforcing court orders restoring possession where a person has been unlawfully evicted from his home. In the present case the applicant has been unlawfully excluded from his home for over two years. The police gave no assistance to court officials in repeated attempts, starting on 11 March 1996, to enforce the order of the court for the eviction of the unlawful occupant, Mr K.V., and tolerated repeated obstruction of the officials in the execution of their duty. Since Mr K.V. moved out in about October 1996, the applicant has attempted, without success so far, to obtain a further court order against a new illegal occupant, Mr Rujević, who appears to have moved into the apartment with the connivance of Mr K.V.

27. With reference to the period before Mr K.V. moved out of the apartment, the Chamber recognises that the authorities responsible for carrying out an eviction may face a difficult task if they are obstructed by people opposed to the eviction, and that they may legitimately find it necessary in some circumstances to delay taking action for reasons of public order. They are bound however to take steps to deal with such a situation. In the context of Article 11 of the Convention the European Court of Human Rights has held that a State is under a positive obligation to take reasonable and appropriate measures to protect lawful demonstrations from violence by counter demonstrators, although the authorities cannot guarantee a successful outcome and have a wide discretion as to the means to be used, (Plattform Ante fur das Leben v. Austria, 1988 Series A No. 139, paras. 30-34). . . .

28. As to the situation since Mr K.V. moved out of the apartment, the Chamber first notes that the court order against Mr K. V. provided that he should leave the apartment at the disposal of the applicant "free of all persons and things." Since he appears not to have complied with that order the Chamber finds it surprising that no further possibility of enforcing the original order should have been open to the applicant. . . .

29. The Chamber therefore concludes that the applicant's rights under Article 8 of the Convention have been violated by reason of the failure of the authorities to enforce the judgement in the applicant's favour and the failure of the Court to deal with sufficient urgency with the second action raised by the applicant.

2. Article 1 of Protocol No. 1 to the Convention

30. Article 1 of Protocol No. 1 to the Convention provides as follows:

> "Every natural or legal person is entitled to the peaceful enjoyment of his possessions. No one shall be deprived of his possessions except in the public interest and subject to the conditions provided for by law and the general principles of international law.

The preceding provisions shall not, however, in any way impair the right of a State to enforce such laws as it deems necessary to control the use of property in accordance with the general interest or to secure the payment of taxes or other contributions or penalties."

31. The European Court of Human Rights has held that this provision "guarantees in substance the right of property" and "comprises three distinct rules." The first rule, in the first sentence of Article 1, lays down the general principle of the peaceful enjoyment of possessions. The second rule, in the second sentence, covers deprivation of possessions and makes it subject to certain conditions. The third rule, in the second paragraph, concerns the State's right to enforce laws controlling the use of property. The second and third rules are concerned with particular instances of interference with the right to peaceful enjoyment of property, (see e.g. Scollo v. Italy, 1995 Series A No. 315, para. 26). Where a measure affecting property is not within the ambit of either the second or the third rule, it is necessary to consider whether there has been a violation of the first rule, for which purpose it must be determined "whether a fair balance was struck between the demands of the general interest of the community and the requirements of the protection of the individual's fundamental rights (Sporrong & Lonnroth v. Sweden, 1982 Series A No. 52, para. 69).

32. As to the present case, the Chamber first notes that the applicant is not the owner of the apartment in question but holds an occupancy right over it. To determine whether Article 1 of Protocol No. 1 is applicable it is therefore necessary to consider whether the occupancy right was a "possession" within its meaning. In this respect it notes that the European Commission and Court of Human Rights have given a wide interpretation to the concept of "possession and have held that it covers a wide variety of rights and interests having economic value (see, e.g., Van Marle v. Netherlands, 1986 Series A No. 101, para. 41; Pressos Compania Naviera S.A. v. Belgium, 1995 Series A No. 332, para. 31). The Chamber has itself held that the concept extends to cover contractual rights under contracts for the purchase of property, even though such contracts did not of themselves give rise to real rights of property (Cases Nos. CH/96/3, 8 & 9, Medan and Others V. State and Federation of Bosnia and Herzegovina, Decision on the Merits delivered on 7 November 1997). The Chamber notes that an occupancy right is a valuable asset giving the holder the right, subject to the conditions prescribed by law, to occupy the property in question indefinitely. In certain circumstances at least it can be transferred. In the Chamber's opinion it is an asset which constitutes a 'possession" within the meaning of Article 1 as interpreted by the European Commission and Court. Article 1 of the Protocol is therefore applicable.

33. The present case is not concerned with an expropriation by the public authorities of the Republika Srpska or with the application of laws controlling the use of property. It relates to a failure by the authorities to

protect the applicant against unlawful interference with his possessions by private individuals. In the Chamber's opinion the case must therefore be considered under the first, general rule in Article 1. This general rule may, like other Convention guarantees, give rise to positive obligations on the authorities to provide effective protection for the individual's rights, (see para. 25 above; see also Application IV o. 20357/92, Whiteside v. United Kingdom, 76A DR p. 80). The Chamber notes, furthermore, that it is implicit in the Court's Judgement in the case of Scollo v. Italy *(sup. cit.)* that such positive obligations may include the provision of necessary assistance in the recovery of property by means of eviction. In the present case the Chamber considers, for essentially the same reasons as it has given in relation to Article 8 of the Convention, that the failure of the authorities to take the necessary measures to enforce the court order obtained by the applicant against Mr K.V., and the failure of the court to proceed with sufficient urgency with the second civil action, involved failures effectively to secure his right to peaceful enjoyment of his possessions. There has therefore been a breach of his rights under Article 1 of Protocol No. 1 to the Convention. . . .

VII. Conclusions

40. For the above reasons the Chamber **decides** as follows: . . .

4. By eleven votes against one to **order** the respondent Party to take effective measures to restore to the applicant possession of the apartment referred to in the relevant orders of the Court of First Instance in Banja Luka;

5. By eleven votes against one to **order** the respondent Party to report to it before 3 February 1998 on the steps taken by it to comply with the above order;

6. By eleven votes against one to **reserve** to the applicant the right to apply to it before 3 March 1998 for any monetary relief or other redress he wishes to claim.

NOTES AND QUESTIONS

1. The process of property restitution following the conflict in Bosnia-Herzegovina has been relatively successful. The Office of High Representative, an international institution that implemented the General Framework for Peace in Bosnia and Herzegovina (typically identified as the Dayton Accords), stated in November 2003 that local housing authorities had resolved 198,197 of 220,225 property claims. *See* Press Release, Office of the High Representative, Property Law Implementation Ratio in November 2003, available at *http://www.ohr.int/ohr-dept/presso/pressr/default.asp?content_id=31459* (last visited on September 3, 2010). Rhodri

C. Williams outlines the two sources that provided the primary framework for the right of restitution during the conflict in Bosnia-Herzegovina. First, Annex 7 of the Dayton Accord states that

> [a]ll refugees and displaced persons have the right freely to return to their homes of origin. They shall have the right to have restored to them, property of which they were deprived in the course of hostilities since 1991 and to be compensated for any property that cannot be restored to them.

See Rhodri C. Williams, *Post-Conflict Restitution and Refugee Return in Bosnia and Herzegovina: Implications for International Standard-Setting and Practice*, 37 N.Y.U.J. INT'L L. & POL. 441, 453 (Spring 2005) (citing General Framework Agreement for Peace in Bosnia Herzegovina, Dec. 14, 1995, Annex 7, ch. 1, art. I(4)). Second, the right of restitution is derived from Article 13(2) of the 1948 Universal Declaration of Human Rights, which states that "[e]very-one has the right to leave any country, including his own, and to return to his country." *Id.* at 458 n. 58 (quoting Universal Declaration of Human Rights, G.A. Res. 217A (III), U.N. GAOR, 2d. Sess. Art. 13(2) at 71, U.N. Doc. A/810 (Dec. 10, 1948)). Section 6 of the Dayton Accords also established the Human Rights Chamber, which provided a key resource in terms of interpreting issues raised under the Dayton Accord. *Id.* at 456.

2. In addition to the sources identified by Williams, the Human Rights Chamber also turned, as it did in *MJ*, to the European Convention for the Protection of Human Rights and Freedom as an important legal framework. How did the Human Rights Chamber use Article 8 to address the failure of the Bosnian legal authorities in removing the squatters from the disputed home?

3. The Chamber also referred to Article 1 of Protocol No. 1 to the Convention. What rights does Article I of Protocol No. 1 to the Convention protect? In particular, the court had to grapple with whether Article I of Protocol No. 1 to the Convention covered the occupancy rights of apartment owners in the former Yugoslavia, which had prohibited the private ownership of homes. How does the court address this issue?

4. Where do you think the "right of return" falls within the traditional framework of the "bundle of rights"? Does it involve the right to use? The right to transfer? The right to exclude?

5. A number of additional resources discuss the "right of return" within context of the Balkan wars of the 1990s. *See, e.g.*, Laura Palmer and Cristina Posa, *The Best-Laid Plans: Implementation of the Dayton Peace Accords in the Courtroom and on the Ground*, 12 HARV. HUM. RTS. J. 361 (1999); Eric Rosand, *The Right of Return Under International Law Following Mass Dislocation: The Bosnia Precedent*, 19 MICH. J. INT'L. L. 1091 (1997-98); Timothy Williams Waters, *The Naked Land: The Dayton Accords, Property Disputes and Bosnia's Real Constitution*, 40 HARV. INT'L L. J. 517 (1999); Lynn Hastings, *Implementation of the Property Legislation in Bosnia Herzegovina*, 37

STAN. J. INT'L L. 221 (2001); Timothy Cornell and Lance Salisbury, *The Importance of Civil Law in the Transition to Peace Lessons from Human Rights*, 35 CORNELL INT'L L. J. 389 (2001).

7.3.2 Guatemala

In the 1980s, violence and repression plagued Guatemala as the government battled insurgent groups. R. Andrew Painter, *Property Rights of Returning Displaced Persons: The Guatemalan Experience*, 9 HARV. HUM. RTS. J 145, 145 (1996). This period was part of the 35 year civil war that began partly in response to President Jacobo Arbenz's 1954 land reform initiatives. *Id.* at 148. The Arbenz government was overthrown in a coup d'etat and replaced with a government that favored private land ownership by a small number of landholders, sparking resistance from rebel groups who favored Arbenz's land distribution policies. *Id.* at 149. The Guatemalan government implemented a "scorched earth" policy under which it attacked and destroyed entire villages thought to support the rebel groups. *Id.* at 150. These attacks forced thousands of Mayan villagers to flee from their homes in the Ixil Triangle, an area in the northwest highlands of Guatemala. *Id.* The government repopulated these "voluntarily" abandoned areas with internally displaced persons from other parts of the country. *Id.* at 150-51. The military created "model villages" and established "civilian patrols" to protect the area from guerrilla attack. *Id.* at 151. The property rights of the former owners were annulled, and new titles were granted to the people brought to the area by the military. *Id.*

As the conflict died down, the internally displaced persons and refugees began to return to their former homes. *Id.* Thousands of land conflicts arose because of the competing interests between the former landowners who fled from violence and the new landowners the military had placed on the land during the repopulation efforts. *Id.* In October 1992, the Permanent Commission of Guatemalan Refugees in Mexico (CCPPs) and the Guatemalan National Service Commission for Repatriates, Refugees and the Displaced (CEAR) signed an agreement addressing the challenges to property ownership faced by returning displaced persons. *Id.* In part, the agreement provided a process to settle land disputes between those returnees who held a definitive land title and second occupiers. *Id.* at 154. Under this procedure, a returnee made a formal claim on the land, and then the government was required to negotiate with the second occupier in an attempt to get him to vacate the land. *Id.* If the second occupier refused to leave, the government was required to inform the returnee of all judicial remedies available. *Id.* If a Verification Agency determined that legal action would cause undue hardship on the returnee, the returnee could waive his rights to the land, and the government had to provide the returnee with other land. *Id.* The returnee was thus guaranteed landownership, even if it was not over the original parcel. *Id.* at 155.

One such conflict was the case of Los Cimientos, an area of the Ixil Triangle. Los Cimientos was part of an ongoing dispute over ownership rights between the Quiché and Ixil communities, both of indigenous Mayan descent. *Id.* at 180-82; Michael Holley, Comment, *Recognizing the Rights of Indigenous People to Their Traditional Lands: A Case Study of an Internally-Displaced Community in Guatemala,* 15 Berkeley J. Int'l L. 119, 123 (1997). In the early 1980s, the government's scorched earth campaign moved through Los Cimientos, *id.* at 121, forcing the Quiché to leave and live as internally displaced persons in other parts of Guatemala, *id.* at 122. When the Quiché tried to return to Los Cimientos in 1990, they found 50 Ixil families living there as part of a "model village" set up by the military. *Id.* The Ixil, backed by the military, challenged the Quiché claim of ownership and prevented the Quiché from returning to Los Cimientos. *Id.*

Even though the Guatemalan government recognized the Quiché's formal title to the land and right to ownership of Los Cimientos, possession was not restored to the community. *Id.* As a result, in 1993, the Human Rights Legal Action Center (CALDH) and the Runujel Junam Council of Ethnic Communities (CERJ) brought a petition to the Inter-American Commission on Human Rights on behalf of the Quiché. *Community of San Vicente Los Cimientos v. Guatemala,* Case No. 11.197, Inter-Am C.H.R., Report No. 68/03, OEA/Ser.L/V/II.118 doc. 70 rev. 2 ¶ 1 (2003). The petition alleged that the State of Guatemala violated various articles of the American Convention of Human Rights, including Article 21, which ensures a right to property. *Id.* With the aid of the Inter-American Commission, the negotiations between CALDH, CERJ, and the Guatemalan government culminated in the signing of a Friendly Settlement Agreement in 2002, excerpted below.

Friendly Settlement Agreement, Community of San Vicente Los Cimientos v. Guatemala

Case No. 11.197, Inter-Am C.H.R., Report No. 68/03, OEA/Ser.L/V/II.1 18 doc. 70 rev. 2 ¶ 36 (2003)

1. [The Guatemalan government, through the Presidential Unit for Conflict Resolution, shall purchase, for the transfer and settlement of the entire population (land owners, land holders, and assigns) of the Los Cimientos Quiché community, the San Vicente Osuna estate and its annex, the Las Delicias estate located in Sinquinalá municipality, Escuintla department.]

The public purchase deed that is to be signed will specify that the San Vicente Osuna estate and its annex, the Las Delicias estate, will become the property of the "Community Association of Residents of Los Cimientos

Xetzununchaj" civic association, comprising all the members of the Los Cimientos Quiché community.

The purchase operation includes all the administrative and registration expenses obligatorily arising from that juridical act. By means of legal mechanisms, the Government authorities, in conjunction with the community's representatives, will negotiate regarding the possibility of securing an exemption and/or special treatment for the tax payments with the corresponding authorities.

The "Community Association of Residents of Los Cimientos Xetzununchaj" civic association represents at least two hundred and thirty-three families who were affected by the violent dispossession inflicted on them, and a commitment exists toward them to make all efforts to raise the living standards of all. . . .

2. The representatives of the Community Association of Residents of Los Cimientos Xetzununchaj expressly note that the estates to be purchased (San Vicente Osuna and its annex, the Las Delicias estate) fully satisfy the land claims of the Los Cimientos Xetzununchaj community in terms of area, quality, and location.

3. This agreement satisfies the past claims made by the members of the Los Cimientos community before the State of Guatemala, before international human rights agencies, and in the framework agreement for negotiations between the Government of the Republic and the community of Los Cimientos, Quiché, signed by the parties on August 21 of this year . . .

4. As a part of the comprehensive, fair, and final solution of this conflict, the community of Los Cimientos, Quiché, through the "Community Association of Residents of Los Cimientos Xetzununchaj" civic association, and the Government of the Republic will jointly identify and negotiate, within 60 days following the settlement of the community, urgent projects to reactivate its productive, economic, and social capacities, with a view to fostering the community's development and wellbeing. . . .

5. Consequently, the purchase and adjudication of the lands indicated in item (1), together with the development and monitoring of the joint and complementary actions established in this document, as applicable, shall represent for the Los Cimientos community the final and satisfactory conclusion of the conflict related to this agreement.

6. The individual land owners, land holders, and assigns of the estates comprising the Los Cimientos community, as a part of the commitments arising from the Government's purchase on their behalf of the estates known as San Vicente Osuna and its annex, the Las Delicias estate, shall cede their current rights of ownership, holding, and inheritance to the Land Fund, in compliance with the provisions of Article 8(h) of the Land Fund Law, Decree No. 24-99.

7. The Government of the Republic shall be responsible for relocating the 233 families of the Los Cimientos, Quiché, community, together with

their property. This shall be affected using appropriate means of transport . . .

8. The Government shall provide the resources necessary to feed the 233 families during their transfer to and establishment in their new homes, and it shall accompany them with a duly equipped mobile unit for the duration of the transfer and until such time as a formal health facility is established in their settlement, in order to cater for any emergency that may arise.

9. For the community's location and resettlement, the Government of the Republic will provide humanitarian assistance, minimal housing, and basic services through the appropriate official agencies. The Government of the Republic will request that the situation be monitored by a commission comprising members of UPRECO, accompanying organizations, the United Nations Verification Mission in Guatemala—Quiché region (MINUGUA), and the Organization of American States (OAS/PROPAZ). . . .

11. . . . We, the individuals appearing herein, having been informed of the content and scope of this document, assume the commitment of complying with it and hereby ratify, accept, and sign it. In Guatemala City, on the eleventh day of September, two thousand and two.

Community of San Vicente Los Cimientos v. Guatemala, Case No. 11.197, Inter-Am C.H.R., Report No. 68/03, OEA/Ser.L/V/II.118 doc. 70 rev. 2 ¶ 36 (2003).

NOTES AND QUESTIONS

1. How are the principles of the CCPP-CEAR agreement reflected in the Friendly Settlement Agreement above?

2. What challenges might arise from guaranteeing returning displaced persons property ownership?

3. The massive displacement of Mayan communities during the Guatemalan civil war severed the indigenous communities' ties with their ancestral lands and drastically changed most communities' culture and lifestyle. Michael Holley, Comment, *Recognizing the Rights of Indigenous People to Their Traditional Lands: A Case Study of an Internally-Displaced Community in Guatemala*, 15 Berkeley J. Int'l L. 119, 132 (1997). These displaced persons relocated to squatter villages, low-land plantations, or model villages near their former homes. *Id.* at 132.

4. Compare Guatemala's approach to resettlement of displaced persons to that seen in *M.J. v. Republicka Srpska*. Which approach is likely to provide the most successful outcome?

5. International law has also begun to recognize criminal remedies for deprivation of property. For example, the International Criminal Tribunal, which has jurisdiction over persons who violated international humanitarian law within the territory of Rwanda, as well as Rwandan

citizens responsible for such violations committed in the territory of neighboring States, can consider criminal penalties for deprivation of property. In particular, Article 23(3) of the Statute of the International Criminal Tribunal for Rwanda states that "[i]n addition to imprisonment, the Trial Chamber may order the return of any property and proceeds acquired by criminal conduct, including by means of duress, to their rightful owners."

TABLE OF CASES

Principal cases appear in italics.

TABLE OF STATUTES

New Jersey

Pennsylvania

South Dakota

Texas

Virginia

INDEX